American Society in
the Twentieth Century

Selected Readings

American Society in the Twentieth Century

Selected Readings

DWIGHT W. HOOVER
C. WARREN VANDER HILL
Editors

John Wiley & Sons, Inc.   New York · London · Sydney · Toronto

For Stow Persons *and the memory of* Harold H. Dunham

Preface

This book examines part of twentieth-century American social history. It describes rather than analyzes some of the changes in social role that have occurred in the United States since 1900. Hopefully, it will supplement the usual political history of the period, which concedes to cultural history a few pages of illustrated art forms but says little about changing social norms. We do not pretend that our survey is complete or that it covers all of America's social experience. We have concentrated on the beginning of the period and its end, leaving the middle less developed.

The theory underlying the book is social role. We contend that the social roles given to certain groups or individuals or assumed by them have changed. We define social role as the part played by an individual, based on group agreement concerning behavior appropriate to that part. This definition implies an ideal situation in which the individual understands the group agreement and such agreement exists. In practice, the roles are often less clear.

Sociologists connect role and status, insisting that the two have a reciprocal relationship. Some also view roles as normative, pressing people into molds made by society. Roles, in this view, are resistant to change. These sociologists support a theory called Functionalism, which conceives of society as a balanced system held together by a glue of common values. As a model, Functionalism leads to a sociology that explains the status quo instead of analyzing change. The consequences of the Functional approach are effectively portrayed in Alvin W. Gouldner's *The Coming Crisis of Western Sociology*. Our emphasis is just the opposite. We believe that one result of a historical look at roles is to show the persistent element of change. We have deliberately concentrated on this element of change to the exclusion of continuity. In doing this, we realize that our position is a minority one.

Several explanations are usually advanced for changes in roles. These explanations assert that change results from (1) contradictions in roles and status in a society that can be resolved only by elimination of the contradictions (for example, an educated black man who works for acceptance in a racist Southern town); (2) role conflict in small groups (for instance, family arguments over a member's duties and privileges); and (3) deliberate choice of an identity different from that assigned by society (a woman deliberately rejecting her conventional role as a mother, for example). We emphasize the third factor, placing ourselves with the existential sociologists such as Gouldner and Robert Nesbit. Part of the attraction of history is a humanistic one that focuses on man's ability to manipulate his own fate. We have concentrated on this ability.

The roles contained in this book are broadly defined—radical, woman, Negro, conservationist, hero, rich, and poor. From an entire spectrum we have chosen only a few roles, and these may be unrepresentative of the United States as a whole. However, these roles are the ones that have become matters of interest, concern, and perplexity to the general public. We have deliberately chosen roles that show the most change, but we recognize the limits of our choice. We have excluded the sharply defined social roles that have changed the least. For example, in selecting women in search of a new social role, we ignore the traditional roles of mother and wife. In describing the change from Negro to black, we overlook the persons remaining comfortable as Negroes. Finally, we use the social conservative (broadly defined) as a starting point, but we do not show the evolution of that role. We think that the social conservative retains a faith in older social roles and does not illustrate change in role expectations. Moreover, the appeal of the traditional role is well known.

The new American social history, which owes a great deal to the French historian, Phillipe Ariés, and his book *Centuries of Childhood: A Social History of Family Life,* emphasizes family role relations. We use a broader approach. Certainly, much can be gained from an intensive study of the evolving roles of the child, the father, and the mother, but we wished to do more. There is a discussion of family roles in Part II, Section B, in connection with roles of women, but little is said about children. We rely almost entirely on adult roles as they were conceived by either the participants themselves or by outside observers.

Admittedly, distortions creep in. Bill Haywood may misrepresent the I.W.W. consciously or unconsciously. Mabel Dodge Luhan could be sui generis. Neither was objective, nor were they concerned directly with the problem of role as a sociologist might be. In a sense (even though obliquely), these individuals were defining themselves; they were seeking roles in which they found satisfaction. Their struggles in an unsympathetic society reveal much about other roles in their own time. Because of the lack of objectivity and the effort to change, these individuals may seem to behave in a puzzling or contradictory fashion. But this shows their common humanity.

We have ignored nonadult roles generally; we also have generally ignored class influence on roles. Undeniably, there are class dimensions to role assignment and performance. For instance, the definition of proper behavior for a woman varies with her group membership. In addition, behavior patterns often originate on one class level and move up or down to others. This migration is the theme of S. P. Fullenwider's *The Mind and Mood of Black America.* The book shows how the lower-class concepts of soul, funk, and "nitty-gritty," which reflect earthy, sensuous experience, are replacing middle-class inhibitions as the black man redefines himself, getting away from the role of the Negro. The case of Mabel Dodge Luhan, which appears in Part II, Section B, shows another direction of role development. Her independence resulted partly from her own wealth. The independence of present-day women in the liberation movement resembles her independence but is based on psychological rather than economic resources. Indeed, many of the liberationists are of lower-middle-class origin. Style of clothes also gives evidence of changing role conceptions through class lines. Historically, children assumed an obsolete dress of their own class. The clothing affected by radical youth of today is that previously worn by the Indian or the black man—both of whom have been assigned inferior roles in the past. Now their styles seem worthy of emulation.

We have included only two class roles: the rich and the poor. The shift in the role definition of the rich, the leaders of society, and high-status persons shows changing cultural values. The self-conscious WASP who gloried in his antecedents and who believed in a high culture based on English sensibilities has changed. As Susan Sontag shows in "Notes on Camp," snobs now find the lowbrow appeal of the movie musical of the 1930s as satisfying as the highbrow appeal of the opera, the pop art of the 1960s as satisfying as the old masters. The rich person no longer needs to dress in his tuxedo to be formal; he may wear turtlenecks and no socks. He no longer needs to go to parties with settings resembling Versailles; he may eat hot dogs with Rockefeller at Coney Island. Not all rich persons would wish to do these things. Mrs. Post in Palm Springs does not eat hot dogs or go without socks; others retain the older role of refined social leader. The roles of the culture leader or rich man are now less rigidly defined, however, and there is more freedom to experiment within these roles.

Connected with the less rigid definition of social leadership, there has been an increase in the prestige of ethnicity. This results from the rise of the descendants of the non-English immigrant, particularly the Jew, in America. E. Digby Baltzell, in his *The Protestant Establishment: Aristocracy and Caste in America,* argues that the WASPs retain a monopoly on status while the Catholics and Jews, who have achieved great power, are denied commensurate status. We believe that Baltzell overemphasizes the lack of status for other religious and ethnic roles. It is no longer necessary to choose between the role of an American citizen and that of a Jewish mother, or between the role of an American worker and that of an Italian husband. The attempts at Americanization at the beginning of this century did distinguish between the roles and placed lower status on the ethnic ones. To become an American it was necessary to assume a public role with mostly English-derived values, and ethnic roles were forced underground. Although the immigrant family retained many of its old values, these values were often concealed from the public and were transmitted with considerable difficulty. Although the melting-pot analogy for Americanization was never a very good one, it did suggest a kind of surface conformity. The growth in the prestige of the ethnic role in middle-class American society is the result of greater tolerance for non-WASP values. Concern with the supposed contradiction between loyalty to an American political order and loyalty to a varying set of social assumptions has lessened. To be Irish and Catholic is not to be un-American. Now the former underground ethnicity has become overt.

As role definitions change and as certain roles become more prestigious, the entire society changes. If we define national character as the total complex of roles available in any given society at any given time, we can conclude that our national character is still changing. We, as Americans, are different from what we used to be. If a young society is one with flexible social roles (loosely defined and held), then perhaps America has become once again a young society. This is the essence of Charles Reich's *The Greening of America*. Although Reich uses three states of consciousness, these states can be equated with different role expectations. Whether Reich is correct or whether America is once again new, however, is not the significant point of our book. The point is that roles are changing and that we can reduce some of the fear and anxiety accompanying the changes if we understand them better.

Dwight W. Hoover
C. Warren Vander Hill

Muncie, Indiana, 1972

Acknowledgments

We thank the following people for their generous advice and assistance during the various stages of preparing this manuscript for publication: Loren Baritz, Mike Bidelman, Lloyd Gardner, Gerald Grob, Neil McMillen, Robert Fogarty, Michael McGiffert, Robin Brooks, George Juergens, and Robert Sklar.

We also thank our student assistants, Danea White, Gary Burbridge, and Dianna Smith, and our typist, Jane Snodgress, for their patience.

D. W. H.
C. W. V. H.

Contents

American Society in
the Twentieth Century

Selected Readings

Part I
MULTINATIONAL AMERICA

The definition of Americanism at the beginning of the twentieth century was monolithic, homogeneous, and restrictive. In *Strangers in the Land,* John Higham says, "From its tiny beginnings at the end of the nineteenth century to its height in the First World War, the movement for Americanization was another indication of the growing urgency of the nationalist impulse." The Americanization movement attempted, through the schools and volunteer societies, to teach both the English language and American ideals. These ideals included a respect for such American institutions as the public school and the legal system, a reverence for American democracy, and an understanding of the American past. While liberal believers in Americanization did not insist on the abandonment of the immigrants' own culture, the more reactionary believers did. These spokesmen wanted a profound change in life style as well as an abandonment of the Old World heritage. The immigrant was to exchange roles, not to fulfill dual ones.

The Americanization movement received support from such organizations as the National Association of Manufacturers and the United States Chamber of Commerce. It reached its peak in 1917, when the National Americanization Committee, headed by Frances Kellar, a pioneer social worker in New York City and a fellow of the College Settlement Movement, proposed that all aliens learn English and apply for naturalization within three years, that all immigrants prove themselves to be Americans, and that aliens be interned wherever anti-American sentiment existed. The Americanization movement lost force in the 1920s when immigration restriction drastically reduced the number of new arrivals, and in the 1930s the immigrant got his political revenge by supporting Franklin Delano Roosevelt.

The role of the newly arrived immigrant as conceived by the Americanization movement was that of a follower of the civil religion. The immigrant would become indistinguishable from the native American in dress, behavior, and attitude. Loyalty to political principles would be matched by acceptance of the values of society as seen by native Americans, an implicit Protestantism and an implicit

1

middle-class orientation, abstinence, hard work, and thrifty habits.

Not all Americans shared this conservative Americanism. Some held a more liberal view, saying that one could retain Old World values and still be an American, that political allegiance did not require cultural uniformity, and that America was richer as a heterogeneous society. Among these people were the philosopher John Dewey and the settlement-house leader Jane Addams. The most articulate although less well-known spokesman for this position was Randolph Bourne, who had excellent family credentials as a native American. He was raised in Bloomfield, New Jersey, in a family that was Republican and Presbyterian and that traced its roots back to seventeenth-century New England. Bourne reacted against his background, perhaps because of physical disability (double curvature of the spine and facial disfigurement), or perhaps because of the exploiting circumstances under which he had to earn his living as a youth. Bourne attended Columbia and studied under John Dewey and Charles Beard. Although he was at first impressed with Dewey's progressivism, Bourne later attacked Dewey for his support of World War I and his instrumentalist position. The latter, Bourne maintained, reflected the more negative values of small-town America. In 1916 in an article, "Trans-National America," Bourne criticized the idea of Americanization, calling for a higher valuation of immigrant culture. He even labeled those who were Americanized as half breeds, sharing the worst of two worlds. These half breeds had given up their role as inheritors of the best that Western culture had to offer while taking only the low culture of the "cheap newspaper, the 'movies,' the popular song, the ubiquitous automobile." Bourne claimed that there was no true native American culture outside of the South and New England, and that even the culture of these areas was dying. For Bourne, the role of the immigrant was to give the best of European culture to a starving America. The future of America lay in cosmopolitanism, which combined the best of several European heritages into a transnational America.

At about the same time, the humanist writer Horace Kallen suggested a similar role for the immigrant. Kallen called his version cultural pluralism. He first expressed his views in 1915, but it was not until 1924 that these views were fully developed in *Culture and Democracy in the United States.* Kallen, who also disavowed the idea of progress, made few converts to his position that true Americanism supported ethnic differences. Among those he did impress was the American Zionist Louis D. Brandeis. Thus, indirectly, Kallen influenced the new nation of Israel. In the United States, however, Kallen remained a spokesman for a minority point of view.

Only in the 1960s have the ideas of Bourne and Kallen seemed to have gained more acceptance. There has been a renewed emphasis on and an elevated status for ethnicity. The selections by Peter Schrag and Walter Kerr demonstrate this fact.

Peter Schrag is a professional journalist and an editor for the *Saturday Review.*

He has written articles concerning the changing American scene in addition to "The Decline of the WASP." The most notable of these is "The Forgotten American," a study of white, working-class citizens who feel aggrieved at their seeming failure to reach the American Dream. In "The Decline of the WASP," Schrag shows how the life style of the WASP is threatened by other life styles, how once-accepted ways of behavior are being supplanted by others. Now it is fashionable to be ethnic and to have a less restricted, more spontaneous life with fewer rules for behavior. Schrag illustrates his thesis with examples drawn from clothes and sports, areas of life that may seem to be relatively insignificant.

There are several obvious problems in Schrag's article. The first is that the role of the WASP is an idealized one. WASP virtues were never completely realized; there was always more diversity behind the stereotype than Schrag concedes. The second is that, contrary to Bourne and Kallen, the ethnic role has a conservative, not a liberating, element in it. Schrag himself points this out. Irish Catholicism is as Puritanical in some ways as American Protestantism; it may be more anti-intellectual. The descendant of the eastern European immigrant has become the typical middle American. It is he who votes for George Wallace. It is he who resists most strongly the demands of blacks for more jobs, better education, and better housing because he feels that it is his job, his school, and his home that are being threatened. Despite the fact that the WASP role never was fully realized in practice and that the ethnic role now is not necessarily the liberal one, the elevation of ethnic traits to as respectable a level as those of the WASPs would gladden the hearts of Bourne and Kallen.

The second selection is a review of *The Education of H*Y*M*A*N K*A*P*L*A*N* by the *New York Times* drama critic, Walter Kerr. It might alternately be titled "The Immigrant's Revenge." Leo Rosten's book from which the play was derived dealt with the attempt to Americanize a Jewish immigrant. The teacher took the role of the typical American; the immigrant assumed the exotic role. The immigrant was the butt of the jokes, his manner was curious, his expectations distorted. The teacher represented the common and the usual. In the play, however, the roles seem reversed. The immigrant role was familiar while the teacher's was strange. What had happened? Did the adaptation change the book? Kerr's answer is that the theme was the same but that he had changed. The Jewish author reflecting on his past had educated the sympathetic American public so well that the roles assumed by his father seemed natural. The work of Jewish authors in the 1960s had made Hyman Kaplan the normal American. Horace Kallen would have found this ironic indeed, but he would have approved.

The continuation of transnational America and cultural pluralism will depend on the confidence and toleration of other Americans. It may well be that the ethnic role becomes respectable only when it is no longer dangerous. It may be only when the immigrant is securely an American that his European, African, or

Asian past can be claimed. It may be that only when immigration is almost a forgotten fact that immigrant ways are respectable. There is little reason to fear that the third-generation Pole will subvert this country by either his Catholicism or his sausage.

Finally, there is the possibility that the ethnicity that Bourne and Kallen desired has vanished, leaving only surface manifestations. We choose to be more optimistic and argue that in the 1970s Americans may choose an ethnic role, that to be an American implies cultural diversity, and that this cultural diversity connects to a significant past.

1 THE DECLINE OF THE WASP

Peter Schrag

For most of us who were born before World War II, America was a place to be discovered; it was imperfect, perhaps—needed some reform, some shaping up— but it did not need to be reinvented. It was all given, like a genetic code, waiting to unfold. We all wanted to learn the style, the proper accent, agreed on its validity, and while our interpretations and our heroes varied, they were all cut from the same stock. Cowboys, pioneers, athletes, entrepreneurs, men of letters: whatever we were offered we took pretty much as our own. Whether we were small-town boys or the children of urban immigrants, we shared an eagerness to become apprentices in the great open democracy, were ready to join up, wanting only to be accepted according to the terms that history and tradition had already established. It never occurred to us to think otherwise.

What held that world together was not just a belief in some standardized version of textbook Americanism, a catalogue of accepted values, but a particular class of people and institutions that we identified with our vision of the country. The people were white and Protestant; the institutions were English; American culture was WASP. We paid lip service to the melting pot, but if, for instance, one's grandmother asked, "Is it good for the Jews?" there wasn't any question in her mind about who was running the country. The critics, the novelist, the poets, the social theorists, the men who articulated and analyzed American ideas, who governed our institutions, who embodied what we were or hoped to be— nearly all of them were WASPs: Hemingway, Fitzgerald, Eliot, MacLeish, Sandburg, Lewis, Steinbeck, Dewey, Santayana, the Jameses, Beard, Parrington, Edmund Wilson, Van Wyck Brooks, Lester Frank Ward, Oliver Wendell Holmes; *The Saturday Evening Post* under George Horace Lorimer (with covers by Norman Rockwell); *The Atlantic* under Edward Weeks; *Harper's* in the days of Frederick

Lewis Allen—to name only a few, and only from the twentieth century. Of all the major figures discussed by Henry Steel Commager in *The American Mind,* not one is a Jew, a Catholic, or a Negro. The American mind was the WASP mind.

We grew up with them; they surrounded us: they were the heroes of the history we studied and of the fantasy life we sought in those Monday-through-Friday radio serials. Even Hollywood, after all the creation of Jewish producers, never did much for pluralism. The stars were often ethnics—show business and sports constituting two major avenues for "outsiders" to make it into the mainstream—but their names and the roles they played rarely, if ever, acknowledged the existence of anything beyond that mainstream. The Hyman Kaplans were lovable jerks, immigrant Sambos; Rochester said, "Yassuh, Mr. Benny" (did we realize that Benny was a Jew?) and anything beginning with Mike, Pat, or Abie was set up for a laugh. Hollywood's Jews sold the American dream strictly in WASP terms.

They—the WASPs—never thought of themselves as anything but Americans, nor did it occur to others to label them as anything special until, about twenty-five years ago, their influence began to decline and they started to lose their cultural initiative and preeminence. There were, to be sure, regional distinctions, but whatever was "American" was WASP. Indeed, there was no "other"—was, that is, no domestic base of social commentary, no voice except their voice, for the discussion of "American" problems. The ethnics had their place and their strong loyalties, but insofar as that place was *American* it was defined by WASPs. We could distinguish Jews, Irishmen, Italians, Catholics, Poles, Negroes, Indians, Mexican-Americans, Japanese-Americans, but not WASPs. When WASPs were alienated it was because, as in the case of Henry Adams, the country had moved away from them, not because, as with the others, they regarded themselves as alien in heritage or tradition. (Southerners who had lost their war and their innocence were—in that respect—alien, ethnically WASPs but also in some sense unwilling immigrants; they were among the first to be out of place in their own country.) For most WASPs, their complaints were proprietary. That is, the old place was going down because the tenants weren't keeping it up properly. They were the landlords of our culture, and their values, with rare exceptions, were those that defined it: hard work, perseverance, self-reliance, puritanism, the missionary spirits, and the abstract rule of law.

They are, of course, still with us—in corporations and clubs, in foundations and universities, in government and the military, maintaining the interlocking directorates that make sociologists salivate and that give the Establishment its ugly name: The Power Structure, the Miliary-Industrial Complex; the rulers of America. But while they still hold power, they hold it with less assurance and with less legitimacy than at any time in history. They are hanging on, men living off their cultural capital, but rarely able or willing to create more. One can almost define their domains by locating the people and institutions that are chronically on the defensive: university presidents and trustees; the large foundations; the corporations; government; the military. They grew great as initiators and entrepreneurs. They invented the country, its culture and its values; they shaped the institutions and organizations. Then they drew the institutions around themselves, moved to the suburbs, and became org-men.

Who and what has replaced them, then, in the invention and production of our culture? Jews and Negroes, Catholics and immigrants. "Of the Americans who have come into notice during the past fifty years as poets, as novelists, as critics, as painters, as sculptors, and in the minor arts," wrote Henry Mencken in 1924, "less than half bear Anglo-Saxon names....So in the sciences, so in the higher reaches of engineering and technology...." Mencken's declaration was premature then; it is an understatement now: Mailer and Roth; Malamud and Bellow; Ellison and Baldwin; Edward Teller and Robert Oppenheimer and Wernher von Braun; Ralph Nader and Cesar Chavez; Noam Chomsky and Allen Ginsberg; John Rock and Jonas Salk; Paul Goodman and Herbert Marcuse; Bruno Bettelheim and Erik Erikson; Eldridge Cleaver and Malcolm X and Martin Luther King. The 1969 Pulitzer Prize for non-fiction was divided between a Jew from Brooklyn (Mailer) and a French immigrant (Rene Dubos); the Pulitzer Prize for fiction was awarded to an American Indian (Scott Momaday). The spokesmen of American literature and culture tend increasingly to represent the pluralistic residues of a melting pot that—for better or worse—never worked as well as some Americans had hoped. It is not simply that many of the major postwar journals of criticism—*Commentary, The New York Review of Books, The New American Review*—are edited by Jews, or that *Time* is edited by a Jewish refugee from Hitler, or that *The Saturday Evening Post* is dead, or that the function of radical muckraking was revitalized by *Ramparts,* originally established as a Catholic magazine, or that William Buckley, a Catholic, is the most articulate conservative in America; we do, after all, still have WASP writers and journals—*Foreign Affairs,* for example, and *The Atlantic* (not to mention *Life* or *Reader's Digest*). It is, rather, that the style, ideas, traumas, perplexities, and passions tend to reflect other backgrounds and interests, and that the integrative capabilities of the WASP style have plunged into precipitous decline. The cultural issues of the 1960s enjoying the greatest cachet were not only ethnic and pluralistic, but also disintegrative—Alienation, the Identity Crisis, Black Power, Doing Your Own Thing, Dropping Out, the White Negro—and it seemed that any kind of material was acceptable as long as it was distinguishable from the old WASP mainstream: the life of the black ghetto, rock music and long hair and pot. Hindu gurus and Zen philosophers, Cuban guerrillas and Catholic radicals, black hustlers and Jewish anarchists. (The first thing I learned, coming from Brooklyn to Amherst in 1949 was that you didn't say "Bullshit" when you disagreed with someone, even your roommate. You said "Yes, but...." Now bullshit is back in style.) For the young, the chief villainy of the age is to be uptight, and who seems to them more uptight than

WASPs, or the Jews and Irishmen trying to be like them? The 1960s was the decade of gaps—missile gaps, credibility gaps, generation gaps—when we became, in many respects, a nation of outsiders, a country in which the mainstream, however mythic, lost its compelling energy and its magnetic attraction. Now that the New Frontier and the Great Society have failed (not only as programs but as verbal rituals) so, at least for the moment, has the possibility of integration and, with it, traditional Americanism. The Average Man has become the Silent Majority. Both of these, of course, are merely convenient political fiction, but the change in labels points to a far deeper crisis of belief.

It is not that WASPs lack power and representation—or numbers—but that the once-unquestioned assumptions on which that power was based have begun to lose their hold. The foundation of WASP dominance in national politics and culture rested on the supposition that WASPdom was the true America, no subculture or special group. Now WASPs are beset by the need to enforce allegiance to something that their very place in power is supposed to take for granted. The problem is then compounded: government can become increasingly gray, trying to represent (or not to offend) "all the people," or it can begin to act as the voice of a distinctive group (the Forgotten Man, the Silent Majority)—in other words, to represent the majority as if it were a minority. (There is a third alternative, which I'll discuss later.) Nixon, characteristically, is trying to do both. When he was first elected in 1968 he brought to Washington a Cabinet of nonentities selected, it seemed, to illustrate the fix we were in: Winton Blount, Clifford Hardin, Maurice Stans, Walter Hickel, the old Agnew. (The exceptions—neither was then a regular Cabinet member—were Daniel Patrick Moynihan, an Irishman, and Henry Kissinger, a Central European immigrant.) They were men without visible personality, class, or place. Something of the same was true in Washington under Eisenhower, but then the Eisenhower atmosphere was tempered by an older lingering sense of independence, of region, a sense—finally—of principle. John Foster Dulles may have been a dangerous moralist, a stubborn Puritan, but he was not plastic. Nixon brought with him no John McCloy, no John Gardner, no Nelson Rockefeller (let alone a George C. Marshall or a Henry Stimson from an even earlier era of WASP assertion) nor does he carry Eisenhower's aura of small-town decency. (Eisenhower's men, like Nixon's, were or are institutional men, but many of them came from a tradition of "service" in which the social purposes of institutions tended to be more important than the problems of management.) We now have a government of "low profiles," gray men who represent no identifiable place, no region, no program. The security of the historic WASP position made regional roots and styles attractive; you weren't just an American but an American from a specific place, with a personality, with foibles and prejudices and attitudes. You didn't have to prove you were a WASP, But where is Nixon from? In what accent does he speak? What is his style, what are his convictions, even his hobbies? Nixon's campaign, his public conduct, and his tastes reflect not only the corporate-organization-man residue of WASPishness; they also symbolize the new insecurity of the mainstream culture.

There are advantages in all this: gray men are not crusaders; they don't speak about massive retaliation or final solutions (or, on the other hand, to be sure, the Great Society). But they are likely to regard any sort of noise as offensive and possibly dangerous. For a moment this afforded us some fun (Spiro Who?), but then Nixon, through the offices of Agnew and Mitchell, turned this quality of his Administration into a serious matter. The noise (of students, of Black Power, of protest) was, and is, scaring them. And for the first time in history—certainly for the first time since the 1920s—the majority has begun to act like a minority, like an ethnic group. The powerful are paranoid about the weak. (And needless to say, many ethnic groups are acting more like ethnic groups than they have at any time since the melting pot was pronounced a success.) This is what makes Agnew potentially more dangerous than Joe McCarthy. McCarthy's quarrels, finally, were those of an outsider attacking the Establishment, and the Establishment, which was still running the country, despite a bad case of nerves, ultimately put him down. But Agnew, Mitchell, and Nixon are the government, and among their most important targets are people who have no money, little organization, and access to nothing except the streets. The threat represented by Nixon's targets is not that of a foreign power, but that of a culture or cultures at odds with the mainstream. Inquisitions and witch-hunts generally mark the end, or the beginning of the end, of an age.

One of the major attributes of the WASP idiom was its self-confidence in its own Americanism. In following the ethic of the small town, in trying to make it, the WASP was operating in a system designed by his people, operated by his people, and responsive to his people. He wasn't trying to stand somebody else's ground or beat somebody else's program. But what is there for a nation that is urban (or suburban), in which the majority has (presumably) already made it, and where size and technology are rendering much of the system impersonal and unresponsive? It is no longer possible for anyone to control the country (or the world) as we once believed we could. With the exception of the balanced ticket (in politics or employment) we have no urban ethic. And so somewhere the self-confidence froze: what in the national spirit and imagery was expansive became conservative and restrictive, enterprise turned to management, ebullience to caution. Most of all, it tended to become dull. One of the most graphic illustrations of these differences in spirit is to be found in a book by John McPhee, *Levels of the Game,* an account of a tennis match between the Negro Arthur Ashe (then the highest-ranking American) and the WASP Clark Graebner (Shaker Heights suburban, churchy, the son of a dentist). Graebner speaks:

I've never been a flashy stylist, like Arthur. I'm a fundamentalist. Arthur is a bachelor. I am married and a conservative. I'm interested in business, in the market, in children's clothes. It affects the way you play the game. He's not a steady player. He's a wristy slapper. Sometimes he doesn't even know where the ball is going....I've never seen Arthur really discipline himself. He plays the game with the lackadaisical, haphazard mannerisms of a liberal. He's an underprivileged type who worked his way up....There is something about him that is swashbuckling, loose. He plays the way he thinks. My style is playmaking—consistent, percentage tennis—and his style is shotmaking.

Ashe speaks:

There is not much variety in Clark's game. It is steady, accurate, and conservative. He makes few errors. He plays stiff, compact Republican tennis.

Blacks, of course, can be disciplined grubbers as much as anyone else, and WASPs certainly never used to lack for swashbuckling types—soldiers, tycoons, ball players, frontiersmen, outlaws. Ashe, obviously, had to grub a lot harder than any white man to break into the big time, or to become a player at all, but he now manages his games with an aristocratic flair, not with what seems to be bourgeois lack of grace. But Graebner's description is otherwise right: he plays percentage tennis, Ashe takes chances. WASPs have learned to live by percentages "steady" (as Ashe says), "accurate, stiff, compact." A little uptight. In taking risks there is more to lost then to gain.

A lot of people, needless to say, have only barely made it, or haven't made it at all: prominent among them Negroes, Puerto Ricans, Poles, Irishmen, Italians, and a good number of underclass WASPs.

For them the decline in confidence tends to be traumatic. At the very moment that they are persuaded, or forced to believe, that the system will work for them—that they can make it, that their children must go to college, and all the rest—the signals from headquarters become confused and indistinct, and the rules seem to change. The children of the affluent march in the streets; long hair and at least the outward signals of sexual freedom are acceptable; hard work, stoicism, and perseverance aren't the ultimate values; individual initiative is not sufficient; the schools are "in trouble." The cultural colonies, forced by "modernization" (the supermarket, urban renewal, automated equipment, Vatican II) to abandon their own styles of life—the hierarchical family, ward politics, closed unions, old neighborhoods, religion, language, food—become witnesses to behavior indicating that the (perhaps mythic) mainstream has begun to stagnate, that a lot of people no longer believe in it, or no longer believe in the old ways of getting there. Those on the move upward and outward have, in other words, no attractive place to go. Which is to say that the underclass tenants have discovered the neglect of the landlord.

Blacks are alienated because they have been kept out of the running. The white ethnics are frustrated because public attention, in defiance of the rhetoric of individual initiative and equality, has gone to blacks. (And because affluent WASPs, who had discriminated against all minorities, are trying to shift the burden of blame on the white underclass.) All of them, sensing the decline of WASP self-confidence and leadership, are left with choices among law and order (meaning militant normalcy, the old ethic), a return to their own cultural and political resources, or exotic combinations of the two. Following the lead, and to their eyes, success, of Black Power and Black Studies, a lot of minorities are trying to redevelop or to invent some exactly corresponding form of ethnic consciousness for themselves. Most of the whites, however, are or in the end will be content to cheer on the cops. For the first time we have Polish vigilantes and a Hebrew posse (the Jewish Defense League). Blacks and honkies, talking like frontiersmen, are buying guns. If the old WASP ethic was the ethic of making it, it isn't surprising that the most militant contemporary exponents of that ethic—those inclined to take its legends of force and action literally—should be among people outside the system trying to break in.

A measure of the decline of the WASP style—perhaps the best measure we have—is the conquest of space. From Lindbergh to NASA (or from Jack Armstrong to Neil Armstrong), from the man who was still a conqueror trusting his own bets and his own skills, and therefore an underdog (no dry runs, no simulators, no mission control) to the org-man, programmed and computerized to the last $24-billion step and the last televised statement, betting his life on the competence and devotion of anonymous technicians: courageous yes, underdog never. A symbol of modern man, to be sure (what if the trains stop or the electricity fails, what if the water becomes polluted and poisonous?), but also a sign of the decline of the great old WASP virtues of self-reliance, initiative, irreverence. Lindbergh was free enterprise; Apollo was the work of a crowd. No ape could have flown the *Spirit of St. Louis* from New York to Paris. But we could have sent an ape to the moon. Or a robot. With a fake flag artificially distended for a dead place where there is no wind.

It was a WASP enterprise all the way. Is it possible to conceive of NASA sending a Negro, a Jew—or a woman? Muhammad Ali perhaps? Joe Namath? Norman Mailer (who wanted to go)? Can one conceive of an astronaut who does not fit absolutely congruously into the background, like Muzak in a supermarket or Spiro Agnew at a picnic of Legionnaires? Can one conceive of an astronaut's wife living in a Jewish section of the Bronx, or expressing an opinion critical of the Vietnam war, or not taking the children to church on Sunday, or having a career of her own? Was it not inevitable that one of the wives would get down on her knees in front of the television set to pray for a safe re-entry? (One can imagine, in that setting, that Walter Cronkite *is* God.) Can one expect Richard Nixon not to say that the mission was the greatest thing since the Creation—or Billy Graham not to suggest, in reply, that perhaps the Resurrection was more important?

What made the moonshot interesting was its unbelievably bad taste, the taste of cultural style that has lost its juice: suburbs and corporation offices, network television and the electric toothbrush, airline pilots and airline hostesses, "the whole mechanical consolidation of force," as Henry Adams wrote in the *Educa-*

tion, "which ruthlessly stamped out the life of the class into which Adams was born, but created monopolies capable of controlling the new energies that America adored." Clearly space travel is technologically impossible except as a collective enterprise. But that is precisely the point. There is no role for the American (i.e. WASP) hero. Heroes presumably defy great odds alone. Gary Cooper has been replaced by Dustin Hoffman.

You ask yourself: Does the Establishment live? And the answer, clearly, is Yes. And yet it does not live in the style to which it was accustomed. Ever since the development of large bureaucracies and tenure systems there has been a tendency among outside intellectuals to overestimate the influence of elites. Not that corporations and institutions are going out of style (and they may, in case of a recession, regain some of their allure to the ambitious because they offer security), but that they have become so large, so stiff, and so beset by critics and complexity as to have lost considerable influence and all the romance of their former connection to success. (In Nixon's Republican party there are disparaging references to "The Eastern Establishment" which suggest that there might now be more than one—meaning, of course, that there is none at all.) Here is Francis T. P. Plimpton, the former Deputy U.S. Ambassador to the U.N., and one of the finest representatives of the old style of WASP culture in America. A gentleman, a man of parts. From *Who's Who in America* (1964-1965):

> *PLIMPTON, Francis T. P., diplomat; b. N.Y.C., N.Y., Dec. 7, 1900; s. George Arthur and Frances Taylor (Pearsons) P.; grad. Phillips Exeter Acad., 1917; A.B., magna cum laude, Amherst Coll., 1922: L.L.B., Harvard University, 1925; LL.D., Colby College, 1960; married Pauline Ames, June 4, 1926; children—George Ames, Francis T. P., Jr., Oakes Ames, Sarah Gay. Admitted to bar, 1926; assoc. with Root, Clark, Buckner & Ballantine. N.Y. City, 1925-32 in charge of Paris office, 1930-31; gen. solicitor, Reconstruction Finance Corp., Washington, D.C., 1932-33; partner Debevoise, Plimpton & McLean, N.Y.C., and predecessor firms, 1933-61; dep. U.S. rep. to UN with rank ambassador E. and P., 1961–. Trustee U.S. Trust Co. of N.Y., Bowery Savs. Bank. Mem. U.S. delegation UN 15th-17th gen. assemblies. Trustee Tchrs. Ins. and Annuity Assn. (pres. trustees of stock), Coll. Retirement Equities Fund Corp., Amherst Coll., Barnard Coll. (vice chmn. bd.), Phillips Exeter Acad. (chmn. bd.), Union Theol. Sem., Athens Coll. (Greece), Lingnan U. (China), Dir. Philharmonic-Symphony Soc. N.Y., Roosevelt Hosp., Am-Italy Soc. Fellow Am. Bar Found.; mem. Am., N.Y. State bar assns., Am. Law Inst., Bar Assn. City N.Y., Fgn. Policy Assn. ....*

The style is responsible, worldly involvement, directing institutions which nourished and arbitrated the culture; schools, universities, hospitals, the Council on Foreign Relations, the United Nations, the Church Peace Union, the missionary college in China, the Philharmonic. They were good institutions all, and many of them still do their good works, but with the possible exception of the federal courts, most of them are no longer sanctified as sources of social and cultural initiative, or even as mediators of conflict. There must have been a time when it was fun to be a university trustee.

The interest and action tend to come from others. George Plimpton, the son of Francis T. P. and probably the best-known WASP dealer in living culture, operates like a Paris salonist among Interesting People (Capote, Mailer, the Kennedys), writing brilliantly of his amateur involvement in The Real Stuff: fighting Archie Moore, playing quarterback for the Detroit Lions, pitching to the Yankees. (All sports are now saturated with ethnics.) It is a new role for the children of privilege. Is there a redeeming social utility in this work? Had Plimpton been Jewish he might have played *schlemiel* in a jockstrap, but as an upper-class WASP perhaps all he can do is represent the man whose dreams of command have turned to fantasy and whose greatest moments of glory come from watching other people do something well. A WASP playing honkie and nigger to find out how it feels to be upward bound. Does the aspiring WASP hero have a choice other than that between Apollo and *Paper Lion?*

The enervation of WASP culture may derive, more than anything, from a loss of place. The geographic and psychic worlds of the old mainstream become less distinct, but certain special neighborhoods, even if they are a generation away, survive as regions of the mind. The sense of place: Salem and Boston and Concord; Zenith and Winesburg; Yoknapatawpha County. It produced people with accents and fashions and biases—personalities—that they carried around as overtly as parasols and walking sticks. And because they knew who they were, they were quite willing to be eccentric and crazy. Now much of that material is gone. The black ghetto still remains as a real place, and so does the memory, if not the fact, of South Boston, of Brooklyn, of rural Mississippi and small-town Texas. But how much of a sense of place can grow in a bedroom suburb? What is the inner sense of Bronxville or Winnetka?

Because WASPs regarded themselves as the proprietors of history and the managers of destiny, there was a double displacement. While they were losing their regions they also began to lose their special role as the intrinsic Americans. When we discovered that the country and the world were no longer easily manageable—when we lost our innocence—it was the WASP role which was most affected. No matter how enthusiastically the ethnics waved the flag, they had always been partial outsiders. (Or perhaps better to say that they enjoyed dual citizenship.) In any case, their culture never depended on the assurance that they were running the show. They were tenants, had learned to survive as minorities. Obviously this produced problems, but it also created the tensions and identities of which modern literature (for example) is made. And these conditions of tenancy haven't yet been destroyed, may, indeed, have been strengthened through the mass media, which have nationalized isolated pockets of minority culture. Moreover, the media help create new minorities, new constituencies: students, for example, and women. What kids or blacks do in one town is now immediately communicated to others. Normalcy doesn't make good television, happenings do.

The greatest effect of the melting pot, ironically, may not have been on immigrants and minorities, but on the mainstream.

The vacuum left by the old arbiters of the single standard—Establishment intellectuals, literary critics, English professors, museum directors, and all the rest—has produced a sort of cultural prison break. And not only by ethnics, by blacks and Indians, or by kids, but by a lot of others, including all sorts of WASPs themselves, who behave as if they have been waiting for this freedom all their lives. That a lot of what results from this new breakout is bad (and who, these days, can get away with saying that?), and that a lot will be transitory is hardly surprising. In a decade hundreds of thousands of "creative" people proclaimed themselves artists and poets, a million amateurs entered the culture biz, and God knows how many gurus, cultists, swamis, and T-group trainers hung out their shingles. No one could expect most of them to be good, or perhaps even to be serious. The wildcatters are working new territory and a lot are going to go bust. But for the moment they're thriving: the Stones and the Beatles, the groups and groupies, Polish Power and Black Studies, liberation schools and free universities, Norman Mailer's ego and Alexander Portnoy's mother, *The Graduate* and *Alice's Restaurant*, rebellious nuns and protesting priests, *Rat* and *Screw* and a hundred other underground papers, mixed-media shows and the Living Theater, bookstores of the occult, Taro cards and freaks and hipsters, miniskirts and maxi coats, beads and joss sticks...all coexisting (barely, uneasily) with Lyndon Johnson's cornpone, Norman Vincent Peale's sermons, *I Love Lucy*, *Reader's Digest*, and Apollo 12. If the 1960s produced the beginning of any sort of renaissance, its characteristic instruments are the hand-held movie camera, the electric guitar, and the mimeograph machine, and if its efforts survive in nothing else, they will undoubtedly be remembered by the greatest outpouring of poster art in all history: peace doves and protest proclamations, the face of John Lennon, the pregnant Girl Scout over the motto "Be Prepared," and the pregnant black woman over the 1968 campaign slogan, "Nixon's The One." This is a counter culture—not high, not low or middle—but eclectic.

Until recently, when encounter groups, public therapy, and other psychic ceremonies became fashionable, reason had been more or less successfully keeping the dark night of the soul within the hidden closets of the mind. And WASPs were the most reasonable people of all. There were, obviously, advantages in that. Most people, I suspect, prefer dispassionate men for airplane pilots, surgeons, and commanders of nuclear armed strategic bombers. Moreover, we may have survived the last twenty-five years precisely because we kept hot men from taking charge. But their style didn't do much for cultural enrichment. Now everything that a graying, nervous civlization kept jammed in those closets is coming out, whether it deserves to or not: sex in all forms, feelings, emotions, self-revelation, and forms of religion and ritual long condemned as superstition. "Honesty" replaces stoicism, and "love," however understood, overwhelms "work." It may well be that the kids are mining McLuhan's non-linear culture, that print and cool reason (and WASPs) will go under together. So far there is no way of knowing. What is certain is that the old media—books, newspapers, magazines— can no longer claim a monopoly on urgent cultural articulation, and that people who work the new territories have moved a long way from the old mainstream.

WASPs seem to have been crippled by their own sanity. They have become too levelheaded. Having confused their particular social order with the Immutability of Things (and with their own welfare), they have defaulted on their birthright of cussedness and irreverence. "This took courage, this took prudence, this took stoutheartedness," thinks Arthur Winner, Jr., James Gould Cozzens' hero, at the end of *By Love Possessed*. (He has just covered up—to his and Cozzens' satisfaction—some $200,000 worth of ledger-de-main perpetrated by one of his partners.) "In this life we cannot have everything for ourselves we might like to have....Victory is not in reaching certainties or solving mysteries; victory is making do with uncertainties, in supporting mysteries." WASPs are willing to be "sick"—meaning that they can have their neuroses and their "reason" too—but never crazy. People who are willing to be crazy are almost invariably Something Else. We no longer have, or seem to have the possibility of having, a figure like Bertrand Russell; we no longer even have an Everett Dirksen or a John L. Lewis.

WASP crimes these days are invariably dull—price fixing, antitrust capers, tax fraud—which is why we are so fascinated by Jimmy Hoffa, Roy Cohn, and the Mafia, why we need the Mafia, would have to invent it were we ever to suspect (as has Daniel Bell) that it doesn't really exist.

Beyond the formal institutions of business and government—the banks, the corporations, the State Department, and Congress—the unique provinces of WASP domination tend to be conservative (in the pure sense) and mediating. WASPs, I think, still regard themselves as the principal heirs of an estate in which the streams flowed clear, the air was clean, and the language pure. In the growing number of conservation societies, and in their almost exclusive dominion over libraries, dictionary-making, and (surprising as it may seem to those familiar with only the current "celebrities" in the profession) the teaching of English, they are trying to preserve some of that estate. But as "the environment" becomes a national issue, they are going to lose ground (you should pardon the pun) even as conservationists. There are going to be new men—technicians, population planners, engineers—who will move in on the Audubon Society, the Sierra Club, and the Izaak Walton League. The urban environment (John Lindsay vs. the New York legislature and Nelson Rockefeller) will demand parity with the environment of Daniel Boone and the bald eagle. On some issues urban and rural conservationists can make common cause, but on others (mass transit, housing, street cleaning, and garbage collection) they cannot.

But it would be unfortunate, perhaps even fatal, if the WASPs mediating function (through courts and other institutions) were also to be seriously eroded. It is inconceivable that America could ever be integrated on ethnic terms. Can one imagine this country as essentially Negro or Italian or Polish; or believe that the

Republican party would nominate anyone named Spiro Agnopopoulos for Vice President; or visualize a trial in which the defendant is white and all the other participants—jude, jurors, lawyers, witnesses—are black? (It did, in fact, happen—in the preliminary proceedings against the Klansmen charged with plotting to murder Charles Evers, the black mayor of Fayette, Mississippi—but it may never happen again.) For if the minorities no longer accept the new style of the mainstream, they are even further from accepting each other. And somebody is going to have to help keep them from tearing each other apart: cops and kids, blacks and blue-collar whites, freaks and squares. Robert Kennedy, I think, recognized this need before he was killed (significantly by a crazy ethnic resenting Kennedy's sympathy with other ethnics). This is also what made the reelection of John Lindsay possible—and significant. The Jews and Negroes of New York may have distrusted him, but they trusted the Italians even less.

Even mediation, however, is no longer feasible on the old standard rigid WASP terms. For the first time, any sort of settlement among competing group interests is going to have to do more than pay lip service to minorities and to the pluralism of styles, beliefs, and cultures. The various commissions on violence and urban riots struggled with that problem but couldn't see beyond their assumptions to the logical conclusion. America is not on the verge of becoming two separate societies, one rich and white, the other poor and black. It is becoming, in all its dreams and anxieties, a nation of outsiders for whom no single style or ethic remains possible. The Constitutional prohibition against an established state religion was adopted because the Jeffersonians understood the destructive consequences of imposing a single set of cultural beliefs beyond the guarantees of freedom and due process.

The Establishment in America has, in part, lost its grip because it devoted itself too much to the management of its game, rather than to the necessary objective of making it possible for everyone to play his own. Minorities—cultural, ethnic, even minorities of one—are fighting over the wreckage of the WASP-abandoned cities and the WASP-forsaken culture. If the WASP Establishment is to act as umpire in this contest—and if we are not to become a police state—it will have to recognize the legitimacy of the contenders. One of the reasons that growing up in America is absurd and chaotic is that the current version of Americanization—what the school people call socializing children—has lost its appeal. We will now have to devise ways of recognizing and assessing the alternatives. The mainstream is running thin.

2 SKIN DEEP IS NOT GOOD ENOUGH

Walter Kerr

Anyone who has managed to get through the last two or three weeks is suddenly aware of how fast history can move. Sometimes, though, we don't notice it moving—until we sit down before an image of ourselves (a poster, a piece of architecture, a play) that has always been accepted as standard and just isn't any more. We blink and realize that a skin has been shed.

It happened last season, I think, with "Hallelujah, Baby!" The Negro gains that the show contented itself with describing no longer seemed real gains at all, certainly nothing worth singing and dancing about. There we were up on the stage, in the comfortable liberal postures we'd grown so used to—patting Negroes on the head as we tried to get them up front on the buses. And instantly we knew that paternalism was dead, had been killed inside us while we were scarcely looking. With so much more at stake in the air that we couldn't help breathing, our posture had changed before our eyes had.

In a quite different way, "The Education of H*y*m*a*n K*a*p*l*a*n" backs into us hard enough to make us realize we weren't standing still. When, some 30 years ago, Leo Rosten first wrote his charming stories about an exuberant Jewish immigrant who hit night school like a ten-strike, they seemed apt. In another 30 years they will probably seem truly quaint. In 1968 they simply seem false.

Now this is a spot of bad luck for a well-meaning musical to run into. The current entertainment at the Alvin has been tidily—if rather solemnly—put together by George Abbott. It has Tom Bosley, the Fiorello of old, to splash proud asterisks between the letters of his name—in living color, hurled at a banner from a paint bucket, the asterisks come out green—and then to subside into dismay as he learns that his beloved Miss Mitnick is to be married to another in the spring. The sight of Mr. Bosley keeping himself wrapped in coat and muffler well into the warm weather, hoping to hold spring at bay, is a nice one. And echoes of the melting-pot humor that once seemed touching and relevant still stir. When Mr. Parkhill, that dedicated teacher, orders his pupils to prepare to "let Shakespeare's thoughts sink into your minds," the silent rustle of minds is delightful: 20 tabula rasas sit up at the ready, welcoming an invasion that will make them all kings. When Mr. Parkhill has finished reading a passage from "Macbeth" and asks "Any questions?", 20 hands shoot skyward like an instant army of lances. We laugh at the wholesale reflex because of course these near-illiterates will have questions. And we laugh again because the questions aren't at all the ones we expected.

But in the meantime we have been puzzled, maybe a little bit dismayed. One of those matronly housewives in the class has responded regularly with a loud

"OY!" No one, naturally enough (though it is not side-splitting now), can pronounce a "w". There is an exercise in giving the opposites of words. For these ardent adult innocents, the opposite of "fresh" is "canned." The opposite of "new" is "second hand." Mr. Bosley is so far from grasping the word "hobo" that he uses it in the sentence "My hobo is hiking" (he means "hobby," which must have seemed unlikely at any time, under any comic sun). At Ellis Island, gateway to the land of opportunity, the immigrants sing, "Maybe we don't belong," but "funny, or not, we're here." An Irish cop on the corner, hustling classmates homeward, barks, "I was a foreigner once meself."

In the theater one's first reaction to this sort of thing is that the jokes are merely stale. "Oy!", after all, was never anything more than a lazy bid for a quick laugh, and if "canned" as the opposite of "fresh" once had an observant neighborhood way-of-life flavor to it, the flavor has long since been lost in the chewing. In point of fact, librettist Benjamin Bernard Zavin has become careless enough to imagine that Abie's Irish Rose is a Rose is a Rose, and blooms freshly. We could have made the jokes when we were 10, going on Potash and Perlmutter.

But something else is wrong. The image of an American is now wrong. As things stand, Mr. Parkhill is the American of the piece, and the immigrants are the good folk who are trying to make themselves over in his likeness. They wish to pronounce "w" as he does, read as he does, hear as he does, think as he does. He, clean-cut and confident, is no doubt what we have come to call a Wasp. A good and earnest and likable Wasp. He is us, and they are they, waiting to become us.

That isn't how our eyes or ears register it any more, though. Looking at the stage, we squint and upset everything. Today, only 25 years back, the immigrants—above all the Jewish immigrants—seem more American than he does. They are the faces and voices and inflections of thought that seem most familiar to us, literally second nature. He is the odd ball, the stranger, the fossil. We glance at him, a bit startled, and say to ourselves, "Where did he go?" We remember him; pale, poised, neatly dressed, briskly sure of himself. And we see him as an outsider, an outlander, a reasonably noble breed in the act of vanishing. He is performing tonight as a molder of minds, but he is no longer in any sense the mold we have in mind. He has stopped being representative, and we didn't notice it until this minute. Not so emphatically, anyway.

A vast transition has reversed what we are looking at. It's not just a matter of having been so exposed to Jewish entertainers and Jewish novelists that their tricks of rhythm have curled up in everyone's ears and come to feel at home there. That's happened, all right. Collecting Yiddish words and dropping them into Madison Avenue sentences has been fashionable for a long time now, so fashionable that it, too, is out of date. The Gentile who can't invert his sentence structure to make it sound pleasantly Jewish probably doesn't exist outside Kansas. (How is it in Kansas? I don't know.) Everybody today has a Jewish mother, whether she is Irish or whatnot. And the Gentile, or for that matter the Jew, who now settles for a fast "all right already" or a sentence beginning with "So" in order to display his credentials as a sophisticate is all too plainly not a sophisticate. That's baby talk, affectation, even less than skin deep.

Skin deep isn't good enough, isn't true enough. What has happened since World War II is that the American sensibility itself has become in part Jewish, perhaps nearly as much Jewish as it is anything else. And this is nothing so superficial as sympathetic identification (because so many Jews were killed) or a playful Gentile gesture of friendliness (because quirks of speech can be charming). It goes right to the bone, all the way in. The literate American mind has come in some measure to think Jewish, to respond Jewishly. It has been taught to, and it was ready to. After the entertainers and the novelists came the Jewish critics, politicians, theologians. Critics and politicians and theologians are by profession molders: they form ways of seeing. And American, at this particular moment in her history, desperately needed a new way of seeing. She had been moved, willy-nilly and by circumstances, into a world environment that called for an unfamiliar response: she had to learn how to deal effectively, courageously, and even humorously with irrational pressures that descended like lightning, with hostility, frustration and despair. An experienced teacher was available.

Well, I should leave the how and why to trained sociologists, I suppose. But the degree of penetration, the spot that is touched when an American says "I," is now so marked that there is scarcely any "they" any more, any quaintness any more. The cast of mind is embedded, firm, on the verge of self-recognition, increasingly flexible. The last sentence of Bernard Malamud's remarkable novel "The Assistant" has become prophetic. All of us, whoever we are or wherever we've come from, in some dim but ineradicable way now share the awareness of the young Italian who has wormed his way into a direct experience of Jewish days and nights. "After Passover he became a Jew."

And so, going to a perfectly ordinary musical for a perfectly ordinary evening's entertainment, we go as someone other than we were when the words were first written down. The story rewrites itself in front of us, and we are thrown slightly off balance. The shoe is on the other foot, now. And whose shoe?

Part 2
RADICAL STYLES

A
From the I.W.W. to the Yippies

[handwritten: MARXISTS]

[handwritten: Haywood = Notorious member of the industrial workers.]

This section examines radicalism on the left, beginning with "Big Bill" Haywood, the most notorious member of the Industrial Workers of the World (I.W.W.), and ends with Abbie Hoffman, the most uninhibited of the Yippies. Selection 4 concerns those who were Marxists in the intervening era. We contend that these individuals shared many common political ideas but that their life styles varied considerably, reflecting changes in their perceptions of society and the role of a revolutionary.

"Big Bill" Haywood was born in Salt Lake City and became a cowboy and miner while still a teenager. His interest in unions began with his work experience and he tried, unsuccessfully, to create a union for cowboys. He later joined the Western Federation of Miners and rose in the hierarchy of the union. In 1901, he achieved the position of secretary-treasurer, leaving the mines for this full-time office. Because he believed that organization was the solution to the miners' problems, Haywood worked hard for the Western Federation of Miners. Disillusionment came with the failure of the union in the Colorado labor disputes of 1903-1905. Violence in Cripple Creek, blamed on the union, furnished the excuse for the governor to deport 79 miners and for local mobs to destroy the union's stores.

In 1905, Haywood met with several other union leaders and political radicals in Chicago to attempt to reform the labor movement. Although Socialist Party leaders Eugene V. Debs and Victor Berger were conspicuous by their absence, those present did agree on 11 principles, including the creation of an industrial union by means of a general convention. The convention met, with Haywood presiding, and the Industrial Workers of the World was born.

Later in the same year the former governor of Idaho, Frank Steunenberg, who had broken a miners' strike in Couer d'Alene in 1899, died of a bomb blast at his front gate. The bomber was Harry Orchard. James McParland, the Pinkerton agent who infiltrated the Molly Maquires, came to Idaho to investigate. He convinced Orchard to implicate Charles Moyer and William D. Haywood, both then

20

officials of the Western Federation of Miners. Although the jury cleared Moyer and Haywood, the effect on Haywood was to radicalize him.

Despite Haywood's exoneration in 1907, he was removed from his office in the Western Federation of Miners. He also was inactive in the I.W.W. until the Lawrence, Massachusetts, strike of 1912. At that time he once again became prominent. From 1914 to 1917, a period of major growth for the I.W.W. Haywood served as the organization's general secretary and treasurer. Arrested again in 1917 on charges of interfering with the war effort, Haywood was imprisoned in Leavenworth until 1919, when he was released on bail pending an appeal. He jumped bail and fled to Russia with other I.W.W. members. By this time Haywood was ill, was drinking heavily, and had been removed from his I.W.W. office. He lived in a Moscow hotel, reminiscing about the past, until his death in 1928.

Haywood's memoirs were written with the aid of ghost writers in his later days in Russia. His recollections fit Haywood's view of himself as a Westerner, rugged individual, and he-man. He dressed to fit the part, with a patch over one eye and a Western hat. In part because of men like Haywood, the I.W.W. became identified with the Western hero. As Robert L. Tyler suggests in "The I.W.W. and the West," the Wobblies are usually the villains in stories; but they are "mythic symbols," "spiky individualists," possessing the attributes of the "earlier mountainmen, cowboys, and sodbusters." As Tyler concludes, the development of the role of the Wobbly is a curious one.

Thus the reflection of the I.W.W. in popular legend and historiography has followed a traceable path, from an organization of dangerous, foreign "Syndicalists," to an organization of wartime saboteurs and traitors to an organization of manly primitives fighting the good fight for freedom, to a jolly band of rogues ushering out the last frontier.

The image of Haywood in Selection 3 is that of the frontier hero. There are cowboys and Indians at the start; there is the mining town complete with the saloon and its companionship and violence. But there is also an element of domesticity and a trace of Benjamin Franklin's uplift spirit as Haywood pictures himself achieving status through his efforts in the Western Federation of Miners. Haywood does not speak of a free life as Abbie Hoffman does; he is committed to a world of work, a world of organization, and to a family as seemingly conventional as those of the mine owners whom he opposed. The limit of his ambition is to become important in the union, to raise wages and improve the working conditions of the miners.

Selection 4 is an account of the radical left from 1912 to 1950 by Daniel Aaron. This account contrasts these radicals with the liberal reformers of the period—Frederic C. Howe, Randolph Bourne, and Herbert Croly. The radicals included in the section are Waldo Frank, V. F. Calverton, and Lincoln Steffens. Like Haywood, Frank, Calverton, and Steffens did have an interest in Communism. Waldo Frank became a Communist; V. F. Calverton joined the Communist

Party for a short time before becoming disillusioned; Lincoln Steffens never became a Communist but did consider migrating to Russia just prior to his death. All shared a pessimism about the prospects of American society much like that of Haywood.

These three radicals, however, were different from "Big Bill" Haywood. They were from middle-class origins, not working-class ones. They also rejected liberal reformism, even though Steffens' muckraking stimulated Progressivism earlier. Their self-images were those of radical critics of society who would effect change by propagandistic means. Unlike Haywood's radicalism, theirs did not originate from personal exploitation; it was a product of vicarious experiences and intellectual conviction.

The Cold War effectively ended the intellectual flirtation with Communism. Although many liberals never were sympathetic to either Communist means or aims, the fear of Russian expansion and the domestic reaction to the experience of the 1930s caused almost all liberals to assume an anti-Communist position. Some who had joined the party—Whittaker Chambers is a good example—switched to a conservative position, abandoning liberalism altogether. The role of the radical intellectual dedicated to overthrowing the system shrank. Like the Wobbly, the Communist became a symbol of an earlier era. The few remaining grew old and their positions seemed dated and stale. The radical as worker or as writer had met his most unrelenting enemy—time.

The 1960s produced another style of radical leftist. This style is illustrated in Selection 5 by Abbie Hoffman, leader of the Yippies, one of the Chicago Seven, and master of the put-on. Given to wearing clothes replicating the flag and being a master of the dramatic gesture, Hoffman started out straight as a product of a Jewish middle-class home and of Brandeis University. He might have become a successful professional man or even a radical intellectual of the type of the 1930s. Instead, he practiced guerrilla theater and courtroom confrontation. Charged with inciting a riot at the Democratic National Convention in 1968, Hoffman and his six codefendants denied almost all of the premises of American jurisprudence. Hoffman discarded his last name because it matched that of the presiding judge; he declared himself to be a citizen of the Woodstock Nation (named after the rock festival and the title of a book he had written) and, in general, behaved in a fashion calculated to shock middle-class Americans. Here Hoffman's trial behavior contrasts sharply with Haywood's, which was much more restrained (the fact that Haywood was on trial for his life on the first occasion might have been sobering).

In Selection 5 Hoffman interviews himself, outlining his methods and goals. Although some of his statements may be deliberately provocative, they reveal much about his conception of the role of the young radical. In the first place, the role is to be anti-ideological. Hoffman disagrees with both Haywood and Calverton on this. In the second place, the role is anti-intellectual. The best things in life are sensual—dancing, making love, listening to music, and having fun. Life is to be composed of hedonistic pleasure. In the third place, the role is anti-middle class. Hoffman rejects the values of work, sacrifice, dedication, and responsibility, as well as the emotions of anger and frustration. The values "Big Bill" Haywood internalized in the service of the I.W.W. are wrong. Nor are the present-day Communists any different in their allegiance to a work ethic. The meeting between Kosygin and President Johnson showed the two participants to be the same, according to Hoffman—dull, bureaucratic, sterile, and puritanical. Hoffman rejects older radicalism as well as older liberalism. Hoffman is radical, not just because he admires the National Liberation Front, the Cuban Revolution, and the Viet Cong attack on the United States Embassy in Saigon, or because he believes that the *Daily News* is more honest than *The New York Times,* or because he considers Robert Kennedy more of an enemy than George Wallace. He is radical in his rejection of political solutions. He does not believe, as Haywood and the Marxist intellectuals did, that a takeover of the governing structure, either by a general strike or violent revolution, is the answer. While earlier radicals were antipolice because the police enforced the law of a capitalistic society, Hoffman is against the police because they represent technological society. Haywood was antitheft, arguing that the present organization of society allowed the capitalist to steal from the worker. Hoffman is in favor of thievery as a way of life. The earlier radicals spoke of a community of shared responsibilities that included submission to authority. When Hoffman speaks of community, he means a community of shared experiences—listening to music, playing in the sun, and taking drugs. Hoffman is hedonistic where the earlier radicals were not. His vision of the good society is utopian, one in which the state no longer exists. This utopia can be reached, according to Hoffman, by a change in social attitude rather than by political change.

Historically, no society treats radicals kindly; they are pressured into conformity, imprisoned, or exiled. American society is no exception, although it is certainly more tolerant of dissent than are authoritarian societies. However, the radicalism of Abbie Hoffman is a much more difficult radicalism to combat than the earlier political radicalism because it is based on different premises. It takes a legitimate role in American society, that of adolescence, and extends it. The adolescent does not have adult responsibilities. He can live in a world without meaningful work, a world where politics is irrelevant, and a world where emotions should be exercised. It is a Peter Pan world but with physically mature participants. The Yippie becomes the romantic primitive who has escaped the constraints of both the superego and social institutions.

The significant feature of radicalism that we have emphasized is the guise that it assumes. Should the radical be a cowboy or an intellectual or a clown? Each assumes the role he chooses because of the impact this role has on him or on the society. Each in his own way reflects the changing views about appropriate behavior held by that society. Hoffman, in the end, will probably be as spectacular a failure as Haywood, but the role he played may reveal as much about contemporary America as Haywood's revealed about the last frontier.

3 SILVER CITY

William D. Haywood

The road to Silver City was through a country that was rugged, bleak, and gray. No habitations except the occasional stations, most of them deserted, and a farm here and there. Not a tree to be seen in the entire distance, nothing but crooked, gnarled sagebrush, greasewood and stretches of browse. At least this was true until one came to the river; there the country was broken up into foot-hills with high mountains behind them.

Approaching the first summit, my thoughts went back to a story told me by Bill Coulter years before, about being chased down this road by Indians when he was driving a stage. I could imagine the flying stage-coach and Bill throwing the buckskin into his team, with a band of Indians behind whooping and yelling but never getting close enough to the galloping horses to shoot an arrow at the driver.

Before I got to Jack Baudoin's I was hungry and thirsty. I had a few dollars in my pocket, but I thought, Hell, what good is money, anyway? Here at least was one place where a car-load of twenty-dollar gold pieces would not buy a square meal. Why should money buy a meal, I wondered; money did not seem to me an equivalent of value, an equivalent of labor, or an equivalent of anything else. This was something that I would have to look into.

At Jordan Valley I turned my horse in to pasture, hung my saddle and bridle up in the livery stable, and took stage for Silver City.

When we got there, I went into a Chinese restaurant, and afterward knocked around the town for an hour or so. I was looking for a place to sleep that night. A man said to me:

"I've got a bed in the old Potosi shaft house. You can roll in with me until your blankets come, but you'd better come up and look at the place so if you happen to come in late you won't stumble and fall down the shaft in the dark."

I went up to the shaft house with him. There were several rolls of blankets scattered about a deep open shaft into the old mine, without any cover or railing around it. I used this place as a lodging house for some days after my blankets arrived. I did not go to the races, but asked the men to get my saddle and horse in Jordan Valley on their way home, and take them back to the ranch.

The first morning I was up early and went to the Blaine mine, rustling a job. I did this for several mornings and sometimes at the noon hour as well, but without success. Hutchinson was the name of the manager; he had been in Nevada years before. I spent all the money I had and went to old Hutch again and told him that I'd have to have some kind of a job.

"What can you do?" he asked me. I told him I could do most anything around a mine.

SOURCE: Reprinted by permission of International Publishers Co., Inc. Copyright © 1929, William D. Haywood, *Bill Haywood's Book. The Autobiography of William D. Haywood.*

"Can you run car?"

"I'm a miner, but I can run car."

"All right. Come on in the morning."

That day I met Dave O'Neill downtown; I had known him in Tuscarora. He handed me a five-dollar gold piece, saying:

"Bill, you might need this."

I said to him, "I am broke, Dave, but I'm going to work in the morning."

"Well," he said, "Keep it anyway. You can hand it to me payday."

Loans of this kind were a general custom among the miners, and it was seldom or never that they were not repaid. Within the last three years Herman Andrigg, with whom I worked in Silver City, where he was champion driller, repaid a loan I made to him more than a quarter of a century ago.

I went to the old shaft house, rolled up my blankets and carried them to the Blaine mine bunk-house. The bunk next to the door was vacant. This just suited me. The bunk-house was a long rambling place with bunks built two high along the walls, accommodating, I suppose, about sixty men. The air was none too good at best, as the opening and shutting of the door was almost the only ventilation.

In the bunk-house, while we sat around the stove or lolled in the bunks, all the old tales of the different mining camps would be related by men who had been on the scene of action, or who had heard the stories at first hand. Bill Pooley, a "Cousin Jack," as we called the Cornishmen, of whom there were many in Silver City, was a good story teller. He once told us about a friend of his who had had smallpox. Bill said:

"When he got well, 'e was so deep pitted that 'e 'ad to shave 'isself with a brace and bit."

Nothing pleased the Cousin Jacks better than to get a lease where they could make wages or a little more. They called this "tributing." A number of them had "tributed" on the Poor Man mine. Simon Harris, the superintendent of the mine, decided to stop this kind of work and to work all the men on wages. Eight or ten of the Cousin Jacks were sitting about a big round table in the Brewery Saloon. They were complaining and lamenting about the loss of their tributes, when one of the group said to another:

"See'ere, Tussy, can't thee pray? Can't thee pray for we tributes?"

Tussy answered; "It's been a long time since I made a prayer, but I'll try." He began:

"Dear Lord, dost thee know Simmon 'Arris, superintendent of the Poor Man mine? If thee know en, we wish for thee to take en and put en in 'Ell, and there let the bugger frizzle and fry, until 'e give us back we just tributes. And when 'e do, dear Lord, we ask thee to take en out of 'Ell again, an' grease en up a bit and turn of en loose. Amen."

All were pleased with the prayer, and bought another gallon of beer in Tussy's honor. Like all prayers, however, it was ineffective. Leasing was abolished and the Cousin Jacks lost their tributes.

There were six or seven car-men in the Blaine mine. We started work ahead of the miners. Our work was to push the cars in the tunnel back to the chutes where the men were working in the stopes above. When we lifted the gates in the chutes the cars would fill without any trouble. It was only from the face of the tunnel, before connections were made with the adjoining Black Jack mine, that we had any shoveling to do. When the cars were loaded, we would push them out, and going down a place called the short cut we would step on the foot-board behind and the cars would gain such speed that we could ride all the way to the dump. The ore we dumped in a bin and from there it was run to the mill which stood in the canyon a few hundred yards below the tunnel.

After a few days I was put to work in the short cut stopes. In my stope, on the opposite shift, worked a man by the name of Matt McLain. When he became shift boss I was working for him. He came into the stope one day where I had a platform rigged up. Leaning his arms on the staging he began talking about old times in Pennsylvania. He said:

"You've heard of the Molly Maguires?"

I said that I had; every one had heard of the Molly Maguires.

"But," he went on, "you never heard how they were trapped. There was a certain Franklin B. Gowen who was manager of one or more of the mines in Shamokin Valley. He decided to wipe out the Molly Maguires, which was a kind of a labor organization that would not stand for a reduction of wages. Gowen employed the Pinkerton Detective Agency, and they sent one of their stool-pigeons whose real name was McParland.

"He came into Pottsville as James McKenna. He had a little bundle tied on the end of a stick over his shoulder when he walked into town and inquired for a place to stop. He found a boarding house that suited him. One evening he went as though by chance into Barney Hogle's saloon and invited everybody in the place to have a drink. When he paid for the drinks, he displayed a roll of bills and incidentally remarked that he had just quit his ship at Philadelphia; that he had got tired of the sea and was going to get a job on land for awhile if he could. He asked Hogle if he could get work in that neighborhood.

"Hogle was one of the bond-masters of the Molly Maguires, that is, he was one of the leaders of this organization that had been transplanted from Ireland and now in Pennsylvania was made up principally of coal miners. Hogle was also a saloon-keeper, and he had seen young McKenna's wad of money. The young Irishman was a good spender and Hogle wanted to cultivate him as a customer. But not wanting to seem anxious in this regard, he answered McKenna by saying that it took a pretty good man to hold a job there.

"McKenna flared up. 'I'm a pretty good man,' he said, buying another drink, 'I'll sing a song, dance a jig, or fight with any man in the house for the whisky for everybody.' He sang an Irish song, he danced an Irish jig. Looking about he saw a likely lad sizing him up. Sidling up to the young miner, he said, 'Is it yez that'll be wanting to try me out?' 'I will that,' was the reply.

"Every one adjourned to the handball court in the rear. McKenna played handball a few minutes, then they stripped for the fight, which was to be a 'fair go.' The audience was all Irish, and nothing tickled their fancy more than a good fight. They selected a referee and squared off. The miner cut McKenna on the cheek, but Mac countered to the jaw with his left, and jabbed his right to the ribs. 'That's the b'y,' shouted a voice. Then with a straight left to the chin the miner drove Mac against the end wall. Mac recovered quickly and with both hands punched the miner about the body, forcing him to a clinch.

"The next round the miner feinted with his left and landed a slam on Mac's nose. The blood spurted as Mac swung and got the young fellow at the point of the jaw, keeling him over. The fight was finished. Every one had been highly pleased. McKenna washed his bloody nose; his right eye was nearly closed. Shaking hands with the young miner, he said, 'Yez were a better man that I thought ye wuz.' Back in the bar-room there were more drinking and dancing. It was declared by all to have been a fine night.

"McKenna patronized this place frequently and got work through the influence of Hogle. All his associates were Molly Maguires. This was just what he wanted. Some time later he was asked to become a Molly Maguire. Of course he readily assented, but said that to be a good Molly Maguire perhaps one ought to have had more experience than had fallen to his lot. It was but a short time after he had joined that he was employed in some kind of official capacity in the organization.

"This gave him the opportunity for which he was looking. Through the skulduggery of this detective, a number of young miners were involved in a murder; at least they were mixed up in it to such an extent that they were charged with murder. A warrant was issued for Tom Hurley. McKenna, who by this time was suspected by the miners, saw Hurley on a train, and started after him. Hurley went to the rear of the train. McKenna and the other dicks who were with him were intercepted here and there in following him, and Hurley had time to drop off the train.

"When the young miners appeared for trial, McKenna testified against them and gave his name as James McParland, a Pinkerton detective. The price the Molly Maguires paid for trusting their affairs to a saloon-keeper was the lives of ten of their members who were executed, and fourteen who were sentenced to from two to seven years in the penitentiary. McParland would probably have been unable to wriggle his slimy way into the organization without Hogle's help."

This was the first time I had ever heard of an agent provocateur. I later learned that it was the first time that such a method had been used against the working-class in America. McLain's story made a deep impression on me.

On June 19, 1896, I was working with two others, cutting out for a station in the Blaine tunnel where they were going to sink a shaft. I was up on a staging, and got down to ask one of the car-men if I could ride his car out. With his assent I started. A big rock on the front end of the car struck the first chute I came to, tipping it up so that my right hand got caught between the car and the bottom of the chute, getting badly mangled. My candle had been put out by the jolt, and I was left in total darkness. I groped my way back to where Big Barney Quigley was working in a cross-cut. I called to him and he came out and walked with me to the doctor's office. We were about three thousand feet in the tunnel then. There was no "first aid," nor bandages, it was just a question of getting there somehow and keeping the bleeding hand from knocking against the wall as we went out. I remember that even at this late season of the year we walked through open cuts where the snow was more than six feet deep.

When we got to the doctor, he said that part of my hand would have to be amputated. I told him that I did not want to go through life doubly crippled. I was already handicapped by the loss of an eye. If there was any chance of saving the hand I wanted him to try to do it. He said:

"We'll try," and dressed the hand. I refused to take an anaesthetic, in spite of the pain, because I was afraid that he would take off the fingers while I was unconscious. After some days the hand showed that it was beginning to mend. It had to be dressed every day and I carried it in a sling a long time.

My wife and little girl had then just come to Silver City. While I was looking for a house to live in we were stopping at the Idaho Hotel. As I was unable to work because of my broken hand, the miners took up a collection and presented me with a purse of money that tided us over this emergency very well. I bought a two-room house from a miner named Schilling who was leaving camp, paying part down and the rest in installments. We moved into our new home.

In the early part of the following August, Edward Boyce, president of the Western Federation of Miners, came to Silver City for the purpose of organizing the miners. Two meetings were held in the county court house, one on the eighth and one on the tenth of August. I attended both, though I did not know then that I would ever be able to go back to work in the mines, as I was still carrying my arm in the sling. But I was greatly interested in what Boyce had to say. Here was a man who had been through the Coeur d'Alenes strike of 1892. He was tall, slender, had a fine head with thin hair. His features were good, but his teeth were prominent. This was due to salivation, contracted while working with quicksilver in a quartz mill. This is a vocational disease met with quite often among mill men.

With more than a thousand other miners he had been arrested by the Federal soldiers when they were sent to the Coeur d'Alenes at the request of Governor Shoup. A bull-pen was built in which the prisoners were confined for more than six months. This was a rough lumber structure two stories high. There was no sanitation provided, and the excrement of the men above dripped through the cracks in the plank floor on the men below. They became vermin-infested and diseased, and some of them died.

The Helena-Frisco mill had been blown up. A story afterward appeared in Collier's weekly, implicating George A. Pettibone. Pettibone was the head of the assembly of the Knights of Labor at Gem. He was already well known among the miners. The story related in a graphic manner how some boxes of powder had been put into the water flume some hundreds of feet up the mountainside. The boxes slid down the flume at a tremendous velocity and exploded when they struck the mill; it was a long gun. The unreliability of the story was shown in the attempt to implicate Pettibone by asserting that he had been so badly injured that he lost one of his arms. I knew Pettibone in after years; neither one of his arms or hands had ever been hurt, though his feelings were badly embittered by the conditions of the mining camps of the Coeur d'Alenes before the strike of '92. He could never forget the maggots in the meat, nor the swathy weasel-faced stool-pigeon called Serengo, in the employ of the Mine Owners' Association organized by John Hays Hammond.

Boyce related how the Western Federation of Miners had been conceived while he and thirteen others were in the Ada county prison at Boise, Idaho. Jim Hawlay, their attorney, who had been a miner, suggested to them that all of the miners of the West should come together in one organization. This thought met the approval of the prisoners, as the miners' unions then in existence were scattered assemblies of the Knights of Labor. Boyce explained how, when they were released, a convention was called on May 13, 1893, in Butte, Montana, and the Western Federation of Miners was organized.

He described the first big strike that occurred after the formation of the W.F.M. This was in Cripple Creek, Colorado, in 1894. Every man in the district had gone on strike to prevent a reduction of wages and to establish the eight-hour day. Some of the mine owners of this district, then reputed to be millionaires, had formed themselves into an organization called the Mine Owners' Association. They knew that they could not depend upon Governor Waite, who had been a miner and was elected on the Populist ticket, but they knew that they could rely on the county commissioners and the sheriff of what was then El Paso county. These officers, at the instigation of the Mine Owners' Association, hired and equipped a small army of deputies, thirteen hundred or more men, who were provided with two hundred saddle horses, gatling guns, and other up-to-date instruments of war.

Previous to this the governor had sent the militia to the district, but upon investigation found that there was no occasion for the presence of the soldiers, and withdrew them. The sheriff mobilized his deputies and started to Cripple Creek. Two hundred of them got as far as Wilbur. The miners learned of their presence and sent a detachment of men against them. There was some shooting and one or two were killed on each side.

Governor Waite now made a personal investigation. He addressed the miners in their hall at Altman. He called out the militia at once and sent them to Cripple Creek with instructions to place themselves between the miners and the hired thugs. The miners were barricaded upon the crest of Bull Hill, where they had a strong fort and proposed to fight to the finish in protection of their wives and families and their rights as workingmen.

The commanding officer, General Brooks, notified the assembled deputies that if they did not disperse he would fire upon them. They left the camp the next day for Colorado Springs. They were so incensed at their failure at Cripple Creek that they tarred and feathered Tarney, the adjutant general of the state, who was in charge of the soldiers at Cripple Creek.

Governor Waite had been elected by the workers of the state. The mine owners knew that they couldn't fool with him, because upon his taking office he had ordered out the militia and had trained their cannon on the city hall in Denver, when the previous office-holders representing the mine owners and their business interests had refused to give up office.

Boyce reminded us that Governor Waite had the distinction of being the only governor in the United States who had ever called out the soldiers to protect the workers.

He told us about the conviction of Ed Lyons and Mike Tully, who had been charged with blowing up the Strong mine. Later they were released from the penitentiary and the stockholders of the mine sued Sam Strong, one of the owners, for the damages resulting from the explosion.

At these meetings Boyce initiated several hundred charter members of the Silver City Miners' Union Number 66 of the Western Federation of Miners.

"That is a good strong pledge," said I to Tom Fry, who was standing at my shoulder. The court room where the meetings were held was crowded. There were miners and mill workers from the Black Jack mine, the Florida mill, the Trade Dollar, the Blaine, the Poor Man, and the smaller mines of the camp. Every seat and every bit of standing room was filled. The charter was held open for some time to allow as many as possible to become charter members.

I was elected a member of the finance committee, and at various times filled the different offices of the union. While I was in Silver City I never missed a meeting of the Miners' Union except when I was working on the night shift, and I always took an active part in the work of the organization.

Two others and myself went as a committee to visit the Black Jack mine and invite one John Taylor who was working there either to become a member of the union, or leave the camp. Taylor became indignant and said that the superintendent told him that he did not need to join the union. We told him that the superintendent was not running the union; "the union is being run by the men of this camp." We had no further discussion with him, but when the shift came out of the mine at noon all of the men around the bunk-house, including the night shift, resolved themselves into a committee of the whole, and told Taylor to roll his blankets and hit the trail. He did this without any loss of time. I met Taylor years later, under strange circumstances.

Stewart, the master mechanic at the Trade Dollar mill, was another man to whom we had to extend a special invitation to join the union. We explained to

him that we could make no distinctions as to men in the camp; that we wanted
to make it a thoroughly organized camp; that he would get as much benefit as
any other member, sick and death benefits as well as hospital service—for the
union very soon owned its own hospital. Stewart joined under protest and in
after years attempted to repay me with interest. But that is another story.

There were nearly a thousand men employed in Silver City. There was a
continual coming and going, but these two were the only men with whom we
had any trouble. The membership included all those working in the mines,
skilled and unskilled alike, and also those in and around the mills. There was
only a slight difference in pay between the skilled and the unskilled men. As
the Western Federation of Miners developed, all of its struggles were for the men
underneath, for the lower paid men, as we came to learn that when the unskilled
worker got a wage upon which he could live decently there was no danger of
the skilled men falling below this level.

All the men in and around the mines worked every day of the week, including
Sundays, and the mills were never closed down even for holidays.

In 1896, in his annual report to the Western Federation of Miners, Ed Boyce
said that he hoped that, before the time of the next convention, the martial
tread of twenty-five thousand armed miners would be heard throughout the West;
that the time had come when the miners would have to protect themselves from
thugs such as were used in the Coeur d'Alenes, in Cripple Creek and in Leadville;
that he trusted every miner would get a modern rifle and a supply of ammunition.

At one time I was on a committee appointed to see Joseph Hutchinson, the
manager of the Trade Dollar Mining Company, about the pay of the men who
were sinking. There was at that time a winze being sunk on the Trade Dollar
Mine for which the men were being paid only three dollars and a half a day,
which was fifty cents less than the union wage for sinking. Hutchinson said:

"Well, that complies with your constitution," taking a copy of the constitution of the union from his desk; "there is no provision here for sinking a winze."

Taking a copy of the constitution from my pocket, I said:

"If you will read this you will see that we have corrected that error. Most
men would rather work in a shaft than in a winze. At least, there is no reason
why the wages should not be the same."

"I agree to that," he told us, "but I wish that when you change your constitution you would be good enough to keep us supplied with the latest issue."

It was not always because of skill or ability that men became superintendents
or managers. One night there was a fire in the Chinese laundry in the back
street. Some one suggested that the place ought to be blown up to keep the fire
from spreading. Joe Hutchinson remarked that a box of powder would do the
work. I told him:

"You don't want to put fifty pounds of powder under that shack! You'd
break every window in town. Four or five pounds will lift it out by the roots."

They got the fire under control without the use of powder. The superintendent had probably never used a pound of powder in his life; he was superintendent through the success of his father.

I haven't described Silver City, which was built in a canyon between two towering peaks, War Eagle and Florida mountains. The bottom of the gulch was full of boulders and rocks which had been turned up by the early gold diggers. The town was but two streets wide, the rear street occupied by prostitutes, black, white and Chinese. There were seventeen saloons in the town, besides other business houses. In the Winter the snow was often packed as deep as the first story windows. The little houses and cabins of the miners would be covered, nothing but the stovepipes sticking up through the snow. I had marked the trail to my house by sticking willows down on either side, and pulling them up as the snow increased in depth.

One night I dropped into the corner saloon. There is a corner saloon in every mining camp, and this one differed little from any of them. There was a billiard and pool table, a stud-poker and a faro game were running. I went over to the faro game, put down a dollar, and won on the turn.

"Give me silver," I said to the dealer, and asking the boys who were standing around to have a drink, we went over to the bar. I noticed a man sitting in a corner with his hat pulled down over his face. I asked Ben Hastings, the bartender:

"Who is that man?" Ben answered, "That's old McCann; he don't drink much, but he'd sell his soul for a dose of morphine."

I called to McCann, "Come on, pardner, have a drink." as he came up, he pushed his hat back a little, and said:

"Hullo, Bill, you don't remember me. I used to know you in Tuscarora."

Staring at his emaciated face, at last I recognized his features, haggard and aged by the use of the drug to which he was addicted.

As I went out later, I noticed McCann speaking to one of the boys who worked in the Trade Dollar mine.

The next morning, on my way to work, I saw light in McCann's cabin, and that evening I heard that he had gone to the stage office early in the morning, having dragged down a box on a hand sled, to be shipped out. The sheriff was at the stage office when McCann arrived there. He took McCann and the box to his office. When the box was opened there it was found to contain a lot of rich ore. McCann was charged with robbery and put in jail.

After several hours in the cell, his cravings began. He called the sheriff and said to him:

"A.B., you know that on account of my nerves I have been taking morphine, and I've got so I can't get along without it. You'll get me some at the post office drug store? If you tell them there it's for me they'll know how much I want."

"Why, sure, Mac, I'll do that," said the sheriff. He went away, and Mac began pacing up and down the cell. Already his temples were throbbing, his body wet with cold sweat. Up and down, up and down he went, more restless and goaded every minute. The hours dragged along, but the sheriff did not come back. In the night he thought he was going to die. His tortured nerves seemed to crack and ravel inside him. Before morning came he longed for death. He called to the guard, his voice shaking:

"I've got to get some morphine. You can get it!"

The guard answered:

"I can't leave here any more than you can. You'll have to wait till the sheriff comes in the morning."

It was late when Crocheron, the sheriff, came back. Mac was standing at the door of the cell. He reached a scrawny arm scarred with many jabs of the hypodermic needle through the bars of the cell, and said desperately:

"Give it to me, sheriff, for God's sake give it to me! I'm dying."

The sheriff pulled the little blue bottle out of his pocket.

"I'll give it to you, Mac. But I must have the names of the men who gave you that ore to ship out."

Mac staggered, tripped on the food pan, and collapsed on the floor. Dragging himself back to the bars, he looked the sheriff in the eyes and said:

"I can't tell you."

The sheriff walked off and left Mac in his agony.

A short time later the court was in session, and Mac, more dead than alive, was brought in for trial. The prosecuting attorney told him:

"McCann, the mining company has no desire to prosecute you. But they do want to know the names of the men who gave you that ore."

McCann, lifting his worn and exhausted face, said:

"I cannot tell you."

He was convicted and sentenced to seven years in the Boise penitentiary and he died there while serving his term. Ben had said he would sell his soul for a dose of morphine. But he suffered untold agonies rather than sell his friends.

On the twenty-eighth of June, 1897, my youngest daughter was born. My wife did not recover her health for months. She was bedfast, and the domestic cares of the family fell entirely upon my shoulders, as there was not a woman or girl in the camp that we could get to work outside her own home. They came up in the evenings after their own work was done, and helped us in neighborly ways, but until the wife of the colored barber came to town I had to do the work myself. The baby from its birth slept with me. Afraid of smothering her if I laid her at my side, every night I put her on my breast. If she had been in a cradle I should not have heard her cry when she was hungry, so soundly did I sleep.

Though I was not working, the butcher and store-keeper and others with who whom I dealt said to me:

"Don't worry, Bill, things will be all right soon. Remember, you can always have anything you want from us."

At that time I gambled some and drank a little, but I quit both. While I had sometimes made winnings, in the long run I had been much the loser.

Sometimes I took my wife to visit the neighbors, the baby in one arm and her in the other. I remember one evening being down to see Mrs. Morris at the foot of the hill. When we started home there had been a drift of snow, and I had my wife on one arm, the baby on the other, and the little girl on my back. I carried them all three up the hill.

The Blaine mine was worked through a tunnel in the side of a mountain, and the mining was done above as well as below the level of the tunnel. Coming out we walked Indian file on a plank laid between the tracks. One day Theodore Buckle, a florid, big, fine-looking young Hollander, was just behind me, and we scuffled and joked as we went along. He went to dinner in a boarding house, I ate my lunch in the blacksmith shop. Going back to the mine after dinner, he was a few minutes ahead of me. Some of the men had to climb a hundred and ten feet to the first level above, and from there to the stopes which were still above this. There were some ahead of Buckle, some behind him. He was just climbing up into his stope when a slab of rock fell and crushed the life out of him. We managed to raise the rock high enough to get his body from under it and carried it down to the hundred-and-ten-foot level. There, for want of a better stretcher, we tied the corpse to a short ladder which we lowered down the man-way to the main tunnel. We sent a committee to town with the body.

On another occasion we heard a shot, back near the station on the same hundred-and-ten-foot level. Then some one called to us and we hurried out to find that MacDonald, who had only been at work a short time, had his entire face blown off. He was still alive and we contrived to lower him down the man-way. One of the boys had run out ahead and sent for a wagon. We got him to the hospital as quickly as we could, where he soon died. MacDonald had evidently been biting a fulminating cap to fasten it on a fuse that he was getting ready to fire his holes. Many of the miners did this instead of using their knives to clinch the cap, or pincers that were made for the purpose.

The question of the eight-hour law was beginning to stir the miners of Idaho, and at the coming session of the legislature they were going to try to have a bill enacted to provide for an eight-hour day for men employed in mines, mills and smelter. Joseph Hutchinson was sent as a lobbyist, supplied with funds by the Trade Dollar Company to work against the bill. This action could be expected from the mine owners, but James R. Sovereign, one-time Master Workman of the Knights of Labor, the editor of the paper owned by the miners' unions of the Coeur d'Alenes, the *Idaho State Tribune*, did a treacherous piece of work in publishing an editorial against the eight-hour law. He proved a faker and sell-out, no better than his predecessor, Powderly. The bill was defeated by the legislature, but later established by the miners. It was the Western Federation of Miners, through its attorney, John H. Murphy, that carried the first eight-hour law passed in the United States, the Utah law, to the United States Supreme Court, where it was declared constitutional. But the miners and the mill men of Utah had to fight to compel its enforcement.

I was elected as a delegate from the Silver City Miners' Union to the convention of the Western Federation of Miners which was held in 1898 in Salt Lake City.

4 IN RETROSPECT: 1912–1950

Daniel Aaron

I

Brooks Adams voted the straight Progressive ticket in 1912, but the Democrats won with a candidate whom Roosevelt in his "elegant billingsgate" later described as a "conscienceless rhetorician," a "logothete," a "very adroit and able (but not forceful) hypocrite," a "silly doctrinaire," and "an utterly selfish and cold-blooded politician." Wilson's hesitancy to involve the United States in a war with Germany (thereby dulling "the national conscience," T.R. complained, and "teaching our people to accept high-sounding words as the offset and atonement for shabby deeds") particularly angered Roosevelt, but the whole tone and direction of Wilson's administration enraged him. However similar the New Nationalism and the New Freedom appeared on the surface, the more genuinely progressive philosophy of the ex-college president different fundamentally from the political theory of the big-game hunter.

Like his opponent in the 1912 campaign, Wilson had also started as a conservative. He had come a long way since the days when he spoke about knocking Bryan into a cocked hat, but he retained his conservative bent and, like Roosevelt again, quite consciously worked to save society from revolution and socialism. Wilson had his counselor, too, in 1912—Louis D. Brandeis, the "people's attorney" and one-time co-worker with Henry Demarest Lloyd. It was Brandeis who convinced Wilson that the New Nationalist-Roosevelt-Adams plan of trust domestication was unworkable. Roosevelt's policies, according to Brandeis, simply legitimized monopolistic practices by making large economic blocks official parts of the government. Under the policy of regulation, the President became, in effect, the chairman of a board of business trustees, a director of a kind of corporate oligarchy. The government that started out to "regulate" would soon be regulated by the forces it ostensibly intended to manage. Only by making certain "that the methods by which monopolies have been built up are legally

SOURCE: From *Men of Good Hope* by Daniel Aaron. Copyright © 1951 by Oxford University Press, Inc. Reprinted by permission.

made impossible," Wilson declared in the spirit of Lloyd and Brandeis, could the American people control their own affairs.

The alternative to a people's government, Wilson argued, was government by a corporation elite. He rejected the system of trustee control, whether the trustees were self-regarding plutocrats or Adams's disinterested administrators, and spoke out eloquently for representation by all the people as against rule by a class "which imagined itself the guardians of the country's welfare." After 1910, Wilson never introduced the naive and irrelevant categories of "good" or "bad" wealth and never, in discussing corporate malpractice, spoke intemperately. Where Roosevelt called names and kept his connections with the objects of his tirades, Wilson saw his opponents as stupid or misguided. He preferred the role of schoolmaster to that of the angry prophet.

And yet, although we admit Wilson's closer kinship to the spirit of progressivism and acknowledge his courageous and persistent attempts to legislate democratic ideas into the law of the land during the early years of his presidency, it must be confessed that he remained a progressive very largely in the latter-day or party sense of the term. The liberal influence of men like Brandeis and George L. Record, the exigencies of the times, and political expediency modified his earlier conservatism and account for his progressive tendencies after 1910. But he held to his conviction that change must proceed in a regular and orderly fashion and that reform should not go too far. After the dramatic success of his New Freedom program, designed to aid the small entrepreneurs in their one-sided struggle against big business, Wilson felt he could relax. The American economy, he thought, had been set back on the highway of free enterprise; the business brigands had reformed and no longer molested the little fellows racing toward El Dorado. So Wilson believed, at any rate, and so he told Congress in his second annual message:

> Our program of legislation with regard to the regulation of business is now virtually complete. It has been put forth, as we intended, as a whole, and leaves no conjecture as to what is to follow. The road at last lies clear and firm before business. It is a road which it can travel without fear or embarrassment. It is the road to ungrudged, unclouded success. In it every honest man, every man who believes that the public interest is part of his own interest, may walk with perfect confidence.

Wilson's remarkable ignorance of the real nature and direction of business enterprise and his never-relinquished faith in the workings of 'free competition' as contrasted with "illicit competition" induced this complacent note of satisfaction. After America entered the war, it became clear that business had not made the honorable capitulation to popular government Wilson had supposed. His second administration helped to undo the reforms of the first, and in 1918 Veblen's absentee owners, who had made enormous profits during the war, were more solidly in control than ever.

To reformers like Frederic C. Howe, who had believed in the New Freedom and hoped for its perpetuation, the President's alliance with men he had formerly denounced seemed particularly shameful. How could a man who had spoken so eloquently in behalf of progressive ideals act so implacably toward those who continued to affirm them? Howe, commenting more regretfully than bitterly, realized that Wilson's commitments abroad distracted him from his domestic responsibilites, but nevertheless he came reluctantly to the following conclusions about his former hero:

> *Conflict disclosed his loneliness, his fearfulness, his hatred of men who chal-*
> *lenged his power. Conflict disclosed the Wilson who had bewildered liberals*
> *while he was President; who turned on old friends, who hated Cabot Lodge,*
> *who excoriated imperialism, and seized Haiti and San Domingo and sent bat-*
> *tleships to Vera Cruz. It disclosed the Wilson who imprisoned men who*
> *quoted him against himself. When he himself was subjected to a personal test,*
> *he abandoned the ideals he had held before America.*

Inadvertently, Wilson betrayed the progressive ideal by covering the mercenary policies of finance capitalism with a fog of perfervid rhetoric; he was either unable or unwilling to see the connection between international peace and the economic and social structures of the powers involved. In the last years of his administration he tried to blend national unity and private profits, service and salesmanship, manifest destiny and dollar diplomacy without any awareness, apparently, that such ingredients would not mix. He saw no paradox, once he had embarked upon his course of war leadership, in conducting the fight against autocracy and militarism abroad and giving the superpatriots a free hand at home. For Wilson, democracy had simply become a battle cry.

It was not that Wilson and the anti-German elements in the United States blundered in breaking our traditional neutrality and siding with the Allies. Veblen, perfectly familiar with the dynamics of imperialism and untouched by the war hysteria, wanted to see Germany defeated for reasons incomprehensible to Colonel Roosevelt and President Wilson. Other progressive-minded men saw in German militarism some of the ruthlessness and terror that another war did not disprove. But Wilson lost his perspective with the rest of the country and failed to offer a postwar program that any genuine progressive could support. The blunt suggestion of his friend George L. Record that Wilson call for the public ownership of the railroads, the utilities, and the trust-controlled natural resources, and the restriction of large fortunes through high inheritance and income taxes, made no impression upon the star-struck President.

The letter recommending these measures which Record sent to Wilson in March of 1919 makes clear just how far the President had drifted from the progressive sentiments of the New Freedom. Record, one of the most remarkable and far-sighted of the later progressives, derived straight from Henry George, whose land theories impressed him deeply, and from Henry Demarest Lloyd. He had been largely instrumental in drafting the progressive program carried through by Wilson during his New Jersey governorship, and he had continued to advise him from time to time in the period following Wilson's election to the presidency. Now in 1919, surveying the wreck of the Democratic party, Record frankly blamed his none-too-appreciative friend for ignoring the "great issue which is slowly coming to the front, the question of economic democracy, the abolition of privilege, and the securing to men the full fruits of their labor or service." It required no special courage, he told the President, to fight for political democracy; that battle had been largely won. Industrial democracy, however, still remained a dream. In proof he cited the recent five to four decision of the Supreme Court (Hammer *v.* Dagenhart), which declared unconstitutional an act of Congress "forbidding the relic of barbarism, the employment of little children in mills." Impossible conditions still obtained in the "industrial slave pens" where poorly paid men worked long hours at monotonous jobs. Record, like his mentor George, repudiated socialism, but he wanted Wilson to fight for a democratic equivalent and to turn his wrath against the powerfully entrenched law-breakers, the profiteers, and the monopolists, and not against the "poor, weak socialists," imprisoned for protesting against what Record termed "the monstrous injustice involved in the immunity of these wealthy criminals, and other similar inequalities of our industrial system." Although he enthusiastically approved of Wilson's championing the League, he challenged his friend to assume an even greater and more imperative task: to "become the real leader of the radical forces in America, and to present to the country a constructive program of fundamental reform."

What Record proposed in 1919, Randolph Bourne, hounded by government agents and driven into silence, had demanded two years before. For Bourne, Deweyan pragmatism led directly into the cul-de-sac of Wilsonian compromise and the suffocation of the progressive ideal. He had been an ardent instrumentalist while keeping a faith in his private utopia. But Bourne suddenly realized that instrumentalism was bankrupt without a vivid poetic vision. The philosophy of "adaptation" or "adjustment," he found out before Woodrow Wilson did, ends in a "radiant cooperation with reality," but it stops there.

> An impossibilist élan that appeals to desire will often carry further. A philosophy of adjustment will not make for adjustment. If you merely try to "meet" situations as they come, you will not even meet them. Instead you will only pile up behind you deficits and arrears that will some day bankrupt you.

Bourne asked the ex-radicals, bogged down in compromise, to construct a valid democratic program if they wished to allay the suspicions of the impossibilist.

> But when [he wrote] the emphasis is on technical organization, rather than organization of ideas, on strategy rather than desires, one begins to suspect that no programme is presented because they have none to present. This burrowing into war-technique hides the void where a democratic philosophy

*should be. Our intellectuals consort with war-boards in order to keep their
minds off the question what the slow masses of the people are really desiring,
or toward what the best hope of the country really drives. Similarly the blaze
of patriotism on the radicals serves the purpose of concealing the feebleness
of their intellectual light.*

Bourne argued that "vision must constantly outshoot technique." The progressive in 1919 had neither vision nor technique, and Brooks Adams's "money
power" (as blind and stupid and reckless, in all but its own peculiar line, as ever
was a drunken soldier, or a crazy Nero') took over in due course as George
Record had predicted.

The defeat of Wilson cannot be attributed solely to Wilson himself. His liberal supporters, even men like Record or Brandeis, who criticized his failure to
prepare an adequate postwar reconstruction program, had no program or organization of their own to sustain him. Isolated more and more from the progressive-
minded rank and file, both by circumstances and by choice, and entirely preoccupied with the Peace Conference and the League, he found it easier to compromise with his conservative critics than to fight them and to saction legislation
(as Howe observed) that he never would have tolerated during the opening years
of his administration. He seemed to have no qualms about sacrificing one set of
ideals in the hope of approximating another. In the end, not even his courage,
sincerity, and audacity were enough to salvage his wrecked administration.

During the next decade, the battered idols of *laisser-faire* were once more en-
shrined in the American temples and the business oracles resumed their glorious
phophecies.

II

By 1920 the progressives found themselves without a party, a leader, or a
philosophy. The old Progressive party had fallen to pieces since the days when
Theodore Roosevelt provided a dubious leadership, and now the insurgents from
the two major parties had no place to go. In the election following the war a
bobtailed Farmer-Labor party managed to poll a quarter of a million votes, and
the Socialist candidate, Eugene Debs, picked up a million more, but the magnitude of the Republican victory left no doubt that whatever progressivism was or
could be, the bulk of the American voters wanted no truck with it.

During the next few years the progressives took stock. Why did they fail and
what now remained for them to do? Did they share a common set of beliefs?
Was it possible to build up a national party that would come to something more
than a loose confederation of malcontent groups, each harboring a different griev-
ance? From the discussion of these questions in the liberal press, one can see
that the answers were not reassuring to the progressive cause.

The various definitions of the "progressive" which cropped up from time to
time did suggest a kind of agreement on the meaning of the term, although most

of them merely expressed a vague liberal creed. The composite progressive turned out to be a person who worked for the wider diffusion of economic, political, and social equality, who sought to approximate the moral code in politics, who combined a zeal for service with a curiosity for facts, who worked for the gradual displacement of the obsolete by the new, who understood the relation between human conduct and unjust economic conditions, who believed in "purposeful change." One contributor to the *Nation* brought these ideas together in the following credo:

> A progressive is one who recognizes the fact that the past does not fit into the present and that the present will not fit into the future. He is one who advocates such changes in our social and economic structure as will best serve the interests of a majority of the people now and present the least resistance to ready adjustments to meet coming needs in the future. He is one who is always ready to take one constructive step forward, even if he cannot go the whole distance. He is one who stands on the past that he may reach farther into the future, but does not try to take the past with him.

Unfortunately, it required more than an enunciation of progressive criteria to launch an effective political party. Progressives could agree on how a progressive ought to feel and what he ought to think, but the more perceptive among them also recognized the ideological conflicts within the movement itself, which had not yet been resolved. Progressivism, as one of them noted, shook and wobbled because it represented little business, which "shades off into big business on the one hand and into labor on the other in such a vague and indefinite fashion that it is inevitable that progressives are divided in their counsels" Both conservative and radical progressives believed in advancing, but they did not agree on how wide the steps should be or how frequently taken.

Even more serious in the eyes of some critics, notably the editors of the *New Republic,* progressivism still smacked of the unreflective insurgency of the Bull Moosers and expended more effort on denunciation than on constructive planning. The progressives emphasized evils rather than remedies; they lacked a "moral and intellectual binder," an "ardent belief in some fundamental principle or purpose which will establish and sharpen the fighting issue between them and their opponents." According to Herbert Croly and his associates, no progressive movement could succeed until large numbers of voters still loyal to the old parties and to the old economic system could be persuaded to abandon their allegiance. A campaign of education was needed to provoke this mass apostasy, which in turn required the formulation of a realistic program. Ideas by themselves were not enough, nor were good intentions. If the farmers and the wage earners were to be won over, they must be made to see that progressivism was a method, not a principle, and that they had something to get by supporting it.

This strong pragmatic approach to politics, which gained currency with some of the progressive theorists in the early 'twenties, had been developing since the outbreak of the First World War. Disgust for Theodore Roosevelt's camp-meeting tactics and Wilsonian rhetoric and a profound respect for power prompted such a man as Herbert Croly to re-examine progressive policies. The defects of progressivism or liberalism, as Walter Lippmann (speaking for his master) wrote in 1919, lay in "its apathy about administration, its boredom at the problem of organization, its failure to make its own what may be called roughly the constructive tradition of Alexander Hamilton." These were Croly sentiments, for Croly combined an admiration for Hamiltonian techniques with an at least ostensible preference for democratic ends. Progressivism, as he understood it, was "fundamentally the attempt to mold social life in the light of the best available knowledge and in the interests of a humane ideal." It lived "by the definite formulation of convictions."

Croly saw the task of the progressives as chiefly one of class reconciliation. In order to achieve this end the progressives had to take the leadership in restoring a larger measure of economic power and social privileges to the masses of farmers and wage earners. Such a restoration of power would do much to relieve class tensions increasingly exacerbated by business rule and to prevent the domination by a single class either from above or from below. Progressives in the past had weakened their position by remaining aloof from the very classes whose support was indispensable, and they could not "repair this mistake," he wrote in 1921, "without reviving the primitive association between liberalism and radicalism and a conscious and militant humanism."

In taking this stand, Croly, for the moment at least, allied himself with the early progressives, but during the next few years he seemed to play down the ideological imperative and concentrate upon naked appeals to economic interests. As the 1924 election approached, the *New Republic* kept hammering at the La Follette supporters not to crusade for social justice, not to talk about helping the oppressed or ameliorating conditions, but to promise a fairer distribution of economic power.

> *It is an illusion [declared an editorial] to suppose that a society like our own which is made up so largely of competing as well as cooperating classes can generate automatically out of this class competition an amount of public spirit and enlightenment which will enable the existing state, which necessarily reflects these prevailing standards, to become the trustworthy agent of a program of social reform.*

Croly's objectives were progressive, but here spoke the Hamiltonian. He stated frankly that any successful party had to be not only numerous but also conscious of its objectives and resolute enough to fight for them. It was up to the progressives to make this issue clear to an electorate who still did not "understand the function of conflict in the social economy of a democratic people," who were satisfied always with "immediate agreements," and who failed to realize "that conscious conflict is often the only means by which the obstacles to co-operation are removable."

The failure of La Follette to win more than a small percentage of the votes in 1924 further testified to the "massive inertia" of the American public and confirmed Croly's conviction that the progressives would never come to power until they had a workable program and an educated following to back it up. The conservatives, he pointed out in December 1924, possessed the program and the personnel to administer it. Until the progressives built up an organization powerful and capable enough to assume power, he advised them to transform themselves into an opposition party whose function it would be to force a clarification of political issues. Two parties, he maintained, now dominated national politics, "neither of which has allowed questions of ultimate political and economic power to become the subject of partizan controversy." Conservatives therefore had no obligation to take a definite stand and administer seriously for the country's welfare. Given a unified radical party instead of the "liberal" Democratic party (which proposed to do "nothing much" instead of "nothing at all"), it might be possible to convert the present negative conservatism of the Republican party into something more nearly resembling the more enlightened Conservative party of England. Certainly "radical progressives" had much more to gain by allowing the businessmen to administer the as yet workable machine of capitalism and forcing upon them the desperate problems they would undoubtedly be obliged to cope with during the next thirty years, than by struggling to gain control over an economy the progressives had not the capacities to manage. An intelligent conservatism, he believed, would respond to the popular demands, preferring to make concessions than to risk the loss of power. Progressives, in turn, might continue their political agitation while preparing themselves to overcome their handicaps. Croly told his fellow progressives they had nothing to fear from the conservatives. Their real enemies were "the stubborn limitations of the existing economic and social system which are created by and confirm the existing disabilities of human nature" and "the lack of a sufficiently alert, conscious and educated body of workers."

Croly's astute diagnosis of progressivism may have stimulated his *New Republic* readers, but it did not halt the dissolution of the progressive movement. The disappointment of the 1924 defeat increased, as the *Nation* had predicted, the "abstention from political life" and the "contaminating cynicism" that had begun to infect many intellectuals since the end of the war. The impregnability of the business system, the huge Republican pluralities, and episodes such as the Sacco-Vanzetti case all seemed to prove the impossibility of compromising with the American rulers. However dull and vulgar their culture, they had apparently devised a system that provided for the physical needs of the citizens if not their spiritual wants. To Herbert Croly, the businessmen were "operating a more efficient and flexible economic and political machine than did the kings and aristocrats of the eighteenth century . . . operating it more efficiently than their opponents would or could."

Four years after Croly's tribute to American business efficiency came the economic collapse that the progressives had neither expected nor prepared for.

III

With the victory of the Democrats in 1932, an administration came into power which at least attempted to continue the progressive struggle for industrial democracy. Franklin Roosevelt was a spiritual descendant of Jefferson and Jackson if not Ralph Waldo Emerson, and his belief in the positive role of government, of government as a popular instrument, resembled closely the attitudes of the men discussed in the preceding chapters.

In many ways, however, Roosevelt stood poles apart from those reformers, even though the liberals at first had him pegged as a lesser Wilson. The ethical tones of nineteenth-century liberalism sounded in his own pronouncements, but he showed hardly a trace of the ideologue. He had little of the evangelist and not a great deal of the practical social architect; in certain respects his notions of government resembled those of Brooks Adams (during Adams's progressive moments) more than those of George or Bellamy. Several years before his election he had observed that "that nation or state which is unwilling by government action to tackle new problems caused by the immense increase of population and the astonishing strides of modern science is headed for a decline and ultimate death from inaction." Roosevelt attempted nothing less, to borrow Henry Adams's metaphor, than to convert "our old Mississippi raft of a confederate state into a brand-new ten-thousand ton, triple screw, armored, line-of-battle ship," a job that Adams predicted would take a thousand years. It required vision to carry out such a scheme, but it also required the combination of firmness and cunning, which many of our successful Presidents, most notably Jefferson and Lincoln, never hesitated to employ.

When Hawthorne called on Lincoln in 1862, he detected in this kindly and sagacious man a touch of slyness, a king "of tact and wisdom," Hawthorne wrote, "that are akin to craft, and would impel him . . . to take an antagonist in flank, rather than make a bull-run at him right in front." Roosevelt had something of that quality variously interpreted by his contemporaries as shrewdness or trickiness, depending on their political orientation. He listened to the theorists and liked them, but the technical aspects of his job appealed to him the most. He saw quite correctly that it was the task of government not only to formulate the national policy but to use "the political technique to obtain so much of that policy as will receive general support; persuading, leading, sacrificing, teaching always—because the greatest duty of statesmen is to educate." Roosevelt served as a salesman for the new progressivism, breaking down the resistance of a people long injured to political and economic superstitions.

The new President showed no more inclination than Theodore Roosevelt or Woodrow Wilson to embark on socialist schemes. He informed his constituents that capitalism, in its unadulterated state, worked well enough, but unfortunately it had been perverted by a group of insiders ("grafters" and "chiselers" in the F.D.R. parlance) who fouled up the engine of private enterprise. Roosevelt compared these business parasites to the carbon in the engine of the car: the engine would not knock quite so loudly, he declared, when the carbon was removed. In other words, the President and his aides looked upon reform as a technical rather than a moral question, even though Roosevelt deeply felt his responsibility to the people and was a sincere humanitarian. As Edmund Wilson remarked in 1933, Roosevelt was at his worst when he imitated the "pastoral unctiousness" of his great Democratic predecessor. "He is himself most impressive," Wilson continued, "not in the role of political prophet, but as a sensible public servant trying to straighten out a bad mess in the interests of what he conceives to be the American democratic tradition." Roosevelt was more interested in increasing the buying power of each citizen than in discussing man's spiritual potentialities, less concerned with plans for developing unplumbed genius than in overcoming the heavy inertia of ignorance and prejudice.

The Rooseveltian strategy of compromise and restraint, of working for realizable goals, of never getting too far ahead of public opinion, of speeding up and slowing down, depending upon national and international exigencies, was understandable and probably necessary. Certainly, a moon-crazed Quixote could never have gone as far toward the liberal goal as the canny Roosevelt, and we can be thankful that a person of his temperament and abilities succeeded to the presidency in 1932.

It does not minimize Roosevelt's achievements to say that New Dealism was a crisis philosophy, reconstructive rather than radical, inconclusive, temporary, makeshift. After acknowledging the valuable legacy of New Deal reforms in the fields of banking, agriculture, labor, and social security (the policy of the do-nothing state was finally and permanently discredited), we can see from the vantage of today that the basic power structure of the country was substantially untouched, even admitting the large and probably lasting gains of organized labor. The tendencies in our society which shocked and frightened the nineteenth-century progressives still exist; unwholesome accumulations of private wealth, inequalities of real opportunity, the monopolization and despoiling of natural resources, the power of special interests to block the majority will. Under the New Deal (once defined by Max Lerner as a "fighting coalition of the productive groups in America headed toward a socialized community, using the technique of democratic planning") it seemed for a time as if ideals and technique really were working in conjunction and that the co-operative commonwealth, so long in the blueprint stage, was at last under construction. By the middle of Roosevelt's second term, however, the movement had already flagged. The inevitable "breathing spell" that follows periods of intense reformist activity set in; the bold experiment had ended.

Historians are still speculating about the reasons for the New Deal relapse, which occurred even before World War II indefinitely postponed its continuation.

But looking back to the Rooseveltian era and judging it by progressive standards, one might say that the New Deal was not radical and far-reaching enough, that it came to terms too readily with the opposition, that the necessity of halting the panic and reviving a sick economy absorbed its early impetus and drained its energies before the real job of reconstruction began. This is the dilemma facing every liberal regime coming to power under similar circumstances; it must undo the work of accumulated stupidity and mismanagement and at the same time surpass the peak performance of the old order whose blundering brought about the collapse. The British Labour Government faces that job today.

The New Deal did not depart very radically from the earlier anti-big-business protests. Like Greenbackism or Populism, New Dealism had utopian overtones, but by and large, it was merely another popular effort to get a larger slice of the American pie. Both Bellamy and Lloyd finally saw the People's party for what it was, and there is little doubt that Veblen, had he lived, would have quickly seen that the New Deal program introduced few if any radical transformations in American life. It was Veblen's utopian bias that enabled him to see the *ideological* nature of the American labor movement and the ineffectuality of liberals dallying along the fringes of reform.

The New Deal succeeded in giving the people a feeling of purpose for a short time, but it based its appeal almost exclusively upon the same desiderata that had motivated the previous Republican administration. In dropping the ethico-religious baggage of the old progressives and in focusing their attentions almost entirely upon raising economic levels and increasing social benefits, the New Deal leaders missed the opportunity of driving home the social and economic lessons of the great depression: that every citizen has obligations as well as rights, that the responsibility for the 1929 debacle could not be foisted upon a small group of corrupt insiders, that the stability and health of a community is not measured by the number of automobiles and washing machines in operation, that reform must be a continuous process and not a short interlude of delirious agitation sandwiched in between decades of reaction and social irresponsibility.

IV

Progressivism, during the 'thirties, had to buck up not only against conservative opposition that bitterly contested almost every New Deal measure (an opposition that arose soon after the panicky days of 1932), but also against a communist opposition unknown in the days of Bellamy and George and hardly formidable until the depression.

The story of communism's rise in the United States is a separate one in itself, but what concerns us here is the defection from the progressive ranks of many intellectuals who, in the space of a few years, became Marxists and party sympathizers. The reasons for this break, already discernible in the middle 'twenties and dramatically evident by 1932, are numerous and varied, but this much can be said by way of explanation.

A number of writers and intellectuals had come to distrust the democratic idealism of the older progressives and the middle-class values they upheld. They saw no hope in either the leadership or the program of progressivism, committed, in their opinion, to the preservation of the *status quo* and to the continued domination of the ruling class. Croly's recommendation that the progressives co-operate with the established powers seemed both cowardly and unworkable. Such a policy brought no immediate relief to the workers and offered further proof that the progressives preferred to sacrifice the rights of the submerged proletariat rather than to cut themselves off from the middle class. What had the progressives done to prevent the "legalized murder" of Sacco and Vanzetti? How could one speak of co-operation with "reactionaries" and "bloodsuckers" who had no compunctions about putting to death anyone who seriously challenged their tyranny? The execution of these two anarchists was more than a miscarriage of justice to many embittered progressives; they saw it as a symbolic capitalist rite that divided America into the "two nations" of John Dos Passos and conclusively exposed the fraudulence of the middle-class ideal.

The depression dispelled what for many radicals was the last myth of capitalism—the myth of prosperity. In place of the vacillation, confusion, and timidity of progressivism, the renegades now turned to a movement that had a creed, a bible, and a cause. The mere example of the Soviet Union, according to one of them, "made all progressive movements and liberal programs seem superficial, long and rather hopeless." Waldo Frank, writing in the *New Masses'* symposium, "How I Came to Communism," in the fall of 1932, expressed the feelings of many former progressives when he remarked: "I have lost my last faith in the middle-classes, in all middle class action, and in the efficacy of middle class groups who are identified, either openly or indirectly, with middle class values." He was ready to agree with Marx that only "the communist society can go forward to the creating of a real *human* culture."

Any such expression of faith in the communist cause would be regarded today as merely another example of leftist rascality or naiveté, but the fact that many honest and idealistic people agreed with Frank in 1932 is highly significant. We cannot minimize its influence by impugning the intelligence or the motives of its supporters. The Communist party challenged a progressivism that hesitated too much and neglected too much. During the early 'thirties, it exhibited a resolution and audacity that made most progressive agitation seem tepid by contrast, and it publicized national evils—race discrimination and the treatment of minorities, for example—with a flair that was new in radical movements. The propagation of Marxist ideas invigorated our universities, stimulated scholarship and teaching. If the results were not always good, a large number, if not all, of the novelists, poets, historians, and critics who passed through and out of the communist phase were none the worse for their experiment; indeed they were better qualified to expose the totalitarian state than the professional "red-baiters," who never took the trouble to understand what they feared and hated. Finally, it must not be forgotten that the fervent sincerity of many communists impressed young men and women who, in an earlier generation, would have turned to the Christian Socialists or to the Fabians. To them, progressivism in the 1930s was "corpse cold," communism a warming fire, a hope, a faith.

All of this is quite understandable in retrospect. What seems harder to comprehend today is why an allegedly cynical and creedless generation could accept so uncritically the communist vision after emphatically rejecting its native middle-class equivalent. The communists distorted reality far more than did the progressives. Bellamy and George had the good sense to project their utopias into the future; the Communist party succeeded in convincing a good many intelligent people that the utopia existed already in the workers' republic across the ocean. The communists and their friends had a touching faith in Soviet statistics and a highly unrealistic notion about the recuperative powers of American capitalism. They sentimentalized the working man as no progressive ever did and placed their faith, as one of them said, in "the proletarians and farmers who *alone* as a class have not been hopelessly corrupted by the sources and methods of the capitalistic order."

The glorification of the proletariat went on simultaneously with the debasement of the bourgeois decadent. During the early 'thirties the strange spectacle could be observed of middle-class writers apologizing for their middle-class origins and acknowledging "that the workers alone can give militant and effective leadership to the fight against reaction." Even the word "people," with its bourgeois overtones, was declared to be a reactionary slogan, whereas the words, "proletariat" and "worker" were considered appropriate symbols for the communist propagandist. The Marxists, in abandoning the middle-class values, also spurned the tactical insights of the progressive agitators, men and women far more familiar with national prejudices and assumptions than their communist successors. The communists were correct enough in seeing progressivism as an embodiment of middle-class values; they simply miscalculated when they concluded that these values were obsolete and irrelevant.

At best the ideas of the nineteenth-century reformers had a kind of historical interest for the radical critics in search of the "usable past" (such men as Lloyd or George or Bellamy were interesting as precursors of scientific socialism and helped to confirm the line that communism was twentieth-century Americanism), but according to the Marxists, the progressive-liberals had nothing to offer the post-Leninist world. Historical liberalism, V. F. Calverton wrote in 1933, was retrogressive and harmful. It found its expression in Wilsonian platitudes and in the "infantile proposals" of La Follette. The outmoded democracy still professed by John Dewey, Charles Beard, Jane Addams, James Harvey Robinson, and others

> *was not the industrial or proletarian democracy of the modern radical but the democracy of the small farmer and the small business man and entrepre-*

Brooched=

neur in the cities. In a word, they were not interested in proletarians as proletarians, but in proletarians as potential bourgeois. They were determined to think of American society as a classless phenomenon, uncognizant that what they were doing was supporting the middle class, first as agrarianites and later as urbanites as well, with its futile stress upon an individualistic economic outlook which has been rendered anachronistic by the technical processes of production and social organization.

Calverton's understanding of the progressive view was correct enough, but we may now wonder why he placed so little stock in the judgment of a John Dewey or a Morris Cohen, why he assumed that they were unaware of the implications of their position, and why he was so certain that nineteenth-century American liberalism was dead.

To Calverton and the other Marxists, the "day of the individual" had passed and the "day of the classes" had arrived. America was at last "Europeanized." The middle class, the source of enlightened leadership for the reformers, would now have to choose, in their disintegrated state, between a rising proletariat and a doomed upper-*bourgeoisie.* A suggestion like Howells's, that the working class vote itself into power, was patently ridiculous, because anyone who had read Marx (or better, his popularizers) knew that no ruling class relinquished power in the manner hoped for by the reformers. Utopianism or gradualism, in fact any theory that seriously broached the possibility of peaceful change, was contemptuously rejected by orthodox communists in the 'thirties. As one of them wrote, "only a liberal could entertain the fantastic notion that the few who run civilization for their profit can be induced to change their purpose by any other method than by shooting them." No plan short of taking over the means of production by the proletariat seemed worth discussing.

The revolutionary radical's impatience with the wishy-washy progressive mentality can be illustrated rather dramatically by Lincoln Steffens's review of Charles Edward Russell's recollections, *Bare Hands and Stone Walls,* which appeared in the *Nation,* December 20, 1933. Russell, a reformist-muck-raking-progressive-socialist, had participated in or observed practically every liberal movement of any significance for the past sixty years and had emerged from the battle with his ideals still whole and his optimism undimmed. His professional duties had taken him all over the world, to New Zealand, Australia, India, Ireland, and Russia. Invariably and characteristically, he sided with the rebels and the underprivileged, but in Russia, to the disgust of Steffens, Russell shied away from Lenin and the Bolsheviks and supported unequivocally the more visionary and soon-to-be liquidated Social Revolutionaries, the men, as he put it, who were shot to death by the rifles of men that professed to want the same things but insisted upon getting them in a different way."

Steffens's observations on this episode are most revealing. Russell said Steffens, represented the predicament of the liberal theoretician who goes through life with an open mind and open mouth and cannot grasp the necessity for action. "There is a time for thinking and planning," he admitted, but after that "there comes a time to close our open minds, shut up talking and go to it. Lest Hitler do things his way. That time is when we don't need good fellows and liberal compromisers who want to get together. The goal is in sight and we must be Bolsheviks and—do it."

As an old friend and co-worker of Russell, Steffens should have known that what disturbed him was not that the Bolsheviks acted (the Social Revolutionaries also had plans as well as visions); he appreciated as well as Steffens the immediate practical tasks that had to be accomplished, and knew that revolutions so long delayed and of such magnitude could not occur without bloodshed. Russell, nevertheless, was shocked by the Bolsheviks' treatment of dissenters, even those who had languished for years in Czarist prisons, and what seemed to him the betrayal of the ideals of the revolution. Steffens accused him, in effect, of sitting back and deploring, of being a "nice socialist" instead of a "socialist." Russell, however, could not reconcile Leninism with socialism or a theocracy (with Lenin as the "titular deity") with democracy. "If so far the story of mankind has taught anything," he remarked, "It is that a people's progress must be self-achieved. You cannot take them by the throat and jab progress into them as a cook stuffs a turkey. The doctrine of doing good to the people because they are too incapable to do anything for themselves is bearded with age. It has been the excuse of every tyrant and bloody minded murderer that ever sat on any throne." The myth of the Soviet paradise flourished in a capitalist wasteland where generous-spirited men and women, disgusted with the callousness and ineptitude of a faltering business civilization, saw their hopes embodied in what they believed to be a vigorous and democratic socialist state; it faded when the nature and tendencies of Soviet Communism became better known. Then Russell's strictures against Leninist tactics could no longer be dismissed as the old-fogyism of a sentimental muckraker.

Morris Cohen, giving his reasons, a year after Steffens's review, why he was not and could not become a member of the Communist party, restated the liberal-progressive creed quietly and eloquently and explained why the liberal must always oppose the communist "fallacy of simplism." Like Russell, he rejected the communist plea "that the denial of freedom is a temporary necessity" as an argument "advanced by all militarists. It ignores the fact," he observed, "that, when suppression becomes a habit, it is not readily abandoned." He could not agree with the Calvertons that liberalism was dead, but even if it were, he said, "I should still maintain that it deserved to live, that it had not been condemned in the court of human reason, but lynched outside of it by the passionate and uncompromisingly ruthless war spirit, common to Communists and Fascists." The liberalism of Morris Cohen, unfortunately for progressivism, did not have a wide appeal in the 'thirties, nor did it carry much weight in the next decade with the managers of the "Progressive party" of Henry Wallace, those of them, at any rate, who did not share Morris Cohen's conviction about the incompati-

Astigmatism =

bility of democracy and dictatorship. The new "Progressives" suffered from political astigmatism; their view of democracy was imperfect and indistinct. Whereas the progressives in the 'eighties and 'nineties felt obliged to denounce Czarist tyranny and capitalist oppression as equally reprehensible, the organizers and strategists of the self-styled "Progressive party" (if not the bulk of the membership) seemed to be more chary with their condemnations, more qualifiedly antitotalitarian, more adept in separating theory from practice. Their failure in the 1948 presidential election to attract more than a scant proportion of the voters can be attributed partly to the fact that they borrowed the rhetoric but rejected the spirit of progressivism and identified what had once been an authentic radical movement with a reactionary ideology.

5 TALKING IN MY SLEEP—AN EXERCISE IN SELF-CRITICISM

"Free"

A mythical interview of questions that are asked and answers that are given. Interviews are always going on. Here's one with myself.

*As I write this, 100,000 tons of garbage are piled up on the streets of New York. I have a vision of the country being totally inundated under this massive garbage pile. Future historians would write that America was destroyed by a nuclear attack when in actuality the people just stopped picking up their trash.

Do you have an ideology?

No. Ideology is a brain disease.

Do you have a movement?

Yes. It's called Dancing.

Isn't that a put-on?

No.

Can you explain that?

Suppose we start the questions again.

OK. Do you have an ideology?

We are for peace, equal rights, and brotherhood.

Now I understand.

I don't. That was a put-on. I don't understand what I said.

I'm getting confused.

Well, let's go on.

SOURCE: From *Revolution for the Hell of It* by Abbie Hoffman. Copyright © 1968, by The Dial Press, Inc. Used by permission of the publisher.

Are you for anything? Do you have a vision of this new society you talk of?

Yes. We are for a free society.

Could you spell that out?

F—R—E—E.

What do you mean free?

You know what that means. America: the land of the free. Free means you don't pay, doesn't it?

Yes, I guess so. Do you mean all the goods and services would be free?

Precisely. That's what the technological revolution would produce if we let it run unchecked. If we stopped trying to control it.

What controls it?

The profit incentive, I guess. Property hang-ups. One task we have is to separate the concept of productivity from work. Work is money. Work is postponement of pleasure. Work is always done for someone else: the boss, the kids, the guy next door. Work is competition. Work was linked to productivity to serve the Industrial Revolution. We must separate the two. We must abolish work and all the drudgery it represents.

Who will do what we now call dirty work, like picking up the garbage?

Well, there are a lot of possibilities. There won't be any dirty work. If you're involved in a revolution you have a different attitude toward work. It is not separate from your vision . . . All work now is dirty work. Lots of people might dig dealing with garbage. Maybe there won't be any garbage. Maybe we'll just let it pile up. Maybe everybody will have garbage disposal. There are numerous possibilities.

Don't you think competition leads to productivity?

Well, I think it did during the Industrial Revolution but it won't do for the future. Competition also leads to war. Cooperation will be the motivating factor in a free society. I think cooperation is more akin to the human spirit. Competition is grafted on by institutions, by a capitalist economy, by religion, by schools. Every institution I can think of in this country promoted competition.

Are you a communist?

Are you an anti-communist?

Does it matter?

Well, I'm tempted to say Yes if I sense you are. I remember when I was young I would only say I was Jewish if I thought the person asking the question was anti-Semitic.

What do you think of Russia?

Ugh! Same as here. Dull, bureaucratic-sterile-puritanical. Do you remember when Kosygin came here and met with Johnson in New Jersey? They looked the same. They think the same. Neither way the wave of the future. Johnson is a communist.

What is the wave of the future?

The National Liberation Front, the Cuban Revolution, the young here and around the world.

Doesn't everybody always place great hope in the young?

Yes, I think so. But young people today are very different from previous generations. I think generational revolt has gone on throughout history. Ortega y Gasset in *Man and Crisis* shows that very dramatically. But there are significant differences. The hydrogen bomb, TV, satellites, jet planes—everything is more immediate, more involving. We are the first internationalists. Vietnam rice paddies are as real to me as the Empire State Building. If you don't live in New York, maybe they are more real. We live in a global village.

Do you like McLuhan?

Let's say I think he is more relevant than Marx. Quentin Fiore, his assistant, is more McLuhan than McLuhan. He's the one who puts the ideas into action. McLuhan still struggles with the printed word. But he is an explorer. He experiments. For an old guy he does well. He understands how to communicate information. It's just that his living style—Catholic, university life, grants, the risks that he takes—is merely academic. Let's say I respect him, but don't love him. What we seek are new living styles. We don't want to talk about them. We want to live them.

Do you consider what you are doing politically relevant?

No.

Is that the best answer you can think of?

Well, when you ask a question like that you trigger off umpteen responses in my head. I believe in the politics of ecstasy.

Can you explain that a little more?

No, but I can touch it, I can small it, I can even dance it. I can even fight it. Politics to me is the way somebody lives his life. Not what they vote for or support or even believe in. I'm more interested in art than politics but, well, see, we are all caught in a word box. I find it difficult to make these kinds of divisions. Northrop, in *Meeting of East and West*, said, "Life is an undifferentiated aesthetic continuum." Let me say that the Vietcong attacking the U.S. Embassy in Saigon is a work of art. I guess I like revolutionary art.

This word game, as you call it. Doesn't that present problems in conveying what you want to say?

Yes, but not in what I want to do. Let me say . . . Did you ever hear Andy Warhol talk?

Yes, or at least I think it was him.

Well, I would like to combine his style and that of Castro's. Warhol understands modern media. Castro has the passion for social change. It's not easy. One's a fag and the other is the epitome of virility. If I was forced to make the choice I would choose Castro, but right now in this period of change in the country the styles of the two can be blended. It's not guerrilla warfare but, well, maybe a good term is monkey warfare. If the country becomes more repressive we must become Castros. If it becomes more tolerant we must become Warhols.

Do you see the country becoming more repressive?

Well, it's very hard to be objective about that. The cops around here are certainly a bunch of bastards. It's winter now and traditionally that's a time of paranoia because it's a time of less action than the summer. Everything has always been geared to the summer. School's out. People in the streets. More action. When you are involved you don't get paranoid. It's when you sit back and try to figure out what's going on, or what you should do. The winter is the hardest time for revolutionists in this country. We probably should hibernate. Everything builds toward the summer. This year it seems more so. Everyday we talk of Chicago and the Festival. Everyday the news carries a prediction of the "long hot summer." The other day I saw a report from Detroit. People, one white line, one black line, lining up at a gun shop. Meanwhile the mayor is trying to cool things with a nice friendly speech on brotherhood. It was some contrast. Every day has a new report on some new police weapon system. Then there is uncertainty and the tendency to re-examine your tactics. Right now I feel like Dwight Eisenhower on an acid trip. "On the one hand this—on the other hand that." I think it's a case of information overload. See, I am conditioned to perform well in chaos—actual chaos. Say a riot. In a riot I know exactly what to do. I'm not good for the winter. This is my last winter in the North. I have to live in total summer if I am to survive.

Will the summer action bring on more repression?

Oh, I suppose so. I see this country as getting simultaneously more repressive and more tolerant. People run off to Hanoi to collaborate with the enemy. Everybody's smoking pot on the streets. People go on TV and radio shows and spell out in detail plans of sabotage. And simultaneously there is repression. The combination of the two is going to produce highly volatile conditions and that's why many different tactics are needed. Right now revolution is anything you can get away with. It has to be that way because of the nature of the opposition.

What is going to accelerate that process?

Well, Vietnam, the black revolution, and most importantly, WE ARE! All three present this system with more unsolvable problems than it can deal with. You see, there is no solution to the Vietnam war. To leave or to stay is a defeat. No matter what the government does in the ghettos it loses. More aid programs increase the appetite for more demands. More repression produces more anger and defensive violence. The same with the young. I know a girl, Peggy Dobbins, who was a teacher at Brooklyn College. She let the students determine the curriculum; before you knew it, the students wanted to grade themselves. She agreed to go along and of course got the ax from the administration. The more you get, the more you want. The more you are prevented from getting what you want, the more you fight to get it. These are trends that are irreversible, because the government cannot deal with these problems—I mean, the government "deals" with problems rather than solving them.

That's pretty political in its analysis. It's New Left in its wording.

Ah, well, it's a regression. I haven't presented any new ideas. But, well, that's the point. All the ideas are in and have been for some time. I guess I just rap on that from force of habit. I was once in the New Left but I outgrew it. Or perhaps it outgrew me. We differ on many things.

Like what?

Fun. I think fun and leisure are great. I don't like the concept of a movement built on sacrifice, dedication, responsibility, anger, frustration and guilt. All those down things. I would say, Look, you want to have more fun, you want to get laid more, you want to turn on with friends, you want an outlet for your creativity, then get out of school, quit your job. Come on out and help build and defend the society you want. Stop trying to organize everybody but yourself. Begin to live your vision. For example, the other night I was at a benefit for a peace group. Great music, light shows, friends all over the place. It was a good time. Some of the money raised goes to arrange rallies at which speakers give boring political speeches. People think it's a drag but that's the sacrifice to get out the politically relevant statement. The point is, nobody listens to politically relevant statements. In Chicago we'll have a huge free music festival. Everybody already knows our feelings on the issues because we are there. It will have a tremendous impact if we can also project the image that we are having all the fun too. When I say fun, I mean an experience so intense that you actualize your full potential. You become LIFE. LIFE IS FUN. Political irrelevance is more effective than political relevance.

I notice as we get further into the interview that your answers get more linear and longer.

You're observant. I'm getting tired.

A few more: I hear you're writing a book. What's it about?

Well, it's called *Revolution for the Hell of It.* Sometimes I think I'm writing it just to see that title on a book jacket. Actually, if I have my way, the book jacket won't have the title on it. The book jacket will have two sleeves, a collar, buttons down the front, and the word BOOK on the back.

Why are you writing it?

Well, 'cause I have no idea how to make a movie. It has some parts I like but the book form is difficult and I write on the run. There is also the time gap. You know, months of delay before it comes out. By then it's a whole new ball game. As far as the medium of print is concerned, I would say I like free street leaflets the best.

Which medium do you like the best of all?

Making love.

Anything else?

Well, I like to experience pleasure, to have fun. I enjoy blowing people's minds. You know, walking up to somebody and saying, "Would you hold this dollar for me while I go in that store and steal something?" The crazier the better. I like being crazy. Letting go. Losing control. Just doing what pops into my mind. I trust my impulses. I find the less I try to think through a situation, the better it comes off.

I've seen things you've written under other names. Is that part of the put-on?

I do that a lot. It is fun because I really get pleasure in doing the act or helping to see it come off. Using false names or other people's makes sense to me. I'm not so sure about it now. You get known. As soon as you do anything in this country you become a celebrity. It's not really the same as being a leader. You can only stimulate actions. Stopping them or controlling them is something leaders can do. I'm not a leader. Nobody is under my command. I haven't the vaguest idea how to stop a demonstration, say, except to go home. I'm really not interested in stopping anything, so I'm not a leader. But this celebrity thing has certain problems. Using false names just tends to increase the myth after a while. Sometimes I do now, and sometimes I don't. If I can get away with it, I do.

Will you use a false name on the book?

If I can get away with it.

Isn't this celebrity or star system alien to your visions of a new society?

Most definitely. I find as you get more and more well known you get less personal freedom. You spend more time doing other people's things than your own. You know, people calling in the middle of the night with their problems. Imagine this scene: You are trying to steal some groceries and some old lady comes up and says how much she likes what you're doing. That's why I use disguises, so I can keep in shape by having to hustle without the myth. The day I can't shoplift, panhandle, or pass out leaflets on my own is the day I'll retire.

The myth, like everything else, is free. Anybody can claim he is it and use it to hustle.

What's the solution? Is there any to the celebrity game?

I don't know. I envision a new life after Chicago. I don't intend to deal with symbolic confrontations. I'm interested in just living with a few friends and building a community. If there is to be confrontration, let it be with the local sheriff rather than LBJ. Maybe this is just a fantasy, though. Maybe it won't happen. I guess everyone dreams of a peaceful life in the country. Especially in the winter.

You're planning to drop out?

Well, dropping out is a continual process. I don't see anything really definite in the future. I just don't want to get boxed-in to playing a predetermined role. Let's say, so much of what we do is theater—in life I just don't want to get caught in a Broadway show that lasts five years, even if it is a success. The celebrity bag is another form of careerism. But you see, celebrity status is very helpful in working with media. It's my problem and I'll deal with it just like any other problem. I'll do the best I can.

Is that why the Yippies were created? To manipulate the media?

Exactly. You see, we are faced with this task of getting huge numbers of people to come to Chicago along with hundreds of performers, artists, theater groups, engineers. Essentially, people involved in trying to work out a new society. How do you do this starting from scratch, with no organization, no money, nothing? Well, the answer is that you create a myth. Something that people can play a role in, can relate to. This is especially true of media people. I'll give you an example. A reporter was interviewing us once and he liked what we were doing. He said "I'm going to tell what good ideas you guys really have. I'm going to tell the truth about the Yippies." We said, "That won't help a bit. Lie about us." It doesn't matter as long as he gets Yippie! and Chicago linked together in a magical way. The myth is about LIFE vs. DEATH. That's why we are headed for a powerful clash.

You don't want the truth told?

Well, I don't want to get philosophical but there is really no such animal. Especially when one talks of creating a myth. How can you have a true myth? When newspapers distort a story they become participants in the creation of the myth. We love distortions. Those papers that claim to be accurate, i.e., the New York *Times, Village Voice, Ramparts, The Nation, Commentary*, that whole academic word scene is a total bore. In the end they probably distort things more than the *Daily News*. The New York *Times* is the American Establishment, not the *Daily News*. The *Daily News* creates a living style. You know: "Pot-smoking, dirty beatnik, pinko, sex-crazy, Vietnik, so-called Yippies." Compare that to the New York *Times:* "Members of the newly formed Youth International Party (YIP)." The New York *Times* is death. The *Daily News* is the closest thing to TV. Look at its front page, always a big picture. It looks like a TV set. I could go on and on about this. It's a very important point. Distortion is essential to myth-making.

Are you saying that you actually like the Daily News?

Not exactly, but I don't consider it the enemy, in the same way that I don't consider George Wallace the enemy. Corporate liberalism, Robert Kennedy, Xerox, David Susskind, the New York *Times,* Harvard University—that is where the real power in America lies, and it is the rejection of those institutions and symbols that distinguishes radicals. That is not to say that I love the *Daily News* but that I consider it more honest than the New York *Times.* I once wanted to start a newspaper called the New York *Liar.* It would be the most honest paper in the country. I would sit in a dark closet and write all the news. The paper would be printed with lemon juice, which is invisible until you heat it with an iron, hence involving the reader. I would write about events without ever leaving the closet. The point is, we all live in dark closets. We all see things through a closet darkly.

That's some fantasy.

Of course. It'll come true, though. Fantasy is the only truth. Once we had a demonstration at the *Daily News* building. About three hundred people smoked pot, danced, sprayed the reporters with Body deodorant, burned money, handed out leaflets to all the employees that began: "Dear fellow member of the Communist conspiracy. . ." We called it an "Alternative Fantasy." It worked great.

What do you mean, it worked great?

Nobody understood it. That is, nobody could explain what it all meant yet everyone was fascinated. It was pure information, pure imagery, which in the end is truth. You see, the New York *Times* can get into very theoretical discussions on the critical level of what we are doing. The *Daily News* responds on a gut level. That's it. The New York *Times* has no guts.

Then being understood is not your goal?

Of course not. The only way you can understand is to join, to become involved. Our goal is to remain a mystery. Pure theater. Free, with no boundaries except your own. Throwing money onto the floor of the Stock Exchange is pure information. It needs no explanation. It says more than thousands of anti-capitalist tracts and essays. It's so obvious that I hesitate to discuss it, since everyone reading this already has an image of what happened there. I respect their images. Anything I said would come on like expertise. "Now, this is what really happened." In point of fact nothin happened. Neither we nor the Stock Exchange exist. We are both rumors. That's it. That's what happened that day. Two different rumors collided.

Can you think of any people in theater that influence you?

W.C. Fields, Ernie Kovacs, Ché Guevara, Antonin Artaud, Alfred Hitchcock, Lenny Bruce, the Marx Brothers—probably the Beatles have the most influence. I think they have the perfect model for the new family. They have unlimited creativity. They are a continual process, always changing, always burying the old Beatles, always dropping out.

Can you pursue that a little?

Well, the Beatles are a new family group. They are organized around the way they create. They are communal art. They are brothers and, along with their wives and girl friends, form a family unit that is horizontal rather than descending vertically like grandparents-parents-children. More than horizontal, it's circular with the four Beatles in inner circle, then their wives and kids and friends. The Beatles are a small circle of friends, a tribe. They are far more than simply a musical band. Let's say, if you want to begin to understand our culture, you can start by comparing Frank Sinatra and the Beatles. It wouldn't be perfect but it would be a good beginning. Music is always a good place to start.

Why is that?

Well, a revolution always has rhythm. Whether it's songs of the Lincoln Brigade, black soul music, Cuban love songs by Jose Marti, or white psychedelic rock. I once heard songs of the Algerian rebels that consisted mostly of people beating guns on wooden cases. It was fantastic. What is the music of the system? Kate Smith singing the National Anthem. Maybe that's Camp, but it's not Soul.

What about dancing?

There too, Arthur Murray. Dance lessons. What a joke. If you need lessons you haven't got the message. Dancing for us is doing anything you want. You have to see a huge throbbing light-rock show. Especially one that is free, because the free-est people only go to free events. You will see people doing all sorts of fantastic dances. Frenzied and smooth. Butterflies and antelopes. Indians and spiders. Swimming and jumping. Lots of people just sit or lie on the floor, which is a nice step too. Nobody takes lessons. In fact, if you liked the way somebody danced and asked them where they learned to do it, they would laugh. Dance schools are about as outmoded as public schools, which really are archaic. In fact, I wouldn't be surprised to find out that Arthur Murray was U.S. Commissioner of Education, and high school was just a training ground for millions of foxtrotters. You can see the difference if you look at one of those silly dance books with the shoe prints. One-Two-Three, One-Two-Three. You know. It would be funny to make one for the new dances, which, by the way, don't have names anymore. I think about two years ago dances stopped having names. Anyway, one of those books would have shoe-prints all over the walls and ceilings. A possible title for this book I'm working on could be The Three

Basic Steps in Modern Dance. One-Two-Free. . . One-Three-T. . . O. . . net wo. . . 10-9-8-7-6-5-4-3-2-1 NOW! That's it. Now you've got it. Turn your motor on and fly. You can go forever.

Forever?

Haven't you heard of nuclear energy? Yes, you can dance forever. That's the Beatles' message. That's why I said before that our movement was called Dancing.

Doesn't all this dancing present a problem for society?

Not for ours, but for the parent culture, the one decaying, most definitely. The cops hate us.

How do you feel about cops?

Cops are our enemy. Not each one as a person, naked, say. We're all brothers when we are naked. Did you ever see a fight in a steam bath? But cops in uniform are a different story. Actually, all uniforms are enemies. Just another extension of machine living. The way we dress—in costumes—is in direct opposition to a uniform culture. Costumes are the opposite of uniforms. Since the cops' uniforms also include clubs, handcuffs, guns, etc., they are particularly hated uniforms. I should also add that I've been arrested seventeen times and beaten by police on at least five occasions. I would no more think of asking a cop for help than shooting arsenic to get high.

Who would you ask for help?

My brothers. None of my brothers are cops. You see a cop's principal role is to protect private property. Our goal is the abolition of property. How could I ever call a cop?

Don't they do more than protect property?

Yeah, they kick the shit out of people who have none. Listen. You should have seen Grand Central Station last week during the YIP-IN. Picture this, thousands, maybe ten thousand people, dancing, singing, throwing balloons in the air. Some people decided to climb on top of the information booth; while they were up there they pulled the hands off the clock. This triggered a police riot, with maybe two hundred cops swinging night-sticks charging into people. No warning. No order to clear. About one hundred people were hospitalized, including my wife and me, and over sixty people arrested. There were the police lined up around the clock, guarding it while others smashed skulls. One kid, Ron Shea, tried to come to my rescue while I was being beaten. He was thrown through a glass door and had both hands broken. He may never be able to use one again. Which hands do you think the cops cared more about, the hands on the clock or Ron Shea's hands?

Why did the kids rip the hands off the clock?

I don't know. Maybe they hate time and schedules. Maybe they thought the clock was ugly. They also decorated the clock with sketches. Maybe they were having fun. When we put on a large celebration the aim is to create a liberated area. People can do whatever they want. They can begin to live the revolution even if only within a confined area. We will learn how to govern ourselves. By the way, this goes on in every revolution. Take Vietnam. In liberated zones the National Liberation Front has schools and theater troupes and hospitals and building programs. The revolutionary experience is far more than just the fighting units.

Do you read revolutionary writings?

Yes, Guevara, Debray, Mao, Giap, McLuhan. I find Giap and McLuhan the most interesting. But of course I am totally caught up with Ché as a hero. His death moved me far more than, say, that of Martin Luther King. Although King's was a shock also.

What do you think of death?

Well, I must say I have no fear of death. I faced it once about two years ago on an internal level. This is hard to explain. I've actually faced the risk of death a number of times but this one time I actually became paranoid. I was overcome with anxiety. It was unclear what was going on. I overcame that state purely on a mind level and realized that I had the power in me not to become paranoid. It's the paranoia, the living in constant fear of death, that is the real bad trip, not the death itself. I will be surprised if I get a chance to live out my life. Gleefuly surprised, but surprised none the less.

Isn't that sort of gloomy?

No! Not really. You can't deny there is a tremendous amount of violence in this country. People who are engaged daily in radical social change are always exposed to that violence. I would rather die fighting for change than surrender. Death in a physical sense is just not seen as the worst of all possible things.

What is?

I don't know. Going to jail. Surrendering. . . . Maybe nothing is really bad, since I am so convinced that we will win the future.

B
From Suffrage to Sisterhood

Sigmund Freud once remarked that he never understood what women really wanted. Despite this uncertainty, he, along with his male contemporaries, accepted a limited role for women. The expectation was that women would bear and rear children, manage the home, and cater to the desires of husbands. Most men, as well as a majority of the women, believed that these roles were naturally or divinely ordained ones and that female happiness depended upon conformity to them. Any other role was subversive of the established order and would lead to unhappiness.

However permanent the domestic roles of the women seemed to nineteenth century observers, the evidence seems to be that these roles had shrunk from their eighteenth-century counterparts. The family in the eighteenth century was more public and less private, with women and children having more in social contacts in the outside world. The family contracted and became more isolated in the nineteenth century. Richard Sennett's study of Union Park, Chicago, *Families Against the City*, shows why. The growth of Chicago after the Civil War threatened the ability of middle-class fathers to understand or control their public lives. Consequently, they withdrew into their families and increasingly separated their public and private lives. This change to a fortress family blocked both women and children from some of the public roles that they had previously enjoyed. There was an actual decline in the number of roles offered by society to these two groups.

Selection 6 should be read with this background in mind. It is an excerpt from William O'Neill's book, *Everyone Was Brave*, a study of the failure of feminism. O'Neill admits that real gains were made in women's rights in the last decades of the nineteenth century. More women did enter universities, work at a greater variety of jobs, and achieve a more nearly equal legal status. However, for a variety of reasons, the movement that culminated in women's suffrage did not produce genuine equality. O'Neill concludes that "the ballot did not materially help women to advance their most urgent causes; even worse, it did not help women to better themselves or improve their status." The resistance to change was too great and the movement too divided.

The primary obstacle to full equality was, as Elizabeth Cady Stanton suggested, woman's role in the family. By an unfortunate juxtaposition of persons and events, discussions of the sexual role of women took a sensational turn. The radical advocacy of free love by Victoria Woodhull, a leading spokesman for women's rights, combined with restrictive Victorian mores, placed those who questioned domesticity in an uncomfortable position. The idea of social purity (which held that women were morally superior to men) along with opposition to birth control (which might enable males to be more promiscuous) led women's-rights advocates to remove even the language of sexual roles from their pleas. By emphasizing the twin virtues of purity and motherhood, these advocates narrowed the range of possible roles. The institutions of marriage and the family were accepted pretty much as defined, leaving the status of women at home quite the same.

Another possibility was proposed by Charlotte Perkins Gilman, who did attempt a reform of the family. She did not attack the existing role of women as wives, although she did say that motherhood was overvalued. She questioned the need for women to be domestic servants. Mrs. Gilman hoped to free women from household duties by the use of child-care centers, neighborhood kitchens and dining facilities, and professional house cleaners. These aids would enable women to become self-sufficient economically. Although Mrs. Gilman persuaded Walter Lippman, she was less successful in convincing the general public. Despite her failure to have her ideas adopted at the time, Mrs. Gilman still inspires feminists, particularly those who advocate child-care centers to aid working mothers.

Neither Victoria Woodhull's view of woman's sexual role nor Charlotte Perkins Gilman's view of woman's domestic role prevailed. The battle for the ballot was won, but this victory changed little in the everyday life of the ordinary woman. The political results of women's suffrage were disappointing. Women did not take a position on issues because they were women, but rather because they were middle-class or lower-class individuals or because they were Republicans or Democrats. Women voted as men did and continued in the roles as wives, mothers, and domestic servants. The larger question of what new roles women should seek remained open. The reason, as O'Neill points out, was that "the great majority of women were afraid, unconsciously at least, to ask it."

One who was not afraid to ask disturbing questions was Mabel Dodge Luhan. Unlike many of her predecessors in the feminist movement, Mrs. Luhan explored the sexual roles of women. Perhaps she could do this because she was rich; perhaps she wanted to do this because of her incessant search, aided by analysts like A. A. Brill, for her self-identity. In any case, Mrs. Luhan explored many possible roles, respectable and otherwise.

Selection 7 is from Christopher Lasch's book, *The New Radicalism in America*, and it catches the spirit of Mabel Dodge Luhan quite well. Mrs. Luhan's tempestuous life involved a search for sexual fulfillment and meaningful outlets for her many talents. She had four husbands and several affairs, as well as being at least a latent homosexual. She evidently found the authority she could respect only in her Indian husband, who represented the uncorrupted primitive to her.

A psychological explanation of Mrs. Luhan's life would probably emphasize her lack of security based on the inability of her weak father to control her strong mother. Using this explanation, it then would follow that had Mrs. Luhan married a strong enough man she would have accepted the normal role of wife and mother. Find the right man, take the right role, and harmony reigns in the social order. This belief is conventional wisdom for all male chauvinists, as well as for many women.

However, as Lasch shows, the solution is not that simple. Mrs. Luhan's quest for immediate experience was combined with a drive for power. At times she wanted to be an intellectual, while at other times she repudiated the intellect in favor of sensuality. Further, she was occupied with sexual rivalry. She wished to submit to men but she also wished to dominate them. She desired attachment to others, but she also wanted to separate herself. She was a complex person who held conflicting views simultaneously. Although she found no role completely satisfying, she was willing to ask questions about women's sexual roles which had been unasked since Victoria Woodhull.

Selection 8 is a catalogue of women's liberation groups with their programs taken from *The New York Times Magazine*. As has seemed typical of all reform movements, the women's liberation movement has fragmented. It includes those who want economic equality—equal pay for equal jobs—and institutional arrangements that make female employment possible—day-care centers for children or shared household responsibility with men. It also includes those who are more interested in a self-conscious examination of what being a woman is, as well as those who reject present male-female relationships. There are those whose major concern is with a male-dominated society. While elements of the older women's-rights movements still remain in women's liberation, the present-day feminists have moved beyond the questions asked by suffragettes in the late nineteenth and early twentieth centuries.

The WITCH group, which is deliberately provocative, is more openly sexual in language than were Victoria Woodhull or Mabel Dodge Luhan. The Redstockings have a flair for dramatization and direct confrontation that resembles that of the earlier women's-rights movement, but the tactics are in the service of the cause of abortion, not the franchise. The Feminists, whom Susan Brownmiller calls one of the most radical groups, do assume that the institution of marriage is partly responsible for the lack of women's freedom. Here, the failure of the first women's movement as seen by O'Neill is remedied. The questions that recur in the meetings of each of these groups center on sexual roles. Societal restriction, which limits the expression of female potential, is attacked, and a strenuous effort is made to create a sense of feminine solidarity. The goals of the contemporary movement are much more wide ranging and openly expressed than the goals of the earlier one. Betty Friedan says, "We're going to redefine the sex roles," and Annie Koedt says, "We're going to be redefining politics."

The first women's-rights movement was unable to challenge the conventional roles of wife and mother. It succeeded only in stretching these roles somewhat by gaining some political and economic concessions. The second women's-rights movement, which incorporates the sexual frankness of our age, wishes to create radically new roles for women. In so doing, the new movement would eliminate some present roles and drastically change others. Both movements started as minority ones, but the first was able to gain much popular acceptance. It remains to be seen whether the second can gain equal acceptance and still retain its more far-reaching goals.

6 THE ORIGINS OF AMERICAN FEMINISM
William L. O'Neill

The Civil War had a powerful effect on the fortunes of women. Having acquired some practical experience and some education outside the home, they were able for the first time to participate actively in a national enterprise. The Union's Sanitary Commission and other relief agencies, although controlled largely by men, gave vast numbers of women public work to do. Thousands served as nurses, and daring individuals such as Clara Barton, Mary Livermore, and Louisa May Alcott, not to mention the eccentric few who became spies, soldiers, and the like, distinguished themselves. On the ideological front, Elizabeth Cady Stanton and Susan B. Anthony formed the National Woman's Loyal League to inspire patriotism, support the Thirteenth Amendment, and secure for women an honorable role in the war effort. Most importantly, perhaps, the war gave Union women a heroic myth which echoed down the generations. Their considerable services lost nothing in the retelling. It quickly became a fixed principle that when the war ended "woman was at least fifty years in advance of the normal position which continued peace would have assigned her." Women understandably needed to believe that large benefits had flowed from their large contribution to a long and horrid war, but in reality they had gained little of permanent use from it. The improvement in their educational opportunities was well under way by 1860, and the war only slightly increased the demand for women teachers and, in a few cases, women undergraduates in colleges depleted by

SOURCE: Reprinted by permission of Quadrangle Books from *Everyone Was Brave: The Rise and Fall of Feminism in America* by William L. O'Neill, Copyright © 1969 by William L. O'Neill. Footnotes in the original have been omitted.

the Army. A few women became government clerks, and after the war some hung on to their ill-paying jobs, but government service did not become an attractive or important occupation for women until the next century. Perhaps an additional hundred thousand women found jobs in industry after 1861, but an army of overworked and underpaid female operatives already existed, and the war had little effect on industry's long-range employment patterns. The war enhanced women's self-confidence, and to some extent it stimulated them organizationally, but the mobilization of women on a national scale did not begin until the 1880s.

For women the most important consequence of the war was not masculine recognition of their services, or (mostly) the lack of it. Rather, it was the passage of the 13th Amendment which crowned the labors of female abolitionists and at the same time touched off a crisis in the women's rights movement with far-reaching consequences. Quickened by their fruitful labors during the war, and certain that the Negro's hour must be theirs also, suffragists assumed in the flush of Union victory that they would soon win the vote. At the first postwar women's rights convention, Theodore Tilton, a liberal journalist, spoke for many when he asked, "Are we only a handful? We are more than formed the Antislavery Society. . . which grew into a force that shook the nation. Who knows but that tonight we are laying the cornerstone of an equally grand movement." The aged Sojourner Truth, ex-slave and a beloved figure in the movement, called for woman's immediate enfranchisement. "I want it done very quick. It can be done in a few years." The youthful Frances Gage assured her listeners that in speaking for temperance around the country she had found her audiences alive to the need for women's votes. "They are ready for this work."

But if the cry of votes for women no longer seemed as bizarre in 1866 as it had in 1848, suffragists were still badly out of step with the rest of America. It soon became apparent that the 14th Amendment would apply to men only, and in 1867, despite great efforts, a woman suffrage referendum was overwhelmingly defeated in Kansas. These two setbacks embittered the more extreme feminists, who concluded after Kansas that men could not be trusted. Years later the authors of *The History of Woman Suffrage* recalled that after their humiliation, "we repudiated man's counsels forevermore; and solemnly vowed that there should never be another season of silence until woman had the same rights everywhere on this green earth, as man." Man could be of little help in the great work, because while he regarded woman as "his subject, his inferior, his slave, their interests must be antagonistic." Also in 1867 feminists attempted to have the word "male" struck from the New York State constitution, with the word "white," over the objections of Horace Greeley who felt with most reformers that it was the Negro's hour and that feminists should wait to press their claims until black suffrage was secured. To which Mrs. Stanton and her friends replied:

*No, no, this is the hour to press woman's claims; we have stood with the
black man in the Constitution over half a century, and it is fitting now that
the constitutional door is open that we should enter with him into the political kingdom of equality. Through all these years he has been the only decent
compeer we have had. Enfranchise him, and we are left outside with lunatics,
idiots and criminals for another twenty years.*

Their shocked disbelief that men would so humiliate them by supporting votes
for Negroes but not for women demonstrated the limits of their sympathy for
black men, even as it drove these former allies further apart. Early in 1869 Elizabeth Cady Stanton observed that at a recent suffrage convention in Washington
several Negroes had said men should always dominate women and that white
women were the Negro's worst enemy. Mrs. Stanton complained that this "republican cry of 'manhood suffrage' creates an antagonism between black men and
all women . . ." This trend, she warned, in language as ominous as it was unfortunate, "will culminate in fearful outrages on womanhood, especially in the
southern states." Additional evidence of the suffragists' hardening attitudes came
when Mrs. Stanton and Miss Anthony aligned themselves with a notorious speculator and bigot, George F. Train, who compaigned with them for woman suffrage
and provided financing for their weekly journal, *Revolution.* With his usual deli-
cacy, Garrison described Train as a "crack-brained harlequin and semi-lunatic,"
a "ranting egotist and low blackguard," and a "nigger-baiter." Train may not
have been all that bad, but he was bad enough to antagonize those friends of
woman suffrage who had not already been put off by the women's fight against
the 14th Amendment. The Stantonites candidly admitted to judging every man
solely on his views toward immediate woman suffrage, and Train was the only
man they knew who did not worry about the effects of equal suffrage on the
Negro's chances. All he asked in return was that *Revolution* carry news of his
financial schemes. Not even Wendell Phillips, a good friend of the suffragists'
cause, was pardoned for thinking that black men needed the vote more than
white women. "Mr. Phillips, with his cry, 'this is the negro's hour,' has done
more to delay justice for woman, and to paralyze her efforts for her own enfranchisement, than any man in the Nation," Mrs. Stanton declared.

By 1869 the Stanton-Anthony forces had worked themselves into an untenable
position. Their policies of simultaneously advancing a wide range of reforms
while taking a hard and narrow line on woman suffrage exerted unbearable strain
on the suffrage movement as a whole. Feminists divided, therefore, into two
groups, with the radical New Yorkers becoming the National Woman Suffrage
Association, and the more conservative Bostonians, led by Henry B. Blackwell,
Lucy Stone, Julia Ward Howe, and T. W. Higginson, among others, forming the
rival American Woman Suffrage Association. The AWSA conceded that this was
indeed "the Negro's hour," but mainly it confined itself to the woman question.
Its position on black suffrage notwithstanding, the National has generally been
admired by historians for the large, generous approach it took to contemporary

social questions. *Revolution* did have a good word to say about every good cause, but its general strategy remained hopelessly confused and obscure. The journal's first issue announced modestly that "we shall show that the ballot will secure for woman equal place and equal wages in the world of work; that it will open to her the schools, colleges, professions and all the opportunities and advantages of life; that in her hand it will be a moral power to stay the tide of crime and misery on every side."

Obviously, if the vote would do all this the Stantonites had good reason to go as far as they did in pursuit of it. But, of course, it would not, and there were those in the group who understood the suffrage's limitations and the importance of advancing other reforms as well. When Boston suffragists (in their own organ, the *Woman's Journal*) attacked *Revolution's* policy of backing every worthy cause, the radicals pointed out that they wanted to vote:

> But we are not dreamers or fanatics; and we know that the ballot when we get it, will achieve for woman no more than it has achieved for man. And to drop all other demands for the sake of uniting to demand the ballot only, may seem the whole duty of the Woman's Journal, but is only a very small part of the mission of the REVOLUTION. The ballot is not even half the loaf; it is only a crust—a crumb. The ballot touches only those interests, either of women or men, which take their root in political questions. But woman's chief discontent is not with her political, but with her social, and particularly her marital bondage. The solemn and profound question of marriage . . . is of more vital consequence to woman's welfare, reaches down to a deeper depth in woman's heart, and more thoroughly constitutes the core of the woman's movement, than any such superficial and fragmentary question as woman's suffrage.

How splendidly put, how true—how confusing to loyal readers whom *Revolution* had previously urged to labor for a right which would of itself secure their emancipation.

Suffragists could not have it both ways. Either the vote was central to woman's freedom, in which case the American was pursuing a proper course, or it was but one of many necessary items, and the National was fully justified in casting a broad net. Time was to show that the Stantonites had reached, however imperfectly, the appropriate conclusions. But their diagnosis was obscured by a habit of using every available argument for woman suffrage, even when they contradicted one another, and by the organization's congenital inability to make those compromises essential to a struggling movement which could ill afford to alienate its friends. Having already lost their allies in the old anti-slavery camp, the radicals quickly proceeded to offend the nascent labor movement. Susan B. Anthony encouraged working women to form trade unions and was a delegate to one of the early National Labor Congresses. Meanwhile, *Revolution* was being printed in a "rat office" (one paying less than the union scale), and Miss Anthony was urging women to better themselves by acting as strikebreakers. Still, when the National Labor Congress refused to readmit Miss Anthony as a delegate in 1869, the radical feminists could see this only as another example of male chauvinism. Elizabeth Cady Stanton concluded that the incident "proved what THE REVOLUTION has said again and again, that the worst enemies of Woman's Suffrage will ever be the laboring classes of men." Having previously consigned Negroes and reformers to that same category, *Revolution* by its own admission had no friends at all and no reason for believing that women would ever get the vote.

. . .

All this having been said, it remains true that the National possessed something of value, the loss of which was greatly to affect the future of American women. Alone of the major women's groups in this period, the NWSA admitted, however fitfully, that the heart of the woman question was domestic and not legal or political; that woman's place in the family system was the source from which her other inequities derived. Marriage, its members believed, was organized exclusively to gratify man's selfish need and wants, and consequently was "opposed to all God's laws." Mrs. Stanton declared:

> *For what man can honestly deny that he has not a secret feeling that where his pleasure and woman's seem to conflict, the woman must be sacrificed; and what is worse, woman herself has come to think so too.*

Mrs. Stanton insisted that she and her friends were not against marriage as such, "only against the present form that makes man master, woman slave. The only revolution that we would inaugurate is to make woman a self-supporting, dignified, independent, equal partner with man in the state, the church, the home." Of course, this is so far from being the case even today that Victorians may be excused for thinking her proposals quite revolutionary enough. Apart from easy divorce, the radical feminists had few other specific proposals to offer. Sex education for boys appealed to some women as one way of insuring a more tender regard for wives, as well as a deterrent to "solitary vice." But these suggestions were bound to seem feeble, perhaps even disingenuous, in view of the impassioned language used to denounce the prevailing sexual norms. Rape appeared to Mrs. Stanton as merely another expression of the general malaise. Citing a recent case, she explained in 1869 that the statutes which "make woman man's chattel slave; theologies that make her his subject, owing obedience; customs that make her his toy and drudge, his inferior and dependent, will ever be expressed by the lower orders of men in such disgusting outrages."

These repeated charges amply warrant our belief that Victorian women generally entertained a low opinion of the sexual act. Yet clearly it does not follow from this that marriage in the nineteenth century was considered a satisfactory expression of sexual refinement, or an adequate defense of female gentility. By today's standards marital sex was perhaps infrequent and decorous, but the double standard of morality and the cult of true womanhood had the curious effect of making such high demands on male continence that few normal men could exhibit the self-control women demanded of them. When the dangers of childbirth were added to the horrors of "conjugal commerce," we ought not to be surprised that sex was something a great many women could readily do without, and that they viewed as loathsome and perverse a system which forced it on them. This was especially true of advanced women, and while most suffragists were married, they tended to marry later, have fewer children, and to be much more divorce-prone than the average woman. Mrs. Stanton did not conform to this pattern. She had five children and only one husband. But in her memoirs she tells us that her life began at fifty when her children could take care of themselves.

It would be wrong to think that Mrs. Stanton was prudish or unreasonable on sexual matters. She was, in fact, one of the very few women reformers who thought that women's willingness to identify chastity with moral worth was a sign of their slave mentality. She never believed, as most other women did, that purity was essential to greatness in either men or women. When in the 1890s the brilliant Irish leader Charles Parnell was driven out of British politics for living in sin with a married woman, she remarked dryly that "if the women of England take up the position there can be no true patriotism without chastity, they will rob some of the most illustrious rulers of their own sex of any reputation for ability in public affairs." She ardently championed the brightest female spirits of her own day, who often led unconventional sex lives. Most American women were scandalized by George Sand; even those like Margaret Fuller who admired her were forced to lament that "a woman of Sand's genius—as free, as bold, and pure from even the suspicion of error might have filled an apostolic station among her people." Others like Harriet Beecher Stowe were less charitable, inspiring Mrs. Stanton on one occasion to declare flatly that "George Sand has done a grander work for women in her pure life and bold utterances of truth, than any woman of her day and generation; while Mrs. Stowe has been vacillating over every demand for her sex, timidly watching the weathercock of public sentiment and ridiculing the advance guard." But few women agreed with Mrs. Stanton. Frances Willard surely represented the great majority when she said, rightly no doubt, that Parnell's disgrace showed the growth of women's influence. With a characteristic disregard for the facts of the case, she cried out,"'God be thanked that we live in an age when men as a class have risen to such an appreciation of women as a class, that the mighty tide of their public sentiment will drown out any man's reputation who is false to woman and the home."

Thus, while the Stanton group's position on marriage was not really very radical, and reflected much the same fear and suspicion of sex which animated most feminists, the fact that it recognized the existence of a marriage question was itself enough to put it beyond the pale. The last serious effort to reunite the suffrage movement failed in 1870, despite the best efforts of Theodore Tilton, when Mrs. Stanton's views on marriage and divorce were strongly condemned at the American Woman Suffrage Association's convention. The split which was originally caused by the Stantonites' refusal to accept Negro suffrage, was now being sustained, personalities apart, by their critique of Victorian marriage. While the National's position on marriage was not especially daring, except by comparison with the prevailing norms exemplified by the American, it was further compromised through the National's association with the fantastic Victoria Woodhull.

Mrs. Woodhull had arrived in New York in 1868 with her sister Tennessee Celeste Claflin, after divorcing her first husband, Dr. Channing Woodhull, a luckless fortune teller and quack nostrums peddler. With the support of Commodore Vanderbilt the sisters entered the brokerage business, but they were most attentive to their periodical *Woodhull and Claflin's Weekly,* a lively magazine devoted to the promotion of feminism, suffrage, spiritualism, and the doctrines of Stephen Pearl Andrews, an eccentric philosopher who had discovered Universology, the key to all knowledge, and had devised Alwato, the scientific universal language. The beautiful and eloquent Victoria rose rapidly to a commanding position in the suffrage movement and scored what was considered a great coup in 1871 when she persuaded the House Judiciary Committee to hold hearings on a proposed constitutional amendment to give women the vote. She testified before the committee to good effect and was subsequently inspired to run for President on her own Cosmo-Political party's ticket. Both Susan B. Anthony and Elizabeth Cady Stanton thought highly of her. Mrs. Stanton wrote her a letter of encouragement from the territory of Wyoming, where women had just been given the vote, which began, "To you, the last victim sacrificed on the altar of woman's suffrage, I send my first word from the land of freedom." Miss Anthony had been roused to a considerable pitch of enthusiasm by the favorable minority report of the House Judiciary Committee on woman suffrage, and wrote Mrs. Woodhull that "I have never in the whole twenty years' good fight felt so full of life and hope. I know now that Mr. Train's prophesy—nay, assertion—three years ago in the Kansas campaign, that 'the women would vote for the next President,' is to be realized. I am sure you and I and all women who shall wish to will vote for somebody, if not for George F. Train or Victoria Woodhull."

Unhappily for the Stantonites, Mrs. Woodhull was an incredibly dangerous woman by virtue of her peculiar temperament and bizarre views. She not only supported every drastic prescription for society's ills, from spiritualism to Marxism, but represented another outcropping of that vein of free love which underlay Victorian monogamy. Free love, or any variant of it, was always a dangerous cause in the nineteenth century. It destroyed Frances Wright's Nashoba community and forced John Humphrey Noyes to move his utopian colony from Vermont to the wilds of western New York. But until the 1870s the relative openness and dispersed character of American society enabled sexual radicals to stay in business. After the Civil War there was a noticeable hardening in American attitudes and institutions, symbolized by the emergence of Anthony Comstock secretary of the New York Society for the Suppression of Vice, who led a nationwide campaign for moral censorship that became known as Comstockery. The Comstock Act itself, which empowered the Post Office to deny mailing privileges to morally offensive works, put a mighty weapon in the hands of censorious Americans and made the transmission of unconventional sexual ideas all but impossible. Opinion was so tense and easily inflamed that even the popular Harriet Beecher Stowe suffered after revealing, for entirely proper reasons, certain colorful facts about Lord Byron's sex life. A poorer time to make a fresh assault on monogamy could hardly be imagined.

Moreover, Victoria Woodhull's intense partisanship and unrestrained invective had given many people good reason to hate her. When Horace Greeley explained that he was against woman suffrage because of its ties with free love, Mrs. Woodhull accused him of wrecking the health and happiness of his wife and causing the deaths of five of his seven children. Although specifically exempting Greeley, she went on to observe that moralizing editors in general were lecherous monsters who, because she was known to favor "social freedom," had made "disgusting revelations of their own natures" to her. Of Catherine Beecher, who had recently been speaking against woman suffrage, Mrs. Woodhull said at the outset of a five-hundred-word sentence:

> If the Catherine Beechers who now clog the wheels of progress, and stand forth as the enemies of their sex, and therefore of the human race, doing their utmost to cement the chains of their degradation, giving to man the same power over them as he possesses over his horses and dogs, and other chattel property, if we say they consider this to be their mission, and they are satisfied to be the puppets of man's caprice—the playthings of his passion—the wretched serfs of his supreme power and authority, and prefer to be voted for in the simplest concerns of life, and dandled upon his knees after the manner of courtesans . . . . let them do so, but not at the expense of other women.

Thus, despite her generous opinions (in an anti-Catholic age she was not afraid to praise religious orders), patriotism (she enthusiastically supported President Grant's attempt to steal Santo Domingo), and many talents, Mrs. Woodhull had no reason to expect much help should she ever get into serious trouble. Indeed, at first she exercised what was for her a degree of caution. She favored licensed prostitution—anathema to virtually all women but not without support in official quarters—in rational and persuasive terms. Noting the efforts of Boston women to redeem and reform prostitutes, she pointed out that of the two approaches used to combat prostitution, rehabilitation and suppression, neither had worked well. Once prostitutes were made they could not easily be rehabilitated, she thought, while making prostitution a crime led only to blackmail and official corruption.

The only repressive agency admissible is a system of police licensing and rigorous visitation. This is not authorizing sin by statute, simply recognizing social and physiological facts. In this way, and in this way alone, until a wholesome moral sentiment can be induced can legislation deal with the subject.

For the customary police tactics the sisters had nothing but contempt. After a mass arrest of prostitutes in Greenwich Street, the *Weekly* noted with heavy irony that "when they come out from their purification, the ninety-four will have been reformed by good teaching; work will be provided for them; and having been washed and regenerated by the humanizing influence of Blackwell's Island, they will not go back to Greenwich street. Oh, no."

These comments were dangerous enough, but even more hazardous was the manner in which the sisters edged closer and closer to openly advocating free love. Their early essays on marriage were suitably obscure and characterized by the usual—among radical feminists—calls for "perfect equality" between the sexes. They also ran occasional pieces by Sarah F. Norton who, according to another contributor, had been expelled from the New York suffrage movement because of her attempts to link equal suffrage with free love. Whether this was literally true or not hardly mattered, for what Miss Norton had to say was serious enough. In a typical effusion she accused *Revolution* of having retreated from its earlier stand on marriage and of being an "orthodox truckler of the weakest type," while announcing that "woman suffrage really means the abolishment of this vile system of marriage."

Apparently tiring of these veiled locutions, Mrs. Woodhull decided to disclose publicly her belief in free love and did so from the stage of Steinway Hall in New York on November 20, 1871. It is difficult to imagine why she expected what was left of her reputation to survive this event. When her intentions became clear, Theodore Tilton, an extraordinarily open-minded person, the author of a flattering biographical pamphlet about her, and perhaps one of her lovers, was the only man of standing in New York willing to preside at the meeting. Nonetheless, Mrs. Woodhull was stunned by the ferocious response to her appeal for a sexual revolution, and when the press and public assailed and harassed her she seemed to lose her reason. After threatening to retaliate against her critics by "carrying the war into Africa," she went on to tell all she knew of the Beecher-Tilton affair. In the November 2, 1872, issue of the *Weekly* she revealed that Henry Ward Beecher, the most famous preacher of his day and a friend of woman suffrage, had for years maintained an affair with Elizabeth Tilton, the wife of her principal champion. Professing to admire Beecher's potent charms, she claimed that her only reason for publicizing the affair was to call attention to Beecher's hypocrisy in not admitting his conversion to the higher sexual morality. Whatever her motives—and they seem to have been remarkably complicated—the result of her outburst was predictable. Tilton sued Beecher, Beecher denied everything, and, although probably guilty, was essentially sustained by both the courts and public opinion. Tilton fled the country a broken man and was soon followed by the Claflin sisters, whose magazine was put out of business by the Post Office Department and whose lives were made unbearable by an indignant populace.

• • •

While the affair had its ludicrous aspects—Beecher's pomposities, Anthony Comstock's efforts to suppress the *Weekly*—it was the greatest scandal of the day, involving as it did America's most popular minister, a well-known editor, and some of the country's more prominent women. And it had the immediate effect of stifling all further discussion of the marriage question. Mrs. Stanton continued to defend free divorce, but otherwise the outburst of public feeling drove radical feminists back from their advanced position and forced them to concentrate more narrowly than before on law and politics. Since the American was already committed to a policy of expedience and compromise as a result of the controversy over black suffrage, the differences between it and the National rapidly diminished. Before long only personal dislikes stood in the way of a reunion which was finally effected in 1890, years after both groups had come to stand for essentially the same things. Nor was this lesson lost on the next generation of suffragists, who were not "distinguished by the breadth of their social views" to begin with. Although sympathetic with the respectable goals of social feminism, the new leaders were determined to avoid complicating the suffrage question by associating it with daring or unconventional speculations, no matter how important. In this manner a vital part of the woman question simply disappeared. Having already taken the economic context of American life as essentially given, feminists went on to do the same thing for the marital and domestic system, accepting, for the most part, Victorian marriage as a desirable necessity. In so doing they assured the success of woman suffrage while guaranteeing that when women did get the vote and enter the labor market in large numbers, the results would be bitterly disappointing.

Neither the Woodhull debacle nor the general climate of Victorian opinion fully explain the feminist position on sex in the late nineteenth century. Also important was the social purity crusade which played a prominent role in the woman movement. Of course, campaigns against prostitution in a century as sexually obsessed as the nineteenth were inevitable, but social purity meant much more than the suppression of vice. Its origins lays in the mothers' associations which began as early as 1815 and, especially during the 1830s and 1840s, developed a considerable interest in suppressing vice and "uplifting" fallen women. Thereafter, maternal societies seem to have lost interest in these matters. It was not until the 1870s that social purity became a coherent and persistent movement, in reaction to the growth of regulated prostitution in both England and the United States. In the 1860s the British Army tried to license prostitution in the continental manner, inspiring a counterattack which spilled over into the United States once regulation had been turned back in England.

The scattered efforts of American vice reformers were crystalized in 1877 when a delegation of English anti-regulationists visited this country. Vigilance committees were formed in New York and elsewhere, and the movement swelled until it reached a peak in 1895 with the formation of the American Purity Alliance. Like all such reforms, social purity progressed erratically. In the early 1880s it languished, but was revived in 1885 by W. T. Stead's exposures of the vice industry, which occasioned almost as great a scandal here as in Britain. Mothers' meetings were held around the country, the WCTU's Social Purity Department was energized, and another department for the suppression of obscene literature added. By the 1890s social purists had not done much to eliminate prostitution, but they had destroyed any chance of regulating it. The physicians, military men, and public health officers who supported regulation had either been persuaded or intimidated, and with this threat removed social purity lost its separate identity.

Social purity was by no means an entirely feminine affair, but its ranks were largely filled with women, and it represented in an especially intense and emotional way the woman movement's characteristic attitudes on sexual questions. It stood for the abolition by law of impure practices, and the censorship for moral reasons of all forms of expression. Famous censors like Anthony Comstock and Josiah W. Leeds of Philadelphia were highly regarded by moral reformers. Female moralists were, however, by no means unsympathetic to the prostitute herself, whom they tended to see as an innocent victim of economic want and masculine lust—as against the still popular view of the inherently depraved harlot.

Less durable than these convictions, which continued to be widely held in the twentieth century, was the Victorian feminists' opposition to birth control. Because the public fight for birth control was won in the United States by a coalition which included emancipated women, it is sometimes assumed that feminists always favored contraception. In the Victorian age, however, organized women invariably opposed it. English feminists consistently preferred continence to contraception and saw birth control as merely another way of encouraging masculine lust. Hence the militants' slogan in 1913, "Votes for Women and Purity for Men." American social purity forces took much the same line, not only out of their fear and hatred of sexual intercourse but because they believed in the conservation of energy. Since they visualized the body as an energy system that was running down, they were eager to avoid the physically depleting effects of coitus.

Social purity, with the Victorian woman's anti-eroticism, completed the work of reorienting feminism away from a serious consideration of sexual issues. Especially after the Woodhull affair it was almost impossible for suffragists to see sexual irregularities as anything but immoral, and immorality as something that could not be suppressed by votes for women. As one suffragist put it while discussing Stead's exposures of the London vice scene, "One thing is evident, without the votes of women no vice that appeals peculiarly to the appetites of man can ever be suppressed or the laws enacted for the suppression of such vice be properly enforced." While there were feminists, particularly after the turn of the century, who did not share these prejudices, the leadership of the woman movement united under the banner of absolute purity. Two important consequences flowed from this. By closing their eyes to the sexual elements regulating the life of women, feminists prevented themselves from developing a satisfactory analysis of the female dilemma. And, as we shall see, when the great changes in female sexual behavior became visible in the 1920s, feminists were unable to react to it in such a way as to command the respect of emancipated young women. It was their sexual views more than anything else that dated the older feminists after World War I, and made it difficult for them either to understand or to speak to a generation moved by quite different ambitions.

This blind spot was true even of a woman like Charlotte Perkins Gilman, almost the only major second-generation feminist to continue attacking the cult of domesticity. The original suffragists were fully aware that "concentrating all woman's thoughts and interests on home life intensifies her selfishness and narrows her ideas in every direction, hence she is arbitrary in her views of government, bigoted in religion and exclusive in society." They also understood that if woman were to be man's equal she would have to occupy the same positions and do the same work. Susan B. Anthony persistently reminded the social purity movement that "whoever controls work and wages, controls morals. Therefore we must have women employers, superintendents, committees, legislators; wherever girls go to seek the means of subsistence, there must be some woman." Although never very precise about the means by which woman's liberation would be effected, the founders always insisted that it meant "emancipation from all political, industrial, social and religious subjection." But while feminism was born out of a revolt against stifling domesticity, and nurtured in the understanding that for women to be really free the entire fabric of their lives had to be rewoven, by the end of the century most feminists had succumbed to what Charlotte Perkins Gilman called the "domestic mythology." Home and family were so revered in the Victorian age that the temptation to exploit rather than resist the current of opinion was irresistible. The original feminists had demanded freedom in the name of humanity; the second generation asked for it in the name of maternity. What bound women into a selfless sisterhood, it was now maintained, was their reproductive capacity. Over and over again feminists asserted that "women stand relatively for the same thing everywhere and their first care is naturally and inevitably for the child."

Maternity was not only a unifying force but the enabling principle which made the entrance of women into public life imperative. As another suffragist put it in 1878, "The new truth, electrifying, glorifying American womanhood today, is the discovery that the State is but the larger family, the nation the old homestead, and that in this national home there is room and a corner and a duty for 'mother.' " Not only was the nation a larger home in need of mothering, but by impinging upon the domestic circle it made motherhood a public role. Jane Addams was a persistent advocate of this doctrine:

> *Many women today are failing properly to discharge their duties to their own families and households simply because they fail to see that as society grows more complicated it is necessary that woman shall extend her sense of responsibility to many things outside of her own home, if only in order to preserve the home in its entirety.*

So the effort to escape domesticity was accompanied by an invocation of the domestic ideal—woman's freedom road circled back to the home from which feminism was supposed to liberate her. In this manner feminism was made respectable by accommodating it to the Victorian ethos which had originally forced it into being.

Given the plausibility and elasticity of this contention, women were, inevitably perhaps, lured into using it to secure their immediate aims. Yet in retrospect it does not seem to have been a completely successful ploy. One historian has recently hailed Frances Willard's "supreme cleverness" in using the WCTU "to advocate woman suffrage and child labor laws and other progressive legislation always in the name of purity and the home." But the history of the WCTU illustrates the weakness of an argument that begins by accepting the opposition's premise. In conceding that better homes were of equal importance to anti-feminists and feminists alike, these women reduced their case from one of principle to a mere quarrel over tactics. To redeem itself the opposition had only to prove that its tactics were superior. This is apparently what happened to the Temperance Union after the death of Frances Willard (which coincided with a significant change in its social composition), when new leaders came to believe that temperance was more crucial to the home than suffrage, child welfare, and other progressive causes. Perhaps this new orientation would have come about in any event, but the suffragists in the WCTU made it all the easier by their willingness to use the cult of domesticity in pursuit of quite separate and distinctively feminist objectives.

The truth was that while femininsts resented the demands made upon them in their roles as wives and mothers, they were not alert to the danger of even a partial accommodation to the maternal mystique. They gravely underestimated the tremendous force generated by the sentimental veneration of motherhood, and assumed they could manipulate the emotions responsible for the condition of women without challenging the principles on which they rested. Moreover, while denying that under present circumstances mothers could be held accountable for the failings of their children, they implied that once emancipated, women could properly be indicted for the shortcomings of their progeny. In 1901 Susan B. Anthony herself went so far as to say that:

Responsibilities grow out of rights and powers. Therefore before mothers can rightfully be held responsible for the vices and crimes, for the general demoralization of society, they must possess all possible rights and powers to control the conditions and circumstances of their own and their children's lives.

Her remark would seem to mean that once granted political equality, mothers would have to answer for all the ills of society—a great weight to lay on posterity. Such statements contributed to the unhealthy and unrealizable expectations which feminism encouraged.

A further hazard stemming from the feminist emphasis on motherhood was the support it gave to the notion that women were not only different from men, but superior to them. Julia Ward Howe, a moderate and greatly admired feminist, persistently reminded women that emancipation was intended to make them better mothers as well as freer persons.

Woman is the mother of the race, the guardian of its helpless infancy, its earliest teacher, its most zealous champion. Woman is also the home-maker; upon her devolve the details which bless and beautify family life. In all true civilization she wins man out of his natural savagery to share with her the love of off-spring, the enjoyment of true and loyal companionship.

Definitions like this left men with few virtues anyone was bound to admire, and inspired women to think of themselves as a kind of super race condemned by historical accident and otiose convention to serve their natural inferiors. Such indeed was the case with some women who, encouraged by the new social sciences—especially anthropology, which demonstrated that matriarchies did exist and may in prehistory have been common if not universal—were moved to take themselves with a seriousness few men could share. Elizabeth Cady Stanton elaborated this hypothesis in 1891 in an impressive paper that she called "The Matriarchate, or Mother-Age." She argued that in prehistoric times women had been superior, or at least equal, to men, but that Christianity and especially Protestantism drove the feminine element out of religion and subordinated women to the rule of men. Society, therefore, lost the beneficent moral and conservative forces of the female intellect and the mother instinct.

With this line of argument Walter Rauschenbusch, no enemy of women's rights, was compelled to take issue. He must have disapproved of the anti-clerical flavor of much feminist thought, but he was specifically motivated by the feminists' moral pretensions.

Many men feel that women are morally better than men. Perhaps it is right that men should instinctively feel so. But it is a different matter when women think so too. They are not better. They are only good in different ways than men.

Rauschenbusch believed in the emancipation of women, but he reminded his readers that the feminine virtues could easily be exaggerated. In recent times, he pointed out, both Christian Science and Theosophy had demonstrated a particular appeal to women, even though both stressed authority and unexamined belief. As Rauschenbusch's observation suggests, the attempt to demonstrate woman's superior nature led only to a dead end. It was really just one more variation of the Victorian mystique, another way of exploiting the belief that women's unique power was rooted in the mystery of her life-giving capacities. Taken one way it led back to a preoccupation with motherhood. Read differently it supported a rejection of men so complete that women could retain their integrity and spirituality only in spinsterhood. Or by subscribing to the principles of Ellen Key, who elevated motherhood even above marriage and made the right to have illegitimate children the central aspect of feminism, women could have their cake and eat it, too. They could realize their generative and instinctual potential without an unseemly dependence on the contaminating male. Having a child in this way meant, of course, a degree of masculine cooperation, but in a delicious reversal of ancient custom man became a passive instrument of woman's purpose and his ungoverned passions the means to her full emancipation. This was radicalism with a vengeance, but a radicalism that had little to do with the normal objects of revolutionary ardor.

· · ·

Seen against this background, Mrs. Gilman's scorching attack on the maternal pieties is all the more impressive. She had suffered as a young wife from the conflict between ambition and motherhood, but she ultimately resolved her problem by divorcing an entirely satisfactory husband and giving up an agreeable child. Having thus cleared her decks she went on to enjoy a successful career as a writer and feminist theoretician—about the only one, in fact, the American movement ever produced. She was able not only to work her way out of the domestic trap, something other women have also done—less brutally one hopes—but to take the next step by confronting intellectually the system that had forced her to take such heroic steps, something no other American woman had managed to do. In bringing her strong and original mind to bear on the large problem of woman's social role she produced, most notably in *Women and Economics,* the best contemporary analysis of it.

Women and Economics, her first book, was written like all her many works—at top speed, sloppily edited, and rushed to print in 1898. Despite its many imperfections the book's arguments were so lucid, its suggestions so original, and its phrases so often brilliant and arresting that Mrs. Gilman became famous almost overnight. She believed that all women needed to work, both for their own sake and for society's, and that the domestic system needed drastic reorganizing to permit this. She advanced her argument on several fronts, claiming that it was both morally necessary and economically desirable that women work in the same way as men. It was morally necessary because while women depended on their husbands for support, they were forced to develop an exaggerated sexuality. The most desirable women got the best husbands and thus, through a process of natural selection, women's sexual attributes became overdeveloped at the expense of other, more important, characteristics. Only when they earned their own living could women form with men those equal partnerships that alone would guarantee marriage's survival. After they married women still needed work in order to continue growing. "Science, art, government, education, industry— the home is the cradle of them all, and the grave if they stay in it. Only as we live, think, feel and work outside the home, do we become humanly developed, civilized, socialized." Apart from developing a finer womanhood, society stood to gain economically from the employment of women who would increase the national output of goods and services.

Mrs. Gilman had a low opinion of housework, and it was at this point that most suffragists began to disagree with her. Since middle-class women did not work and apparently did not want to work, feminists generally claimed that inequality in the home derived from society's failure to value properly the contribution housewives made to the domestic economy. Mrs. Gilman easily disposed of the inflated claims for domestic work by pointing out that no matter how good a housekeeper a woman was, her standard of living was unrelated to her performance. "What she gets out of life is not proportioned to her labors, but to his." Over and over again Mrs. Gilman called on women to distinguished between the essential and nonessential aspects of their social role. "When women are wise enough to be free, and free enough to be wise, they will learn to dissociate the joys of love, the status of marriage, the blessings and cares of motherhood, from the plain trade of cooking, and the labors of personal service."

What made Mrs. Gilman's failure to win many converts to her position so important for the future of women was, as Aileen Kraditor has pointed out, that if the work they did at home was as valuable as the work men did outside it, then "no fundamental economic change would be necessary in home relationships for women to achieve equality." While suffragists wanted every woman to have the same vocational opportunities as men, they expected most women to stay at home most of the time. Since they accepted the domestic system as unalterable, this meant that, in effect, they thought women's domestic inequities could be remedied by changed attitudes and symbolic reorientations. Hence the vote, while it would not affect family life in any direct way, would improve women's domestic status by raising their self-esteem. Similarly, some feminists thought husbands should pay their wives a salary in recognition of their contributions to the familial economy. It was natural for suffragists to think this way because they venerated motherhood and, for the most part, subscribed to the prevailing domestic pieties. When they did not, they had to appear to in order not to offend people who did. Moreover, to admit that women's dilemma was institutional and not simply a matter of bad habits and poor attitudes, was to admit the need for a domestic revolution—something few suffragists wanted.

It was Mrs. Gilman's principal virtue that she accepted the logic of her own position. If domesticity crushed woman's spirit and weakened her morals, then the home would have to be replaced by something better. Nor was Mrs. Gilman afraid to suggest what that better something might be. She envisioned large housing units which would provide nurseries, central kitchens, maid service, and the like, thereby freeing wives and mothers for productive work. By putting cooking, cleaning, and child care on a professional basis they would be done better than by a horde of amateur housewives, the scale of operation would create economies, and, of course, to meet the added expenses each family would have the wife's salary. The concept was not unique to Mrs. Gilman (indeed, *Woodhull and Claflin's Weekly* once predicted that urban families would some day live in residential hotels which would free women from housework), but she became its most forceful proponent and the idea was always associated with her. From Walter Lippmann's point of view, Mrs. Gilman's plan made simple good sense. While it was no more than the domestic counterpart of the rationalization and reorganization transforming the national economy, it would also assist those processes which Lippman was eager to see consummated. By enabling women to specialize, either outside the cooperatives or as cooks or housekeepers within them, it would break down the narrowness and individualism through which women clogged the wheels of progress. "One of the supreme values of feminism is that it will have to socialize the home," Lippmann wrote in 1914. "When women seek a career they have to specialize. When they specialize they have to cooperate. They have to abandon more and more the self-sufficient individualism of the older family."

Lippmann's enthusiasm for cooperative housekeeping in this sense derived, of course, from his hopes for the nationalization of American life rather than from any special desire to emancipate women. But he was probably right in thinking that it would advance both causes. Mrs. Gilman was herself a socialist, eager to reduce women's parochialism, but the immediate virtue of her plan was that it could be put into effect immediately, at least on a small scale, and need not await the social revolution. Yet it took little time for her to recognize that the traditional family and the myths on which it rested were much stronger than most people realized. Even though the falling birthrate, the increased number of working women, and the decline of the family as a unit of production, among other things, were popularly supposed to be destroying the family, domestic life seemed little changed. Accordingly, Mrs. Gilman delivered an even mightier blow against the system in a devastating book entitled simply *The Home* (1903).

This witty and savage attack on the cult of domesticity included some of her best writing. "The home," she conceded, "is the cradle of all the virtues, but we are in a stage of social development where we need virtues beyond the cradle size." One by one she destroyed the clichés that supported domesticity. Was the home not sacred? On the contrary, the home was devoted principally to eating, sleeping, resting, and other such elemental processes. They were necessary functions, of course, "but are they more hallowed than the others?" By this token, were not learning, working, and the like equally sacred, was not, in fact, the school more sacred than the home because more valuable to civilization? What about the privacy of the home? But who, Mrs. Gilman asked, has any real privacy in the home? Not the children,

> under the close, hot focus of loving eyes, every act magnified out of all natural proportion by the close range, the child soul begins to grow. Noticed, studied, commented on, and incessantly interfered with; forced into miserable self-consciousness by this unremitting glare; our little ones grow permanently injured in character, by this lack of one of humanity's most precious rights—privacy.

Nor was privacy possible to the wife who must supervise her children, deal with tradesmen and callers, and entertain her friends. Perhaps the husband, if he had a den or study of his own, could gain some privacy, but as a rule the best way to gain peace was to have your servants tell everyone you were not at home. Thus, "to be in private, you must claim to be out of it."

The worship of motherhood did not escape Mrs. Gilman's withering pen. "Matriolatry" seemed to her one of the most dangerous of all social myths because it encouraged women to think that their reproductive capacities alone assured their success as mothers. The care of children required reason, not instinct, and clearly this was in short supply. Who but mothers "raised our huge and growing crop of idiots, inbeciles, cripples, defectives, and degenerates, the vicious and the criminals; as well as all the vast mass of slow-minded, prejudiced, ordinary people who clog the wheels of progress?"

The temptation is to go on quoting from this remarkable book for, although its theme is much like the attack on domestic myths and realities in *Women and Economics,* Mrs. Gilman rang as many changes on it as wit and invention could devise. Persistently, ingeniously, sometimes elegantly, she hunted down every loose thought, wrung the truth from every careless phrase, and exploded the pretensions of every piece of nonsense anyone had ever uttered about domestic life. *The Home* was a *tour de force,* in its own way more impressive than *Women and Economics,* yet it had no discernible effects. This was not because of any flaws in Mrs. Gilman's reasoning. The cult of domesticity and the inefficiencies of private housing certainly inhibited the development of women and perpetuated their inferiority. Self-culture and improved educational opportunities did not cancel out the narrowing influences of home life because "it is use, large, free, sufficient use that the mind requires, not mere information." It followed logically from this that to free woman, particularly during the middle years when they had large families to manage, more was required than the simple elimination of discriminatory laws and customs which, when swept away, would still leave women in a state of *de facto* inferiority by reason of their domestic entrapment.

• • •

Broadly speaking, the emancipation of women in this sense could be accomplished in only two ways. One method would be to erect a welfare state, as Sweden was to do, which through a system of nurseries, paid maternity leaves, and similar benefits would ease the burdens of motherhood and make women genuinely competitive with men in the job market. The other, and by no means antagonistic, way was to reorganize domestic customs and institutions to achieve the same end. These were not mutually exclusive alternatives, but they demanded quite different strategies. Building the welfare state called for political action, while reforming the domestic system involved social action, propaganda, experimentation, persuasion, and the other techniques by which individuals are induced to change their behavior. It would appear that Mrs. Gilman took this latter course because there were no true welfare states in existence yet to show how the thing was done. Moreover, the utopian socialist tradition was still strong in America, not only on account of the many communitarian societies which had flourished here, but because the whole idea of effecting social change by example rather than by edict was congenial to the American temperament.

Our experience in this century suggests that the advantages of Mrs. Gilman's strategy were less clear-cut than they seemed at the time. The welfare state has contributed, in Europe at least, to the emancipation of women, while nowhere in the West has the effort to change the basic patterns of domestic life met with much success. It is true that the development of a welfare state has proceeded much more slowly in the United States than in any other developed Western nation, and in this sense Mrs. Gilman was not wrong to think that the prospects for effective action on a national scale to emancipate married women were poor. What she could not have guessed in 1898 was the extraordinary affection Americans would demonstrate for the detached, self-contained, single family dwelling. The retreat to suburbia had already begun, thanks to the streetcar, but in the twentieth century it became a rout. After World War II the G.I. Bill, the Federal Housing Administration, and similar developments made it possible not only for the middle but for the regularly employed working classes to enjoy the benefits of suburbia. Housing projects snaked out from and around every major city, laying waste the countryside and erecting in place of meadow and woodland acres of identical domestic boxes and forests of utility poles and TV antennas. The cities which, for all their problems, had seemed at the turn of the century to be alive with possibilities for new and better ways of living, were abandoned to the very rich and the very poor.

The crucial point about the suburban explosion is not that tract housing is inferior; indeed, for most people such a home, no matter how drab, monotonous, or aridly situated, represents an improvement over their previous quarters. What is important about these sprawling new developments is that they freeze the domestic pattern. To the wife's other roles is now added that of chauffeur, because the automobile, while it made tract housing feasible for the masses, corroded the system of public transportation. In cities the proximity of schools, nurseries, jobs, shops, and the like, and the transit facilities which service them, make it possible, if not easy, for wives to stretch themselves beyond the home. But in suburbs housewifery is itself a full-time job. Thus the laws which make it easy to build and sell houses on a massive scale, the business customs and institutions that are geared to this type of residential construction and none other, and the durability of Victorian domestic concepts have conspired to frustrate the hopes of visionaries and perpetuate woman's functional inferiority in the great world.

There remained a further alternative which Mrs. Gilman did not explore. She attacked the home because it seemed to her the weakest point in the domestic system. In effect she accepted marriage and the family while proposing to change the physical shell enclosing them. It remained theoretically possible, however, to do just the opposite: to take the home as given and instead to redefine marriage and the family. This was the direction radical feminists were taking before the Woodhull affair, and while their nerve was shattered by it, the stream of criticism directed against Victorian marital and familial patterns lasted well into the twentieth century. The decline of communitarianism and the suppression of Mormon bigamy may have reduced the visible alternatives to monogamy, but radical sexual ideas continued to be advanced. Ellen Key's advocacy of motherhood without marriage involved quite a different sense of what constituted a family. Similarly, Judge Ben Lindsey's appeal for "companionate marriages" broke sharply with the conventional notion of marriage as a lifelong sexual union. Mrs. Havelock Ellis' suggestions for a "novitiate for marriage" (trial marriage) and "semi-detached marriage" (separate domiciles for each spouse) had the same effect. But Mrs. Gilman was unable to speculate on these matters, not only because of her own rigidly conventional views on sex but because the entire area was out of bounds to serious feminists. The movement was just large enough to contain her socialism and her critique of domesticity and motherhood, even while rejecting it. No one could go any further and keep the confidence of organized American womanhood.

From this survey it should be clear that well before 1917 the woman movement, while not altogether bankrupt intellectually, had lost its original verve and openness to new ideas. It had, moreover, embraced a code of sexual morality that precluded serious attention to the social context of emancipation and would cost it the full attention and respect of the generation that came of age in the 1920s. But what would in the long run be fatal to the movement was not so much prudery as its inability to ask fundamental questions about itself. Hardcore feminists, having firmly rejected their own radical origins, were, by the turn of the century, too respectable and too certain that women's rights was a simple political matter to learn much from Mrs. Gilman—who was unique in any event.

Woman suffrage thus became a substitute for all the things feminists were unwilling to do or consider. As their vision narrowed, the emotional weight they invested in the ballot became all the greater, and their need to exaggerate its value all the more urgent. After the 1890s, therefore, ardent feminists became increasingly obsessed with the suffrage question, and to understand the dead end into which this led them we must examine in more detail what they expected from the vote.

7 MABEL DODGE LUHAN: SEX AS POLITICS
Christopher Lasch

Mabel Dodge Luhan—born Mabel Ganson in 1879—was the daughter of a rich banker in Buffalo, New York. She was educated in boarding schools; St. Margaret's in Buffalo, Miss Graham's School in New York, Chevy Chase School in Maryland. A summer in France with her mother completed her education. In 1900 she married Karl Evans, son of a prominent Buffalo family like her own. She bore him a son, but the marriage, she said later, was as loveless as that of her own parents, between whom she could remember only a single show of affection. ("He bent over her, with no more ease than he would have shown had he been trying to pluck berries with his lips from some thorny bush. He approached her gingerly. She gave him a brusque push backward as his mouth drew near her cold cheek. 'Oh, get out!' she said, and the kiss slid off and dissolved in the darkness.") This first marriage ended abruptly when Evans was killed in a hunting accident in 1902. The widow suffered a nervous breakdown and was sent off to Europe—as standard a cure for neurasthenic young matrons as it was an education for girls. On the boat she met Edwin Dodge, a Boston architect of independent means, and in 1903 they were married and established residence in a villa near Florence. Mabel Dodge lived there until 1912, when she returned to the United States and established her well-known *salon* at 23 Fifth Avenue. Estranged from her husband, she plunged into a highly publicized affair with John Reed, twice accompanying him to Europe. From the second of these trips she came home alone, to begin an affair with the painter and sculptor Maurice Sterne, whom she married, once more with a notable lack of enthusiasm, in 1916. They lived for a time on a farm near Croton, New York. In 1917 they went to Taos, New Mexico, already something of an art colony, so that Sterne could sculpt the Indians. There Mrs. Sterne fell in love with Antonio Luhan, a Pueblo Indian; bought a ranch outside Taos; and dismissing Sterne, began a new life in the desert. In 1923 she and Luhan were married. Thereafter she devoted

SOURCE: From Chapter 4 of *The New Radicalism in America, 1889-1963*, by Christopher Lasch. Copyright © 1965 by Christopher Lasch. Reprinted by permission of Alfred A. Knopf, Inc. Footnotes in the original have been omitted.

herself to philanthropic efforts on behalf of the Indians, to collecting writers and artists (of whom the most renowned was D. H. Lawrence), and to writing her enormous autobiography, the published portions of which alone run to five volumes. She died in 1962.

Mrs. Luhan's autobiography consists of four volumes collectively entitled *Intimate Memories—Background* (1933), *European Experiences* (1935), *Movers and Shakers* (1936), and *Edge of Taos Desert* (1937)—together with a memoir of Lawrence, *Lorenzo in Taos* (1932), which is also autobiographical. (The last of these was published first, but written after the first two volumes of *Intimate Memories*, and a portion of the third, had already been completed.) In addition, Mrs. Luhan published two other books during her lifetime, neither of them of more than passing interest: *Winter in Taos* (1935) and *Taos and Its Artists* (1947). The bulk of her works, however, remain unpublished. Five other books were designated as part of *Intimate Memories* but withheld from publication, presumably on the ground that they might offend living people (although the same objection could have been raised against the published volumes). These were "Green Horses," a 314-page continuation of the account of her life in Buffalo; "Una and Robin" (1933), a study of Robinson Jeffers and his wife; "Notes upon Awareness" (1938), "a consecutive summation of the attempts of one manic-depressive character to discover how to free herself of her disability & vacillation, & the various 'Methods' she encountered on her way thro' the Jungle of Life!; "The Statue of Liberty. An Old-Fashioned Story of Taboos' (1947); and "The Doomed: A Tragic Legend of Hearsay and Observation" (1953). Besides these, Mrs. Luhan also left a number of other volumes described as having a "distinctly autobiographical character": "Family Affairs, a Recapitulation" (1933); "Doctors" (1954), subtitled "Fifty Years of Experience"; "Mexico in 1930"; "On Human Relations, A Personal Interpretation" (1938); and two novels. All these works, together with her correspondence after 1914 (the correspondence before 1914 was accidentally burned), were deposited by Mrs. Luhan in the Yale University Library, but her son, John Evans, has forbidden anyone to look at the unpublished memoirs until the year 2000.

Except for her vast memoir, an extraordinary effort to introspection, the life of Mable Dodge Luhan was that of another rich and restless woman, a footnote in the cultural history of Bohemia. It is as such that one occasionally hears of her; for her autobiography is nowadays very seldom read. One comes across references to her *salon*, where Bill Haywood and Emma Goldman once held forth—"the only successful salon I have ever seen in America," in the opinion of Lincoln Steffens. One reads that she had something to do with backing the Armory Show of modern art; or again, that she helped to organize the Paterson strike pageant staged in Madison Square Garden, in which the workers themselves acted out the story of the strike. For the rest, Mrs. Luhan hovers on the fringes of the Lawrence legend, a marginal figure in literary as in social history. Her memoirs created a small stir when they appeared in the thirties, but except for the Greenwich Village volume, *Movers and Shakers*, they have long since fallen into oblivion. Even at the time, they seemed as dated as Mah-Jongg, relics of a period which the depression had made ancient history. At a time when political involvement was the fashion among intellectuals, Mrs. Luhan's painstaking investigations of the intricacies of personal intercourse could hardly have commanded a following. The confessional had gone out of vogue; and even when it reappeared in the forties, in the form of "confessions" by ex-Communists, Mrs. Luhan by her continuing indifference to the great issues of the day forfeited her chance for a reputation. She had no sins to confess except those which were bound up with a devotion to the private life as frivolous, it seemed now, as it was impossibly selfish.

Yet those who read Mrs. Luhan's autobiography with care are more likely to be struck by the familiarity of its theme and tone than by the remoteness of the setting in which the story sometimes unfolds. One does not need to travel very far in the contemporary world—no farther, certainly, than the nearest academic community—to encounter the same intense involvement in group personal relations that was characteristic of Mrs. Luhan and her friends forty-five years ago; the same need jointly and publicly to analyze them in all their details; the same absence of compelling interests outside the circle of friendship which might relieve the pressure under which it is forced to operate. Literary fashions change; but if the intensely analyzed emotional life, of which Mrs. Luhan's autobiography provides such a classic record, was a passing literary fancy, it also represents a tendency inherent in modern life. It is a result of the withering away of the larger social context of existence, which causes people in their loneliness to seek an intimacy even in casual friendships which hitherto was expected only of a few special relationships, if indeed it was expected at all.

The very idea of intimacy as a mutual baring of souls, a mutual examination of the psyche, seems to be an invention of the last two hundred years. When the community disappeared, intimacy not only displaced sociability as the ideal mode of human intercourse, it tended even to displace sexuality itself, notwithstanding the enormous apparent increase of interest in sex. The modern world in its ignorance of the past believed that it had discovered sex, had rescued it from the grip of "Puritanism"; but what had really happened was that sex for the first time had come to be seen as an avenue of communication rather than simply as a means of mutual pleasure. By insisting that sex was in fact the highest form of love, the highest form of human discourse, the modern prophets of sex did not so much undermine the prudery against which they appeared to be in rebellion (itself a comparatively recent development) as invert it. In effect, they took the position that sex, far from being "dirty," was more "spiritual" than the spirit itself, having its ultimate sanction in the communion of souls which sex alone, it was now thought, could provide.

When the community was a reality, most of life's events derived their meaning at least partly from that fact. As long as government remained essentially a local matter, the community represented the collective authority of the leading families, and the continuity between public and private life was therefore almost perfect. Birth, courtship, marriage, and death were public as well as private events, matters of general concern which could not be left to the discretion of the individuals most immediately involved. Marriage in particular, the union not merely of individuals but of families, involved questions of property and power in which the whole community had an immediate stake. In a sense, the private life did not exist at all. The concept of self-fulfillment as the aim of existence could not flourish, if it could exist at all, in a setting in which so much emphasis was placed upon the duties and responsibilities of life, so little upon its opportunities for new forms of experience. What one owed to others was always so much more apparent than what one owed to oneself. All the details of personal intercourse, moreover, were circumscribed by elaborate forms and conventions, as if to emphasize their quasi-public character; and under those conditions there was little opportunity for the naked embrace of the spirit which the modern world has since learned to understand as the essence of love and friendship, the essence of life itself. Communication even between lovers took the form of a stylized dialogue in which both participants remained acutely conscious of all that their respective roles, as defined by tradition, demanded of them. All this set limits to experience, but it also gave it a charm and beauty, a serenity and dignity, which it afterwards largely lost. Life was both enriched and impoverished by the waning of the conventions of communal existence.

By the end of the nineteenth century the close-knit communities which had once been the characteristic form of society throughout the Western world, eroded by a long process of national centralization, had disappeared, except in backwaters isolated from the mainstream of modern life. The most immediate evidence of what was happening was the dissolution of the old-style family, which had once served as the link between the individual and the community, the personal and the public modes of being. To some people this development came as a disaster; to others it symbolized better than anything else the release from outworn conventions which it seemed the special destiny of modern civilization to realize. The debate over the family, turning on the question of the rights of women and children, was waged with an intensity which suggests the importance of the changes that were taking place; but it missed what was perhaps the central point, that the dissolution of the family mirrored the dissolution of the community as a whole. The two institutions were intertwined. If the community was a collective family, the family was also a miniature state, the father a king, lord of all he surveyed. His authority over his wife and children was almost absolute in theory, however beneficently it was exercised. But it depended on his wider authority outside the family. The father was not only head of his household but the visible embodiment of the larger life beyond it. The whole community stood imposingly behind his authority at home. Not the winning of women's rights or the more permissive attitude toward children, but the disappearance of the community, destroyed that authority. When government was centralized and politics became national in scope, as they had to be to cope with the energies let loose by industrialism, and when public life became faceless and anonymous and society an amorphous democratic mass, the old system of paternalism (in the home and out of it) collapsed, even when its semblance survived intact. The patriarch, though he might still preside in splendor at the head of his board, had come to resemble an emissary from a government which had been silently overthrown. The mere theoretical recognition of his authority by his family could not alter the fact that the government which was the source of all his ambassadorial powers had ceased to exist.

The decline of patriarchal authority and the havoc it left behind make themselves immediately felt in Mabel Dodge Luhan's account of her early life, an account by turns nostalgic and harsh. "I like my Buffalo as I knew it," she announced at the outset, only to add in the same sentence that she had come to understand the adults who surrounded her as a child and to admire the gallantry and courage with which they endured "the terrible emptiness of their lives." Her own life was empty too, insofar as the absence of familial authority left an emptiness at its center. Like Randolph Bourne, Mabel Ganson practically brought herself up. She might have been orphaned at birth, for all the demands her parents made upon her obedience or for that matter upon her affection. A stranger alike to love and authority, she knew only her father's sporadic gusts of impotent rage; and when this unfortunate man sought belatedly to arrest the anarchy in his own household, his wife undercut him with her silent contempt. Doubtless it was from her mother, in the first instance, that Mabel Ganson imbibed the scorn of men which was so often to assert itself in her later life. When her father flew into one of his jealous rages and "stamped and shouted and called her names," her mother hid "her cold, merciless, expressionless contempt behind her book or newspaper." The girl "tried to imitate her look." The father "would shout and fling his arms about and his face would seem to break up into fragments from the running passion in him," but her mother refused even to acknowledge his presence. "And when he could shout no more he would stamp out of the room and mount the stairs and presently we would hear his door slam far away in the house. Sometimes, then, she would raise her eyes from the pretense of reading and, not moving her head, she would glance at me sideways and drawing down the corners of her mouth, she would grimace a little message of very thin reassurance to me."

Mabel Luhan's was the generation of which Walter Lippmann wrote: "We inherit freedom, and have to use it. The sanctity of property, the patriarchal family, hereditary caste, the dogma of sin, obedience to authority—the rock of ages, in brief, has been blasted for us. Those who are young to-day are born into a world in which the foundations of the older order survive only as habits or by default." Beyond the chaos in the Ganson family, beyond the erosion of parental authority, one also senses the erosion of society itself. The Gansons belonged

prominently to Buffalo "society," but society in the larger sense never seems to
have entered their lives. Certainly it is completely missing from their daughter's
autobiography. She never refers to a public event of any kind, never refers to
her father's role in the world, gives only the barest hint of his occupation. Nor
does her mother seem to have had any existence, in the girl's imagination, beyond
the walls of the family mansion. Mabel suspected that her mother had "beaux";
but that was all. She could imagine for her mother no connection with a world
outside the family except one which was by definition clandestine and illicit—
secret meetings with faceless men in unknown hotels. And even that, as she later
realized, was perhaps no more than a fantasy of her own. "Was she a deep and
secret woman ... or did I invent all that about her?"

The houses of the rich had become fortresses against intrusion. Even the
architecture of the period reflected the tendency of each family to withdraw into
a world of its own making. To the outsider these edifices presented a massive
wall of impenetrable stone, into which doors and windows were deeply set, mere
slits, like those of the medieval castles to which the buildings of Richardson and
his imitators obscurely alluded. The effect of the heavy doors and ponderous
draperies was not only to shut out intruders but to stifle the human sounds within. A pervasive silence descended. Life came to be lived behind locked doors.
In her mother's bureau, concealed in a handkerchief case, Mabel Ganson found
a copy of Boccaccio.

In such a setting the tenderer human emotions, muffled and stifled, thwarted
and denied, could struggle to light only in shy and timorous gestures, taking on
twisted and hardly recognizable forms. An aunt of a family down the street had
a secret, like Mrs. Ganson. One evening when the other adults were away, she
put on men's clothes, which she had hidden away in her room. She "wooed"
Mabel and her friends with "an air of magical attractiveness." She danced with
them, pressing them "to her hard shirt front." "She danced with us each in
turn, and soon we were pushing each other aside to get into her arms again. She
wrinkled her nose at us and laughed a kind of wild laugh and lighted cigarettes
one from the other."

Only twenty years, a single generation, separated Jane Addams from Mabel
Dodge, but the disintegration of family life seemed already to have entered a
new phase. Life in respectable families no longer seemed merely boring and
pointless; it gave off now an atmosphere of actual decay. Or was it only that
Mabel Ganson was a little obsessed with secrets? But if she was, that was significant in itself; it was the state of mind that middle-class family life now seemed
all too often to induce. Whether her perceptions of that life were accurate or
distorted, it is enough that they were of the darkest sort, intimations of a vast
moral wreckage; and that they led very early to a longing to escape more urgent
by far, more exaggerated, and at the same time more ambiguous and inconclusive
to its expression, than anything Jane Addams seems to have felt. The very air
in her family's house seemed to the girl unbearably oppressive and overripe.

Even in the dead of winter, Mrs. Luhan says, she used to sleep with her head under a wide-open window.

Very early, Mabel Ganson seems to have come to the conclusion that the world into which she was born was hopelessly corrupt, destined to imminent extinction. Yet it was not until forty years later that she announced her break with it, and even then the break was far from complete. The very depth of her loathing for middle-class life seemed ever more fully to implicate her in it. Long after she had undertaken her symbolic withdrawal to New Mexico, all the conflicts of her early life still remained unresolved. Jane Addams's more modest rebellion was much more decisive in its outcome than Mabel Luhan's melodramatic one. In Jane Addams's case, rebellion led at last to something like contentment; in Mrs. Luhan's it turned in upon itself, renewing old dissatisfactions. And although Mrs. Luhan's narrative of her struggle purported, like Jane Addams's, to be a record of the successful resolution of an emotional crisis, it was in actuality a prolonged cry of despair.

The crises themselves took outwardly similar forms. From the time of her first marriage, Mrs. Luhan displayed the now familiar symptoms of neurasthenia. Bored, weary, endlessly ill, she felt her life to be devoid of purpose. Lacking Jane Addams's Protestant conscience, she took a certain pleasure in her own misery. Perhaps the uninhibited self-indulgence of the one, the unremitting self-reproach of the other, was the great difference between them. Mabel Luhan liked to surround herself with sympathizing men: doctors, psychoanalysts, authors, anybody to whom she could recite her misfortunes. In Florence, she says, she grew to enjoy complaining to her doctor as she sat in her "shaded bedroom, away from the unbecoming light from the window." "But if I woke with early morning tears, and felt too sad to get up and bathe and dress in one of my pretty peignoirs, then, when he came and the butler announced him, I would send down word I was not well enough to see him that morning, for I felt I could only receive him when I was looking my best." For such women, confessors who should be at the same time objects of casual flirtation had become an abiding need.

Like Jane Addams, Mabel Luhan decided that her unhappiness was a function of the habit of living at second hand. Both women, moreover, saw the habit as the peculiar curse of their class, the curse of an excessive refinement and cultivation of the intellect at the expense of the emotions. Mrs. Luhan was appalled to find that the habit continued even after she moved to Taos. One day she came upon a garden in the desert.

"Shakespearean," I thought, and then quickly dismissed the analogy. Was one to be forever reminded of something else and never to experience anything in itself at first-hand? My mind seemed to me a waste-basket of the world, full of scraps that I wanted to throw away and couldn't. I longed for an immersion in some strong solution that would wipe out forever the world I had known so I could savor, as though it were all there was to savor, this life of natural beauty and clarity that had never been strained into Art or Literature.

The thought reminds one of Jane Addams's disgust when she discovered that even her own uselessness presented itself in the borrowed imagery of De Quincey. There is a further resemblance: in both cases, the realization that books and learning stood in the way of experience coincided with a mounting sense that excessive intellection cut one off also from the springs of femininity. Thus Jane Addams envied the "active, emotional life" of her grandmothers. Mrs. Luhan characteristically saw the matter in the context of a sexual competition: if domination was masculine and submission feminine, then her relations with men revealed an alarming sexual inadequacy, since she seemed always to end by playing the stronger part. The association of overcivilization with a betrayal of woman's nature expressed itself in her conversion to the simpler way of life of the Indians—an event analogous to the revelation that came to Jane Addams at the bullfight in Madrid. Her decision to turn her back on civilization coincided with the discovery of a man to whom she thought she could unequivocally submit. But the violence with which she expressed her resolution was all her own; there is no parallel to it in anything Jane Addams ever wrote. When she came to realize, she says, that she belonged to Antonio Luhan, that she was "his" and could never dispute his decisions or seek to impose her will against his, she began to wish to

> *leave the world I had been so false in, where I had always been trying to play a part and always feeling unrelated, a world that was on a decline so rapid one could see people one knew dropping to pieces day by day, a dying world with no one appearing who would save it, a decadent unhappy world, where the bright, hot, rainbow flashes of corruption were the only light high spots. Oh, I thought, to leave it, to leave it all, the whole world of it and not to be alone. To be with someone real at last, alive at last, unendingly true and untarnished.*

Not only the intensity of her desire "to leave it all" but the scope of her indictment of civilization distinguished Mabel Luhan from Jane Addams and other radicals, for whereas they tended to define the culture against which they were in rebellion as the culture of a particular class or nationality (the "Anglo-Saxon"), she brought the whole of the white race within the sweep of her rhetorical condemnation. Perhaps because she had not merely visited the continent but had lived there for a period of years, she could not share Randolph Bourne's belief that "Puritanism" was a peculiarly Anglo-American phenomenon. Nor did she look to the working class to find the spontaneity missing in the life of the middle class. She turned instead to the Indians, whom she proceeded to romanticize, however, exactly as other intellectuals romanticized Europeans, proletarians, and children.

There is one final difference between Mrs. Luhan and most of the other cultural radicals of her time. Like Jane Addams, like Bourne, like John Dewey, Mrs. Luhan upheld "experience" against intellection. But she defined experience much more narrowly than they did. Whereas they referred to any direct perception of life, any perception that was not filtered through the perceptions of others, she tended to restrict the concept of experience to the purely biological. All thought was treacherous in her view; the senses alone could be trusted to speak the truth. She insisted, moreover, on the primacy not of the senses in general but of the particular sensations associated with sexual excitement. Mrs. Luhan may be regarded as a pioneer in the cult of the orgasm, which has since not only captivated so many other intellectuals but permeated the entire culture. Her conversion in the desert presented itself as an upwelling of triumphant heterosexuality. Until her submission to Tony Luhan, she had known only a single "satisfactory sexual experience," as a more erudite generation would have put it. In Buffalo her first husband had rudely and abruptly taken her on the floor of the hall of her parents' house. Since that "first surprising involuntary orgasm," she maintained, "actually nothing real had happened" to her until she came to Taos. But now "I was by grace born in the flash as I should have been years, years ago; inducted into the new world."

"It is indeed the happy woman who has no history, for by happy we mean the loving and beloved, and by history we designate all those relatable occurrences on earth caused by the human energies seeking other outlets than the biological one. ... That I have so many pages to write signifies, solely, that I was unlucky in love. Most of the pages are about what I did instead." Thus Mabel Dodge Luhan summed up the story of her life: a sad story with a happy ending, her spiritual regeneration "on the edge of Taos desert." Having found a biological "outlet" for her energies, she had no further history to record.

Unfortunately for the plausibility of this interpretation of her life, Mrs. Luhan had already produced what was in effect another volume of memoirs, in the disguise of an essay on D. H. Lawrence, which gave a quite different version of her life in Taos. Although it appeared before any of the volumes of her *Intimate Memories, Lorenzo in Taos* dealt with events more recent than any covered in that work. It showed how little was changed by Mrs. Luhan's renunciation of the white race and her marriage to an Indian. In fact, it showed that the writing of the *Intimate Memories,* the ostensible record of her triumph, was itself an act of desperation, undertaken as a kind of therapy during a depression which appears to have been at least as severe as anything she had experienced before. It may be that the therapy was so effective that it produced an unprecedented state of contentment which Mrs. Luhan, when she came to the last volume, then projected back to the beginning of her life in Taos. However that may be, the earlier account flatly contradicts the later, and since the former consists largely of contemporary letters, whereas the second is purely retrospective, there is no question as to which is the more dependable of the two.

By the fall of 1924, seven years after her arrival in Taos and a year after her fourth marriage, Mrs. Luhan had reached a crisis in her affairs, one of those onsets of boredom, frustration, and melancholy which recurred at regular intervals throughout her life. In 1922 she had lured D. H. Lawrence and his wife to Taos. Lawrence had misgivings about coming, but "I willed him to come. Before I went to sleep at night, I drew myself all in to the core of my being where there is a live, plangent force lying passive—waiting for direction. ... 'Come, Lawrence! Come to Taos!' became, in me, Lawrence in Taos. This is not prayer," Mrs. Luhan added, "but command. Only those who have exercised it know its danger."

At first, Lawrence was captivated by Mrs. Luhan in spite of himself. He suggested that they collaborate on a novel based on her life. He drafted the first chapter of the book, but the project soon collapsed in a series of quarrels. The friendship itself collapsed. In October 1924 Lawrence went to Mexico, and although he returned to the United States for a few months in 1925, Mrs. Luhan had no further contact with him. On top of Lawrence's departure, she found herself at an impasse with her new husband. She now had to admit that their "different cultures" had "taken different directions." "There is practically nothing for us unavoidably to *do* together," she wrote to Lawrence. "For he likes Mexican dances and I don't. He likes the simple movements of life, like the plaza life, and I don't. And there is little we can talk about of *current* life. About general essentials and the eternities we are in agreement and can speak together about them. If we sit in a room, it is in silence." Her boredom, as always, tended to immobilize her. The smallest decisions became "a kind of agony." She felt herself sinking under a "terrible inertia." From this familiar "gummed-up" state there were only two forms of release that she had been able to discover, falling in love and writing. "If one can do some writing for someone, then after it the world appears mild, sober, lovely, or interesting." She began to play with the notion of writing an autobiography. This thought, it is interesting to note, was bound up with her decision to return to psychoanalysis. She had been analyzed in New York some time before, first by Smith Ely Jeliffe and then by A. A. Brill, and she now decided to lease Finney Farm, where she had lived with her third husband, and to return to the care of Dr. Brill. After these arrangements had been completed, she wrote to Lawrence:

> *Now both you and Brill feel I have to do all the work this winter. With guidance I have to do the thing, whatever it is.*
> *Can you tell me what this thing literally is? Finding myself? I believe I've been a kind of werewolfess.*

Lawrence had urged her to "try, above all things, to be still and to contain yourself."

> *What kind of control and discipline did you mean? Would writing do as a cure and a help? Shall I try to start a life-history or something? Save this letter if you think it would help Brill. It's so hard for me to formulate things, maybe it would aid him.*

Lawrence with characteristic bluntness told her that she hadn't enough "restraint" for creative writing but that she could "make a document." "If you want to write your apologia pro vita sua, do it as honestly as you can—and if it's got the right thing in it, I can help you with it once it's done." Thus encouraged, Mrs. Luhan set to work and completed the first volume within a year—"a real effort," she thought, "to see *Mabel*." Within another year she finished the second volume and sent it to Lawrence, as she had sent the first, for his opinion.

He was impressed with it in spite of himself. At the same time he found the manuscript "frightfully depressing"—"the most heart-destroying revelation of the American life process that ever has or ever will be produced." Not art—"because art always gilds the pill, and this is hemlock in a cup"—it was nevertheless, he thought, "the most serious 'confession' that ever came out of America." It seemed to him "so horribly hear the truth" that it made him "sick in my solar plexus, like death itself." "My dear Mabel, I do think it was pretty hard lines on all of you, to start with. Life gave America gold and a ghoulish destiny. Heaven help us all!"

Notwithstanding her insistence (an afterthought, it would seem) that her childhood was "all right" and that she "would not have had it different," Mrs. Luhan knew that she had written a depressing book. "It is indeed the happy woman who has no history." But it was not depressing for the reason she herself supposed—because it recorded the sublimation of biological energies into other channels. Mrs. Luhan's garbled interpretations of Freud and Jung, with which she unfortunately burdened so much of her narrative, were of little interest. What mattered, what rescued *Intimate Memories* from banality and at the same time accounted for the depressing quality of the work, was the "long, long indictment of our civilisation," as Lawrence noted; that, and what he called the "strange focussing of female power, upon object after object, in the process of decreation: or uncreation: as a sort of revenge," he speculated, "for the compulsion of birth and procreation." This last theme, the theme of sexual rivalry and hostility, was the real subject of the work, the subject of practically everything Mrs. Luhan wrote, as it was the favorite subject of Lawrence himself. The difference between them was that Lawrence ruthlessly dragged what he knew about the battle of the sexes to consciousness and managed, moreover, to write about himself with a rare honesty; Mrs. Luhan, on the other hand, allowed most of her understanding of sexual conflict to remain only half articulated, buried under layers of ideology. Her chief fault as a writer was perhaps not so much artistic, as Lawrence first suspected, as intellectual; a fatal susceptibility to intellectual quackery in all its forms. She was forever hitting upon some new nostrum that was to cure all her emotional complaints. First it was Freud, then Jung, then Dr. Gurdjieff's institute at Fontainebleau in France. Her letters to Lawrence, filled with intricate diagrams of psychic principles and with talk of introverts and extroverts, made him despair of her. She reveled in the paraphernalia of pseudo-science, and her efforts to understand herself inevitably collapsed under this ponderous freight. Only when the descriptive writer triumphed over the ideologue did understanding struggle to the surface, too often to be crushed again under the weight of her latest intellectual enthusiasm.

The record of her unhappiness remains, however, and when one strips it of the dubious interpretations she herself inflicted on it, its outlines emerge with a good deal of clarity. Her Lesbianism is a case in point. Mrs. Luhan tends to treat it for the most part as a clinical detail, the consequence of an early breast-fixation. There is a whole section in Background on "The Breast," in which bosom after bosom is realized in graphic detail: "round they were and with a deep cleft between them"; "white [and] flowery ... with their pointed nipples leaning towards me"; "large, ballooning, billowing ..., firm and resilient and with a stout, springing nipple." What is important, however, is not that Mabel Ganson as a child was fascinated by breasts or that she later had a number of passing schoolgirl affairs, but that as she grew older her homosexual tendencies revealed themselves more and more as an aspect of the will to power which pervaded all her sexual relations with women and men alike.

Consider her friendship with Violet Shillito, with its dreary sequel—the climatic episode of *Background*, and the central event, perhaps, of the entire autobiography. The friendship itself is described with tenderness; Lawrence found it almost "the only ... touch of real love" in the book; but even that, he added, was "deathly." Violet, the daughter of American parents living permanently in France, was the sister of Mary Shillito, a classmate of Mabel's at Miss Graham's School in New York. Her accomplishments, as Mary recited them, were legendary. She had taught herself Italian in order to read Dante, Greek in order to read Plato. Later she studied higher mathematics at the Sorbonne; "for the beauty," she explained. Mary made a kind of cult of her absent sister, into which she inducted Mabel, a cult at the center of which was a shared passion for what Mary and Violet called *"la grande vie intérieure."* Mary persuaded her new friend to make a pilgrimage to Paris. For Mabel and her mother it was a pilgrimage also, such as so many American girls and their mothers had undertaken before, to the temple of culture and tradition; and the daughter's reaction to Europe differed very little from that of innumerable other Americans who went abroad around the turn of the century. She came away with a sense that the old civilization had played itself out.

Violet herself was an intimation of the death of a way of life. Prematurely wise, she was to die prematurely shortly thereafter, hard on the Gansons' departure. High-strung, aristocratic, she lived in an atmosphere of overripe romanticism. She seemed to her friend "weary"; she suggested "civilization coming to pieces." She had an intuition that Götterdämmerung lay close at hand; she spoke of the "debacle" ahead, "of everything going under." She played Chopin and Beethoven while her sister wept. But it was Wagner to whom they were all three most perfectly attuned—Wagner, who "voiced for the white race its desire for annihilation." At Bayreuth they strolled hand in hand about the grounds. In the Shillitos' country house Mabel turned to Violet in the night, and "there arose all about us, it seemed a high, sweet singing." *Je ne savais pas que je sois sensuelle,"* Violet said, *"mais il paraît que je le suis." "Et pourquoi pas?"* asked her friend, "for it seemed to me if that was what was meant by *sensualité* it was exquisite and commendable and should be cultivated." But Violet seemed more than ever weary and resigned. "That sweet, rueful, loving smile was on her face now all the time we were together, and it was called there by that glad life of our blood, which for want of a better term I must call music—but that she had named to me by the term *sensualité.*"

The Gansons went home to American, Mabel to the Chevy Chase School, her debut in Buffalo ("I was never so bored in my life"), her marriage to Karl Evans, his early death. When she returned to Europe, Violet was dead and she herself was engaged to Edwin Dodge. Mary Shillito now lived with a girl named Marcelle, who had been devoted to Violet, "a girl with a strong, independent character, the kind of character that a man is supposed to have." Both of them disapproved of Mabel's impending marriage; there were quarrels; Mabel went off to Florence with Dodge. By the time she next visited Mary, her own emotional life had settled into the pattern it continued thereafter to follow. Finding Mary jealous and spiteful and the atmosphere in the château oppressive, she "began," she says, "to try to throw a little net around Marcelle." She succeeded without difficulty in "lighting a little fire in her," and "night after night Marcelle gave herself up to the luxury of streaming love that passed out of her across to me." Mary reacted with "rabbity alarm." One night she burst in on the pair; a terrible scene ensued; Mabel took Marcelle away to Aix-les-Bains for three days. Then she went back to her husband in Italy. "I missed Marcelle ... I hated to grow cold again."

Thus *la grande vie intérieure* played itself out in a sordid little struggle for power. "I began to try to throw a little net around Marcelle." One begins to understand why Mrs. Luhan's lovers are so often described as victims. Twice she uses a striking image in this connection, writing of a girl at the Chevy Chase School that she "lay in her bed like a sacrifice, straight and relaxed," and of Violet that "she lay beside me, a long, stiff effigy in the white light from the moon shining on the wall."

It was in her relations with men that Mrs. Luhan, as she herself was at least intermittently aware, most fully gave play to her impulse to dominate. It was not, she explained, that she wished to dominate her men; it was only that she had never met a man to whom she could submit. "The fact is, like most real women, all my life I had needed and longed for the strong man who would take the responsibility for me and my decisions. I wanted to lie back and float on the dominating decisive current of an all-knowing, all-understanding man. I had never known any such man." But why did sex present itself in the first place as a struggle, a question of resistance or submission?

It was not simply that she had somehow never known "any such man." In her more candid moments Mrs. Luhan acknowledged a conflict within herself.

Something in us wants men to be strong, mature, and superior to us so that we may admire them, thus consoled in a measure for our enslavement to them. ... But something else in us wants them to be inferior, and less powerful than ourselves, so that obtaining the ascendancy over them we may gain possession, not only of them, but of our own souls, once more.

Mrs. Luhan treated her husbands and lovers like possessions of the same order as the beautiful objects with which she filled her houses. She collected people and arranged them like flowers. Her New York *salon* was only one of many; wherever she went, she loved to combine people in startling new juxtapositions. Sometimes she staged a little tableau in which she herself played a part. In Florence she loved to torment her husband by engaging in harmless flirtations, just as she tormented Mary Shillito by "lighting a little fire" in Marcelle. Her pleasure lay in Edwin Dodge's having to be present at the scene of her conquests; the conquests themselves were nothing more than the amusement of a moment. When she tired of Dodge, she tired of the game as well. In Taos the pattern repeated itself. Lawrence was convinced that she had *"caused* [Luhan] to take a violent prejudice against" him. Not content with playing off Lawrence against Luhan, Mabel meanwhile sent her son around the neighborhood with the report that "my mother is tired of those Lawrences who sponge on her."

All the time she was pushing people here and there, she longed only to "lie back and float" on the current of dominating masculinity; so that her triumphs of manipulation brought her in the long run little satisfaction. She wanted her life to be "very comfortable and orderly"; she longed for "intimate, domestic pleasures." With John Reed, the only one of her lovers whom she did not eventually marry, she tried particularly hard to adopt the role of the submissive wife and help-meet. But it was impossible to submit to Reed because Reed himself was in so many ways a child. At the same time his masculine independence, which should have pleased her if she was "tired of trying to be emancipated," irritated her beyond measure. When she went to Chicago to see him off to Mexico, where his articles on the revolution were to win him a reputation as a war correspondent, she was disappointed "that he looked merely rather glad instead of overjoyed." "The man in him was already on the job," she observed bitterly. "The woman's place was in the home." And when she went with him to Europe in 1914, she found that Reed's real mistress was the war. "Panting with pleasurable activity, his eyes shining ... he rushed with his friends into the affair of the war." Eventually Reed ran off with another woman. She herself lapsed back into invalidism. "I stayed in bed a good deal of the time. Lifeless."

Maurice Sterne, her next acquisition, was more pliable than Reed, but his very pliability made him contemptible. When she met Sterne, he was a painter, She insisted he ought to be a sculptor instead. He obligingly turned to sculpture, changing his career to suit her. She pretended "a kind of deference" to him. "For as long as I lived with him I had to try and look up to him, but it was an effort that constantly failed."

Perhaps, after all, she had been "unlucky in men"; "or perhaps something in me had engaged me only with those men with whom I could successfuly contend." But with Tony Luhan, she insisted, it was different. "From the first I never disputed his decisions." So Mrs. Luhan claimed in her memoirs. She forgot all those occasions, which she herself had recorded in *Lorenzo in Taos*, when she successfully pitted her will against his. Luhan, for instance, at first disapproved of inviting Lawrence to Taos. "His instinct somewhat opposed it. ... But I overruled it, and he gave way." He also objected to taking Lawrence to an Apache festival, "but I made him!" "I am always *making* him do things," she added. So much for her "submission" to Luhan.

Nor did she submit to the Indian way of life, though she was always talking about it. Having loudly renounced the "sick old world of art and artists," she still filled her life, as Lawrence reported, with "suppers and motor drives and people dropping in." She loved "to play the patroness," he complained; and her relation to the Indians was that of the great lady to her wards. In fact, it was exactly the relation Randolph Bourne mistakenly imagined Jane Addams had to the immigrants—a patronizing "appreciation" of their curious old folkways. As Lawrence quickly discovered, she "hates the white world and loves the Indian out of hate." That is, she loved whatever was exotic and picturesque in Indian life, whatever was not white. The glory of the Indians, she once announced in public, was that they did not want progress; they did not want "a dismal accretion of cars, stoves, sinks, *et al.*"; "the blood of their fore-runners is still stronger in them than new needs for THINGS." She herself at that time had just moved into a new house, as Harry T. Moore has noted, "with soundproof bedrooms, a magnificent kitchen, and several fine bathrooms." A young Indian, addressing her in a letter to the local paper, angrily proposed that they exchange places. "You can have all the horse and buggies you want and I'll have your nice new cars. You drink muddy water from the mountains and I and my wife and five children will drink nice clean water from your faucets." What she did not understand, he said, was that "we want to live like humans and not like animals." For Mrs. Luhan, however, their living like animals was the very source of the Indians' charm. It meant (as she erroneously believed) that they had not yet learned to sublimate their biological energies. If sublimation was the root of evil, the Indians still lived in an innocent Eden. It is a pity the Indians did not know more about Freud and Jung (as interpreted by Mrs. Luhan). They would have taken comfort in knowing that their illiteracy and squalor were enviable cultural advantages.

When D. H. Lawrence cried: "Back to your tents, O America!" Americans such as Walter Lippmann and Mabel Dodge took him literally. When Lawrence urged Americans to "take up life where the Red Indian, the Aztec, the Maya, the Incas, left it off," and "to listen to your own, don't listen to Europe," they assumed that he was glorifying the noble savage. Lippmann felt called upon to instruct Lawrence in the elements of American history: America had no native culture, but was "a nation of emigrants who took possession of an almost empty land." Anyone who had read Lawrence's *Studies in Classic American Literature* might have seen that he was pleading with American writers to cultivate their own literary traditions; but it was characteristic of American radicals that they could see Lawrence only as a reformer with a bold new program for the regeneration of Western man. They forgot that he was first and foremost a writer whose chief concern was the process whereby life is translated into literature. That process was precisely what did not interest American radicals; they would have dismissed Lawrence as a believer in the heresy of "art for art's sake," had they suspected that he cared about it. It was as a prophet armed with a new religion that he caught their imagination and as a prophet that they accepted or rejected him. Mrs. Luhan solemnly explained: "Lawrence had a belief ... that it was his destiny to [destroy] the old modes, the evil, outworn ways of the world" and "that if he could overcome evil and destroy it, he would have fulfilled his destiny." She simply could not get it into her head that Lawrence was mainly interested in writing books. She could see him only as a Faustian figure wrestling with "Satanic powers." As for his writings, she seemed to have enjoyed only his travel books, if indeed she had even read the others. She cared so little about art in general that when she was presented with the manuscript of *Sons and Lovers,* in payment for the ranch which she tried to give to Frieda Lawrence and which Lawrence refused to allow his wife to accept as a gift, she gave the manuscipt to Dr. Brill, "for helping a friend of mine." She took pride in this gesture, which symbolized her liberation from the "world of art and artists." "I supposed [Brill] still has it," she airily remarked. "I never asked him."

Since Lawrence's American friends believed him to be essentially a propagandist who wanted white men to live like Indians, these friends were secretly pleased to find that real Indians made him uncomfortable. This discovery made them feel superior to him; they themselves, they imagined, had such easy and natural contact with red men. Witter Bynner, one of the ornaments of the Taos literary colony, professed amusement at the spectacle of Lawrence "extolling the noble savage in print while he dreaded or disliked him in person." Mabel Luhan was convinced that Lawrence felt inadequate in the presence of her husband. When she and Luhan met the Lawrences' train, the car broke down and Luhan got out to fix it. Frieda Lawrence urged her husband to help him, whereupon Lawrence confessed: "I am a failure. I am a failure as a man in the world of men." If Mrs. Luhan's account is inherently improbable—for, as Professor Moore has pointed out, Lawrence hated machines and "thought that Indians who knew how to fix them were corrupt"—it nevertheless reveals once again her obsession with masculinity, femininity, and sexual rivalry. From the beginning, her relations with the Lawrences assumed in her mind a complicated pattern of competition, Luhan pitted against Lawrence, herself against Frieda Lawrence, Lawrence and Frieda against each other, and above all Lawrence against herself: a four-way battle of wills.

Thus she was convinced that "there was never a moment of sympathy" between Lawrence and her husband after Luhan laughed at Lawrence's first attempts to ride a horse. Lawrence assured her that he had "nothing against" Luhan, but that altered in no way Mrs. Luhan's habit of seeing all human relations as a form of politics. Love, friendship, and sex all continued in her imagination to constitute a struggle for mastery; life itself was a struggle for mastery; and she was later convinced that Lawrence had died, in fact, not of tuberculosis (a consideration altogether beneath her notice), but "because he scorned to learn the mundane mastery that may insure a long, smooth life if the living impulse is emasculated and overcome." He "made a mess of living and of friendship and love ... because he never learned to 'control' himself, but let life rule." Lawrence in turn thought that Mrs. Luhan was unhappy precisely because she was so intent on willing her happiness. "You have striven so hard, and so long, to *compel* life. Can't you now slowly change, and let life slowly drift into you." But he had already answered his own question. Within a few weeks of meeting Mabel Luhan, he had discovered her "terrible will-to-power." She had a "passion," he said afterward, "for breaking other people's eggs and making a mess instead of an omelette, which is really dangerous. She seems to hate anybody to care for anybody—even for herself—and if anybody *does* care for anybody, she must upset it—even if she falls herself out of the apple-cart." "A woman," he decided, "*must* upset any apple-cart that's got two apples in it: just for the fun."

No sooner had the Lawrences arrived in Taos than Mrs. Luhan capitalized on the existing tension between Lawrence and his wife in order to drive a rift between them. Frieda Lawrence had to admire the "terrific energy ... resources and intelligence" with which Mrs. Luhan set about her task; but "why were you so bossy?" she wailed afterward. The proposed novel which Lawrence and Mrs. Luhan were to write became the means of rescuing him from what Mrs. Luhan regarded as a disastrous marriage. Frieda resisted the novel from the first. "I did not want this. I had always regarded Lawrence's genius as given to me." Terrible quarrels ensued—"the vileness of 1923," Lawrence referred to them subsequently. Mrs. Luhan told Frieda that she was not "the right woman for Lawrence," and Frieda was "miserable thinking that Lawrence had given her the right to talk like this to me." Lawrence railed by turns at Frieda and at Mrs. Luhan. Finally he and Frieda "left Mabel's ambient" and moved to a neighboring ranch. In the spring they escaped to Mexico.

The struggle with Frieda, Mrs. Luhan discovered, "released ... all my desire for domination." She strove not only to win Lawrence away from his wife but "to seduce his spirit so that I could make him carry out certain things." She wanted him "to take *my* experience, *my* material, *my* Taos, and to formulate it all into a magnificent creation." Knowing that "the strongest, surest way to the soul is through the flesh," she simulated a physical passion for him. "I persuaded my flesh and my nerves that I wanted him." It was really "his soul I needed for my purpose, his soul, his will." But "the only way to obtain the ascendancy over these essential tools was by way of the blood."

That is one of the things we know, Jeffers [she wrote, addressing herself to the poet to whom her narrative was dedicated]; realists like you know it. The idealists, as they call themselves—masking under a nice word their short-sightedness—they never know it. Of course some people stop short of the gate of blood. They are satisfied with that. But others, all those who get things done—they go on from there.

I was always trying to get things done: I didn't often even try to do anything myself. I seemed to want to use all my power upon delegates to carry out the work. This way—perhaps a compensation for that desolate and barren feeling of having nothing to do!—I achieved a sense of fruitfulness and activity vicariously.

Beside her own confessions, Lawrence's strictures on Mrs. Luhan's "will-to-power" seem mild enough; yet she became convinced that Lawrence wished to "destroy" her. After the Lawrences' return to New Mexico in the spring of 1924, matters came rapidly to a head. One night in July the caldron of accumulated bitterness boiled over. The Lawrences had come down to Taos from their ranch, accompanied by Dorothy Brett, a viscount's daughter who had worshipfully followed Lawrence to the New World. Mrs. Luhan had two other house guests, Alice Sprague, a childhood friend from Buffalo, and her own latest admirer and retainer, Clarence Thompson, a young aesthete from New York whom she described as "extremely sophisticated and exquisite." After supper Tony Luhan drove off on some errand, and the rest of the party "strolled over to the studio." Lawrence and Clarence disappeared for half an hour and returned surprisingly, for Lawrence rarely drank, with a bottle of moonshine whiskey. "As the unaccustomed alcohol ran through our veins, we all drew together, feeling more convivial than usual, more cosy and reassured." Somebody put a record on the gramophone and Clarence and Mrs. Luhan began to dance. Then Clarence danced with Frieda, "in a dignified, dreamy way." Mrs. Luhan seized Lawrence, who danced as seldom as he drank, and "led him round and round in a one-step." But when they stopped for more drinks, "there began to rise between us all that feeling of division and comparison that is so odious." They danced again. Between the two couples "a fiercer and more sinister emotion had sprung up." Clarence and Frieda, dancing gracefully "in an evident trance of self-satisfaction," pretended not to notice Lawrence and Mrs. Luhan, who flew about the room "bumping into them as hard as we could at every round!" Gathering speed and momentum, the couples collided ever more violently. "Lorenzo kicked Frieda as often as he could." Mrs. Luhan was in transports of delight. "That night, for once, and for only that once, I was able to join to his all my physical energy, and my will, destructive or not, in a mutual effort against the outside world. This was no deep, invisible 'flow' of life between us, reinforcing each the other [such as Lawrence was always commending to her as the best form of friendship]. No, it was his use of my strength for a battering-ram."

At last they all stopped for breath. Frieda and Clarence slipped silently out into the night. "I couldn't believe my eyes. That was simply not done among us. I mean, no one ever went out of sight of all the others. What one did we all did. There were no tête-à-têtes, no dialogues, nothing that was not in plain sight of all the others." But Frieda and Clarence, innocent of the rules, were gone. Lawrence went to bed. Tony came home. Mrs. Luhan went to bed and lay awake wondering what had become of the lovers, as she now imagined them. Finally she went out to look for them. She had reached the courtyard when Tony appeared, shouting: "Come back here!" She felt herself, however, "compelled to go on." Tony jumped in his car and drove angrily away; he did not return until the next morning. Meanwhile Mrs. Luhan found Clarence preparing for bed. "What *have* you been doing, Clarence?" He had been talking to Frieda, he said. "Frieda has told me *the Truth!*" The truth was that Lawrence had vowed to "destroy" Mabel Luhan. Mrs. Luhan "was shaking all over—trembling with the shock and the strangeness. It sounded true. It *was* true."

Next morning Clarence confronted Lawrence. "You devil! I *know* you now!" The Lawrences and Brett went back to their ranch, in all likelihood none too clear as to exactly what had happened. Such were the hazards of group life. Couple pitted against couple, the party had become a tiny court of intrigue, but a court with no world beyond itself, an oasis of intrigue in the middle of an uninhabited desert.

That such a scene could have taken place was a measure of the social vacuum in which modern life had come to be lived. But the central element in the scene was quite possibly a complete fabrication of Mrs. Luhan's. According to Dorothy Brett, usually a more reliable observer of facts, it was *she* who danced with Lawrence, bumping into Clarence and his partner, and Clarence's partner was not Frieda but Mrs. Luhan herself. ("Wild, elfish humour seizes [Lawrence]: as we pass Mabel and Clarence, decorously dancing the American dance, we bump into them, [Lawrence] with a wicked laugh, until Clarence, furious, rushes out of the studio. Frieda follows him—and Mabel vanishes, too. Then suddenly [Lawrence] tire[s]." But it makes no difference. What matters is that Mrs. Luhan could have imagined the scene as she did, seeing herself as Lawrence's "batteringram."

In the fall of that year, she and Lawrence went their separate ways, Lawrence to Mexico, Europe, and death, Mrs. Luhan to her analyst in New York. She set out determined to will her will into submission. But how tedious, after all, these analysts were! One had to deal with them like babies, holding their hands. "With these analysts one has to be so careful, one has to weigh everything lest one give them more than they can swallow and they turn and rend one for it! Unless one fits oneself into their systems and formulas so they can pigeon-hole one into a type or a case, they grow puzzled or angry or sad. ... One has, then, to be continually assuaging them and measuring down to them out of sheer, kind-heartedness. When I think of the time I have spent assuaging analysts at twenty dollars an hour!"

Happily, Mrs. Luhan could afford the sport; and she could take added consolation, if she needed it, in knowing that in the forthcoming struggle with Dr. Brill the odds, as usual, were all on her own side.

8 SISTERHOOD IS POWERFUL

Susan Brownmiller

A member of the Women's Liberation Movement explains what it's all about

Women are an oppressed class. Our oppression is total, affecting every facet of our lives. We are exploited as sex objects, breeders, domestic servants and cheap labor. We are considered inferior beings whose only purpose is to enhance men's lives...

Redstocking Manifesto

While we realize that the liberation of women will ultimately mean the liberation of men from the destructive role as oppressor, we have no illusion that men will welcome this liberation without a struggle...

Manifesto of the New York Radical Feminists

There is a small group of women that gathers at my house or at the home of one or another of our 15 members each Sunday evening. Our ages range from early twenties to the late forties. As it happens, all of us work for a living, some at jobs we truly like. Some of us are married, with families, and some are not. Some of us knew each other before we joined the group and some did not. Once we are settled on the sofa and the hard-backed chairs brought in from the kitchen, and the late-comers have poured their own coffee and arranged themselves as best they can on the floor, we begin our meeting. Each week we explore another aspect of what we consider to be our fundamental oppression in a male-controlled society. Our conversation is always animated, often emotional. We rarely adjourn before midnight.

Although we are pleased with ourselves and our insights, we like to remind each other now and then that our small group is not unique. It is merely one of many such groups that have sprung up around the city in the last two years under the umbrella of that collective term, the women's liberation movement. In fact, we had been meeting as a group for exactly four Sundays when one of us got a call from a representative of C.B.S. asking if we would care to be filmed in our natural habitat for a segment on the evening news with Walter Cronkite. We discussed the invitation thoroughly, and then said no.

Women's liberation is hot stuff this season, in media terms, and no wonder.

In the short space of two years, the new feminism has taken hold and rooted in territory that at first glance appears an unlikely breeding ground for revolutionary ideas: among urban, white, college-educated, middle-class women generally considered to be a rather "privileged" lot by those who thought they knew their politics, or knew their women. From the radical left to the Establishment middle, the women's movement has become a fact of life. The National Organization for Women (NOW), founded by Betty Friedan in 1966, has 35 chapters across the country. Radical feminist groups—creators of the concept of women's liberation, as opposed to women's rights—exist in all major cities side by side with their more conservative counterparts.

Without doubt, certain fringe aspects of the movement make "good copy," to use the kindest term available for how my brethren in the business approach the subject matter. ("Get the bra burning and the karate up front," an editor I know told a writer I know when preparing one news magazine's women's liberation story.)

But the irony of all this media attention is that while the minions of C.B.S. News can locate a genuine women's liberation group with relative ease (they ferreted out our little group before we had memorized each other's last names), hundreds of women in New York City have failed in their attempts to make contact with the movement. I have spoken to women who have spent as much as three months looking for a group that was open to new members. Unclaimed letters have piled up at certain post office box numbers hastily set up and thoughtlessly abandoned by here-today-and-gone-tomorrow "organizations" that disappeared as abruptly as they materialized. The elusive qualities of "women's lib" once prompted the writer Sally Kempton to remark, "It's not a movement, it's a state of mind." The surest way to affiliate with the movement these days is to form your own small group. That's the way it's happening.

Two years ago the 50 or so women in New York City who had taken to calling themselves the women's liberation movement met on Thursday evenings at a borrowed office on East 11th Street. The official title of the group was the New York Radical Women. There was some justification at the time for thinking grandly in national terms, for similar groups of women were beginning to form in Chicago, Boston, San Francisco and Washington. New York Radical Women came by its name quite simply: the women were young radicals, mostly under the age of 25, and they come out of the civil rights and/or peace movements, for which many of them had been full time workers. A few years earlier, many of them might have been found on campuses of Vassar, Radcliffe, Wellesley and the larger coed universities, a past they worked hard to deny. What brought them together to a women-only discussion and action group was a sense of abuse suffered at the hands of the very protest movements that had spawned them. As "movement women," they were tired of doing the typing and fixing the food while "movement men" did the writing and leading. Most were living with or married to movement men who, they believed, were treating them as convenient sex objects or as somewhat lesser beings.

Widely repeated quotations, such as Stokeley Carmichael's wisecrack dictum to S.N.C.C., "The position of women in our movement should be prone," and, three years later, a similar observation by Black Panther Eldridge Cleaver had reinforced their uncomfortable suspicion that the social vision of radical men did not include equality for women. Black power, as practiced by black male leaders, appeared to mean that black women would step back while black men stepped forward. The white male radical's eager embrace of *machismo* appeared to include those backward aspects of male supremacy in the Latin culture from which the word *machismo* is derived. Within their one-to-one relationships with their men, the women felt, the highly touted "alternate life style" of the radical movement was working out no better than the "bourgeois" life style they had rejected. If man and wife in a suburban split-level was a symbol of all that was wrong with plastic, bourgeois America, "man and chick" in a Lower East Side tenement flat was hardly the new order they had dreamed of.

In short, "the movement" was reinforcing, not eliminating, their deepest insecurities and feelings of worthlessness as women—feelings which quite possibly had brought them into radical protest politics to begin with. So, in a small way, they had begun to rebel. They had decided to meet regularly—without their men—to talk about their common experience. "Our feminism was very underdeveloped in those days," says Anne Koedt, an early member of the group. "We didn't have any idea of what kind of action we could take. We couldn't stop talking about the blacks and Vietnam."

In Marxist canon, "the woman question" is one of many manifestations of a sick, capitalist society which "the revolution" is supposed to finish off smartly. Some of the women who devoted their Thursday evening meeting time to New York Radical Women believed they were merely dusting off and stream-lining an orthodox, ideological issue. Feminism was bad politics and a dirty word since it excluded the larger picture.

But others in the group, like Anne Koedt and Shuli Firestone, an intense and talkative young activist, had begun to see things from a different, heretical perspective. Woman's oppressor was Man, they argued, and not a specific economic system. After all, they pointed out, male supremacy was still flourishing in the Soviet Union, Cuba and China, where power was still lodged in a male bureaucracy. Even the beloved Che wrote a guidebook for revolutionaries in which he waxed ecstatic over the advantages to a guerrilla movement of having women along in the mountains—to prepare and cook the food. The heretics tentatively put forward the idea that feminism must be a separate movement of its own.

New York Radical Women's split in perspective—was the ultimate oppressor Man or Capitalism?—occupied endless hours of debate at the Thursday evening meetings. Two warring factions emerged, dubbing each other "the feminists" and "the politicos." But the other things were happening as well. For one thing, new women were coming in droves to the Thursday evening talk fest, and a growing feeling of sisterhood was permeating the room. Meetings began awkwardly and shyly, with no recognized chairman and no discernible agenda. Often the suggestion, "Let's sit closer together, sisters," helped break the ice. But once the evening's initial awkwardness had passed, volubility was never a problem. "We had so much to say," an early member relates, "and most of us had never said it to another woman before."

Soon *how* to say it became an important question. Young women like Carol Hanisch, a titian-haired recruit to the civil rights movement from a farm in Iowa, and her friend Kathie Amatniek, a Radcliffe graduate and a working film editor, had spent over a year in Mississippi working with S.N.C.C. There they had been impressed with the Southern-revival-style mass meeting at which blacks got up and "testified" about their own experience with the "Man." Might the technique also work for women? And wasn't it the same sort of thing that Mao Tse-tung had advocated to raise political consciousness in Chinese villages? As Carol Hanisch reminded the group, Mao's slogan had been "Speak pain to recall pain"— precisely what New York Radical Women was doing!

The personal-testimony method encouraged *all* women who came to the meeting to speak their thoughts. The technique of "going around the room" in turn brought responses from many who had never opened their mouths at male-dominated meetings and were experiencing the same difficulty in a room full of articulate members of their own sex. Specific questions such as, "If you've thought of having a baby, do you want a girl or a boy?" touched off accounts of what it meant to be a girl-child—the second choice in a society that prizes boys! An examination of "What happens to your relationship when your man earns more money than you, and what happens when *you* earn more money than him?" brought a flood of anecdotes about the male ego and money. "We all told similar stories," relates a member of the group. "We discovered that, to a man, they all felt challenged if we were the breadwinners. It meant that we were no longer dependent. We had somehow robbed them of their 'rightful' role."

"We began to see our 'feminization' as a two-level process," says Anne Koedt. "On one level, a woman is brought up to believe that she is a girl and that is her biological destiny. She isn't supposed to want to achieve anything. If, by some chance, she manages to escape the psychological damage, she finds that the structure is prohibitive. Even though she wants to achieve, she finds she is discouraged at every turn and she still can't become President."

Few topics, the women found, were unfruitful. Humiliations that each of them had suffered privately—from being turned down for a job with the comment, "We were looking for a man," to catcalls and wolf whistles on the street—turned out to be universal agonies. "I had always felt degraded, actually turned into an object," said one woman. "I was no longer a human being when a guy on the street would start to make those incredible animal noises at me. I never was flattered by it, I always understood that behind that whistle was a masked hostility. When we started to talk about it in the group, I discovered that every

woman in the room had similar feelings. None of us knew how to cope with
this street hostility. We had always had to grin and bear it. We had always
been told to dress as women, to be very sexy and alluring to men, and what
did it get us? Comments like 'Look at the legs on that babe' and 'would I like
to—her.' " (My small group has discussed holding a street action of our own on
the first warm day of spring. We intend to take up stations on the corner of
Broadway and 45th Street and whistle at the male passers-by. The confrontation, we feel, will be educational for all concerned.)

"Consciousness-raising," in which a woman's personal experience at the hands
of men was analyzed as a *political* phenomenon, soon became a keystone of the
women's liberation movement.

In 1963, *before* there was a women's movement, Betty Friedan published what
eventually became an American classic, "The Feminine Mystique." The book
was a brilliant, factual examination of the post-World War II "back to the home"
movement that tore apart the myth of the fulfilled and happy American housewife. Though "The Feminine Mystique" held an unquestioned place as *the* intellectual mind-opener for most of the young feminists—de Beauvoir's "The Second Sex,"
a broad, philosophical analysis to the cultural restraints on women, was runner-up
in popularity—few members of New York Radical Women had ever felt motivated
to attend a meeting of Friedan's National Organization for Women, the parlia-
mentary-style organization of professional women and housewives that she
founded in 1966. Friedan, the mother of the movement, and the organization
that recruited in her image were considered hopelessly bourgeois. NOW's emphasis on legislative change left the radicals cold. The generation gap created real
barriers to communication.

"Actually, we had a lot in common with the NOW women," reflects Anne
Koedt. "The women who started NOW were achievement-oriented in their
professions. They began with the employment issue because that's what they
were up against. The ones who started New York Radical Women were achievement-oriented in the radical movement. From both ends we were fighting a male
structure that prevented us from achieving."

Friedan's book had not envisioned a movement of young feminists emerging
from the college campus and radical politics. "If I had it to do all over again,"
she says, "I would rewrite my last chapter." She came to an early meeting of
New York Radical Women to listen, ask questions and take notes, and went
away convinced that her approach—and NOW's—was more valid. "As far as I'm
concerned, we're *still* the radicals," she says emphatically. "We raised our consciousness a long time ago. I get along with the women's lib people because
they're the way the troops we need come up. But the name of the game is confrontation and action, and equal employment *is* the gut issue. The legal fight is
enormously important. Desegregating The New York Times help-wanted ads
was an important step, don't you think? And NOW did it. The women's movement *needs* its Browns versus Boards of Education."

Other older women, writers and lifetime feminists, also came around to observe, and stayed to develop a kinship with girls young enough to be their daughters. "I almost wept after my first meeting. I went home and filled my diary," says Ruth Herschberger, poet and author of "Adam's Rib," a witty and unheeded expostulation of women's rights published in 1948. "When I wrote 'Adam's Rib,' I was writing for readers who wouldn't accept the first premise. Now there was a whole roomful of people and a whole new vocabulary. I could go a whole month on the ammunition I'd get at one meeting."

In June of 1968, New York Radical Women produced a mimeographed booklet of some 20 pages entitled "Notes from the First Year." It sold for 50 cents to women and $1.00 to men. "Notes" was a compendium of speeches, essays and transcriptions of tape-recorded "rap sessions" of the Thursday evening group on such subjects as sex, abortion and orgasm. Several mimeographed editions later, it remains the most widely circulated source material on the New York women's liberation movement.

The contribution to "Notes" that attracted the most attention from both male and female readers was a one-page essay by Anne Koedt entitled, "The Myth of Vaginal Orgasm." In it she wrote:

"Frigidity has generally been defined by men as the failure of women to have vaginal orgasms. Actually, the vagina is not a highly sensitive area and is not physiologically constructed to achieve orgasm. The clitoris is the sensitive area and is the female equivalent of the penis. All orgasms (in women) are extensions of sensations from this area. This leads to some interesting questions about conventional sex and our role in it. Men have orgasms essentially by friction with the vagina, not with the clitoris. Women have thus been defined sexually in terms of what pleases men; our own biology has not been properly analyzed. Instead we have been fed a myth of the liberated woman and her vaginal orgasm, an orgasm which in fact does not exist. What we must do is redefine our sexuality. We must discard the 'normal' concepts of sex and create new guidelines which take into account mutual sexual enjoyment. We must begin to demand that if a certain sexual position or technique now defined as 'standard' is not mutually conducive to orgasm, then it should no longer be defined as standard."

Anne Koedt's essay went further than many other women in the movement would have preferred to go, but she was dealing with a subject that every woman understood. "For years I suffered under a male-imposed definition of my sexual responses," one woman says. "From Freud on down, it was men who set the standard of my sexual enjoyment. *Their* way was the way I should achieve nirvana, because their way was the way it worked for them. Me? Oh, I was simply an 'inadequate woman!'"

By September, 1968, New York Radical Women felt strongly enough to attempt a major action. Sixty women went to Atlantic City in chartered buses to picket the Miss America pageant. The beauty contest was chosen as a target because of the ideal of American womanhood it extolled—vacuous, coiffed, cosmeticized and with a smidgin of talent.

But New York Radical Women did not survive its second year. For one thing, the number of new women who flocked to the Thursday evening meetings made consciousness-raising and "going around the room" an impossibility. The politico-feminist split and other internal conflicts—charges of "domination" by one or another of the stronger women were thrown back and forth—put a damper on the sisterly euphoria. An attempt to break up the one large group into three smaller ones—by lot—proved disastrous.

Several women felt the need for a new group. They had become intrigued with the role of the witch in world history as representing society's persecution of women who dared to be different. From Joan of Arc, who dared to wear men's clothes and lead a men's army, to the women of Salem who dared to defy accepted political, religious mores, the "witch" was punished for deviations. Out of this thinking grew WITCH, a handy acronym that the organizers announced, half tongue-in-cheek, stood for Women's International Terrorist Conspiracy from Hell.

Much of WITCH was always tongue-in-cheek, and from its inception its members were at great pains to deny that they were feminists. The Yippie movement had made outrageous disruption a respectable political tactic of the left, and the women of WITCH decided it was more compatible with their thinking to be labeled "kooks" by outsiders than to be labeled man-haters by movement men.

In the WITCH philosophy, the patriarchy of the nuclear family was synonymous with the patriarchy of the American business corporation. Thus, four women took jobs at a branch of the Travelers Insurance Company, where a fifth member was working, and attempted to establish a secret coven of clerical workers on the premises. (For the Travelers' project, WITCH became "Women Incensed at Travelers' Corporate Hell.") In short order, the infiltrators were fired for such infractions of office rules as wearing slacks to work. Undaunted, a new quintet of operatives gained employment in the vast typing pools at A.T.&T. "Women Into Telephone Company Harassment" gained three sympathizers to the cause before Ma Bell got wise and exorcised the coven from her midst. Two WITCHes were fired for insubordination; the rest were smoked out and dismissed for being "overqualified" for the typing pool.

WITCH's spell over the women's movement did not hold. "At this point," says Judith Duffet, an original member, "you could say that WITCH is just another small group in women's liberation. We're concerned with consciousness-raising and developing an ideology through collective thinking. We don't do the freaky, hippie stuff any more."

While WITCH was brewing its unusual recipe for liberation, another offshoot of New York Radical Women emerged. The new group was called Redstockings, a play on *bluestockings*, with the blue replaced by the color of revolution. Organized by Shuli Firestone and Ellen Willis, an articulate rock-music columnist for the New Yorker and a serious student of Engels's "Origins of the Family," Redstockings made no bones about where it stood. It was firmly committed to feminism and action.

Redstockings made its first public appearance at a New York legislative hearing on abortion law reform in February, 1969, when several women sought to gain the microphone to testify about their own abortions. The hearing, set up to take testimony from 15 medical and psychiatric "experts"—14 were men—was hastily adjourned. The following month, Redstockings held its *own* abortion hearing at the Washington Square Methodist Church. Using the consciousness-raising technique, 12 women "testified" about abortion, from their own personal experience, before an audience of 300 men and women. The political message of the emotion-charged evening was that *women* were the only true experts on unwanted pregnancy and abortion, and that every woman has an inalienable right to decide whether or not she wishes to bear a child.

Redstockings' membership counts are a closely held secret, but I would estimate that the number does not exceed 100. Within the movement, Redstockings push what they call "the pro-woman line." "What it means," says a member, "is that we take the woman's side in *everything.* A woman is never to blame for her own submission. None of us need to change ourselves, we need to change men." Redstockings are also devout about consciousness-raising. "Whatever else we may do, consciousness-raising is the ongoing political work," says Kathie Amatniek. For the last few months, the various Redstocking groups have been raising their consciousness on what they call "the divisions between women that keep us apart"—married women *vs.* single, black women *vs.* white, middle class *vs.* working class, etc.

While Redstockings organized its abortion speak-out, the New York chapter of NOW formed a committee to lobby for repeal of restrictive abortion legislation. These dissimilar approaches to the same problem illustrate the difference in style between the two wings of the women's movement.

But within New York NOW itself, a newer, wilder brand of feminism made an appearance. Ti-Grace Atkinson, a Friedan protégée and the president of New York NOW, found herself in increasing conflict with her own local chapter and Friedan over NOW's hierarchical structure, a typical organization plan with an executive board on top. Ti-Grace, a tall blonde who has been described in print as "aristocratic looking," had come to view the power relationship between NOW's executive board and the general membership as a copycat extension of the standard forms of male domination over women in the society at large. She proposed to NOW that all executive offices be abolished in favor or rotating chairmen chosen by lot from the general membership. When Atkinson's proposal came up for a vote by the general membership of the New York chapter in October, 1968, and was defeated, Ti-Grace resigned her presidency on the spot and went out and formed her own organization. Named the October 17th Movement—the date of Ti-Grace's walkout from NOW—it made a second debut this summer as The Feminists, and took its place as the most radical of the women's liberation groups. (New York NOW suffered no apparent effects from its first organizational split. Over the last year it has gained in membership as feminism has gained acceptabiltty among wider circles of women.)

The Feminists made anti-elitism and rigorous discipline cardinal principles of their organization. As the only radical feminist group to take a stand against the institution of marriage they held a sit-in at the city marriage license bureau last year, raising the slogan that "Marriage Is Slavery." Married women or women living with men may not exceed one-third of the total membership.

Differences over such matters as internal democracy, and the usual personality conflicts that plague all political movements, caused yet another feminist group and another manifesto to make their appearance this fall. In November, Shuli Firestone and Anne Koedt set up a plan for organizing small groups—or "brigades," as they prefer to call them—on a neighborhood basis, and named their over-all structure the New York Radical Feminists. Eleven decentralized neighborhood units (three are in the West Village) meet jointly once a month.

The Radical Feminists co-exist with the Feminists and the Redstockings without much rivalry, although when pressed, partisans of the various groups will tell you, for instance, that Redstockings do too much consciousness-raising and not enough action, or that the Feminists are "fascistic," or that the Radical Feminists are publicity hungry. But in general, since interest in the women's liberation movement has always exceeded organizational capacity, the various groups take the attitude of "the more the merrier."

Despite the existence of three formal "pure radical feminist" organizations, hundreds of women who consider themselves women's liberationists have not yet felt the need to affiliate with any body larger than their own small group. The small group, averaging 8 to 15 members and organized spontaneously by friends calling friends has become *the* organizational form of the amorphous movement. Its intimacy seems to suit women. Fear of expressing new or half-formed thoughts vanishes in a friendly living-room atmosphere. "After years of psychoanalysis in which my doctor kept telling me my problem was that I wouldn't accept—quote—*my female role*," says a married woman with two children who holds a master's degree in philosophy, "the small group was a revelation to me. Suddenly, for the first time in my life, it was O.K. to express feelings of hostility to men." Says another woman: "In the small group I have the courage to think things and feel feelings, that I would never have dared to think and feel as an individual."

The meetings have often been compared to group therapy, a description that most of the women find irritating. "Group therapy isn't political and what we're doing is highly political," is the general response. In an early paper on the nature and function of the small group, Carol Hanisch once wrote, "Group therapy implies that we are sick and messed up, but the first function of the small group is to get rid of self-blame. We start with the assumption that women are really 'neat' people. Therapy means adjusting. We desire to change the objective conditions."

The groups are usually leaderless and structureless, and the subjects discussed at the weekly meetings run the gamut of female experience. The Radical Femi-

nists offer to new groups they organize a list of consciousness-raising topics
that includes:

• Discuss your relationships with men. Have you noticed any recurring
patterns?

• Have you ever felt that men have pressured you into sexual relationships?
Have you ever lied about orgasm?

• Discuss your relationships with other women. Do you compete with wom-
en for men?

• Growing up as a girl, were you treated differently from your brother?

• What would you most like to do in life? What has stopped you?

"Three months of this sort of thing," says Shuli Firestone, "is enough to
make a feminist out of any woman."

The kind of collective thinking that has come out of the women's liberation
movement is qualitatively different from the kinds of theorems and analyses that
other political movements have generated. "Women are different from all other
oppressed classes," says Anne Koedt. "We live in isolation, not in ghettos, and
we are in the totally unique position of having a master in our own houses."
It is not surprising, therefore, that marriage and child care are two subjects that
receive intensive scrutiny in the small group.

If few in the women's movement are willing to go as far as the Feminists and
say that marriage is slavery, it is hard to find a women's liberationist who is not
in some way disaffected by the sound of wedding bells. Loss of personal identity
and the division of labor within the standard marriage (the husband's role as pro-
vider, the wife's role as home maintenance and child care) are the basic points at
issue. "I have come to view marriage as a built-in self-destruct for women," says
one divorcee after 12 years of marriage. "I married early, right after college, because it was expected of me. I never had a chance to discover who I was. I was
programmed into the housewife pattern." Many married women's liberationists
will no longer use their husbands' last names; some have gone back to their maid-
en names, and some even to their mothers' maiden names.

One paper that has been widely circulated within the movement is entitled
"The Politics of Housework," by Pat Mainardi, a Redstocking who is teacher and
painter. "Men recognize the essential fact of housework right from the beginning,"
she wrote. "Which is that it stinks. You both work, you both have careers, but
you are expected to do the housework. Your husband tells,you, 'Don't talk to
me about housework. It's too trivial to discuss.' MEANING: *His* purpose is to
deal with matters of significance. *Your* purpose is to deal with matters of in-
significance. So *you* do the housework. Housework trivial? Just try getting
him to share the burden. The measure of his resistance is the measure of your
oppression."

Not only the oppression of housework, but the oppression of child care has become a focus of the women's movement. Much of the energy of young mothers in the movement has gone into setting up day-care collectives that are staffed on an equal basis by mothers and fathers. (Thus far they have proved difficult to sustain.) "Some of the men have actually come to understand that sharing equally in child care is a political responsibility," says Rosalyn Baxandall, a social worker and an early women's liberationist. Rosalyn and her husband, Lee, a playwright, put in a morning a week at an informal cooperative day nursery on the Lower East Side where their 2-year-old, Finn, is a charter member.

In November, at the Congress to Unite Women, a conference that drew over 500 women's liberationists of various persuasions from the New York area, a resolution demanding 24-hour-a-day child care centers was overwhelmingly endorsed. Women in the movement have also suggested plans for a new kind of life style in which a husband and wife would each work half-day and devote the other half of the day to caring for their children. Another possibility would be for the man to work for six months of the year while the woman takes care of the child-rearing responsibilities—with the roles reversed for the next six months.

The "movement women" who did not endorse the separatism of an independent radical feminist movement last year and chose to remain in what the feminists now call "the male left" have this year made women's liberation a major issue in their own political groups. Even the weatherwomen of Weatherman meet separately to discuss how to combat male chauvinism among their fellow revolutionaries. The women of Rat, the farthest out of the underground radical newspapers, formed a collective and took over editorial management of their paper last month, charging that their men had put out a product filled with sexist, women-as-degraded-object pornography. Twenty-two-year-old Jane Alpert, free on bail and facing conspiracy charges for a series of terrorist bombings, was spokesman for the Rat women's *putsch*. A black women's liberation committee functions within S.N.C.C., and its leader, Frances M. Beal, has said publicly, "To be black and female is double jeopardy, the slave of a slave."

The new feminism has moved into some surprisingly Establishment quarters. A spirited women's caucus at New York University Law School forced the university to open its select national scholarship program to women students. Women's caucuses exist among the editorial employees at McGraw Hill and Newsweek. Last month, 59 women in city government, sent a petition to Mayor Lindsay demanding that he actively seek qualified women for policy-making posts. The movement is a story without an end, because it has just begun. The goals of liberation go beyond a simple concept of equality. Looking through my notebook, I see them expressed simply and directly. *Betty Friedan: "We're going to redefine the sex roles." Anne Koedt: "We're going to be redefining politics."* Brave words for a new movement, and braver still for a movement that has been met with laughter and hostility. Each time a man sloughs off the women's movement with the comment, "They're nothing but a bunch of lesbians and frustrated bitches," we quiver with collective rage. How can such a charge be answered in rational terms? It cannot be. (The supersensitivity of the movement to the lesbian issue, and the existence of a few militant lesbians within the movement once prompted Friedan herself to grouse about "the lavender menace" that was threatening to warp the image of women's rights. A lavender *herring*, perhaps, but surely no clear and present danger.)

The small skirmishes and tugs of war that used to be called "the battle of the sexes" have now assumed ideological proportions. It is the aim of the movement to *turn men around*, and the implications in that aim are staggering. "Men have used us all their lives as ego fodder," says Anne Koedt. "They not only control economics and the government, they control us. There are the women's pages and the rest of the world." It is that rest of the world, of course, that we are concerned with. There is a women's rights button that I sometimes wear and the slogan on it reads, "Sisterhood is Powerful." If sisterhood were powerful, what a different world it would be.

Women as a class have never subjugated another group; we have never marched off to wars of conquest in the name of the fatherland. We have never been involved in a decision to annex the territory of a neighboring country, or to fight for foreign markets on distant shores. Those are the games men play, not us. *We* see it differently. We want to be neither oppressor nor oppressed. The women's revolution is the final revolution of them all.

How does a sympathetic man relate to a feminist woman? Thus far, it has not been easy for those who are trying. The existence of a couple of *men's* consciousness-raising groups—the participants are mostly husbands of activist women—is too new to be labeled a trend. "When our movement gets strong, when men are forced to see us as a conscious issue, *what are they going to do?*" asks Anne Koedt. And then she answers: "I don't know, but I think there's a part of men that really wants a human relationship, and that's going to be the saving grace for all of us."

C
From Back to Front

This section is about the change in role of the black man in America. The change is from a role given by white America to one that is self-defined. It is the transformation from Negro to black, from peasant to cultural innovator. This section does not consider the merits of specific civil-rights programs. The industrial education proposed by Booker T. Washington, the talented tenth advocated by W. E. B. DuBois, and the cultural nationalism suggested by Julius Lester all reflect changing historical conditions that have contributed to role change. The reader who is interested in these programs and changes is advised to read Francis L. Broderick and August Meier's *Negro Protest Thought in the Twentieth Century* or Harold Cruse's insightful *The Crisis of the Negro Intellectual.*

Selection 9 appeared in the old *Saturday Evening Post* at the beginning of the twentieth century. The author, Thomas Dixon, has been described by the historian Thomas R. Cripps as a "sometime preacher, a professional Southerner and a fretful Negrophobe." His best known work was the novel, *The Clansman*, a romanticized view of the Ku Klux Klan. The novel served as the basis for the movie, *The Birth of a Nation*, one of the first to exploit the potentiality of the medium and containing a singularly racist theme.

What role does Dixon see for the Negro? What natural abilities and cultural experiences combine to make him suitable for a part in American life? As might be expected, Dixon sees few possibilities for the black man. The black man possesses baser instincts than the white man. These instincts are the consequence of the Negro being on a lower rung of the evolutionary ladder. As a result, the Negro has greater sexual desire and the race, as a whole, increases faster than the white majority. If permitted to multiply without check, the Negro race will swamp the white. Therefore, the Negro ought to remain under the control of enlightened white men. These white men will provide the best examples for the Negro to imitate; Dixon holds that the Negro has no culture worth considering. He waxes eloquent in his erroneous descriptions of Africa. The Negro, then, can be a sharecropper, or better yet, a household servant. In either case, he is to be directed by his white superior. He is to be treated gently and to share the intimacy of the family, but he is to remain subservient.

What about future roles for the Negro? Dixon is pessimistic about the chances for racial harmony based on a dominant-submissive relationship. He sees in the racial Christianity of the time, which emphasized the superior religious qualities of the Negro caused by poverty, a threat of social amalgamation. If the white Christian recognizes the virtues of the Negro Christian, he may desire to associate with him on more equal terms. Further, there is also the threat of Negro education. The Negro shows signs of wanting economic betterment, of wanting to become a middle-class entrepreneur, of wanting to become self-sufficient, all attitudes promoted by Booker T. Washington and his Tuskegee Institute. Dixon correctly recognizes that the ideology of Washington is preindustrial, aimed at creating a class of independent Negro farmers and businessmen. The drive for independence and the movement toward amalgamation would lead to tragedy, according to Dixon. Negro aspirations to an equal place in American society will be blocked by white resistance, which may take the extreme form of racial war and extermination. Given the conflict in role expectations between the white and black man, it would be kinder to both to colonize the Negro in Africa.

While Dixon's obviously racist view cannot be taken as representative of the broad spectrum of white opinion, it does reflect the assumptions of a sizable section of the American populace. Dixon believed in distinctive roles based on supposed racial characteristics and maintained, if necessary, by physical separation. His separatist position is based on a belief in the natural inferiority of the Negro and on the fear of Negroes contaminating whites.

Selection 10 is a short article written by the outstanding Negro leader W. E. B. DuBois, which appeared in the *Chicago Defender*, a well-known Negro newspaper. DuBois lived to be 95 and became, perhaps, the most significant spokesman for the black man in twentieth-century America. During his long career, DuBois took many different positions, some contradictory but all challenging. These positions on the tactics and strategy of the civil-rights movements were carefully prepared and convincingly presented. They justly earned him his role as the leading black man of his time.

DuBois was born in Massachusetts and was educated at Fisk University. He did graduate study at Harvard University and at the University of Berlin. It was at the latter school that he acquired the costume of the student. After teaching at Wilberforce, the University of Pennsylvania, and Atlanta University, DuBois left the academic world to join the administrative staff of the National Association for the Advancement of Colored People, which he had helped to found. He served as Director of Publicity and Research and as editor of the *Crisis*, the journal of the NAACP. He was forced out of office in the NAACP in 1934 because of his militant views and returned to Atlanta University. Ten years later, he joined the NAACP staff again as Director of Special Research. He held this position for four years. In 1961, DuBois ended his leftward migration by joining the Communist Party. He spent the last years of his life in Africa after he had become a citizen of Ghana.

While DuBois was always interested in Africa and did attend several Pan-African Conferences, his original position was against a return to Africa. He believed that the role of the black man was to be integrated into American society. World developments, he felt, showed the gradual merger of the races. DuBois' vision of the role of the black man in America led him to attack Booker T. Washington's plans of education as insufficient. In 1934, however, when DuBois broke with the NAACP over its lack of energy and insufficiently radical program, he had begun to question the feasibility of integration as a short-term goal. He believed that greater effort to achieve economic equality in segregated circumstances might be more productive. In the 1950s, DuBois' interest in Africa rekindled with the emergence of independent states in that area. He had become more sympathetic with those American black men who looked to Africa as a refuge.

Despite his position changes and his opposition to the orthodoxy of his own time, DuBois' personal role remained remarkably consistent. It was the role of an intellectual and scholar. It was to be one who was at home with the best ideas and the best of the many cultures of the world. While DuBois' civil rights proposals may have seemed radical, his conception of the scholar's role was conservative. This is clearly indicated in Selection 10 with its reflection on clothes and food. DuBois' cane illustrates the fact that the conscious snobbery of the German student and his tastes in dining—an unpretentious California wine and the necessary demitasse—would not offend the most discriminating disciple of the Galloping Gourmet. Not for DuBois were the dashiki or sandals or chitterlings. His life style would probably have put Dixon's to shame.

Selection 11 shows how far the wheel has turned. The standards of DuBois are rejected. Instead, the lower-class values of black society are the most accepted. The black intellectual like DuBois may be a "marginal man," a concept borrowed from Kelly Miller and Robert Park by Julius Lester. The "marginal man" accepts too much of the dominant culture and becomes a stranger to his own roots. This latest reaction against the highest standards would be unwelcome news to DuBois. As S. P. Fullenwider says in *The Mind and Mood of Black America*:

> *If building a community on the concept of "nitty-gritty" and on the closely related concept of "funk" must have disturbed Martin Luther King and those who followed the Southern Christian Leadership Conference, it would have appalled W. E. B. DuBois. The idea of eating hog's head cheese would have turned his New England stomach. And the sight described by Jack Newfield of the SNCC worker he saw on the 1965 Selma to Montgomery march in sunglasses, goatee, and overalls, singing, "Do What the Spirit Say Do," was best not seen by DuBois in his goatee, kid gloves and cane.*

The rejection of white standards and the change from the role of Negro, a white creation, to black, a self-definition, is ironic, because the weaknesses supposedly seen by Dixon in the Negro have become virtues in the black. Black culture is more vital than white culture because it is not based on upper-middle-class intellectuality; rather, it is based on lower-class sensual experience. The black man should remain apart from the white man because white culture might dilute the superior black culture. Like Dixon, Lester desires two separate societies, but for opposite reasons.

The supreme irony is that the conception of the black man's role as that of existential hero, as expressed by Normal Mailer in "The White Negro" and by Eldridge Cleaver in *Soul on Ice,* is now recommended to whites. The white man must learn to be physical, to achieve greater sensual abandonment. He must get his body, says Cleaver, as blacks must get their heads. Cleaver's advice seems to have been taken by those who have deliberately tried to imitate blacks—Janis Joplin and the Beatles in music and by members of the counterculture in clothes. In their search for alternate cultures and roles, young middle-class white Americans have attempted to realize the richness of black life styles. Nor has this search been confined to black America. The life style of the Indian has also been idealized and copied, from fringed jacket and headband to ecological economy. The transformation of Negro to black and the elevation of supposedly inferior qualities to a position of respect surely can be called moving from the back to the front.

9   BOOKER T. WASHINGTON AND THE NEGRO

Thomas Dixon, Jr.

Some Danger Aspects of the Work of Tuskegee

For Mr. Booker T. Washington as a man and leader of his race I have always had the warmest admiration. His life is a romance which appeals to the heart of universal humanity. The story of a little ragged, barefooted piccaninny who lifted his eyes from a cabin in the hills of Virginia, saw a vision and followed it, until at last he presides over the richest and most powerful institution of learning in the South, and sits down with crowned heads and Presidents, has no parallel even in the Tales of the Arabian Nights.

The spirit of the man, too, has always impressed me with its breadth, generosity and wisdom. The aim of his work is noble and inspiring. As I understand it from his own words, it is "to make Negroes producers, lovers of labor, honest, independent, good." His plan for doing this is to lead the Negro to the goal

SOURCE: From *The Saturday Evening Post,* August 19, 1905.

through the development of solid character, intelligent industry and material acquisition.

Only a fool or a knave can find fault with such an ideal. It rests squarely on the eternal verities. And yet it will not solve the Negro problem nor bring us within sight of its solution. Upon the other hand, it will only intensify that problem's dangerous features, complicate and make more difficult its ultimate settlement.

It is this tragic fact to which I am trying to call the attention of the nation.

I have for the Negro race only pity and sympathy, though every large convention of Negroes since the appearance of my first historical novel on the race problem has gone out of its way to denounce me and declare my books caricatures and libels on their people. Their mistake is a natural one. My books are hard reading for a Negro, and yet the Negroes, in denouncing them, are unwittingly denouncing one of their best friends.

I have been intimately associated with Negroes since the morning of my birth during the Civil War. My household servants are all Negroes. I took them to Boston with me, moved them to New York, and they now have entire charge of my Virginia home. The first row I ever had on the Negro problem was when I moved to Boston from the South to take charge of a fashionable church at the Hub. I attempted to import my baby's Negro nurse into a Boston hotel. The proprietor informed me that no "coon" could occupy a room in his house in any capacity, either as a guest or servant. I gave him a piece of my mind and left within an hour.

As a friend of the Negro race I claim that he should have the opportunity for the highest, noblest and freest development of his full, rounded manhood. He has never had this opportunity in American, either North or South, and he never can have it. The forces against him are overwhelming.

My books are simply merciless records of conditions as they exist, conditions that can have but one ending if they are not honestly and fearlessly faced. The Civil War abolished chattel slavery. It did not settle the Negro problem. It settled the Union question and created the Negro problem. Frederic Harrison, the English philosopher, declared that the one great shadow which clouds the future of the American Republic is the approaching tragedy of their reconcilable conflict between the Negro and White Man in the development of our society. Mr. James Bryce recently made a similar statement.

The Argument of the Ostrich Man

If allowed to remain here the Negro race in the United States will number 60,000,000 at the end of this century by their present rate of increase. Think of what this means for a moment and you face the gravest problem which ever puzzled the brain of statesman or philosopher. No such problem ever before confronted the white man in his recorded history. It cannot be whistled down by opportunists, politicians, weak-minded optimists or female men. It must be squarely met and fought to a finish.

Several classes of people at present obstruct any serious consideration of this question—the pot-house politician, the ostrich man, the pooh-pooh men, and the benevolent old maid. The politician is still busy over the black man's vote in doubtful States. The pooh-pooh man needs no definition—he was born a fool. The benevolent old maid contributes every time the hat is passed and is pretty sure to do as much harm as good in the long run to any cause. The ostrich man is the funniest of all this group of obstructionists, for he is a man of brains and capacity.

I have a friend of this kind in New York. He got after me the other day somewhat in this fashion: "What do you want to keep agitating this infernal question for? There's no danger in it unless you stir it. Let it alone. I grant you that the Negro race is a poor, worthless parasite, whose criminal and animal instincts threaten society. But the Negro is here to stay. We must train him. It is the only thing we can do. So what's the use to waste your breath?" "But what about the future when you have educated the Negro?" I asked timidly.

"Let the future take care of itself!" the ostrich man snorted. "We live in the present. What's the use to worry about Hell? If I can scramble through this world successfully I'll take my chances with the Hell problem!"

My friend forgets that this was precisely the line of argument of our fathers over the question of Negro slavery. When the constructive statesmen of Virginia (called pessimists and infidels in their day) foresaw the coming baptism of fire and blood ('61 to '65) over the Negro slave, they attempted to destroy the slave trade and abolish slavery. My friend can find his very words in the answers of their opponents. "Let the future take care of itself! The slaves are here and here to stay. Greater evils await their freedom. We need their labor. Let the question alone. There is no danger in it unless you stir it."

The truth which is gradually forcing itself upon thoughtful students of our national life is that no scheme of education or religion can solve the race problem, and that Mr. Booker T. Washington's plan, however high and noble, can only intensity its difficulties.

This conviction is based on a few big fundamental facts, which no pooh-poohing, ostrich-dodging, weak-minded philanthropy or political rant can obscure.

The first one is that no amount of education of any kind, industrial, classical or religious, can make a Negro a white man or bridge the chasm of the centuries which separate him from the white man in the evolution of human civilization.

Expressed even in the most brutal terms of Anglo-Saxon superiority there is here an irreducible fact. It is possibly true, as the Negro, Professor Kelly Miller, claims, that the Anglo-Saxon is "the most arrogant and rapacious, the most exclusive and intolerant race in history." Even so, what answer can be given to his cold-blooded proposition: "Can you change the color of the Negro's skin, the kink of his hair, the bulge of his lip or the beat of his heart with a spelling-book or a machine?"

What Abraham Lincoln Said

No man has expressed this idea more clearly than Abraham Lincoln when he said: "There is a physical difference between the white and black races which, I believe, will forever forbid them living together on terms of social and political equality."

Whence this physical difference? Its secret lies in the gulf of thousands of years of inherited progress which separates the child of the Aryan from the child of the Africa.

Buckle in his *History of Civilization* says: "The actions of bad men produce only temporary evil, the actions of good men only temporary good. The discoveries of genius alone remain: it is to them we owe all that we now have; they are for all ages and for all times; never young and never old, they bear the seeds of their own lives; they are essentially cumulative."

Judged by this supreme test, what contribution to human progress have the millions of Africans who inhabit this planet made during the past four thousand years? Absolutely nothing. And yet, Mr. Booker T. Washington in a recent burst of eloquence over his educational work boldly declares: "The Negro race has developed more rapidly in the thirty years of its freedom than the Latin race has in one thousand years of freedom."

Think for a moment of the pitiful puerility of this statement falling from the lips of the greatest and wisest leader the Negro race has yet produced!

Italy is the mother of genius, the inspiration of the ages, the creator of architecture, agriculture, manufactures, commerce, law, science, philosophy, finance, church organization, sculpture, music, painting and literature, and yet the American Negro in thirty years has outstripped her thousands of years of priceless achievement!

Education is the development of that which *is*. The Negro has held the Continent of Africa since the dawn of history, crunching acres of diamonds beneath his feet. Yet he never picked one up from the dust until a white man showed to him its light. His land swarmed with powerful and docile animals, yet he never built a harness, cart or sled. A hunter by necessity, he never made an ax, spear or arrowhead worth preserving beyond the moment of its use. In a land of stone and timber, he never carved a block, sawed a foot of lumber or built a house save of broken sticks and mud, and for four thousand years he gazed upon the sea yet never dreamed a sail.

Who is the greatest Negro that ever lived according to Mr. Booker T. Washington? Through all his books he speaks this man's name with bated breath and uncovered head—"Frederick Douglass of sainted memory!" And what did Saint Frederick do? Spent a life in bombastic vituperation of the men whose genius created the American Republic, wore himself out finally drawing his salary as a Federal office-holder, and at least achieved the climax of Negro sainthood by marrying a white woman!

What Education Cannot Do

Says the author of Napoleon, Honorable Thomas E. Watson: "Education is a good thing, but it never did and never will alter the essential character of any man or race of men."

I repeat, education is the development of that which *is*. Behold the man whom the rags of slavery once concealed—nine millions strong! This creature, with a racial record of four thousand years of incapacity, half-child, half-animal, the sport of impulse, whim and conceit, pleased with a rattle, tickled with a straw, being who, left to his will, roams at night and sleeps in the day, whose native tongue has framed no word of love, whose passions once aroused are as the tiger's—equality is the law of our life!—when he is educated and ceases to fill his useful sphere as servant and peasant, what are you going to do with him?

The second big fact which confronts the thoughtful, patriotic American is that the greatest calamity which could possibly befall this Republic would be the corruption of our national character by the assimilation of the Negro race. I have never seen a white man of any brains who disputes this fact. I have never seen a Negro of any capacity who did not deny it.

One thought I would burn into the soul of every young American (and who thinks of a Negro when he says "American?")—this: Our Republic is great not by reason of the amount of dirt we possess, or the size of our census roll, but because of the genius of the race of pioneer white freemen who settled this continent, dared the might of kings, and blazed the way through our wilderness for the trembling feet of liberty.

A distinguished Negro college professor recently expressed himself as to the future American in one of our great periodicals as follows:

> *All race prejudice will be eradicated. Physically, the new race will be much the stronger. It will be endowed with a higher intelligence and clearer conception of God than the whites of the West have ever had. It will be much less material than the American white of to-day. It will be especially concerned with the things of the mind, and moral excellence will become the dominant factor in the life of the new nation. The new race is to gain more from the Black element than from the White.*

We have here an accurate statement of the passionate faith of ninety-nine Negroes out of every hundred. Professor Du Bois, author of *The Souls of Black Folk*, undoubtedly believes this. His book is a remarkable contribution to the literature of our race problem. In it for the first time we see the naked soul of a Negro beating itself to death against the bars in which Aryan society has caged him! No white man with a soul can read this book without a tear. Mr. Charles W. Chesnutt, the Negro novelist, believes in amalgamation, for he told me so. Professor Kelly Miller, the distinguished Negro teacher of Washington, believes it. In a recent article he declares:

It is, of course, impossible to conceive of two races occupying the same area, speaking the same language, worshipping according to the same ritual, and endowed with the same political and civil privileges without ultimately fusing. Social equality is not an individual matter, as many contend, but is rigorously under the control of public sentiment.

I commend the solid logic of these sentences from a thoughtful Negro to the illustrious Society of Pooh-Poohs.

What is the attitude of Mr. Booker T. Washington on this vital issue? You will search his books and listen to his lectures in vain for any direct answer. Why? Because, if he dared to say what he really in his soul of souls believes, it would end his great career, both North and South. In no other way has he shown his talent as an organizer and leader of his people with such consummate skill as in the dexerity with which he has for twenty years dodged this issue, holding steadily the good-will of the Southern white man and the Northern philanthropist. He is the greatest diplomat his race has ever produced.

Yet he who reads between the lines of his written and spoken words will find the same purpose and the same faith which his more blunt and fearless brethren have honestly and boldly proclaimed. He shows this in his worship of Frederick Douglass. In his book, *The Future of the American Negro*, we find this careful sentence: "To state in detail just what the place the black man will occupy in the South as a citizen when he has developed in the direction named is beyond the wisdom of any one."

Yet on page 69 he says: "The surest way for the Negro to reach the highest positions is to prepare himself to fill well at the present the basic occupations"—independent industries, of course—for, mark you, *"Tuskegee Institute is not a servant-training school!"*

Again on pages 83 and 85 we are told: "There is an unmistakable influence that comes over a white man when he sees a black man living in a two-story brick house that has been paid for. I need not stop to explain. Just in so far as we can place rich Negroes in the South who can loan money to white men, this race question will disappear."

Why?

The conclusion is obvious: The Negro who holds a mortgage on a white man's house will ultimately demand and receive social recognition from him.

On page 66 of his *Future of the American Negro* he says: "The Jew, who was once in about the same position as the Negro is to-day, has now recognition because he has entwined himself about America in a business and industrial way."

Again his conclusion is obvious. The absurdity of the comparison, however, is the important point in this sentence, not only for the pathetic ignorance of history it displays but for the revelation of the writer's secret hopes and dreams.

The Jew has not been assimilated into our civil and social life because of his money—but for a very different reason. The Jew belongs to our race, the same great division of humanity. The Semitic group of the white race is, all in all, the greatest evolved in history. Their children have ever led the vanguard of human progress and achievements. A great historian and philosopher once said: "Show me a man of transcedent genius at any period of the world's history and I'll show you a man with Hebrew blood in his veins." Our prejudice against the Jew is not because of his inferiority, but because of his genius. We are afraid of him, we Gentiles who meet him in the arena of life, get licked and then make faces at him. The truth is the Jew had achieved a noble civilization—had his poets, prophets, priests and kings—when our Germanic ancestors were still in the woods cracking cocoanuts and hickory-nuts with monkeys. We have assimilated the Jew because his daughter is beautiful and his son strong in mind and body!

The Danger of a Nation Within a Nation

The trouble with Mr. Booker T. Washington's work is that he is silently preparing us for the future heaven of Amalgamation—*or he is doing something equally dangerous,* namely, he is attempting to build a nation inside a nation of two hostile races. In this event he is storing dynamite beneath the pathway of our children—the end at last can only be in bloodshed.

Mr. Washington is not training Negroes to take their place in any industrial system of the South in which the white man can direct or control him. He is not training his students to be servants and come at the beck and call of any man. He is training them *all* to be masters of men, to be independent, to his own and operate their own industries, plant their own fields, buy and sell their own goods, and in every shape and form destroy the last vestige of dependence on the white man for anything.

I do not say this is not laudable—I do not say that is not noble. I only ask what will be its end for the Negro when the work is perfect? Every pupil who passes through Mr. Washington's hands ceases forever to work under a white man. Not only so, but he goes forth trained as an evangelist to preach the doctrine of separation and independence.

The Negro remains on this Continent for one reason only. The Southern white man has needed his labor, and therefore has fought every suggestion of his removal. But when he refuses longer to work for the white man, then what?

Mr. Booker T. Washington says on page 65 of his book: "The Negro must live for all time beside the Southern white man."

On what sort of terms are they to live together? As banker and borrower? Hardly, if the Negro is the banker. Even now, with the white man still hugging the hoary delusion that he can't get along without the Negro, he is being forced to look to the Old World for labor. The simple truth is, the South will lag behind the world industrially in just so far as she depends on Negro labor. The idea that a white man cannot work in the fields of the South is exploded. Only one-third of the cotton crop is to-day raised by Negro labor. Even now the relations of the races, with the Negro an integral part of the white man's industrial scheme, become more and more difficult.

A Gulf that Grows Wide

Professor Kelly Miller says: "It is a matter of common observation that the races are growing further and further apart."

Mr. Washington says on this point: "For the sake of the Negro and the Southern white man there are many things in the relations of the two races that must soon be changed" (page 65). The point I raise is that education necessarily drives the races further and further apart, and Mr. Washington's brand of education makes the gulf between them if anything a little deeper. If there is one thing a Southern white man cannot endure it is an educated Negro. What's to be the end of it if the two races are to live forever side by side in the South?

Mr. Washington says: "Give the black man so much skill and brains that he can cut oats like the white man—then he can compete with him."

And then the real tragedy will begin. Does any sane man believe that when the Negro ceases to work under the direction of the Southern white man, this "arrogant," "rapacious" and "intolerant" race will allow the Negro to master his industrial system, take the bread from his mouth, crowd him to the wall and place a mortgage on his house? Competition is war—the most fierce and brutal of all its forms. Could fatuity reach a sublimer height than the idea that the white man will stand idly by and see this performance? What will he do when put to the test? He will do exactly what his white neighbor in the North does when the Negro threatens his bread—kill him!

Abraham Lincoln foresaw this tragedy when he wrote his Emancipation Proclamation, and he asked Congress for an appropriation of a billion dollars to colonize the whole Negro race. He never believed it possible to assimilate the Negro into our national life. This nation will yet come back to Lincoln's plan, still so eloquently advocated by the Negro Bishop, Henry M. Turner.

It is curious how the baldheaded assertion of a lie can be repeated and repeated until millions of sane people will accept the bare assertion as an established fact. At the close of the War, Mr. Lincoln, brooding over the insoluble problem of the Negro's future which his proclamation had created, asked General Benjamin F. Butler to devise and report to him immediately a plan to colonize the Negroes. General Butler, naturally hostile to the idea, made at once his famous, false and facetious report, "that ships could not be found to carry the Negro babies to Africa as fast as they are born!" The President was assassinated a few days later. This lie is now forty odd years old, and Mr. Booker T. Washington actually repeats it as a verbal inspiration though entirely unconscious of its historic origin.

We have spent about $800,000,000 on Negro education since the War. One-half of this sum would have been sufficient to have made Liberia a rich and powerful Negro state. Liberia is capable of supporting every Negro in America. Why not face this question squarely? We are temporizing and playing with it. All our educational schemes are compromises and temporary makeshifts. Mr. Booker T. Washington's work is one of noble aims. A branch of it should be immediately established in Monrovia, the capital of Liberia. A gift of ten millions would do this, and establish a colony of half a million Negroes within two years. They could lay the foundations of a free black republic which within twenty-five years would solve our race problem on the only rational basis within human power. Colonization is not a failure. It has never been tried.

We owe this to the Negro. At present we are deceiving him and allowing him to deceive himself. He hopes and dreams of amalgamation, forgetting that self-preservation is the first law of Nature. Our present attitude of hypocrisy is inhuman toward a weaker race brought to our shores be the sins of our fathers. We owe him a square deal, and we will never give it to him on this Continent.

10   THE GUILT OF THE CANE

W. E. B. DuBois

When I attended the Friedrich Wilhelm's University in Berlin in 1892 to 1893, the insignia of a student which were absolutely compulsory were gloves and cane. There I acquired the cane habit and have carried one ever since. It is useless and silly, but also harmless and cheap. So I still carry a cane, an incorrigible habit. Once as I was revisiting Germany, I found in a little shop on the Friedrichstrasse, now in ghastly ruins, an enticing umbrella cane. It was a thin silk umbrella with a removable wooden outer sheath. I bought it forthwith and carried it for years until it wore out.

Recently in an old umbrella shop on Forty-fifth street, New York, what did I see but an umbrella cane almost a replica of my old one! I inquired the price— it was much too high and I left. But the temptation was irresistible. Twice I returned, and finally I bought it at a ridiculous price, which I then increased by equipping it with a silver band engraved with name and address. I took singular satisfaction in this toy. It renewed my youth; it brought back a land and a culture forever dead; it healed and revived memories.

I fared west, talking to groups of varied complexions of mind and body; eating a delicious Thanksgiving dinner with my friends the Lochards; seeing Des Moines again fifty-one years after my wedding, at Cedar Rapids, and finally landing in Union Station, Chicago, on my way home. Here is a restaurant, where I have a favorite seat. Pushing the Third World War firmly into the background, I had a

SOURCE: From *The Chicago Defender,* January 17, 1948. Copyright © *The Chicago Defender.* Reprinted by permission.

trout from the North Woods, an appetizing salad, a small bottle of sauterne (albeit Californian), and a demi-tasse in a dainty cup—not a bowl. I then strolled leisurely to my sleeping-car, at peace with a cockeyed world, until I laid my precious cane-umbrella on the bed: the cane sheath was missing! It was made of turned wood from Sweden and folded sweetly into a warm brown roll. I had the umbrella. I had the engraved silver address but the cane-cover was gone. I had dropped it! I had lost it! It was irreplaceable! I had the sick feeling which, whether it rises from the fall of the world or the flick of a finger, spells doom. Suddenly a whole group of memories, experiences, hopes, triumphs, and failures of fifty years, rose and curled themselves around that lost cane-cover. To the porter's astonishment, I rushed out and began to search the depot floors and platforms.

As you may know, the Chicago Union Station occupies upward of two acres, fairly full of feet and traveling bags. I threaded doggedly through passengers, looking in vain, and porters eyed me askance. I finally flew back to the Pullman and again searched there. It was still gone. Ah! I remembered, the restaurant! I hurried there. It was closed! The connecting lunch counter was open however. I rushed in there and laid my case feelingly before the pretty counter-girl and the sympathetic head waitress. I was led on to the closed restaurant and searched the check-room. No trace! "But," said the waitress brightly, "How about the Lost and Found?" In vain! There was nothing there but a yellow stick with a ribbon! My time was running short. I began to have that feeling, not simply of loss, but of loss of nothing, which still seemed of fundamental importance, because it linked to this world the dream of another that had been born and died— I was unbelievably and illogically dejected and disillusioned. After all, what was the use—and just then I saw it! It lay quietly folded in its soft, brown roll, cunningly hidden under the desk of the Pullman agent, where I had checked in an hour since.

I fell upon it. I rubbed it gently and slipped it carefully in place. I became suddenly quite voluble. I explained to the Pullman agent, the Gateman, the Pullman porter—until finally I began to sense obscurely but definitely that to none of these did the matter seem of that cosmic importance which it did to me. Then I went to bed.

11 CULTURAL NATIONALISM

Julius Lester

Blacks have always been made to view their predicament in terms of whites. They have been the "outs" trying to get "in." This immediately gives those who are "in" a power. It is their decision whether or not you will get in. They set the qualifications. Black people have to qualify for a job or enter a school according to standards set by whites. Life for a black person can be nothing more than a series of tests with a nation of white schoolteachers grading every step you take, every breath you breathe. In the South you can fail the test if you wear a white shirt and tie. In the North you can fail if you don't wear a shirt and tie. By saying that America has a "Negro Problem," the burden for solving it has been put on the one who carries the burden of being oppressed. "If Negroes would do this and do the other, we wouldn't have this problem." It is always the Negro who is wrong.

It has been impossible for blacks not to fall victims to this white assessment of themselves, while at the same time resisting it. Black people are what the sociologist Robert Park has characterized as "marginal men." We exist in two cultural worlds and in two different societies at the same time, without being totally a part of either. What is more pathetic and sad than a wedding in the ghetto, the bride in her lovely white gown posing for pictures on the stoop of a slum building and walking past the fallen garbage cans to a car at the curb to which someone has tied a few cans to announce the glad tidings as she and her groom drive away together. She has had her wedding just as it was described in the magazines. She had had her six-tiered cake with a little white bride and groom at the top. She has stuffed a piece of cake into her new husband's mouth. She has walked down the aisle with a little girl walking behind, holding her train. She has done it all, all, including the big diamond on her third finger, left hand, and she would've been more comfortable and gotten her marriage off to a better start if she'd danced for four hours to James Brown and Aretha, drunk liquor, had a good time, and then gone to the marital bed with her new husband. But she wanted it done the way she thought it was supposed to be done. She threw her bouquet and they threw rice on her.

This is the marginality with which blacks have to live. It is particularly difficult for the intellectual, who has roots in the black experience, yet lives a life where he must compete with whites. He has to learn new ways in those integrated schools, and this learning makes him a stranger to his people while he comes no closer to overcoming his alienation from the white world. "Marginal men" are created whenever two different historical and cultural peoples come into contact.

SOURCE: Reprinted from *Look Out, Whitey! Black Power's Gon' get Your Mama* by Julius Lester. Copyright © 1968 by Julius Lester. Used by permission of the publisher, The Dial Press. Footnotes in the original have been omitted.

No black person has escaped this marginality. He has been constantly bombarded by the symbols of the dominant culture. He has seen his own culture ridiculed by whites. Western culture has equated the evil of the world with black—black as sin, "the blackest day of my life," "blackball," etc. There are over sixty synonyms in *Roget's Thesaurus* for black, and all of them have connotations of something not good. Is it any wonder, then, that black people have devoted so much time trying to erase their blackness? They have tried to solve the pain of their marginality by denying what they are, or at least, by hiding it, covering it up, because to deny it has been impossible.

Since the earliest days of slavery a program of cultural genocide has been conscious on the part of whites, because the success of their lives depended on it. First, the white man tried to stamp out any vestiges of culture in Africans. Blacks from the same tribes were not allowed to remain together. Thus, Africans from different tribes found that they could communicate in only one language—English. The white man then moved to reinforce this by saying that blacks had never contributed anything to civilization. And any knowledge that spoke to the contrary was suppressed. Next came the creation of class distinctions among the blacks. The house servant received more favors than did the field hand. The mulatto was the most prized of all and was quite often educated by the master, his father. In some instances, whites were so successful in wiping out feelings of separate identity in the slaves that there was a small number of black slaveholders in the South.

This program of cultural genocide was backed up by laws forbidding blacks to do, in essence, anything whites didn't want them to do. This amounted to everything except work. The law's authority came from the barrel of a gun or the noose of a rope. Even after the laws were off the books, custom did not change. A nigger is a nigger is a nigger.

Yet, while whites were denigrating black culture, they were stealing it. While saying that blacks had no culture, ol' boss on the plantation didn't have a ball where John didn't fiddle and Sam pick the banjo. Some slaves were professional musicians who did nothing but make music when the white man wanted music. Whites loved to go to black churches for the music. They heard jazz in New Orleans and tried to imitate it. They couldn't, but they recorded it, got the money, and had their thing called "legitimate." This process has never abated. King Oliver and Paul Whiteman (appropriate name) were contemporaneous band leaders, but who earned the money? Not black King Oliver. The musical contribution of black people is recognized today. Jazz is the only indigenous music America has, but now the ploy is to say, well, it may be true that this is Negro music, but now it belongs to the world. Says who? We didn't give it to anybody. You came and got it, took the money and the credit, and then come back and tell me what a great thing I've done by giving the world this music.

The dances whites have tried to do have come from blacks. The mambo, samba, tango, merengue, are all religious dances from Africa, Brazil, or Haiti. These dances have been divested of meaning by people of an alien culture. The twist, watusi, boogaloo, and monkey have come from the black community and have been appropriated by whites who have no idea that these are, in essence, religious dances, rich with sexual adumbrations.

The white attitude toward black culture is another instance where the rhetoric has been the reverse of the actions, for whites have not failed to adopt the music, dance, speech, and fashions of a culture that they have declared nonexistent. (Men's fashions invariably come from the ghetto and generally there is a two-year lag before they enter white America. In women's fashions, 1967 seemed to be the year that African designs were to be appropriated by white America. The February *Harper's Bazaar* featured clothes modeled on African dresswear. The clothes were beautiful, but those white skins killed the vibrancy of the colors.)

Even though blacks have believed what whites told them, that which was uniquely black within them refused to be stilled. The black preacher tried to preach a logical sermon, going deliberately from point to point, but he just couldn't do it. He had to shout and get happy. He had to throw his arms in the air and move around, jump up and down and roundabout. He had to do what the spirit said, do it like the spirit told him to do.

The uniqueness of black culture can be explained in that it is a culture whose emphasis is on the nonverbal, i.e., the nonconceptual. The lives of blacks are rooted in the concrete daily experience. When the black preacher shouts, "God is a living God!" don't argue. Get ready to shake hands with the Lord Almighty. "I talked to God this morning and I said, 'Now, listen here, Lord. You got to do something about these white folks down here. Lord, they giving us a hard time. You got to do something!' " God is like a personal friend, an old buddy, whom you talk to man-to-man. The black church congregation doesn't want to be told about God, it wants to feel Him, see Him, and touch Him. It is the preacher's responsibility to see that they do.

In black culture it is the experience that counts, not what is said. The rhythm-and-blues singer and the gospel quartets know that their audiences want to feel the song. The singers are the physical embodiment of the emotions and experiences of the community. They are separate from the community only in that they have the means to make the community experience through music that no-good man who left, the pain of loneliness, the joy of love, physical and religious.

Perhaps the essence of the nonverbalism of black culture is found in rhythm. In any speech by Martin Luther King, one can hear his unconscious understanding of black rhythm and voice timbre. It is there, in the black preacher, the music, and the day-to-day speech. It is there in the color sense of black people. It is there, not only in the way we dance, but in the way we walk. It is African, not American.

With Western culture's emphasis upon the verb, the result has been the creation of a subject-object relationship between man and his experience. The verb-oriented culture separates man from his experience in such a way that for a man to relate his experience he must set himself on one side, the experience on the other, and the verb in between to connect the two. Thus, for example, for the German mystic Meister Eckhart to state his oneness with God, he had to say "I am God," which to his congregation sounded like the highest egotism. If Meister Eckhart had been African, he would simply have been possessed by the rhythm of his particular god and exemplified the dynamic Oneness.

This difference between verb-oriented and non-verb-oriented cultures is most apparent when one considers art in the two cultures. The artist is essentially a revolutionary whose aim is to change people's lives. He wants people to live better, and one way of doing it is to make them see, hear, and feel what he has seen, felt, and heard. The artist is not concerned with beauty, but with making man's life better. Thus, it is an insult when a work of music is applauded for the pleasant vibrations which have come to the ear. The Western concept of art is, in essence, antiart. If the listeners had opened their beings to the music, it would be impossible for them to applaud. If they applauded, it would not be a polite coming together of the hands in rapid motion, but exulting cries. People would run out into the streets and hug everyone in sight, shout, throw off their clothes, and become new men. Instead, they respond by saying, "How beautiful!" Poor Van Gogh. He sacrificed his life to put on canvas the way he saw the world, and his reward is people who can't see beyond the vibrant colors and the agitated brushstrokes. Once something is called "art," it is put in a category. It is no longer something to be experienced directly; it is to be commented upon, studied, and understood. To understand is not to experience. Yet, Western culture and education are aimed at the rational.

The black man knows the inherent irrationality of life. Thus, black culture is aimed at the experience. The congregation responds to the preaching by patting the foot and shouting. The blues singer's audience yells back at him, "Take you time, now. Tell it." The audience demands that the performer (preacher, singer, or what have you) relate to them at this level. It is his responsibility. White teen-agers go to hear the Beatles and scream through their entire performance. It isn't because of the music. Their screams obliterate it. It is because of an involvement with the singers. Yet, you never hear a black teen-ager gush over the Temptations like whites do over the Beatles. You will hear black-teenagers sing every line of the Temptations' current song and all their past ones. You will see them imitate every movement the performers make on stage. You can sit in restaurants in the black community and if a particularly meaningful record is played on the jukebox, every person in the place will suddenly start singing.

These two very different cultures met under what cannot be considered auspicious circumstances. The dominant culture sought to destroy the new one. It did not totally succeed, but through slavery, intimidation, and murder it did create in the members of the minority culture a desire to deny that culture and assume the characteristics and ways of the dominant one. The black American may feel that black is bad, but even while he is saying it one can hear in the rising and falling of his voice the sound of the African dialects and drums.

Of the minority groups in this country, blacks are the only one having no language of their own. Language serves to insulate a group and protect it from outsiders. Lacking this strong protection, black people are more victims of the American lie of assimilation than the Puerto Rican, Italian, or Jew, who can remove himself from America with one sentence in his native language. America is not a melting pot. It is a nation of national minorities, each living in well-defined areas and retaining enough of the culture of the native land to maintain an identity other than that of an American. The black person also has two native lands: America and Africa. But both have deliberately been denied him.

This denial of America and Africa has created the central psychological problem for the black American. Who am I? Many avoid their blackness as much as possible by trying to become assimilated. They remove all traces of blackness from their lives. Their gestures, speech, habits, cuisine, walk, everything they can consciously control, becomes as "American Dream" as possible. Generally, they are the "responsible ones," the undercover, button-down-collar Uncle Toms who front for the white man at a time of "racial crisis," reassuring white folks that "responsible Negroes deplore the violence and looting and we ask that law and order be allowed to prevail." A small minority avoid the crux of their blackness by going to another extreme. They identify completely with Africa. Some do so to the extent of wearing African clothes, celebrating African holidays, and speaking Swahili. They, however, are only unconsciously admitting that the white man is right when he says American blacks have nothing of their own.

For other blacks the question of identity is only now being solved by the realization of those things that are theirs. Black people do have a language of their own. The words may be English, but the way a black person puts them together and the meaning that he gives them creates a new language. He has another language, too, and that language is rhythm. This has been recognized by black people for some time, and they call it "soul." In Africa they speak of negritude. The two are the same. It is the recognition of those things uniquely ours which separate us from the white man.

This consciousness has come about through the teachings of the Honorable Elijah Muhammad, Malcolm X, and most recently, SNCC. More than any other person, Malcolm X was responsible for the growing consciousness and new militancy of black people. He said aloud those things which blacks had been saying among themselves. He even said those things we had been afraid to say to each other. His clear, uncomplicated words cut through the chains on black minds like a giant blowtorch. His words were not spoken for the benefit of the press. He was not concerned with stirring the moral conscience of America, because he knew—America has no moral conscience. He spoke directly and eloquently to black men, analyzing their situation, their predicament, events as they happened, explaining what it all meant for a black man in America.

Now blacks are beginning to study their past, to learn those things that have been lost, to re-create what the white man destroyed in them, and to destroy that which the white man put in its stead. They have stopped being Negroes and have become black men, in recognition of this new identity, their real identity. In the November, 1967, *Ebony*, Lerone Bennett, Jr., quotes Ossie Davis on the difference between a Negro and a black man.

> *I am a Negro. I am clean, black and I smile a lot. Whenever I want something—to get a job in motion pictures, for instance, or on television or to get a play produced on Broadway, whenever I need a political favor—I got white folks. White folks have money. I do not. White folks have power, I do not. All of my needs—financial, artistic, social, my need for freedom—I must depend on white folks to supply. That is what is meant by being a Negro.*
>
> *Malcolm X used to be a Negro, but he stopped. He no longer depended upon white folks to supply his needs—psychologically or sociologically—to give him money or lead his fight for freedom or to protect him from his enemies or to tell him what to do. Malcolm X did not hate white folks, nor did he love them. Most of all, he did not need them to tell him who he was. Above all, he was determined to make it on his own.... Malcolm was a man, a black man! A black man means not to accept the system as Negroes do but to fight hell out of the system as Malcolm did. It can be dangerous. Malcolm was killed for it....*

Blacks now realize that "Negro" is an American invention which shut them off from those of the same color in Africa. They recognize now that part of themselves is in Africa. Some feel this in a deeply personal way, as did Mrs. Fannie Lou Hamer of Mississippi, who cried when she was in Africa, because she knew she had relatives there and she would never be able to know them. Her past would always be partially closed to her.

All across the country now one can find blacks wearing their hair "Afro" style. For the girls it means they no longer go to the beauty parlor to have their hair straightened with hot combs. They wear it as it was before the hot combs and grease got to it. Howard University's Homecoming Queen of 1966 was a former SNCC worker who wears her hair *au naturel.* For the men it means letting the hair grow long. Not only is this true of young blacks directly involved in "the movement," but of teen-agers in the urban centers.

This new cultural awareness has produced numerous conferences of black intellectuals around the country in the past couple of years. Newspapers and small magazines have sprung up whose sole purpose is the furtherance of black consciousness. Friends are often admonished to "think black." People are often criticized for "sounding too much like whitey." When a man is rude to a black woman, he is criticized for not treating his "sister" properly. You no longer "hang out" on the block with your friends, you "hang out with the brothers."

Black consciousness is more than this, however. It is fundamental to Black Power. Anne Braden defined black consciousness when she wrote:

Negroes ... need to eliminate from their thinking and feeling the patterns that have been put there by a society that is essentially built on the concept of the superiority of the white man.... Negroes need to reject the unconscious idea that what is white is better. And because they do live in a society that holds to that idea, they will begin to think and feel differently only when they realize their own history, their own worth as a people, their own ties with dark-skinned people elsewhere in the world.

Black consciousness is an essential part of speaking and defining for ourselves. It is the foundation for Black Power.

Part 3
STYLES OF LIFE

A
Myths in Celluloid

The twentieth century has witnessed a considerable increase in communications media. The use of radio, the movies, and television as instruments of mass manipulation is of recent origin. According to Marshall McLuhan, these new technological developments have not only increased the amount of information people possess but have also changed the people themselves. He says that the media has imposed "on us a particular pattern of perceiving and thinking that controls us to an extent we scarcely suspect." "Our human senses, of which all media are extensions, are also fixed charges on our personal energies ... they also configure the awareness and experience of each one of us." While McLuhan has rightly been attacked for his extreme claims for the media, it must be admitted that we are influenced to a considerable extent by our means of communication. We contend in this section that there is a reciprocal relationship between the changing life styles of Americans and the media.

We have chosen examples of the mutual interaction of life styles and media primarily from material about the movies. The first two selections deal with the content of some movies; the last involves the showing of movies on television. We chose movies to demonstrate the thesis for several reasons, among them the facts that the movies have most nearly spanned the twentieth century, preceding commercial radio by at least ten years; that movies have attracted more critical attention than have radio and television; and that the visual aspect of the movies has made possible more specific representations of social role than has the more limited aural aspect of radio. In selecting the movies, we realize we may have omitted material from other media that may have been as appropriate as that which we included.

We have not surveyed the history of the movies nor have we traced significant trends in this popular art. This is not to say that such efforts are unrewarding. A good case can be made that the social fantasies of the 1930s musical reflect accurately the ostentation and vulgarity of the newly rich Hollywood community. Similarly, the college comedies of the same era show the vision of persons who never went to college. The campus queen and the football hero are stereotypes made by outsiders. The war movies of the twentieth century reveal changing attitudes toward collective violence. The chauvinism of movies made during the wars—World War I, World War II, the Korean War, and the Vietnam War—is expressed differently by the characterization of the heroes in each. The super-hero of World War II, as exemplified by John Wayne in the *Sands of Iwo Jima*, has become the more complex, less heroic, tortured Alan Arkin in *Catch-22*. (Although *Catch-22* concerns World War II, it reflects attitudes of the Vietnam War.) The difference between the two types is measured less in time than in social attitude. Even the war movies with an intentional pacifistic message differ. The sentimental tragedy of *All Quiet on the Western Front* resembles the black comedy of *M*A*S*H* as much as *Rebecca of Sunnybrook Farm* resembles *The Diary of a Mad Housewife*. In both war films the event represented is a decade old and in both there is horror aplenty—in living color in *M*A*S*H*—but the message of futility in the latter case is much more subliminal. The two heroes vary immensely; one can only compare the mad antics of Elliot Gould with the quiet desperation of Lew Ayres.

Changing attitudes toward sex and sexual roles are obvious in the development of the movies. The present commonness of nudity recalls the 1920s, when the naked human body was also seen, although in much shorter sequences. The explicit sexuality of the movies of the last decade is a new development. It is not that pornography is new. It seems to have developed contemporaneously with each new medium of communication. Its audience, however, has been limited because of the high cost and because of its illegality. The early movie makers moved to Hollywood in part because of its proximity to Mexico—hence the ease in distributing illegitimate films. The change in our time has not been the making of pornographic films; it has been the increase in the market. Earlier blue movies were shown either in the private screening rooms of the rich or in the back room of the American Legion hall—thus limiting the audience. The more recent frankness has made the audience a more public one, particularly increasing the exposure of the middle-class male and female. Sexual behavior openly portrayed on the screen does reflect and influence attitudes on sexual roles.

The roles of radicals and women have also changed. The image of the radical evolved from the bewhiskered, incompetent bomb thrower satirized by Buster Keaton in one of his early silent films to the threatening saboteur of the post-World War II film, *I Was a Communist for the F.B.I.*, to the campus radical of the 1960s in *The Strawberry Statement*. Few films have treated alternate roles for women in any sophisticated fashion. However, the change in attitude toward career women can be found by comparing the career-girl roles played by Rosalind Russell in the 1930s with those seemingly more natural roles portrayed in contemporary movies.

The movies show changing heroic roles, sexual roles, and radical roles. Different kinds of appropriate behavior are suggested with differing statuses attached.

Not all the nuances of the roles are explored nor are movies consistent, but they are a rich source of information on social history.

Selection 12 illuminates the ideal roles of a conservative social order. *The Birth of a Nation* is one of the first modern movies because of the aesthetic brilliance of D. W. Griffith, but the subject of the movie perpetuates the myths of the antebellum South. The black man should be a slave because he is a beast with consuming appetites. Here, the ideas of Dixon, contained in Selection 9, become visually realized. The social purity that hindered the women's-rights movement also becomes embodied in the Southern girl. Her innocence stands in sharp contrast to the sexual passion of the black man. The ideal society is a hierarchical one, with domestic harmony and little social mobility. The metaphor used in the movie to describe this society is a familiar one. The South was the body—warm, kind, and emotional—while the North was the head—cold, harsh, and rational. (The metaphor now is used by Eldrige Cleaver to distinguish between black and white men, with black men having the body and white ones the head. Dixon would find it ironic indeed that even his metaphors were turned against him.) *The Birth of a Nation* spoke for reactionary social roles, which denied any greater freedom to black men or white women.

Selection 13 involves a genre rather than a single film. This genre is that of the Western movie, which is a peculiarly American product and which began with the beginnings of the movie industry. Even today it survives on television and is a staple product of European film makers as well. Because of its origin, the Western, as Robert Warshow suggests, radiates American social values. While the Western has assumed a conventional form because of its long evolution, it also retains many implicit assumptions about proper behavior for both men and women, heroes and villains.

The earlier cowboy movies do not interest Warshow; neither do the movies of the 1930s and 1940s built around the cult of a star—Tom Mix, Roy Rogers, or Gene Autry. He prefers others that, although using a formula, illustrate a changing American ethos. The simple heroes and villains of the earlier movies were men of action and moral certitude. They have been replaced by more complex men who must decide on unclear moral issues. The gunfighter still must kill, but the killing exacts considerable psychic cost. In the end, the gunfighter is defeated because he is unable to achieve even his limited goals in an imperfect world. He must play out his role to the end, even if he no longer believes in it.

What changes have occurred in the Western movie that reflect changing American attitudes? The role of the Westerner was traditionally that of a man who achieves identity through violent means. He was a man alone with little in the way of social ties or personal possessions. Defined this way, the Westerner was the ideal American man, reflecting the myth of American individuality and lack of a sense of community that were so much a part of the nineteenth century. By the 1950s the role of both the Westerner and the audience that perceived this role had changed. The Westerner was less successful with his violence; the audience expected him to meet defeat. Perhaps this is because violence had become much more commonplace. Warshow thinks that World War II ended the cinematic use of lynching to eliminate the worst of villains. The role of the Western hero has become tempered; the hero is less omnipotent; he has more social ties; he is less successful in his violence. If the role of cowboy furnished the base for the fantasies of small boys, these fantasies are now much more limited.

Selection 14 is a reaction to the rerunning of movies of different periods on television by the critic Pauline Kael. One would think that there would be a jumble because the assumptions underlying the movies were so different, that there would be no clear-cut roles for the viewer to imitate. In part, this has happened. Yet Kael believes that the compression of time does bring insight. We watch old movies when we have forgotten other parts of our earlier life because movies give us a sense of our own existence. We can recreate the past or we can understand what was not clear at the time. What did our parents regard as threatening in the roles in movies that we were forbidden by them to see? Was it the sexual precocity of Rita Hayworth? Was it the possibility of our becoming gangsters like Edward G. Robinson? Kael even sees the physical triumph of the immigrant as the leading man changes in appearance. The standards of handsomeness have changed to include those who were previously thought ugly. Old movies on T.V. do show what changes have occurred in our views on what behavior and appearance were appropriate for various roles.

Television addicts are not likely to be all members of an older, nostalgic generation. Some are young enough never to have known a televisionless existence. How are they to make sense of a medium using materials wrenched out of their own times? How are they to gain a semblance of consistency in viewing ideal roles? Pauline Kael suggests two possibilities. The first is that some actors become identified with certain roles—James Dean as the misunderstood youth, Gary Cooper as the taciturn cowboy, and Humphrey Bogart as the tough, cynical man of the world. These roles are time resistant. The other possibility is that there is a deadening of sensibilities because of the sheer quantity of materials. The television generation accepts all roles as possible and internalizes none. Perhaps in television the pluralistic view of Horace Kallen is realized.

The three selections in the section illustrate how possible life styles can be handled by the media. The first, on *The Birth of a Nation*, shows how a movie can perpetuate older assumptions about black men and women. The second shows how a movie convention, the Western, does change through time, reflecting external opinions about the nature and use of violence by the Westerner. The last shows how a medium, television, has made possible, through the showing of old movies, the simultaneous presentation of many different role possibilities, leading to either confusion or toleration. We believe that the changes in communications have made possible increasing alternatives of behavior in our time.

12 CULTURAL HISTORY WRITTEN WITH LIGHTING: THE SIGNIFICANCE OF *THE BIRTH OF A NATION*

Everett Carter

On February 20, 1915, David Wark Griffith's long film, *The Clansman*, was shown in New York City. One of the spectators was Thomas Dixon, the author of the novel from which it was taken, who was moved by the power of the motion picture to shout to the wildly applauding spectators that its title would have to be changed. To match the picture's greatness, he suggested, its name should be *The Birth of a Nation*. Only by a singular distortion of meaning could the film be interpreted as the story of a country's genesis; the birth it did herald was of an American industry and an American art; any attempt to define the cinema and its impact upon American life must take into account this classic movie. For with the release of *The Birth of a Nation* "significant motion picture history begins." Its prestige became enormous. It was the first picture to be played at the White House, where Woodrow Wilson was reported to have said: "it is like writing history with lightning." By January 1916 it had given 6,266 performances in the area of greater New York alone. If we conservatively estimate that five hundred patrons saw each performance, we arrive at the astounding total of over three million residents of and visitors to New York who saw the picture, and forever viewed themselves and their country's history through its colorations. And not only significant motion picture history begins, but most of the problems of the art's place in our culture begins too. The picture projects one of the most persistent cultural illusions; it presents vividly and dramatically the ways in which a whole people have reacted to their history; its techniques in the narrowest sense are the fully realized techniques of the pictorial aspects of the motion picture; in the widest sense, its techniques are a blend of the epical and the symbolically realistic, and each part of this mixture has developed into a significant genre of cinematic art.

Griffith was a Kentuckian, a devout believer in Southern values; and these values, he was certain, were embodied in *The Clansman*, a sentimental novel of the Reconstruction which had appeared in 1905, had been widely read, had been seen in dramatic form throughout the South, and whose author had dedicated it "To the memory of a Scotch-Irish leader of the South, my Uncle, Colonel Leroy McAfee, Grand Titan of the Invisible Empire Ku Klux Klan." In his introduction, Dixon went on to describe his theme: "How the young South, led by the reincarnated souls of the Clansmen of Old Scotland, went forth under this cover and against overwhelming odds, daring exile, imprisonment, and a felon's death, and saved the life of a people, forms one of the most dramatic chapters in the history of the Aryan race." This strong suggestion that the South's struggle is a racial

SOURCE: From *American Quarterly*, Vol. XII (Fall 1960). Copyright, 1960, Trustees of the University of Pennsylvania. Reprinted by permission. Footnotes in the original have been omitted.

epic, involving all the people of one blood in their defense against a common ancestral enemy, became, as we shall see, a major influence upon Griffith's conception of his cinematic theme. And, in addition, the novel in so many ways served as what would later be called a "treatment" from which the story would be filmed, that we must examine the book closely before we can understand the significance of the film.

The Clansman told the story of "Thaddeus Stevens' bold attempt to Africanize the ten great states of the American Union...." It interpreted the history of the Reconstruction as the great Commoner's vengeance, motivated partly by economics: the destruction of his Pennsylvania iron mills by Lee's army; partly by religion: in his parlor there was "a picture of a nun ... he had always given liberally to an orphanage conducted by a Roman Catholic sisterhood"; but mainly by lust: his housekeeper was "a mulatto, a woman of extraordinary animal beauty ..." who became, through her power over Austin Stoneman (the fictional name for Stevens) "the presiding genius of National legislation." Stoneman was shown in private conference with Lincoln, whose words in his Charleston debate with Douglas were directly quoted: "I believe there is a physical difference between the white and black races which will forever forbid their living together on terms of political and social equality." Stoneman's instruments in the South were all described as animals, demonstrating that the Civil War was fought to defend civilization against the barbaric and bestial. Silas Lynch, the carpetbagger, "had evidently inherited the full physical characteristics of the Aryan race, while his dark yellowish eyes beneath his heavy brows glowed with the brightness of the African jungle." The Negro leader, Alack, had a nose "broad and crushed flat against his face," and jaws "strong and angular, mouth wide, and lips thick, curling back from solid teeth set obliquely...." The Cameron family of the Old South were the principal victims; Gus, a renegade Negro, ravished Marion Cameron, the sixteen-year-old "universal favourite" who embodied "the grace, charm, and tender beauty of the Southern girl...." Silas Lynch attempted to violate Elsie Stoneman, the betrothed of Ben Cameron. The actual rape was a climax of a series of figurative violations of the South by the North, one of which was the entry of Stoneman into the black legislature, carried by two Negroes who made "a curious symbolic frame for the chalk-white passion of the old Commoner's face. No sculptor ever dreamed a more sinister emblem of the corruption of a race of empire-builders than this group. Its black figures, wrapped in the night of four thousand years of barbarism, squatted there the 'equal' of their master, grinning at his forms of Justice, the evolution of forty centuries of Aryan genius." These figurative and literal ravishments provoked the formation of the Ku Klux Klan, whose like "the world had not seen since the Knights of the Middle Ages rode on their Holy Crusades." The Klan saved Elsie, revenged Marion, brought dismay to the Negro, the carpetbagger, and the scalawag; and, in the final words of the book "Civilisation has been saved, and the South redeemed from shame."

The picture followed the book failthfully in plot, character, motivation, and theme, and became a visualization of the whole set of irrational cultural assumptions which may be termed the "Plantation Illusion." The Illusion has many elements, but it is based primarily upon a belief in a golden age of the ante bellum South, an age in which feudal agrarianism provided the good life for wealthy, leisured, kindly, aristocratic owner and loyal, happy, obedient slave. The enormous disparity between this conception and the reality has been the subject of Gaines' *The Southern Plantation* and Stampp's *The Peculiar Institution*. But our concern is not with the reality but with what people have thought and felt about the reality; this thinking and feeling is the Illusion, and the stuff of the history of sensibility. The Illusion was embodied in Kennedy's *Swallow Barn* (1832), developed through Carruthers' *The Cavaliers of Virginia* (1834), and firmly fixed in the national consciousness by Stephen Foster's "Old Folks at Home" (1851), "My Old Kentucky Home" and "Massa's in the Cold, Cold Ground" (1852) and "Old Black Joe," songs which nostalgically describe a "longing for the old plantation..." In 1905 Dixon summarized it in the assertion that the South before the Civil War was ruled by an "aristocracy founded on brains, culture, and blood," the "old fashioned dream of the South" which "but for the Black curse—could be today the garden of the world."

This was the image realized almost immediately at the beginning of *The Birth of a Nation*. A scene of Southern life before the Civil War is preceded by the title: "In the Southland, life runs in a quaintly way that is no more." A primitive cart is shown trundling up a village street, filled with laughing Negroes: there is further merriment as a few children fall from the cart and are pulled into it; then appears a scene of a young aristocrat helping his sister into a carriage; she is in white crinoline and carries a parasol; the young southerner helps her gallantly from the carriage, and the title reads: "Margaret Cameron, daughter of the old South, trained in manners of the old school." With the two levels of feudal society established, the scene is then of the porch of the plantation house. Dr. and Mrs. Cameron are rocking; he has a kitten in his arms, and puppies are shown playing at his feet. A pickaninny runs happily in and out among the classic columns while the Camerons look indulgently on; a very fat and very black servant claps her hands with glee.

A corollary of this aspect of the Southern Illusion, one might even say a necessary part of it, is the corresponding vision of the North as the land of coldness, harshness, mechanical inhumanity; expressed most generously, it is the description of the North as "head" and the South as the warm human "heart" which was Sidney Lanier's major metaphor in his Reconstruction poems. Although Lanier had called for the reunion of the heart and head, a modern Southerner, John Crowe Ransom, has scolded Lanier for preaching reconcilliation when, Ransom said, what should have been preached was the "contumacious resistance" of the warm, agrarian South against the harsh industrialism and rationalism of the North. *The Clansman* had emphasized the contrast between warm South and cold North by rechristening Thaddeus Stevens, "Austin Stoneman"—the man of stone; the radical Republican who is the obdurate villain of the picture. He has a clubfoot and moves angularly and mechanically; his house, his dress, are gloomy, dark, and cold, as opposed to the warmth and lightness of the Southern plantation garments and scene. In the novel, Dixon had identified him as the owner of Pennsylvania iron mills, and Griffith took the hint, giving him clothes to wear and expressions to assume which, in their harshness and implacability, suggest the unyielding metal. The sense of commercialism, combined with rigidity and pious hypocrisy, is identified with the North, too, by showing the presumed beginnings of slavery in America. We see a Puritan preacher sanctimoniously praying while two of the elect arrange the sale of a cringing slave; the following scene is of Abolitionists demanding the end of slavery; the grouping of the two scenes, the dress and features of the characters in both, make the point strongly that these are the same people; the montage is a dramatization of Ben Cameron's assertion in the novel, that "our slaves were stolen from Africa by Yankee skippers.... It was not until 1836 that Massachusetts led in Abolition—not until all her own slaves had been sold to us at a profit....

In these opening scenes, too, we have the complete cast of characters of the Plantation Ideal. The Camerons are shown as they go down to the fields to mingle with the happy and trusting slaves. A title tells us that "in the two hour interval for dinner given in their working day from six to six the slaves enjoy themselves"; then appears a view of slaves clapping hands and dancing. Ben Cameron places his hand paternally upon the shoulder of one, and shakes hands with another who bobs in a perfect frenzy of grateful loyalty: in several seconds a wonderful summary of a hundred years of romantic tradition in which "a beautiful felicity of racial contact has been presented, not as occasional but as constant; an imperious kindness on the part of the whites, matched by obsequious devotion on the part of the blacks."

The Plantation Ideal had to explain the obvious fact that during the war and Reconstruction, many Negroes fought with the Union and greeted Emancipation with joy. The Illusion protected itself by explaining that the true, southern, full-blooded Negro remained loyal throughout and after the war. It expanded the truth of individual instances of this kind into a general rule. In the Civil War sequences of *The Birth of a Nation*, the Camerons' slaves are shown cheering the parade of the Confederate soldiers as they march off to defend them against their freedom. The fat Negro cook and the others of the household staff are described as "The Faithful Souls"; they weep at Southern defeat and Northern triumph; they rescue Dr. Cameron from his arrest by Reconstruction militia.

While the Illusion persistently maintained the loyalty of the true slave, it premised the disaffection of other Negroes upon several causes, all of them explicable within the framework of the Plantation Ideal. The major explanation was the corruption of the Negro by the North. The freed Negro, the Union soldier, is a monster of ingratitude, a renegade from the feudal code, and only evil can be expected of him. The picture shows The Faithful Soul deriding one such abolitionist; the title reads, "You northern black trash, don't you try any of your airs on me." And a little later, we see her lips saying, and then read on the screen, "Those free niggers from the north sho' am crazy." The second explanation was that the mulatto, the person of mixed blood, was the arch-villain in the tragedy of the South. Stoneman, the radical Republican leader, is shown, as he was in the novel, under the spell of his mulatto housekeeper. A scene of Stoneman lasciviously fondling his mistress is preceded by the title: "The great leader's weakness that is to blight a nation." The mistress, in turn, has as a lover another mulatto, Silas Lynch, who is described as the principal agent in Stoneman's plans to "Africanize" the South. This dark part of the Plantation Illusion is further represented in the twin climaxes of the picture, both of which are attempted sexual assaults on blond white girls, one by a Northern Negro, and the other by the mulatto, Silas Lynch.

The sexual terms into which this picture translated the violation of the Southern Illusion by the North underscore the way in which the film incorporates one of the most vital of the forces underlying the Illusion—the obscure, bewildering complex of sexual guilt and fear which the Ideal never overtly admits, but which is, as Stampp and Cash and Myrdal have pointed out, deeply woven into the Southern sensibility. The mulatto, while he occasionally would be the offspring of the lowest class of white woman and the Negro, much more commonly was the result of the debasement of the Negro woman by the white man, and, not infrequently, by the most aristocratic of the characters in the plantation conception. At the very least, then, the deep convictions of the Protestant South about the nature of sin would cause the Southern Illusion to regard the living, visible evidence of a parent's lust as evil in itself, and at the most, and worst, and most debilitating, as a reminder of the burden of guilt the white must bear in the record of sexual aggression against the Negro. The Birth of a Nation gives all aspects of these sexual fears and guilts full expression. Typically, the burden of guilt is discharged by making the mulatto the evil force in the picture, evincing both the bestial, animal sensuality of the unrestrained Negro, and the perverted intellectual powers of the white. And the full-blooded, but renegade, black justifies any excess of the Klan, by accomplishing that final, most dreaded act of the sexual drama, the violation of the blond "little sister." The book had made the rape actual: "A single tiger-spring," it narrated, "and the black claws of the beast sank into the soft white throat." The picture shows us the little sister as she jumps off a cliff to escape dishonor; but a scene of Gus, kneeling blackly over the white-clad, broken body, makes the sexual point without the overt act. And this point is further reinforced by a description of Lynch's attempts to possess Elsie Stoneman, by a portrayal of the passage of the first law of the black Reconstruction legislature legalizing miscegenation, and by a scene of Negroes who carry signs reading "Equal rights, equal marriage."

The descriptions of Gus as "tiger-like" and of Stoneman's mistress as a leopard, bring us to the last element of the Plantation Illusion—the defense of the system on the basis of the essential non-humanity of the Negro. The book had been blatant in its statement of this position; the picture projects this attitude by its shots of the eyes of mulatto and Negro displaying animal lust and ferocity, and by its view of Gus as a slinking animal, waiting, crouching, springing.

As the record of a cultural illusion, then, *The Birth of a Nation* is without equal. Furthermore, it is the film to which, as the historian of the art declares, "much of subsequent filmic progress owes its inspiration." In order to understand its significance, one has to remind oneself of the nature of the motion picture art. It is not an art of external events and the people who perform them; it is an art of the camera and the film. Before Griffith, the camera was treated as a fixed object, much like the spectator of the drama. The interpretation was by the actors, by their bodies, by their faces, by physical objects, and by the settings before which these performed. Griffith made the ordering and interpretation—the art, in brief—one of the location, the angle, the movement of the camera, and of the juxtaposition of the images the camera records by means of cutting and arranging these images to bring out their significance. An example of the first technique—camera position—was the famous scene of Sherman's march to the sea. The camera shows the serpentine line of Union troops in the distance, winding over the landscape. War is distant; it is simply a move of masses over territory; the camera turns slowly until it includes, in the left foreground, the figures of a weeping mother and child. Immediately a perspective is achieved; what was remote and inhuman becomes close and humanized; the human implications of such mass movements are illustrated clearly, sharply, and poignantly, simply by the perspective of the camera.

An example of the second aspect of the purely filmic technique was Griffith's juxtaposition of the two parallel scenes in the introduction to the Plantation Ideal: Negro cart and white carriage. Alone the first shot would be at worst meaningless, at best a bit of atmosphere; the second would serve merely to introduce two characters who might have been presented in an indefinite variety of ways. Placed together, both scenes become significant forms because of the two elements they have in common: means of transportation, and the perfect fitness of each group of characters to that means; the juxtaposition thus serves to summarize the feudal theory—the rightness of each part of society in its place.

A second aspect of this editorial technique—the cutting and arranging of images—was also brought to its fullness of possibility in *The Birth of a Nation* after Griffith had experimented with it in earlier films. This was the intercutting of parallel scenes occurring at different locations in space, but at the same location in time, each of which has a bearing upon the other, with the meanings of both carefully interwoven, and with the tensions of either relieved only when the two are finally brought together. The famous example of this, an example which has been followed faithfully from then on, was the intercutting of shots of Lynch's attempted forced marriage to Elsie Stoneman with shots of the gathering of the Klan which will effect her rescue. A series of six shots of Lynch and Elsie is superseded by seven shots of the gathering of the Klan; then two single shots of the Klan and two of the attempted ravishment are quickly alternated; fourteen shots of Lynch and Elsie are followed by one of the Klan; a shot of long duration during which the Elsie-Lynch struggle becomes more intense is then followed by seven shots of the Klan's ride to the rescue; and so it goes until both sequences are joined in space when the Klan finally reaches Elsie. As an early critic described the meaning of this achievement: "Every little series of pictures ... symbolizes a sentiment, a passion, or an emotion. Each successive series, similar yet different, carries the emotion to the next higher power, till at last, when both of the parallel emotions have attained the *nth* power, so to speak, they meet in the final swift shock of victory and defeat." To these epoch-making achievements of camera placement, significant juxtaposition and inter-cutting, Griffith added the first uses of night photography, or soft-focus photography, and of moving camera shots, and the possibilities of film art were born.

And with it were born most of the problems of those of us who wish to take the art seriously. For what can we make of so awkward a combination of sentimental content and superb technique? We must admit, first of all, that the effect of the film's detachable content was pernicious. It served the ugliest purposes of pseudo-art, giving people a reflection of their own prejudices—sentimental at best, vicious at worst—and a restatement of their easy explanations of the terrible complexities of their history as Americans. It demonstrated how easily and how successfully the art could pander to the sentimentality of the public, how effectively and profitably it could transfer melodrama from the stage and false values from the novel. The enormous commercial success of the film at a time when men like Louis B. Mayer, later to become the head of the greatest studio, were starting their careers as exhibitors, cannot but have fixed the melodramatic, the cheap and obviously emotional, as the index to the potential economic success of a film.

But it showed, as well, two directions in which the film would move: one is in the direction of the epic, and the other in what may be termed "symbolic realism." Its move in the first direction, of course, was an immense and shocking perversion. Griffith apparently sensed the truth that great epics are involved with the destiny of whole races and nations, and had seized upon Dixon's hint that the South's struggle was part of an "Aryan" saga. The Klan was described in the book, and on the screen, as part of an "Aryan" tradition. The term is used again at a crucial point in the screen narrative, when a mob of Negro soldiers attack the embattled whites. The battle of the Caucasians, the title on the screen tells us, is "in defense of their Aryan birthright." Griffith improved upon Dixon in emphasizing the "epical" quality of the story: before they ride, the Klansmen are shown partaking of a primitive barbaric rite; they dip a flag into the blood of the blond white virgin before they go out to destroy.

The picture is no epic, but rather an epic manque: partial, fragmentary, and therefore necessarily inartistic; in its attempt to be the saga of a shattered fragment of a nation, in its attempt to erect upon false premises a series of racial responses reputedly instinctive, it was immediately self-defeating. An epic is justified in its radical simplification, its stereotypes, its primitive terms, by its appeal to a real national unity of belief, and by its power to reinforce that unity. The oversimplifications of *The Birth of a Nation,* however, are not the controlled and ordering images of an art based upon a set of beliefs to which an entire people subscribe, images which emotionally order and control the world of that people's experience; instead it is the projection of images of disorder, an attack upon cultural and moral unity; the images of the film are the debilitating images of a false myth, a pseudo-epic.

The picture did, however, provide another cinematic genre with many of its basic situations. In 1908, with the "Bronco Billie" series, the Western setting had begun to be realized as particularly suitable to the enactment of the drama of simple primitive faith and national aspirations. After *The Birth of a Nation,* its images of elemental struggle and black and white moral values, and its techniques for making these exciting and significant, were transferred to the "Western." The epic qualities of *The Birth of a Nation* were false and vicious because they impinged upon contemporary reality and oversimplified both actual history and contemporary social circumstances; transferred to a realm of pure mythology—the Western scene of Richard Dix, *Stagecoach* and *High Noon*—and to the moral blackness of outlaw and moral whiteness of law, these simplifications, and the techniques for pictorializing them, have given us something much more artistically valid.

But more important, *The Birth of a Nation* pointed in the second, and the major, direction of the motion picture art. This direction we can call "symbolic realism"—the apparent imitation of actuality which brings out the symbolic or representational meaning of that apparent reality. This "significant" or "symbolic" realism was demonstrated to be effective in the portrayal of either deep psychological or wide universal meanings. To take a rather titillating example in *The Birth of a Nation* of the first kind of surface realism arranged to illustrate unexpressed psychological truths: Lillian Gish played an innocent love scene with the hero, returned to her room, and seated herself dreamily on the bed; the bed happened to be a four-poster each of whose posts was almost embarrassingly suggestive of masculinity; she dreamily embraced and caressed the bedpost. Some years later, Greta Garbo, as Queen Christina, after three days in bed with John Gilbert, used the bedpost in similar fashion. More significant, perhaps, is the way in which images were juxtaposed in this pioneering picture so as to bring out the universal significance of the concrete instance. The view of the army winding past the mother and child to symbolize the agony and displacements of war; the cart and the carriage as symbols of feudal levels of society; Stoneman's clubfoot representing the maimed wrathful impotence of the mechanical North; little sister adorning her coarse post bellum dress with a bit of cotton rescued from the destroyed plantation fields—these were but a few of the large number of symbolic extensions of the surface, and they pointed the way toward the great documentary symbolic realism of Flaherty, and the imaginative symbolic realism of *The Informer, Sous les Toits de Paris, The River,* and the whole run of wonderful Italian neorealistic films: *Open City, Paisan, The Bicycle Thief,* and *LaStrada.*

A preliminary examination of a significant motion picture, then, has yielded some profit as well as some disappointment. The disappointment is largely in the failure of this pioneering picture to measure up to standards of artistic greatness: its failure to achieve that fusion of content and technique which together make up a great work of art. Its failure is doubly disappointing, because it involves an inversion and debasement of epic powers in which those powers pander to popular taste instead of attempting to reach a whole vision, sinewed with moral responsibility. But in this very failure lies some of its profits for us as students of American civilization; better than any other art work, it summarizes every aspect of the Plantation Illusion which is so vigorous a force in the history of American Sensibility; for the student of the art form, it will demonstrate the beginnings of techniques which both rescue *The Birth of a Nation* from ugliness, and which, when used to embody more aesthetically malleable content, give us the possibilities of the art of the movie.

13 MOVIE CHRONICLE: THE WESTERNER

Robert Warshow

They that have power to hurt and will do none,
That do not do the thing they most do show,
Who, moving others, are themselves as stone,
Unmoved, cold, and to temptation slow;
They rightly do inherit heaven's graces,
And husband nature's riches from expense;
They are the lords and owners of their faces,
Others but stewards of their excellence.

The two most successful creations of American movies are the gangster and the Westerner: men with guns. Guns as physical objects, and the postures associated with their use, form the visual and emotional center of both types of films. I suppose this reflects the importance of guns in the fantasy life of Americans; but that is a less illuminating point than it appears to be.

The gangster movie, which no longer exists in its "classical" form, is a story of enterprise and success ending in precipitate failure. Success is conceived as an increasing power to work injury, it belongs to the city, and it is of course a form

SOURCE: From *The Immediate Experience* (New York: Doubleday and Company, Inc., 1962). Reprinted by permission of Paul Warshow.

of evil (though the gangster's death, presented usually as "punishment," is perceived simply as defeat). The peculiarity of the gangster is his unceasing, nervous activity. The exact nature of his enterprises may remain vague, but his commitment to enterprise is always clear, and all the more clear because he operates outside the field of utility. He is without culture, without manners, without leisure, or at any rate his leisure is likely to be spent in debauchery so compulsively aggressive as to seem only another aspect of his "work." But he is graceful, moving like a dancer among the crowded dangers of the city.

Like other tycoons, the gangster is crude in conceiving his ends but by no means inarticulate; on the contrary, he is usually expansive and noisy (the introspective gangster is a fairly recent development), and can state definitely what he wants: to take over the North Side, to own a hundred suits, to be Number One. But new "frontiers" will present themselves infinitely, and by a rigid convention it is understood that as soon as he wishes to rest on his gains, he is on the way to destruction.

The gangster is lonely and melancholy, and can give the impression of a profound worldly wisdom. He appeals most to adolescents with their impatience and their feeling of being outsiders, but more generally he appeals to that side of all of us which refuses to believe in the "normal" possibilities of happiness and achievement; the gangster is the "no" to that great American "yes" which is stamped so big over our official culture and yet has so little to do with the way we really feel about our lives. But the gangster's loneliness and melancholy are not "authentic"; like everything else that belongs to him, they are not honestly come by: he is lonely and melancholy not because life ultimately demands such feelings but because he has put himself in a position where everybody wants to kill him and eventually somebody will. He is wide open and defenseless, incomplete because unable to accept any limits or come to terms with his own nature, fearful, loveless. And the story of his career is a nightmare inversion of the values of ambition and opportunity. From the window of Scarface's bulletproof apartment can be seen an electric sign proclaiming: "The World Is Yours," and, if I remember, this sign is the last thing we see after Scarface lies dead in the street. In the end it is the gangster's weakness as much as his power and freedom that appeals to us; the world is not ours, but it is not his either, and in his death he "pays" for our fantasies, releasing us momentarily both from the concept of success, which he denies by caricaturing it, and from the need to succeed, which he shows to be dangerous.

The Western hero, by contrast, is a figure of repose. He resembles the gangster in being lonely and to some degree melancholy. But his melancholy comes from the "simple" recognition that life is unavoidably serious, not from the disproportions of his own temperament. And his loneliness is organic, not imposed on him by his situation but belonging to him intimately and testifying to his completeness. The gangster must reject others violently or draw them violently to him. The Westerner is not thus compelled to seek love; he is prepared to accept it, perhaps, but he never asks of it more than it can give, and we see him constantly in situations where love is at best an irrelevance. If there is a woman he loves, she is usually unable to understand his motives; she is against killing and being killed, and he finds it impossible to explain to her that there is no point in being "against" these things: they belong to his world.

Very often this woman is from the East and her failure to understand represents a clash of cultures. In the American mind, refinement, virtue, civilization, Christianity itself, are seen as feminine, and therefore women are often portrayed as possessing some kind of deeper wisdom, while the men, for all their apparent self-assurance, are fundamentally childish. But the West, lacking the graces of civilization, is the place "where men are men"; in Western movies, men have the deeper wisdom and the women are children. Those women in the Western movies who share the hero's understanding of life are prostitutes (or, as they are usually presented, barroom entertainers)—women, that is, who have come to understand in the most practical way how love can be an irrelevance, and therefore "fallen" women. The gangster, too, associates with prostitutes, but for him the important things about a prostitute are her passive availability and her costliness: she is part of his winnings. In Western movies, the important thing about a prostitute is her quasi-masculine independence: nobody owns her, nothing has to be explained to her, and she is not, like a virtuous woman, a "value" that demands to be protected. When the Westerner leaves the prostitute for a virtuous woman—for love—he is in fact forsaking a way of life, though the point of the choice is often obscured by having the prostitute killed by getting into the line of fire.

The Westerner is *par excellence* a man of leisure. Even when he wears the badge of a marshal or, more rarely, owns a ranch, he appears to be unemployed. We see him standing at a bar, or playing poker—a game which expresses perfectly his talent for remaining relaxed in the midst of tension—or perhaps camping out on the plains on some extraordinary errand. If he does own a ranch, it is in the background; we are not actually aware that he owns anything except his horse, his guns, and the one worn suit of clothing which is likely to remain unchanged all through the movie. It comes as a surprise to see him take money from his pocket or an extra shirt from his saddlebags. As a rule we do not even know where he sleeps at night and don't think of asking. Yet it never occurs to us that he is a poor man; there is no poverty in Western movies, and really no wealth either: those great cattle domains and shipments of gold which figure so largely in the plots are moral and not material quantities, not the objects of contention but only its occasion. Possessions too are irrelevant.

Employment of some kind—usually unproductive—is always open to the Westerner, but when he accepts it, it is not because he needs to make a living, much less from any idea of "getting ahead." Where could he want to "get ahead" to? By the time we see him, he is already "there"; he can ride a horse faultlessly, keep his countenance in the face of death, and draw his gun a little faster and shoot it a little straighter than anyone he is likely to meet. These are sharply defined acquirements, giving to the figure of the Westerner an apparent moral clarity which corresponds to the clarity of his physical image against his bare landscape; initially, at any rate, the Western movie presents itself as being without mystery, its whole universe comprehended in what we see on the screen.

Much of this apparent simplicity arises directly from those "cinematic" elements which have long been understood to give the Western theme its special appropriateness for the movies: the wide expanses of land, the free movement of men on horses. As guns constitute the visible moral center of the Western movie, suggesting continually the possibility of violence, so land and horses represent the movie's material basis, its sphere of action. But the land and the horses have also a moral significance: the physical freedom they represent belongs to the moral "openness" of the West—corresponding to the fact that guns are carried where they can be seen. (And, as we shall see, the character of land and horses changes as the Western film becomes more complex.)

The gangster's world is less open, and his arts not so easily identifiable as the Westerner's. Perhaps he too can keep his countenance, but the mask he wears is really no mask: its purpose is precisely to make evident the fact that he desperately wants to "get ahead" and will stop at nothing. Where the Westerner imposes himself by the appearance of unshakable control, the gangster's pre-eminence lies in the suggestion that he may at any moment lose control; his strength is not in being able to shoot faster or straighter than others, but in being more willing to shoot. "Do it first," says Scarface expounding his mode of operation, "and keep on doing it!" With the Westerner, it is a crucial point of honor *not* to "do it first"; his gun remains in its holster until the moment of combat.

There is no suggestion, however, that he draws the gun reluctantly. The Westerner could not fulfill himself if the moment did not finally come when he can shoot his enemy down. But because that moment is so thoroughly the expression of his being, it must be kept pure. He will not violate the accepted forms of combat though by doing so he could save a city. And he can wait. "When you call me that—smile!"—the villain smiles weakly, soon he is laughing with horrible joviality, and the crisis is past. But it is allowed to pass because it must come again: sooner or later Trampas will "make his play," and the Virginian will be ready for him.

What does the Westerner fight for? We know he is on the side of justice and order, and of course it can be said he fights for these things. But such broad aims never correspond exactly to his real motives; they only offer him his opportunity. The Westerner himself, when an explanation is asked of him (usually by a woman), he is likely to say that he does what he "has to do." If justice and order did not continually demand his protection, he would be without a calling. Indeed, we come upon him often in just that situation, as the reign of law settles over the West and he is forced to see that his day is over; those are the pictures which end with his death or with his departure for some more remote frontier. What he defends, at bottom, is the purity of his own image—in fact his honor. This is what makes him invulnerable. When the gangster is killed, his whole life is shown to have been a mistaken, but the image the Westerner seeks to maintain can be presented as clearly in defeat as in victory: he fights not for advantage and not for the right, but to state what he is, and he must live in a world which permits that statement. The Westerner is the last gentleman, and the movies which over and over again tell his story are probably the last art form in which the concept of honor retains its strength.

Of course I do not mean to say that ideas of virtue and justice and courage have gone out of culture. Honor is more than these things: it is a style, concerned with harmonious appearances as much as with desirable consequences, and tending therefore toward the denial of life in favor of art. "Who hath it? he that died o' Wednesday." On the whole, a world that leans to Falstaff's view is a more civilized and even, finally, a more graceful world. It is just the march of civilization that forces the Westerner to move on; and if we actually had to confront the question it might turn out that the woman who refuses to understand him is right as often as she is wrong. But we do not confront the question. Where the Westerner lives it is always about 1870—not the real 1870, either, or the real West—and he is killed or goes away when his position becomes problematical. The fact that he continues to hold our attention is evidence enough that, in his proper frame, he presents an image of personal nobility that is still real for us.

Clearly, this image easily becomes ridiculous: we need only look at William S. Hart or Tom Mix, who in the wooden absoluteness of their virtue represented little that an adult could take seriously; and doubtless such figures as Gene Autry or Roy Rogers are no better, though I confess I have seen none of their movies. Some film enthusiasts claim to find in the early, unsophisticated Westerns a "cinematic purity" that has since been lost; this idea is as valid, and finally as misleading, as T. S. Eliot's statement that *Everyman* is the only play in English that stays within the limitations of art. The truth is that the Westerner comes into the field of serious art only when his moral code, without ceasing to be compelling, is seen also to be imperfect. The Westerner at his best exhibits a moral ambiguity which darkens his image and saves him from absurdity; this ambiguity arises from the fact that, whatever his justifications, he is a killer of men.

In *The Virginian*, which is an archetypal Western movie as *Scarface* or *Little Caesar* are archetypal gangster movies, there is a lynching in which the hero (Gary Cooper), as leader of a posse, must supervise the hanging of his best friend for stealing cattle. With the growth of American "social consciousness," it is no longer possible to present a lynching in the movies unless the point is the illegality and injustice of the lynching itself; *The Ox-Bow Incident*, made in 1943, explicitly puts forward the newer point of view and can be regarded as a kind of "anti-Western." But in 1929, when *The Virginian* was made, the present inhibition about lynching was not yet in force; the justice, and therefore the necessity, of the hanging is never questioned—except by the schoolteacher from the East, whose refusal to understand serves as usual to set forth more sharply the deeper seriousness of the West. The Virginian is thus in a tragic dilemma where one moral absolute conflicts with another and the choice of either must leave a moral stain. If he had chosen to save his friend, he would have violated the image of himself that he had made essential to his existence, and the movie would have had to end with his death, for only by his death could the image have been restored. Having chosen instead to sacrifice his friend to the higher demands of the "code"—the only choice worthy of him, as even the friend understands—he is none the less stained by the killing, but what is needed now to set accounts straight is not his death but the death of the villain Trampas, the leader of the cattle thieves, who had escaped the posse and abandoned the Virginian's friend to his fate. Again the woman intervenes: Why must there be *more* killing? If the hero really loved her, he would leave town, refusing Trampas's challenge. What good will it be if Trampas should kill him? But the Virginian does once more what he "has to do," and in avenging his friend's death wipes out the stain on his own honor. Yet his victory cannot be complete: no death can be paid for and no stain truly wiped out; the movie is still a tragedy, for though the hero escapes with his life, he has been forced to confront the ultimate limits of his moral ideas.

This mature sense of limitation and unavoidable guilt is what gives the Westerner a "right" to his melancholy. It is true that the gangster's story is also a tragedy—in certain formal ways more clearly a tragedy than the Westerner's—but it is a romantic tragedy, based on a hero whose defeat springs with almost mechanical inevitability from the outrageous presumption of his demands: the gangster is *bound* to go on until he is killed. The Westerner is a more classical figure, self-contained and limited to begin with, seeking not to extend his dominion but only to assert his personal value, and his tragedy lies in the fact that even this circumscribed demand cannot be fully realized. Since the Westerner is not a murderer but (most of the time) a man of virtue, and since he is always prepared for defeat, he retains his inner invulnerability and his story need not end with his death (and usually does not); but what we finally respond to is not his victory but his defeat.

Up to a point, it is plain that the deeper seriousness of the good Western films comes from the introduction of a realism, both physical and psychological, that was missing with Tom Mix and William S. Hart. As lines of age have come into Gary Cooper's face since *The Virginian,* so the outlines of the Western movie in general have become less smooth, its background more drab. The sun still beats upon the town, but the camera is likely now to take advantage of this illumination to seek out more closely the shabbiness of buildings and furniture, the loose, worn hang of clothing, the wrinkles and dirt of the faces. Once it has been discovered that the true theme of the Western movie is not the freedom and expansiveness of frontier life, but its limitations, its material bareness, the pressures of obligation, then even the landscape itself ceases to be quite the arena of free movement it once was, but becomes instead a great empty waste, cutting down more often than it exaggerates the stature of the horseman who rides across it. We are more likely now to see the Westerner struggling against the obstacles of the physical world (as in the wonderful scenes on the desert and among the rocks in *The Last Posse*) than carelessly surmounting them. Even the horses, no longer the "friends" of man or the inspired chargers of knight-errantry, have lost much of the moral significance that once seemed to belong to them in their careering across the screen. It seems to me the horses grow tired and stumble more often than they did, and that we see them less frequently at the gallop.

In *The Gunfighter*, a remarkable film of a couple of years ago, the landscape has virtually disappeared. Most of the action takes place indoors, in a cheerless saloon where a tired "bad man" (Gregory Peck) contemplates the waste of his life, to be senselessly killed at the end by a vicious youngster setting off on the same path. The movie is done in cold, quiet tones of gray, and every object in it—faces, clothing, a table, the hero's heavy mustache—is given an air of uncompromising authenticity, suggesting those dim photographs of the nineteenth-century West in which Wyatt Earp, say, turns out to be a blank untidy figure posing awkwardly before some uninteresting building. This "authenticity," to be sure, is only aesthetic; the chief fact about nineteenth-century photographs, to my eyes at any rate, is how stonily they refuse to yield up the truth. But that limitation is just what is needed: by preserving some hint of the rigidity of archaic photography (only in tone and décor, never in composition), *The Gunfighter* can permit us to feel that we are looking at a more "real" West than the one the movies have accustomed us to—harder, duller, less "romantic"—and yet without forcing us outside the boundaries which give the Western movie its validity.

We come upon the hero of *The Gunfighter* at the end of a career in which he has never upheld justice and order, and has been at times, apparently, an actual criminal; in this case, it is clear that the hero has been wrong and the woman who has rejected his way of life has been right. He is thus without any of the larger justifications, and knows himself a ruined man. There can be no question of his "redeeming" himself in any socially constructive way. He is too much the victim of his own reputation to turn marshal as one of his old friends has done, and he is not offered the sentimental solution of a chance to give up his life for some good end; the whole point is that he exists outside the field of social value. Indeed, if we were once allowed to see him in the days of his "success," he might become a figure like the gangster, for his career has been aggressively "anti-social" and the practical problem he faces is the gangster's problem: there will always be somebody trying to kill him. Yet it is obviously absurd to speak of him as "anti-social," not only because we do not see him acting as a criminal, but more fundamentally because we do not see his milieu as a society. Of course it has its "social problems" and a kind of static history: civilization is always just at the point of driving out the old freedom;

there are women and children to represent the possibility of a settled life; and there is the marshal, a bad man turned good, determined to keep at least his area of jurisdiction at peace.   But these elements are not, in fact, a part of the film's "realism," even though they come out of the real history of the West; they belong to the conventions of the form, to that accepted framework which makes the film possible in the first place, and they exist not to provide a standard by which the gunfighter can be judged, but only to set him off.   The true "civilization" of the Western movie is always embodied in an individual, good or bad is more a matter of personal bearing than of social consequences, and the conflict of good and bad is a duel between two men.   Deeply troubled and obviously doomed, the gunfighter is the Western hero still, perhaps all the more because his value must express itself entirely in his own being—in his presence, the way he holds our eyes—and in contradiction to the facts.   No matter what he has done, he *looks* right, and he remains invulnerable because, without acknowledging anyone else's right to judge him, he has judged his own failure and has already assimilated it, understanding—as no one else understands except the marshal and the barroom girl—that he can do nothing but play out the drama of the gun fight again and again until the time comes when it will be he who gets killed.   What "redeems" him is that he no longer believes in this drama and nevertheless will continue to play his role perfectly: the pattern is all.

The proper function of realism in the Western movie can only be to deepen the lines of that pattern.   It is an art form for connoisseurs, where the spectator derives his pleasure from the appreciation of minor variations within the working out of a pre-established order.   One does not want too much novelty: it comes as a shock, for instance, when the hero is made to operate without a gun, as has been done in several pictures (e.g., *Destry Rides Again*), and our uneasiness is allayed only when he is finally compelled to put his "pacifism" aside.   If the hero can be shown to be troubled, complex, fallible, even eccentric, or the villain given some psychological taint or, better, some evocative physical mannerism, to shade the colors of his villainy, that is all to the good.   Indeed, that kind of variation is absolutely necessary to keep the type from becoming sterile; we do not want to see the same movie over and over again, only the same form.   But when the impulse toward realism is extended into a "reinterpretation" of the West as a developed society, drawing our eyes away from the hero if only to the extent of showing him as the one dominant figure in a complex social order, then the pattern is broken and the West itself begins to be uninteresting.   If the "social problems" of the frontier are to be the movie's chief concern, there is no longer any point in re-examining these problems twenty times a year; they have been solved, and the people for whom they once were real are dead.   Moreover, the hero himself, still the film's central figure, now tends to become its one unassimilable element, since he is the most "unreal."

The Ox-Bow Incident, by denying the convention of the lynching, presents us with a modern "social drama" and evokes a corresponding response, but in doing so it almost makes the Western setting irrelevant, a mere backdrop of beautiful scenery. (It is significant that *The Ox-Bow Incident* has no hero; a hero would have to stop the lynching or be killed in trying to stop it, and then the "problem" of lynching would no longer be central.) Even in *The Gunfighter* the women and children are a little too much in evidence, threatening constantly to become a real focus of concern instead of simply part of the given framework; and the young tough who kills the hero has too much the air of juvenile criminality: the hero himself could never have been like that, and the idea of a cycle being repeated therefore loses its sharpness. But the most striking example of the confusion created by a too conscientious "social" realism in the celebrated *High Noon*.

In *High Noon* we find Gary Cooper still the upholder of order that he was in *The Virginian*, but twenty-four years older, stooped, slower moving, awkward, his face lined, the flesh sagging, a less beautiful and weaker figure, but with the suggestion of greater depth that belongs almost automatically to age. Like the hero of *The Gunfighter*, he no longer has to assert his character and is no longer interested in the drama of combat; it is hard to imagine that he might once have been so youthful as to say, "When you call me that—smile!" In fact, when we come upon him he is hanging up his guns and his marshal's badge in order to begin a new, peaceful life with his bride, who is a Quaker. But then the news comes that a man he had sent to prison has been pardoned and will get to town on the noon train; three friends of this man have come to wait for him at the station, and when the freed convict arrives the four of them will come to kill the marshal. He is thus trapped; the bride will object, the hero himself will waver much more than he would have done twenty-four years ago, but in the end he will play out the drama because it is what he "has to do." All this belongs to the established form (there is even the "fallen woman" who understands the marshal's position as his wife does not). Leaving aside the crudity of building up suspense by means of the clock, the actual Western drama of *High Noon* is well handled and forms a good companion piece to *The Virginian*, showing in both conception and technique the ways in which the Western movie has naturally developed.

But there is a second drama along with the first. As the marshal sets out to find deputies to help him deal with the four gunmen, we are taken through the various social strata of the town, each group in turn refusing its assistance out of cowardice, malice, irresponsibility, or venality. With this we are in the field of "social drama"—of a very low order, incidentally, altogether unconvincing and displaying a vulgar anti-populism that has marred some other movies of Stanley Kramer's. But the falsity of the "social drama" is less important than the fact that it does not belong in the movie to begin with. The technical problem was to make it necessary for the marshal to face his enemies alone; to explain *why* the other townspeople are not at his side is to raise a question which does not exist in the proper frame of the Western movie, where the hero is "naturally" alone and it is only necessary to contrive the physical absence of those who might be his allies, if any contrivance is needed at all. In addition, though the hero of *High Noon* proves himself a better man than all around him, the actual effect of this contrast is to lessen his stature: he becomes only a rejected man of virtue. In our final glimpse of him, as he rides away through the town where he has spent most of his life without really imposing himself on it, he is a pathetic rather than a tragic figure. And his departure has another meaning as well; the "social drama" has no place for him.

But there is also a different way of violating the Western form. This is to yield entirely to its static quality as legend and to the "cinematic" temptations of its landscape, the horses, the quiet men. John Ford's famous *Stagecoach* (1938) had much of this unhappy preoccupation with style, and the same director's *My Darling Clementine* (1946), a soft and beautiful movie about Wyatt Earp, goes further along the same path, offering indeed a superficial accuracy of historical reconstruction, but so loving in execution as to destroy the outlines of the Western legend, assimilating it to the more sentimental legend of rural America and making the hero a more dangerous Mr. Deeds. (*Powder River*, a recent "routine" Western shamelessly copied from *My Darling Clementine*, is in most ways a better film; lacking the benefit of a serious director, it is necessarily more concerned with drama than with style.)

The highest expression of this aestheticizing tendency is in George Stevens' *Shane*, where the legend of the West is virtually reduced to its essentials and then fixed in the dreamy clarity of a fairy tale. There never was so broad and bare and lovely a landscape as Stevens puts before us, or so unimaginably comfortless a "town" as the little group of buildings on the prairie to which the settlers must come for their supplies and to buy a drink. The mere physical progress of the film following the style of *A Place in the Sun*, is so deliberately graceful that everything seems to be happening at the bottom of a clear lake. The hero (Alan Ladd) is hardly a man at all, but something like the Spirit of the West, beautiful in fringed buckskins. He emerges mysteriously from the plains, breathing sweetness and a melancholy which is no longer simply the Westerner's natural response to experience but has taken on spirituality; and when he has accomplished his mission, meeting and destroying in the black figure of Jack Palance a Spirit of Evil just as metaphysical as his own embodiment of virtue, he fades away again into the more distant West, a man whose "day is over," leaving behind the wondering little boy who might have imagined the whole story. The choice of Alan Ladd to play the leading role is alone an indication of this film's tendency. Actors like Gary Cooper or Gregory Peck are in themselves, as material objects, "realistic," seeming to bear in their bodies and their faces mortality, limitation, the knowledge of good and evil. Ladd is a more "aesthetic" object, with some of the "universality" of a piece of sculpture; his special quality is in his physical smoothness and serenity, unworldly and yet not innocent, but suggesting that no experience can really touch him. Stevens has tried to freeze the Western myth once and for all in the immobility of Alan Ladd's countenance. If *Shane* were "right," and fully successful, it might be possible to say there was no point in making any more Western movies; once the hero is apotheosized, variation and development are closed off.

Shane is not "right," but it is still true that the possibilities of fruitful variation in the Western movie are limited. The form can keep its freshness through endless repetitions only because of the special character of the film medium, where the physical difference between one object and another—above all, between one actor and another—is of such enormous importance, serving the function that is served by the variety of language in the perpetuation of literary types. In this sense, the "vocabulary" of films is much larger than that of literature and falls more readily into pleasing and significant arrangements. (That may explain why the middle levels of excellence are more easily reached in the movies than in literary forms, and perhaps also why the status of the movies as art is constantly being called into question.) But the advantage of this almost automatic particularity belongs to all films alike. Why does the Western movie especially have such a hold on our imagination?

Chiefly, I think, because it offers a serious orientation to the problem of violence such as can be found almost nowhere else in our culture. One of the well-known peculiarities of modern civilized opinion is its refusal to acknowledge the value of violence. This refusal is a virtue, but like many virtues it involves a certain willful blindness and it encourages hypocrisy. We train ourselves to be shocked or bored by cultural images of violence, and our very concept of heroism tends to be a passive one: we are less drawn to the brave young men who kill large numbers of our enemies than to the heroic prisoners who endure torture without capitulating. In art, though we may still be able to understand and participate in the values of the Iliad, a modern writer like Ernest Hemingway we find somewhat embarrassing: there is no doubt that he stirs us, but we cannot help recognizing also that he is a little childish. And in the criticism of popular culture, where the educated observer is usually under the illusion that he has nothing at stake, the presence of images of violence is often assumed to be in itself a sufficient ground for condemnation.

These attitudes, however, have not reduced the element of violence in our culture but, if anything, have helped to free it from moral control by letting it take on the aura of "emancipation." The celebration of acts of violence is left more and more to the irresponsible: on the higher cultural levels to writers like Céline, and lower down to Mickey Spillane or Horace McCoy, or to the comic books, television, and the movies. The gangster movie, with its numerous variations, belongs to this cultural "underground" which sets forth the attractions of violence in the face of all our higher social attitudes. It is a more "modern" genre than the Western, perhaps even more profound, because it confronts industrial society on its own ground—the city—and because, like much of our advanced art, it gains its effects by a gross insistence on its own narrow logic. But it is anti-social, resting on fantasies of irresponsible freedom. If we are brought finally to acquiesce in the denial of these fantasies, it is only because they have been shown to be dangerous, not because they have given way to a better vision of behavior.[1]

In war movies, to be sure, it is possible to present the uses of violence within a framework of responsibility. But there is the disadvantage that modern war is a co-operative enterprise; its violence is largely impersonal, and heroism belongs to the group more than to the individual. The hero of a war movie is most often simply a leader, and his superiority is likely to be expressed in a denial of the heroic: you are not supposed to be brave, you are supposed to get the job done and stay alive (this too, of course, is a kind of heroic posture, but a new—and "practical"—one). At its best, the war movie may represent a more civilized point of view than the Western, and if it were not continually marred by ideological sentimentality we might hope to find it developing into a higher form of drama. But it cannot supply the values we seek in the Western.

Those values are in the image of a single man who wears a gun on his thigh. The gun tells us that he lives in a world of violence, and even that he "believes in violence." But the drama is one of self-restraint: the moment of violence must come in its own time and according to its special laws, or else it is valueless. There is little cruelty in Western movies, and little sentimentality; our eyes are not focused on the sufferings of the defeated but on the deportment of the hero. Really, it is not violence at all which is the "point" of the Western movie, but a certain image of man, a style, which expresses itself most clearly in violence. Watch a child with his toy guns and you will see: what most interests him is not (as we so much fear) the fantasy of hurting others, but to work out how a man might look when he shoots or is shot. A hero is one who looks like a hero.

Whatever the limitations of such an idea in experience, it has always been valid in art, and has a special validity in an art where appearances are everything. The Western hero is necessarily an archaic figure; we do not really believe in him and would not have him step out of his rigidly conventionalized background. But his archaicism does not take away from his power; on the contrary, it adds to it by keeping him just a little beyond the reach both of common sense and of absolutized emotion, the two usual impulses of our art. And he has, after all, his own kind of relevance. He is there to remind us of the possibility of style in an age which has put on itself the burden of pretending that style has no meaning, and, in the midst of our anxieties over the problem of violence, to suggest that even in killing or being killed we are not freed from the necessity of establishing satisfactory modes of behavior. Above all, the movies in which the West-

[1] I am not concerned here with the actual social consequences of gangster movies, though I suspect they could not have been so pernicious as they were thought to be. Some of the compromises introduced to avoid the supposed bad effects of the old gangster movies may be, if anything, more dangerous, for the sadistic violence that once belonged only to the gangster is now commonly enlisted on the side of the law and thus goes undefeated, allowing us (if we wish) to find in the movies a sort of "confirmation" of our fantasies.

erner plays out his role preserve for us the pleasures of a complete and self-contained drama—and one which still effortlessly crosses the boundaries which divide our culture—in a time when other, more consciously serious art forms are increasingly complex, uncertain, and ill-defined.

14 MOVIES ON TELEVISION
Pauline Kael

A few years ago, a jet on which I was returning to California after a trip to New York was instructed to delay landing for a half hour. The plane circled above the San Francisco area, and spread out under me were the farm where I was born, the little town where my grandparents were buried, the city where I had gone to school, the cemetery where my parents were, the homes of my brothers and sisters, Berkeley, where I had gone to college, and the house where at that moment, while I hovered high above, my daughter and my dogs were awaiting my return. It was as though my whole life was suspended in time—as though no matter where you'd gone, what you'd done, the past were all still there, present, if you just got up high enough to attain the proper perspective. Sometimes I get a comparable sensation when I turn from the news programs or the discussion shows on television to the old movies. So much of what formed our tastes and shaped our experiences, and so much of the garbage of our youth that we never thought we'd see again—preserved and exposed to eyes and minds that might well want not to believe that this was an important part of our past. Now these movies are there for new generations, to whom they cannot possibly have the same impact or meaning, because they are all jumbled together, out of historical sequence. Even what may deserve an honorable position in movie history is somehow dishonored by being so available, so meaninglessly present. Everything is in hopeless disorder, and that is the way new generations experience our movie past. In the other arts, something like natural selection takes place: only the best or the most significant or influential or successful works compete for our attention. Moreover, those from the past are likely to be touched up to accord with the taste of the present. In popular music, old tunes are newly orchestrated. A small repertory of plays is continually reinterpreted for contemporary meanings—the great ones for new relevance, the not so great rewritten, tackily "brought up to date," or deliberately treated as period pieces. By contrast, movies, through the accidents of commerce, are sold in blocks or packages to television, the worst with the mediocre and the best, the successes with the failure, the forgotten with the half forgotten, the ones so dreary you

SOURCE: From *Kiss Kiss Bang Bang* by Pauline Kael. Reprinted by permission of Atlantic-Little, Brown and Co. Copyright © 1965, 1966, 1967, 1968 by Pauline Kael; originally appeared in *The New Yorker*.

don't know whether you ever saw them or just others like them with some so famous you can't be sure whether you actually saw them or only imagined what they were like. A lot of this stuff never really made it with any audience; it played in small towns or it was used to soak up the time just the way TV in bars does.

There are so many things that we, having lived through them, or passed over them, never want to think about again. But in movies nothing is cleaned away, sorted out, purposefully discarded. (The destruction of negatives in studio fires or deliberately, to save space, was as indiscriminate as the preservation and resale.) There's a kind of hopelessness about it: what does not deserve to last lasts, and so it all begins to seem one big pile of junk, and some people say, "Movies never really were any good—except maybe the Bogarts." If the same thing had happened in literature or music or painting—if we were constantly surrounded by the piled-up inventory of the past—it's conceivable that modern man's notions of culture and civilization would be very different. Movies, most of them produced as fodder to satisfy the appetite for pleasure and relaxation, turned out to have magical properties—indeed, to be magical properties. This fodder can be fed to people over and over again. Yet, not altogether strangely, as the years wear on it doesn't please their palates, though many will go on swallowing it, just because nothing tastier is easily accessible. Watching old movies is like spending an evening with those people next door. They bore us; and we wouldn't go out of our way to see them; we drop in on them because they're so close. If it took some effort to see old movies, we might try to find out which were the good ones, and if people saw only the good ones maybe they would still respect old movies. As it is, people sit and watch movies that audiences walked out on thirty years ago. Like Lot's wife, we are tempted to take another look, attracted not by evil but by something that seems much more shameful—our own innocence. We don't try to reread the girls' and boys' "series" books of our adolescence—the very look of them is dismaying. The textbooks we studied in grammar school are probably more "dated" than the movies we saw then, but we never look at the old schoolbooks, whereas we keep seeing on TV the movies that represent the same stage in our lives and played much the same part in them—as things we learned from and, in spite of, went beyond.

Not all old movies look bad now, of course; the good ones are still good—surprisingly good, often, if you consider how much of the detail is lost on television. Not only the size but the shape of the image is changed, and, indeed, almost all the specifically visual elements are so distorted as to be all but completely destroyed. On television, a cattle drive or a cavalry charge or a chase—the climax of so many a big movie—loses the dimensions of space and distance that made it exciting, that sometimes made it great. And since the structural elements—the rhythm, the buildup, the suspense—are also partly destroyed by deletions and commercial breaks and the interruptions incidental to home viewing, it's amazing that the bare bones of performance, dialogue, story, good directing, and (especially important for close-range viewing) good editing can still make an old movie more entertaining than almost anything new on television. (That's why old movies are taking over television—or, more accurately, vice versa.) The verbal slapstick of the newspaper-life comedies—*Blessed Event, Roxie Hart, His Girl Friday*—may no longer be fresh (partly because it has been so widely imitated), but it's still funny. Movies with good, fast, energetic talk seem better than ever on television—still not great but, on television, better than what is great. (And as we listen to the tabloid journalists insulting the corrupt politicians, we respond once again to the happy effrontery of that period when the targets of popular satire were still small enough for us to laugh at without choking.) The wit of dialogue comedies like Preston Sturges's *Unfaithfully Yours* isn't much diminished, nor does a tight melodrama like *Double Indemnity* lose a great deal. Movies like Joseph L. Mankiewicz's *A Letter to Three Wives* and *All About Eve* look practically the same on television as in theatres, because they have almost no visual dimensions to lose. In them the camera serves primarily to show us the person who is going to speak the next presumably bright line—a scheme that on television, as in theatres, is acceptable only when the line is bright. Horror and fantasy films like Karl Freund's *The Mummy* or Robert Florey's *The Murders in the Rue Morgue*—even with the loss, through miniaturization, of imaginative special effects—are surprisingly effective, perhaps because they are so primitive in their appeal that the qualities of the imagery matter less than the basic suggestions. Fear counts for more than finesse, and viewing horror films is far more frightening at home than in the shared comfort of an audience that breaks the tension with derision.

Other kinds of movies lose much of what made them worth looking at—the films of Von Sternberg, for example, designed in light and shadow, or the subtleties of Max Ophuls, or the lyricism of Satyajit Ray. In the box the work of these men is not as lively or as satisfying as the plain good movies of lesser directors. Reduced to the dead grays of a cheap television print, Orson Welles' *The Magnificent Ambersons*—an uneven work that is nevertheless a triumphant conquest of the movie medium—is as lifelessly dull as a newspaper wirephoto of a great painting. But when people say of a "big" movie like *High Noon* that it has dated or that it doesn't hold up, what they are really saying is that their judgment was faulty or has changed. They may have overresponded to its publicity and reputation or to its attempt to deal with a social problem or an idea, and may have ignored the banalities surrounding that attempt; now that the idea doesn't seem so daring, they notice the rest. Perhaps it was a traditional drama that was new to them and that they thought was new to the world; everyone's "golden age of movies" is the period of his first moviegoing and just before—what he just missed or wasn't allowed to see. (The Bogart films came out just before today's college kids started going.)

Sometimes we suspect, and sometimes rightly, that our memory has improved a picture—that imaginatively we made it what we knew it could have been or should have been—and, fearing this, we may prefer memory to new contact. We'll remember what it meant to us. The nostalgia we may have poured over a performer or over our recollections of a movie has a way of congealing when we try to renew the contact. But sometimes the experience of reseeing is wonderful—a confirmation of the general feeling that was all that remained with us from childhood. And we enjoy the fresh proof of the rightness of our responses that reseeing the film gives us. We reexperience what we once felt, and memories flood back. Then movies seem magical—all those madeleines waiting to be dipped in tea. What looks bad in old movies is the culture of which they were part and which they expressed—a tone of American life that we have forgotten. When we see First World War posters, we are far enough away from their patriotic primitivism to be amused at the emotions and sentiments to which they appealed. We can feel charmed but superior. It's not so easy to cut ourselves off from old movies and the old selves who responded to them, because they're not an isolated part of the past held up for derision and amusement and wonder. Although they belong to the same world as stories in Liberty, old radio shows, old phonograph records, an America still divided between hayseeds and city slickers, and although they may seem archaic, their pastness isn't so very past. It includes the last decade, last year, yesterday.

Though in advertising movies for TV the recentness is the lure, for many of us what constitutes the attraction is the datedness, and the earlier movies are more compelling than the ones of the fifties or the early sixties. Also, of course, the movies of the thirties and forties look better technically, because, ironically, the competition with television that made movies of the fifties and sixties enlarge their scope and their subject matter has resulted in their looking like a mess in the box—the sides of the image lopped off, the crowds and vistas a boring blur, the color altered, the epic themes incongruous and absurd on the little home screen. In a movie like *The Robe,* the large-scale production values that were depended on to attract TV viewers away from their sets become a negative factor. But even if the quality of the image were improved, these movies are too much like the ones we can see in theatres to be interesting at home. At home, we like to look at those stiff, carefully groomed actors of the thirties, with their clipped, Anglophile stage speech and their regular, clean-cut features—walking profiles, like the figures on Etruscan vases and almost as remote. And there is the faithless wife—how will she decide between her lover and her husband, when they seem as alike as two wax grooms on a wedding cake? For us, all three are doomed not by sin and disgrace but by history. Audiences of the period may have enjoyed these movies for their action, their story, their thrills, their wit, and all this high living. But through our window on the past we see the actors acting out other dramas as well. The Middle European immigrants had children who didn't speak the king's English and, after the Second World War, didn't even respect it so much. A flick of the dial and we are in the fifties amid the slouchers, with their thick lips, shapeless noses, and shaggy haircuts, waiting to say their lines until they think them out, then mumbling something that is barely speech. How long, O Warren Beatty, must we wait before we turn back to beautiful stick figures like Phillips Holmes?

We can take a shortcut through the hell of many lives, turning the dial from the social protest of the thirties to the films of the same writers and directors in the fifties—full of justifications for blabbing, which they shifted onto characters in oddly unrelated situations. We can see in the films of the forties the displaced artists of Europe—the anti-Nazi exiles like Conrad Veidt, the refugees like Peter Lorre, Fritz Kortner, and Alexander Granach. And what are they playing? Nazis, of course, because they have accents, and so for Americans—for the whole world—they become images of Nazi brutes. Or we can look at the patriotic sentiments of the Second World War years and those actresses, in their orgies of ersatz nobility, giving their lives—or, at the very least, their bodies—to save their country. It was sickening at the time; it's perversely amusing now—part of the spectacle of our common culture.

Probably in a few years some kid watching *The Sandpiper* on television will say what I recently heard a kid say about *Mrs Miniver:* "And to think they really believed it in those days." Of course, we didn't accept nearly as much in old movies as we may now fear we did. Many of us went to see big-name pictures just as we went to *The Night of the Iguana,* without believing a minute of it. The James Bond pictures are not to be "believed," but they tell us a lot about the conventions that audiences now accept, just as the confessional films of the thirties dealing with sin and illegitimacy and motherhood tell us about the sickly-sentimental tone of American entertainment in the midst of the Depression. Movies indicate what the producers thought people would pay to see—which was not always the same as what they would pay to see. Even what they enjoyed seeing does not tell us directly what they believed but only indirectly hints at the tone and style of a culture. There is no reason to assume that people twenty or thirty years ago were stupider than they are now. (Consider how we may be judged by people twenty years from now looking at today's movies.) Though it may not seem obvious to us now, part of the original appeal of old movies— which we certainly understood and responded to as children—was that, despite their sentimental tone, they helped to form the liberalized modern consciousness. This trash—and most of it was, and is, trash—probably taught us more about the world, and even about values, than our "education" did. Movies broke down barriers of all kinds, opened up the world, helped to make us aware. And they were almost always on the side of the mistreated, the socially despised. Almost all drama is. And, because movies were a mass medium, they had to be on the side of the poor.

Nor does it necessarily go without saying that the glimpses of something really good even in mediocre movies—the quickening of excitement at a great performance, the discovery of beauty in a gesture or a phrase or an image—made us understand the meaning of art as our teachers in art-appreciation courses never could. And—what is more difficult for those who are not movie lovers to grasp—even after this sense of the greater and the higher is developed, we still do not want to live only on the heights. We still want that pleasure of discovering things for ourselves; we need the sustenance of the ordinary, the commonplace, the almost-good as part of the anticipatory atmosphere. And though it all helps us to respond to the moments of greatness, it is not only for this that we want it. The educated person who became interested in cinema as an art form through Bergman or Fellini or Resnais is an alien to me (and my mind goes blank with hostility and indifference when he begins to talk). There isn't much for the art-cinema person on television; to look at a great movie, or even a poor movie carefully designed in terms of textures and contrasts, on television is, in general, maddening, because those movies lose too much. (Educational television, though, persists in this misguided effort to bring the television viewer movie classics.) There are few such movies anyway. But there are all the not-great movies, which we probably wouldn't bother going to see in museums or in theatre revivals—they're just not that important. Seeing them on television is a different kind of experience, with different values—partly because the movie past hasn't been filtered to conform to anyone's convenient favorite notions of film art. We make our own, admittedly small, discoveries or rediscoveries. There's Dan Dailey doing his advertising-wise number in *It's Always Fair Weather,* or Gene Kelly and Fred Astaire singing and dancing "The Babbitt and the Bromide" in Ziegfeld Follies. And it's like putting on a record of Ray Charles singing "Georgia on My Mind" or Frank Sinatra singing "Bim Bam Baby" or Elisabeth Schwarzkopf singing operetta, and feeling again the elation we felt the first time. Why should we deny these pleasures because there are other, more complex kinds of pleasure possible? It's true that these pleasures don't deepen, and that they don't change us, but maybe that is part of what makes them seem our own—we realize that we have some emotions and responses that don't change as we get older.

People who see a movie for the first time on television don't remember it the same way that people do who saw it in a theatre. Even without the specific visual loss that results from the transfer to another medium, it's doubtful whether a movie could have as intense an impact as it had in its own time. Probably by definition, works that are not truly great cannot be as compelling out of their time. Sinclair Lewis's and Hemingway's novels were becoming archaic while their authors lived. Can *On the Waterfront* have the impact now that it had in 1954? Not quite. And revivals in movie theatres don't have the same kind of charge, either. There's something a little stale in the air, there's a different kind of audience. At a revival, we must allow for the period, or care because of the period. Television viewers seeing old movies for the first time can have very little sense of how and why new stars moved us when they appeared, of the excitement of new themes, of what these movies meant to us. They don't even know which were important in their time, which were "hits."

But they can discover something in old movies, and there are few discoveries to be made on dramatic shows produced for television. In comedies, the nervous tic of canned laughter neutralizes everything; the laughter is as false for the funny as for the un-funny and prevents us from responding to either. In general, performances in old movies don't suffer horribly on television except from cuts, and what kindles something like the early flash fire is the power of personality that comes through in those roles that made a star. Today's high-school and college students seeing *East of Eden* and *Rebel Without a Cause* for the first time are almost as caught up in James Dean as the first generation or adolescent viewers was, experiencing that tender, romantic, marvellously masochistic identification with the boy who does everything wrong because he cares so much. And because Dean died young and hard, he is not just another actor who outlived his myth and became ordinary in stale roles—he is the symbol of misunderstood youth. He is inside the skin of moviegoing and television-watching youth—even educated youth—in a way that Keats and Shelley or John Cornford and Julian Bell are not. Youth can respond—though not so strongly—to many of our old heroes and heroines: to Gary Cooper, say, as the elegant, lean, amusingly silent romantic loner of his early Western and aviation films. (And they can more easily ignore the actor who sacrificed that character for blubbering righteous bathos.) Bogart found his myth late, and Dean fulfilled the romantic myth of self-destructiveness, so they look good on television. More often, television, by showing us actors before and after their key starring roles, is a myth-killer. But it keeps acting ability alive.

There is a kind of young television watcher seeing old movies for the first time who is surprisingly sensitive to their values and responds almost with the intensity of a moviegoer. But he's different from the moviegoer. For one thing, he's housebound, inactive, solitary. Unlike a moviegoer, he seems to have no need to discuss what he sees. The kind of television watcher I mean (and the ones I've met are all boys) seems to have extreme empathy with the material in the box (new TV shows as well as old movies, though rarely news), but he may not know how to enter into a conversation, or even how to come into a room or go out of it. He fell in love with his baby-sitter, so he remains a baby. He's unusually polite and intelligent, but in a mechanical way—just going through the motions, without interest. He gives the impression that he wants to withdraw from this human interference and get back to his real life—the box. He is like a prisoner who has everything he wants in prison and is content to stay there. Yet, oddly, he and his fellows seem to be tuned in to each other; just as it sometimes seems that even a teen-ager locked in a closet would pick up the new dance steps at the same moment as other teen-agers, these television watchers react to the same things at the same time. If they can find more intensity in this box than in their own living, then this box can provide constantly what we got at the movies only a few times a week. Why should they move away from it, or talk, or go out of the house, when they will only experience that as a loss? Of course, we can see why they should, and their inability to make connections outside is frighteningly suggestive of ways in which we, too, are cut off. It's a matter of degree. If we stay up half the night to watch old movies and can't face the next day, it's partly, at least, because of the fascination of our own movie past; they live in a past they never had, like people who become obsessed by places they have only imaginative connections with—Brazil, Venezuela, Arabia Deserta. Either way, there is always something a little shameful about living in the past; we feel guilty, stupid—as if the pleasure we get needed some justification that we can't provide.

For some moviegoers, movies probably contribute to that self-defeating romanticizing of expectations which makes life a series of disappointments. They watch the same movies over and over on television, as if they were constantly returning to the scene of the crime—the life they were so busy dreaming about that they never lived it. They are paralyzed by longing, while those less romantic can leap the hurdle. I heard a story the other day about a man who ever since his school days had been worshipfully "in love with" a famous movie star, talking about her, fantasizing about her, following her career, with its up and downs and its stormy romances and marriages to producers and agents and wealthy sportsmen and rich businessmen. Though he became successful himself, it never occurred to him that he could enter her terrain—she was so glamorously above him. Last week, he got a letter from an old classmate, to whom, years before, he had confided his adoration of the star; the classmate—an unattractive guy who had never done anything with his life and had a crummy job in a crummy business—had just married her.

Movies are a combination of art and mass medium, but television is so single in its purpose—selling—that it operates without that painful, poignant mixture of aspiration and effort and compromise. We almost never think of calling a television show "beautiful," or even of complaining about the absence of beauty, because we take it for granted that television operates without beauty. When we see on television photographic records of the past, like the pictures of Scott's Antarctic expedition or those series on the First World War, they seem almost too strong for the box, too pure for it. The past has a terror and a fascination and a beauty beyond almost anything else. We are looking at the dead, and they move and grin and wave at us; it's an almost unbearable experience. When our wonder and our grief are interrupted or followed by a commercial, we want to destroy the ugly box. Old movies don't tear us apart like that. They do something else, which we can take more of and more easily: they give us a sense of the passage of life. Here is Elizabeth Taylor as a plump matron and here, an hour later, as an exquisite child. That charmingly petulant little gigolo with the skinny face and the mustache that seems the most substantial part of him— can he have developed into the great Laurence Olivier? Here is Orson Welles as a young man, playing a handsome old man, and here is Orson Welles as he has really aged. Here are Bette Davis and Charles Boyer traversing the course of their lives from ingenue and juvenile, through major roles, into character parts—

back and forth, endlessly, embodying the good and bad characters of many styles, many periods. We see the old character actors put out to pasture in television serials, playing gossipy neighbors or grumpy grandpas, and then we see them in their youth or middle age, in the roles that made them famous—and it's startling to find how good they were, how vital, after we've encountered them caricaturing themselves, feeding off their old roles. They have almost nothing left of that young actor we responded to—and still find ourselves responding to—except the distinctive voice and a few crotchets. There are those of us who, when we watch old movies, sit there murmuring the names as the actors appear (Florence Bates, Henry Daniell, Ernest Thesiger, Constance Collier, Edna May Oliver, Douglas Fowley), or we recognize them but can't remember their names, yet know how well we once knew them, though I cannot remember the names of my childhood companions or of the prizefighter I once dated, or even of the boy who took me to the senior prom. We are eager to hear again that line we know is coming. We hate to miss anything. Our memories are jarred by cuts. We want to see the movie to the end.

The graveyard of *Our Town* affords such a tiny perspective compared to this. Old movies on television are a gigantic, panoramic novel that we can tune in to and out of. People watch avidly for a few weeks or months or years and then give up; others tune in when they're away from home in lonely hotel rooms, or regularly, at home, a few nights a week or every night. The rest of the family may ignore the passing show, may often interrupt, because individual lines of dialogue or details of plot hardly seem to matter as they did originally. A movie on television is no longer just a drama in itself; it is part of a huge ongoing parade. To a new generation, what does it matter if a few gestures and a nuance are lost, when they know they can't watch the parade on all the channels at all hours anyway? It's like traffic on the street. The television generation knows there is no end; it all just goes on. When television watchers are surveyed and asked what kind of programming they want or how they feel television can be improved, some of them not only have no answers but can't understand the questions. What they get on their sets is television—that's it.

B

From the "Survival of the Fittest" to the Survival of Us All

Another of today's most pressing concerns is the transformation of the natural environment by the necessities of modern industrial society. The issue of pollution challenges the issues of race relations and the Vietnam War for primacy, and a renewed interest in natural ways marks the generation of today. This interest is expressed in the use of organically grown foods, in the reading of the *Whole Earth Catalog,* and in the return to rural subsistence living, in private isolation in Alaska or in communes in various parts of the country. Even persons who eat supermarket food and work at the same old desk now talk glibly about ecology and conservation. These ideas, which formerly were the property of the National Park Service or the Sierra Club, have become commonplace. As the concepts have spread, spokesmen for them have become more concerned with the survival of life on this planet.

It is in this context that the role of the conservationist will be considered. We contend that the role has changed from mystic to scientist to Cassandra and that this change is illustrated by three men—John Muir, Aldo Leopold, and Paul Ehrlich, all outstanding advocates of conservation. Each considered man's relation to nature differently, although the later naturalists incorporated ideas of the earlier ones. Each reflects the value assumptions of his time. Each sets out goals and means to reach these goals.

John Muir was the most significant publicist of the idea of the American wilderness at the beginning of the twentieth century. He arrived at this position after a long journey. Muir was born in Scotland but emigrated to the United States with his parents in 1849. The family settled on a farm in central Wisconsin. Muir worked at various trades and attended the University of Wisconsin for two and one half years, but he changed his career plans drastically when an industrial accident almost blinded him. At this crucial juncture, Muir became a wanderer in America's wildernesses. He walked a thousand miles from Indiana to the Gulf of Mexico. He then went west to California and found his natural home, the Sierras. There he began to write, soon achieving fame. He used this

169

fame to preach the message of conservation of the natural environment for spiritual purposes. Muir not only wrote about the wilderness; he was a pioneer in the movement to preserve it. He lobbied to make a national park out of an area in the King's river region, was the basic planner for Yosemite National Park, and was one of the original founders of the Sierra Club, now one of the oldest and most prestigious conservation groups in the United States. Muir early bridged the gap between those who wanted to conserve national resources but also to permit selected exploitation—timber harvesting and livestock grazing—and those who wished no introduction of lumberer or drover at the start. By 1898, however, he was won over to the no-development position. Muir later also helped to gain national park status for the Grand Canyon.

Selection 15 concerns Muir's fight to prevent the damming of Hetch Hetchy Valley in Yosemite Park, one of his last battles. In this selection his ideas are poetically expressed and quasi-religious, resembling the ideas of Emerson, whom Muir had met and admired. The conservationist is described by Muir as one who intuits moral values directly from nature. Man should live to achieve a natural harmony; he should eschew the benefits of civilization; he should not interfere with the environment. Muir, speaking in terms of a nineteenth-century aesthetic, believed it was appropriate to use senses other than reason to appreciate the remaining elements of the American wilderness. He also urged preservation because the natural world reflected God's beneficence.

Aldo Leopold was a pioneer in constructing the intellectual underpinning of the science of ecology. Born in Iowa, Leopold was educated at Yale. Following his graduation, he remained another year at the Forestry School in order to qualify for the United States Forest Service. He joined the service and was first assigned to the Southwest, Arizona and New Mexico. In this, and in subsequent assignments, Leopold specialized in game preservation and recreation. He spent nine years in the Forest Service, resigned and served as secretary of the Alburquerque Chamber of Commerce for a year, and then rejoined the Forest Service. Here he was converted to a Muirlike position on keeping the National Forests alive. In 1924, Leopold went to Madison, Wisconsin to become assistant director of the Forest Service's Forest Products Laboratory. Leopold continued to write articles promoting the wilderness concept and calling for the preservation of specific threatened areas, such as the Gila Wilderness Reservation.

In the 1930s, Leopold became a specialist in game management for the University of Wisconsin and a proponent of ecology. Roderick Nash in *Wilderness and the American Mind* attributes the latter change to a vacation trip to the Sierra Madre in Mexico. Nash quotes Leopold as saying, "It was here that I first clearly realized that land is an organism, that all my life I had seen only sick land, whereas here was a biota still in perfect aboriginal health." Now Leopold had gone beyond Muir. Preservation of the wilderness was not to provide just an escape from the pressures of civilization. It was also to demonstrate how all land should be. From this example, man could derive an ethic that encompassed land use and man's relation to other living things.

Selection 16, entitled "The Round River," represents Leopold's later thinking. In it, Leopold speaks in terms almost as poetic as Muir, but he conceives of the conservationist as one who must restore man to a proper place in nature everywhere. Leopold seems as religious as Muir, but without transcendental or metaphysical overtones. There is a sense of harmony that Leopold finds not only in the wilderness but also in cultivated areas when man truly joins the biotic community. There is still a sense of optimism in the work; Leopold believes that the conservationist is an educator who will see the triumph of knowledge over ignorance. Further, there is the confidence, inspired by scientific training, that man will take the path of ecological sanity.

Selection 17 was written by Dr. Paul H. Ehrlich, a contemporary scientist. He represents a more recent point of view that we are rapidly approaching the crisis point on this planet, that the problem is no longer whether the wilderness can be saved to provide moral uplift or whether a proper land ethic can be developed. The question is, can man survive? The title of Barry Commoner's book is most appropriate, *Science and Survival.*

Dr. Ehrlich's career pattern differs from those of Muir and Leopold. Like Leopold, Ehrlich is associated with a university, but he did not come to the university as a game-management expert. He is typical of a generation of professors who had a highly trained, professional scientific background. Ehrlich, who is professor of biology and director of graduate study for the department of biological sciences at Stanford, has earned a scholarly reputation as a population biologist. He has written books aimed at mass audiences and designed as calls to action. His most famous one is *The Population Bomb,* which sees population expansion as the major cause of pollution. Unlike Muir and Leopold, Ehrlich starts with man's propensity to reproduce himself. It is this conception that is the most strikingly modern.

Selection 17 is entitled "Eco-Catastrophe" and is a fictional account of a future happening. It is pessimistic in tone, reflecting Ehrlich's view that man's life on earth can end soon. It does not share the peace found in Muir's Hetch Hetchy Valley or in Leopold's Round River. The concept of nature and man coexisting in mutual harmony is lacking in "Eco-Catastrophe." The style is not poetic; it is instead the style of a scientific report containing statistical projections and inter-acting variables. It reflects the author who, as a scientist, provides the answer regardless of its emotional cost.

The article shows the conservationist in a new role. He is still the educator, but his means are not those of persuasion. Rather, they are those of threats of disaster. Time is short; the sense of urgency is most compelling. The ecologist has become Cassandra, and he demands attention. Recent American society has given its scientists much esteem, but has failed to listen when these same scientists attempt to influence public policy. It remains to be seen whether Ehrlich or others can change this tendency. Perhaps the ultimate irony would occur if Ehrlich's attempt to prevent ecological disaster were no more effective, despite his professional credentials, than were those of the amateur naturalist, John Muir, to save Hetch Hetchy.

15 HETCH HETCHY VALLEY

John Muir

Yosemite is so wonderful that we are apt to regard it as an exceptional creation, the only valley of its kind in the world; but Nature is not so poor as to have only one of anything. Several other yosemites have been discovered in the Sierra that occupy the same relative positions on the range and were formed by the same forces in the same kind of granite. One of these, the Hetch Hetchy Valley, is in the Yosemite National Park about twenty miles from Yosemite and is easily accessible to all sorts of travelers by a road and trail that leaves the Big Oak Flat Road at Bronson Meadows a few miles below Crane Flat, and to the mountaineers by way of Yosemite Creek basin and the head of the middle fork of the Tuolumne.[1]

It is said to have been discovered by Joseph Screech, a hunter, in 1850, a year before the discovery of the great Yosemite. After my first visit to it in the autumn of 1871, I have always called it the "Tuolumne Yosemite," for it is a wonderfully exact counterpart of the Merced Yosemite, not only in its sublime rocks and waterfalls but in the gardens, groves and meadows of its flowery park-like floor. The floor of Yosemite is about 4000 feet above the sea; the Hetch Hetchy floor about 3700 feet. And as the Merced River flows through Yosemite, so does the Tuolumne through Hetch Hetchy. The walls of both are of gray granite, rise abruptly from the floor, are sculptured in the same style and in both every rock is a glacier monument.

Standing boldly out from the south wall is a strikingly picturesque rock called by the Indians, Kolana, the outermost of a group 2300 feet high, corresponding with the Cathedral Rocks of Yosemite both in relative position and form. On the opposite side of the Valley, facing Kolana, there is a counterpart of the El Capitan that rises sheer and plain to a height of 1800 feet, and over its massive brow flows a stream which makes the most graceful fall I have ever seen. From the edge of the cliff to the top of an earthquake talus it is perfectly free in the air for a thousand feet before it is broken into cascades among talus boulders. It is in all its glory in June, when the snow is melting fast, but fades and vanishes toward the end of summer. The only fall I know with which it may fairly be compared is the Yosemite Bridal Veil; but it excels even that favorite fall both in

SOURCE: From John Muir, *The Yosemite* (New York: The Century Company, 1912).

[1] Hetch Hetchy Valley is flooded by a reservoir. The dam is reached by auto from the Big Oak Flat highway, via Mather.

height and airy-fairy beauty and behavior. Lowlanders are apt to suppose that mountain streams in their wild career over cliffs lose control of themselves and tumble in a noisy chaos of mist and spray. On the contrary, on no part of their travels are they more harmonious and self-controlled. Imagine yourself in Hetch Hetchy on a sunny day in June, standing waist-deep in grass and flowers (as I have often stood), while the great pines sway dreamily with scarcely perceptible motion. Looking northward across the Valley you see a plain, gray granite cliff rising abruptly out of the gardens and groves to a height of 1800 feet, and in front of it Tueeulala's silvery scarf burning with irised sun-fire. In the first white outburst at the head there is abundance of visible energy, but it is speedily hushed and con-cealed in divine repose, and its tranquil progress to the base of the cliff is like that of a downy feather in a still room. Now observe the fineness and marvelous distinct-ness of the various sun-illumined fabrics into which the water is woven; they sift and float from form to form down the face of that grand gray rock in so leisurely and unconfused a manner that you can examine their texture, and patterns and tones of color as you would a piece of embroidery held in the hand. Toward the top of the fall you see groups of booming, comet-like masses, their solid, white heads separate, their tails like combed silk interlacing among delicate gray and purple shadows, ever forming and dissolving, worn out by friction in their rush through the air. Most of these vanish a few hundred feet below the summit, changing to varied forms of cloud-like drapery. Near the bottom the width of the fall has increased from about twenty-five feet to a hundred feet. Here it is composed of yet finer tissues, and is still without a trace of disorder—air, water and sunlight woven into stuff that spirits might wear.

So fine a fall might well seem sufficient to glorify any valley; but here, as in Yosemite, Nature seems in nowise moderate, for a short distance to the eastward of Tueeulala booms and thunders the great Hetch Hetchy Fall, Wapama, so near that you have both of them in full view from the same standpoint. It is the counterpart of the Yosemite Fall, but has a much greater volume of water, is about 1700 feet in height, and appears to be nearly vertical, though considerably inclined, and is dashed into huge outbounding bosses of foam on projecting shelves and knobs. No two falls could be more unlike—Tueeulala out in the open sunshine descending like thistledown; Wapama in a jagged, shadowy gorge roaring and thundering, pounding its way like an earthquake avalanche.

Besides this glorious pair there is a broad, massive fall on the main river a short distance above the head of the Valley. Its position is something like that of the Vernal in Yosemite, and its roar as it plunges into a surging trout-pool may be heard a long way, though it is only about twenty feet high. On Ranch-eria Creek, a large stream, corresponding in position with the Yosemite Tenaya Creek, there is a chain of cascades joined here and there with swift flashing plumes like the one between the Vernal and Nevada Falls, making magnificent shows as they go their glacier-sculptured way, sliding, leaping, hurrahing, covered with crisp clashing spray made glorious with sifting sunshine. And besides all these a few small streams come over the walls at wide intervals, leaping from ledge to ledge with bird-like song and watering many a hidden cliff-garden and fernery, but they are too unshowy to be noticed in so grand a place.

The correspondence between the Hetch Hetchy walls in their trends, sculpture, physical structure, and general arrangement of the main rock-masses and those of the Yosemite Valley has excited the wondering admiration of every observer. We have seen that the El Capitan and Cathedral Rocks occupy the same relative positions in both valleys; so also do their Yosemite points and North Domes. Again, that part of the Yosemite north wall immediately to the east of the Yosemite Fall has two horizontal benches, about 500 and 1500 feet above the floor, timbered with golden-cup oak. Two benches similarly situated and timbered occur on the same relative portion of the Hetch Hetchy north wall, to the east of Wapama Fall, and on no other. The Yosemite is bounded at the head by the great Half Dome. Hetch Hetchy is bounded in the same way, though its head rock is incomparably less wonderful and sublime in form.

The floor of the Valley is about three and a half miles long, and from a fourth to half a mile wide. The lower portion is mostly a level meadow about a mile long, with the trees restricted to the sides and the river banks, and partially separated from the main, upper, forested portion by a low bar of glacier-polished granite across which the river breaks in rapids.

The principal trees are the yellow and sugar pines, digger pine, incense cedar, Douglas spruce, silver fir, the California and golden-cup oaks, balsam cottonwood, Nuttall's flowering dogwood, alder, maple, laurel, tumion, etc.[2] The most abundant and influential are the great yellow or silver pines like those of Yosemite, the tallest over two hundred feet in height, and the oaks assembled in magnificent groves with massive rugged trunks four to six feet in diameter, and broad, shady, wide-spreading heads. The shrubs forming conspicuous flowery clumps and tangles are manzanita, azalea, spiraea, brier-rose, several species of ceanothus, calycanthus, philadelphus, wild cherry, etc.; with abundance of showy and fragrant herbaceous plants growing about them or out in the open in beds by themselves— lilies, Mariposa tulips, brodiaeas, orchids, iris, spraguea, draperia, collomia, collinsia, castilleja, nemophila, larkspur, columbine, goldenrods, sunflowers, mints of many species, honeysuckle, etc. Many fine ferns dwell here also, especially the beautiful and interesting rock-ferns—pellaea, and cheilanthes of several species— fringing and rosetting dry rock-piles and ledges; woodwardia and asplenium[3] on damp spots with fronds six or seven feet high; the delicate maidenhair in mossy nooks by the falls, and the sturdy, broad-shouldered pteris[4] covering nearly all the dry ground beneath the oaks and pines.

It appears, therefore, that Hetch Hetchy Valley, far from being a plain, com-

[2] Douglas spruce: Douglas Fir. California oak: California black oak. Balsam cottonwood: Black cottonwood. Tumion: California nutmeg, Torreya californica.
[3] Athyrium.
[4] Pteridium.

mon, rock-bound meadow, as many who have not seen it seem to suppose, is a grand landscape garden, one of Nature's rarest and most precious mountain temples. As in Yosemite, the sublime rocks of its walls seem to glow with life, whether leaning back in repose or standing erect in thoughtful attitudes, giving welcome to storms and calms alike, their brows in the sky, their feet set in the groves and gay flowery meadows, while birds, bees, and butterflies help the river and waterfalls to stir all the air into music—things frail and fleeting and types of permanence meeting here and blending, just as they do in Yosemite, to draw her lovers into close and confiding communion with her.

Sad to say, this most precious and sublime feature of the Yosemite National Park, one of the greatest of all our natural resources for the uplifting joy and peace and health of the people, is in danger of being dammed and made into a reservoir to help supply San Francisco with water and light, thus flooding it from wall to wall and burying its gardens and groves one or two hundred feet deep. This grossly destructive commercial scheme has long been planned and urged (though water as pure and abundant can be got from sources outside of the people's park, in a dozen different places), because of the comparative cheapness of the dam and of the territory which it is sought to divert from the great uses to which it was dedicated in the Act of 1890 establishing the Yosemite National Park.

The making of gardens and parks goes on with civilization all over the world, and they increase both in size and number as their value is recognized. Everybody needs beauty as well as bread, places to play in and pray in, where Nature may heal and cheer and give strength to body and soul alike. This natural beauty-hunger is made manifest in the little windowsill gardens of the poor, though perhaps only a geranium slip in a broken cup, as well as in the carefully tended rose and lily gardens of the rich, the thousands of spacious city parks and botanical gardens, and in our magnificent National Parks—the Yellowstone, Yosemite, Sequoia, etc.—Nature's sublime wonderlands, the admiration and joy of the world. Nevertheless, like anything else worth while, from the very beginning, however well guarded, they have always been subject to attack by despoiling gain-seekers and mischief-makers of every degree from Satan to Senators, eagerly trying to make everything immediately and selfishly commercial, with schemes disguised in smug-smiling philanthropy, industriously, sham-piously crying, "Conservation, conservation, panutilization," that man and beast may be fed and the dear Nation made great. Thus long ago a few enterprising merchants utilized the Jerusalem temple as a place of business instead of a place of prayer, changing money, buying and selling cattle and sheep and doves; and earlier still, the first forest reservation, including only one tree, was likewise despoiled. Ever since the establishment of the Yosemite National Park, strife has been going on around its borders and I suppose this will go on as part of the universal battle between right and wrong, however much its boundaries may be shorn, or its wild beauty destroyed.

The first application to the Government by the San Francisco Supervisors for the commercial use of Lake Eleanor and the Hetch Hetchy Valley was made in 1903, and on December 22nd of that year it was denied by the Secretary of the Interior, Mr. Hitchcock, who truthfully said:

> *Presumably the Yosemite National Park was created such by law because of the natural objects of varying degrees of scenic importance located within its boundaries, inclusive alike of its beautiful small lakes, like Eleanor, and its majestic wonders, like Hetch Hetchy and Yosemite Valley. It is the aggregation of such natural scenic features that makes the Yosemite Park a wonderland which the Congress of the United States sought by law to reserve for all coming time as nearly as practicable in the condition fashioned by the hand of the Creator—a worthy object of National pride and a source of healthful pleasure and rest for the thousands of people who may annually sojourn there during the heated months.*

In 1907 when Mr. Garfield became Secretary of the Interior the application was renewed and granted; but under his successor, Mr. Fisher, the matter has been referred to a Commission, which as this volume goes to press still has it under consideration.

The most delightful and wonderful camp-grounds in the Park are its three great valleys—Yosemite, Hetch Hetchy, and Upper Tuolumne; and they are also the most important places with reference to their positions relative to the other great features—the Merced and Tuolumne Canyons, and the High Sierra peaks and glaciers, etc., at the head of the rivers. The main part of the Tuolumne Valley is a spacious flowery lawn four or five miles long, surrounded by magnificent snowy mountains, slightly separated from other beautiful meadows, which together make a series about twelve miles in length, the highest reaching to the feet of Mount Dana, Mount Gibbs, Mount Lyell and Mount McClure. It is about 8500 feet above the sea, and forms the grand central High Sierra camp-ground from which excursions are made to the noble mountains, domes, glaciers, etc.; across the Range to the Mono Lake and volcanoes and down the Tuolumne Canyon to Hetch Hetchy. Should Hetch Hetchy be submerged for a reservoir, as proposed, not only would it be utterly destroyed, but the sublime canyon way to the heart of the High Sierra would be hopelessly blocked and the great camping-ground, as the watershed of a city drinking system, virtually would be closed to the public. So far as I have learned, few of all the thousands who have seen the park and seek rest and peace in it are in favor of this outrageous scheme.

One of my later visits to the Valley was made in the autumn of 1907 with the late William Keith, the artist. The leaf-colors were then ripe, and the great god-like rocks in repose seemed to glow with life. The artist, under their spell, wandered day after day along the river and through the groves and gardens, studying the wonderful scenery; and, after making about forty sketches, declared with enthusiasm that although its walls were less sublime in height, in picturesque beauty and charm Hetch Hetchy surpassed even Yosemite.

That anyone would try to destroy such a place seems incredible; but sad experience shows that there are people good enough and bad enough for anything. The proponents of the dam scheme bring forward a lot of bad arguments to prove that the only righteous thing to do with the people's parks is to destroy them bit by bit as they are able. Their arguments are curiously like those of the devil, devised for the destruction of the first garden—so much of the very best Eden fruit going to waste; so much of the best Tuolumne water and Tuolumne scenery going to waste. Few of their statements are even partly true, and all are mis-leading.

Thus, Hetch Hetchy, they say, is a "low-lying meadow." On the contrary, it is a high-lying natural landscape garden, as the photographic illustrations show.

"It is a common minor feature, like thousands of others." On the contrary it is a very uncommon feature; after Yosemite, the rarest and in many ways the most important in the National Park.

"Damming and submerging it 175 feet deep would enhance its beauty by forming a crystal-clear lake." Landscape gardens, places of recreation and worship, are never made beautiful by destroying and burying them. The beautiful sham lake, forsooth, would be only an eyesore, a dismal blot on the landscape, like many others to be seen in the Sierra. For, instead of keeping it at the same level all the year, allowing Nature centuries of time to make new shores, it would, of course, be full only a month or two in the spring, when the snow is melting fast; then it would be gradually drained, exposing the slimy sides of the basin and shallower parts of the bottom, with the gathered drift and waste, death and decay of the upper basins, caught here instead of being swept on to decent natural burial along the banks of the river or in the sea. Thus the Hetch Hetchy dam-lake would be only a rough imitation of a natural lake for a few of the spring months, an open sepulcher for the others.

"Hetch Hetchy water is the purest of all to be found in the Sierra, unpolluted, and forever unpollutable." On the contrary, excepting that of the Merced below Yosemite, it is less pure than that of most of the other Sierra streams, because of the sewerage of campgrounds draining into it, especially of the Big Tuolumne Meadows camp-ground, occupied by hundreds of tourists and mountaineers, with their animals, for months every summer, soon to be followed by thousands from all the world.

These temple destroyers, devotees of ravaging commercialism, seem to have a perfect contempt for Nature, and, instead of lifting their eyes to the God of the mountains, lift them to the Almighty Dollar.

Dam Hetch Hetchy! As well dam for water-tanks the people's cathedrals and churches, for no holier temple has ever been consecrated by the heart of man.

16 THE ROUND RIVER
Aldo Leopold

One of the marvels of early Wisconsin was the Round River, a river that
flowed into itself, and thus sped around and around in a never-ending circuit.
Paul Bunyan discovered it, and the Bunyan saga tells how he floated many a log
down its restless waters.

No one has suspected Paul of speaking in parables, yet in this instance he did.
Wisconsin not only *had* a round river, Wisconsin *is* one. The current is the
stream of energy which flows out of the soil into plants, thence into animals,
thence back into the soil in a never-ending circuit of life. 'Dust unto dust' is a
desiccated version of the Round River concept.

We of the genus *Homo* ride the logs that float down the Round River, and by
a little judicious 'burling' we have learned to guide their direction and speed.
This feat entitles us to the specific appellation *sapiens.* The technique of burling is called economics, the remembering of old routes is called history, the selection of new ones is called statesmanship, the conversation about oncoming riffles
and rapids is called politics. Some of the crew aspire to burl not only their own
logs, but the whole flotilla as well. This collective bargaining with nature is
called national planning.

In our educational system, the biotic continuum is seldom pictured to us as
a stream. From our tenderest years we are fed with facts about the soils, floras,
and faunas that comprise the channel of Round River (biology), about their origins in time (geology and evolution), about the technique of exploiting them
(agriculture and engineering). But the concept of a current with drouths and
freshets, backwaters and bars, is left to inference. To learn the hydrology of the
biotic stream we must think at right angles to evolution and examine the collective behavior of biotic materials. This calls for a reversal of specialization; instead of learning more and more about less and less, we must learn more and
more about the whole biotic landscape.

Ecology is a science that attempts this feat of thinking in a plane perpendicu-
lar to Darwin. Ecology is an infant just learning to talk, and, like other infants,
is engrossed with its own coinage of big words. Its working days lie in the future. Ecology is destined to become the lore of Round River, a belated attempt
to convert our collective knowledge of biotic materials into a collective wisdom
of biotic navigation. This, in the last analysis, is conservation.

Conservation is a state of harmony between men and land. By land is meant
all of the things on, over, or in the earth. Harmony with land is like harmony
with a friend; you cannot cherish his right hand and chop off his left. That is
to say, you cannot love game and hate predators; you cannot conserve the waters

and waste the ranges; you cannot build the forest and mine the farm. The land is one organism. Its part, like our own parts, compete with each other and co-operate with each other. The competitions are as much a part of the inner workings as the co-operations. You can regulate them—cautiously—but not abolish them.

The outstanding scientific discovery of the twentieth century is not television, or radio, but rather the complexity of the land organism. Only those who know the most about it can appreciate how little is known about it. The last word in ignorance is the man who says of an animal or plant: 'What good is it?' If the land mechanism as a whole is good, then every part is good, whether we understand it or not. If the biota, in the course of aeons, has built something we like but do not understand, then who but a fool would discard seemingly useless parts? To keep every cog and wheel is the first precaution of intelligent tinkering.

Have we learned this first principle of conservation: to preserve all the parts of the land mechanism? No, because even the scientist does not yet recognize all of them.

In Germany there is a mountain called the Spessart. Its south slope bears the most magnificent oaks in the world. American cabinetmakers, when they want the last word in quality, use Spessart oak. The north slope, which should be the better, bears an indifferent stand of Scotch pine. Why? Both slopes are part of the same state forest; both have been managed with equally scrupulous care for two centuries. Why the difference?

Kick up the litter under the oak and you will see that the leaves rot almost as fast as they fall. Under the pines, though, the needles pile up as a thick duff; decay is much slower. Why? Because in the Middle Ages the south slope was preserved as a deer forest by a hunting bishop; the north slope was pastured, plowed, and cut by settlers, just as we do with our woodlots in Wisconsin and Iowa today. Only after this period of abuse was the north slope replanted to pines. During this period of abuse something happened to the microscopic flora and fauna of the soil. The number of species was greatly reduced, i.e., the digestive apparatus of the soil lost some of its parts. Two centuries of conservation have not sufficed to restore these losses. It required the modern microscope, and a century of research in soil science, to discover the existence of these 'small cogs and wheels' which determine harmony or disharmony between men and land in the Spessart.

For the biotic community to survive, its internal processes must balance, else its member-species would disappear. That particular communities *do* survive for long periods is well known: Wisconsin, for example, in 1840 had substantially the same soil, fauna, and flora as at the end of the ice age, i.e. 12,000 years ago. We know this because the bones of its animals and the pollens of its plants are preserved in the peat bogs. The successive strata of peats, with their differing abundance of pollens, even record the weather; thus around 3000 B.C. an abundance of ragweed pollen indicates either a series of drouths, or a great stamping of buffalo, or severe fires on the prairie. These recurring exigencies did not prevent the survival of the 350 kinds of birds, 90 mammals, 150 fishes, 70 reptiles, or the thousands of insects and plants. That all these should survive as an internally balanced community for so many centuries shows an astonishing stability in the original biota. Science cannot explain the mechanisms of stability, but even a layman can see two of its effects: (1) Fertility, when extracted from rocks, circulated through such elaborate food chains that it accumulated as fast as or faster than it washed away. (2) This geological accumulation of soil fertility paralleled the diversification of flora and fauna; stability and diversity were apparently interdependent.

American conservation is, I fear, still concerned for the most part with show pieces. We have not yet learned to think in terms of small cogs and wheels. Look at our own back yard: at the prairies of Iowa and southern Wisconsin. What is the most valuable part of the prairie? The fat black soil, the chernozem. Who built the chernozem? The black prairie was built by the prairie plants, a hundred distinctive species of grasses, herbs, and shrubs; by the prairie fungi, insects, and bacteria; by the prairie mammals and birds, all interlocked in one humming community of co-operations and competitions, one biota. This biota, through ten thousand years of living and dying, burning and growing, preying and fleeing, freezing and thawing, built that dark and bloody ground we call prairie.

Our grandfathers did not, could not, know the origin of their prairie empire. They killed off the prairie fauna and they drove the flora to a last refuge on railroad embankments and roadsides. To our engineers this flora is merely weeds and brush; they ply it with grader and mower. Through processes of plant succession predictable by any botanist, the prairie garden becomes a refuge for quack grass. After the garden is gone, the highway department employs landscapers to dot the quack with elms, and with artistic clumps of Scotch pine, Japanese barberry, and Spiraea. Conservation Committees, en route to some important convention, whiz by and applaud this zeal for roadside beauty.

Some day we may need this prairie flora not only to look at but to rebuild the wasting soil of prairie farms. Many species may then be missing. We have our hearts in the right place, but we do not yet recognize the small cogs and wheels.

In our attempts to save the bigger cogs and wheels, we are still pretty naïve. A little repentance just before a species goes over the brink is enough to make us feel virtuous. When the species is gone we have a good cry and repeat the performance.

The recent extermination of the grizzly from most of the western stock-raising states is a case in point. Yes, we still have grizzlies in the Yellowstone. But the species is ridden by imported parasites; the rifles wait on every refuge boundary; new dude ranches and new roads constantly shrink the remaining range; every year sees fewer grizzlies on fewer ranges in fewer states. We console ourselves with the comfortable fallacy that a single museum-piece will do, ignoring the clear dictum of history that a species must be saved *in many places* if it is to be saved at all.

• • •

We need knowledge—public awareness—of the small cogs and wheels, but sometimes I think there is something we need even more. It is the thing that *Forest and Stream*, on its editorial masthead, once called "a refined taste in natural objects." Have we made any headway in developing "a refined taste in natural objects"?

In the northern parts of the lake states we have a few wolves left. Each state offers a bounty on wolves. In addition, it may invoke the expert services of the U.S. Fish and Wildlife Service in wolf-control. Yet both this agency and the several conservation commissions complain of an increasing number of localities where there are too many deer for the available feed. Foresters complain of periodic damage from too many rabbits. Why, then, continue the public policy of wolf-extermination? We debate such questions in terms of economics and biology. The mammalogists assert the wolf is the natural check on too many deer. The sportsmen reply they will take care of excess deer. Another decade of argument and there will be no wolves to argue about. One conservation inkpot cancels another.

In the lake states we are proud of our forest nurseries, and of the progress we are making in replanting what was once the north woods. But look in these nurseries and you will find no white cedar, no tamarack. Why no cedar? It grows too slowly, the deer eat it, the alders choke it. The prospect of a cedarless north woods does not depress our foresters; cedar has, in effect, been purged on grounds of economic inefficiency. For the same reason beech has been purged from the future forests of the Southeast. To these voluntary expungements of species from our future flora, we must add the involuntary ones arising from the importation of diseases: chestnut, persimmon, white pine. Is it sound economics to regard any plant as a separate entity, to proscribe or encourage it on the grounds of its individual performance? What will be the effect on animal life, on the soil, and on the health of the forest as an organism? 'A refined taste in natural objects' perceives that the economic issue is a separate consideration.

• • •

We who are the heirs and assigns of Paul Bunyan have not found out either what we are doing to the river or what the river is doing to us. We burl our logs of state with more energy than skill.

We have radically modified the biotic stream; we had to. Food chains now begin with corn and alfalfa instead of oaks and bluestem, flow through cows, hogs, and poultry instead of into elk, deer, and grouse, thence into farmers, flappers, and freshmen instead of Indians. That the flow is voluminous you can determine by consulting the telephone directory, or the roster of government agencies. The flow in this biotic stream is probably much greater than in the pre-Bunyan eras, but curiously enough science has never measured this.

Tame animals and plants have no tenacity as links in the new food chain; they are maintained, artificially, by the labor of farmers, aided by tractors, and abetted by a new kind of animal: the Professor of Agriculture. Paul Bunyan's burling was self-taught; now we have a 'prof' standing on the bank giving free instruction.

Each substitution of a tame plant or animal for a wild one or an artificial waterway for a natural one, is accompanied by a readjustment in the circulating system of the land. We do not understand or foresee these readjustments; we are unconscious of them unless the end effect is bad. Whether it be the President rebuilding Florida for a ship canal, or Farmer Jones rebuilding a Wisconsin meadow for cow pasture, we are too busy with new tinkerings to think of end effects. That so many tinkerings are painless attests the youth and elasticity of the land organism.

One of the penalties of an ecological education is that one lives alone in a world of wounds. Much of the damage inflicted on land is quite invisible to laymen. An ecologist must either harden his shell and make believe that the consequences of science are none of his business, or he must be the doctor who sees the marks of death in a community that believes itself well and does not want to be told otherwise.

The government tells us we need flood control and comes to straighten the creek in our pasture. The engineer on the job tells us the creek is now able to carry off more flood water, but in the process we have lost our old willows where the owl hooted on a winter night and under which the cows switched flies in the noon shade. We lost the little marshy spot where our fringed gentians bloomed.

Hydrologists have demonstrated that the meanderings of a creek are a necessary part of the hydrologic functioning. The flood plain belongs to the river. The ecologist sees clearly that for similar reasons we can get along with less channel improvement on Round River.

Now to appraise the new order in terms of the two criteria: (1) Does it maintain fertility? (2) Does it maintain a diverse fauna and flora? Soils in the first stages of exploitation display a burst of plant and animal life. The abundant crops that evoked thanksgiving in the pioneers are well known, but there was also a burst of wild plants and animals. A score of imported food-bearing weeds had been added to the native flora, the soil was still rich, and landscape had been diversified by patches of plowland and pasture. The abundance of wildlife reported by the pioneers was in part the response to this diversity.

Such high metabolism is characteristic of new-found lands. It may represent normal circulation, or it may represent the combustion of stored fertility, i.e., biotic fever. One cannot distinguish the fever from normality by asking the biota to bite a thermometer. It can only be told *ex post facto* by the effect on the soil. What was the effect? The answer is written in gullies on a thousand fields. Crop yields per acre have remained about stationary. The vast technological improvements in farming have only offset the wastage in soil. In some regions, such as the dust bowl, the biotic stream has already shrunk below the point of navigability, and Paul's heirs have moved to California to ferment the grapes of wrath.

As for diversity, what remains of our native fauna and flora remains only because agriculture has not got around to destroying it. The present ideal of agriculture is clean farming; clean farming means a food chain aimed solely at economic profit and purged of all non-conforming links, a sort of *Pax Germanica* of the agricultural world. Diversity, on the other hand, means a food chain aimed to harmonize the wild and the tame in the joint interest of stability, productivity, and beauty.

Clean farming, to be sure, aspires to rebuild the soil, but it employs to this end only imported plants, animals, and fertilizers. It sees no need for the native flora and fauna that built the soil in the first place. Can stability be synthesized out of imported plants and animals? Is fertility that comes in sacks sufficient? These are the questions at issue.

No living man really knows. Testifying for the workability of clean farming is northeastern Europe, where a degree of biotic stability has been retained (except in humans) despite the wholesale artificialization of the landscape.

Testifying for its non-workability are all the other lands where it has ever been tried, including our own, and the tacit evidence of evolution, in which diversity and stability are so closely intertwined as to seem two names for one fact.

. . .

I had a bird dog named Gus. When Gus couldn't find pheasants he worked up an enthusiasm for Sora rails and meadowlarks. This whipped-up zeal for unsatisfactory substitutes masked his failure to find the real thing. It assuaged his inner frustration.

We conservationists are like that. We set out a generation ago to convince the American landowner to control fire, to grow forests, to manage wildlife. He did not respond very well. We have virtually no forestry, and mighty little range management, game management, wildflower management, pollution control, or erosion control being practiced voluntarily by private landowners. In many instances the abuse of private land is worse than it was before we started. If you don't believe that, watch the strawstacks burn on the Canadian prairies; watch the fertile mud flowing down the Rio Grande; watch the gullies climb the hillsides in the Palouse, in the Ozarks, in the riverbreaks of southern Iowa and western Wisconsin.

To assuage our inner frustration over this failure, we have found us a meadowlark. I don't know which dog first caught the scent; I do know that every dog on the field whipped into an enthusiastic backing-point. I did myself. The meadowlark was the idea that if the private landowner won't practice conservation, let's build a bureau to do it for him.

Like the meadowlark, this substitute has its good points. It smells like success. It is satisfactory on poor land which bureaus can buy. The trouble is that it contains no device for preventing good private land from becoming poor public land. There is danger in the assuagement of honest frustration; it helps us forget we have not yet found a pheasant.

I'm afraid the meadowlark is not going to remind us. He is flattered by his sudden importance.

· · ·

Considering the prodigious achievements of the profit motive in wrecking land, one hesitates to reject it as a vehicle for restoring land. I incline to believe we have overestimated the scope of the profit motive. Is it profitable for the individual to build a beautiful home? To give his children a higher education? No, it is seldom profitable, yet we do both. These are in fact, ethical and aesthetic premises which underlie the economic system. Once accepted, economic forces tend to align the smaller details of social organization into harmony with them.

No such ethical and aesthetic premise yet exists for the condition of the land these children must live in. Our children are our signature to the roster of history; our land is merely the place our money was made. There is as yet no social stigma in the possession of a gullied farm, a wrecked forest, or a polluted stream, provided the dividends suffice to send the youngsters to college. Whatever ails the land, the government will fix it.

I think we have here the root of the problem. What conservation education must build is an ethical underpinning for land economics and a universal curiosity to understand the land mechanism. Conservation may then follow.

17   ECO-CATASTROPHE
Paul R. Ehrlich

I

The end of the ocean came late in the summer of 1979, and it came even more rapidly than the biologists had expected. There had been signs for more than a decade, commencing with the discovery in 1968 that DDT slows down photosynthesis in marine plant life. It was announced in a short paper in the technical journal, *Science*, but to ecologists it smacked of doomsday. They knew that all life in the sea depends on photosynthesis, the chemical process by which green plants bind the sun's energy and make it available to living things. And

SOURCE: Reprinted with the permission of Paul R. Ehrlich and the Editors of *Ramparts*.

they knew that DDT and similar chlorinated hydrocarbons had polluted the entire surface of the earth, including the sea.

But that was only the first of many signs. There had been the final gasp of the whaling industry in 1973, and the end of the Peruvian anchovy fishery in 1975. Indeed, a score of other fisheries had disappeared quietly from over-exploitation and various eco-catastrophes by 1977. The term "eco-catastrophe" was coined by a California ecologist in 1969 to describe the most spectacular of man's attacks on the systems which sustain his life. He drew his inspiration from the Santa Barbara offshore oil disaster of that year, and from the news which spread among naturalists that virtually all of the Golden State's seashore bird life was doomed because of chlorinated hydrocarbon interference with its reproduction. Eco-catastrophes in the sea became increasingly common in the early 1970's. Mysterious "blooms" of previously rare microorganisms began to appear in offshore waters. Red tides—killer outbreaks of a minute single-celled plant—returned to the Florida Gulf coast and were sometimes accompanied by tides of other exotic hues.

It was clear by 1975 that the entire ecology of the ocean was changing. A few types of phytoplankton were becoming resistant to chlorinated hydrocarbons and were gaining the upper hand. Changes in the phytoplankton community led inevitably to changes in the community of zooplankton, the tiny animals which eat the phytoplankton. These changes were passed on up the chains of life in the ocean diminished, its stability also decreased.

Other changes had taken place by 1975. Most ocean fishes that returned to fresh water to breed, like the salmon, had become extinct, their breeding streams so dammed up and polluted that their powerful homing instinct only resulted in suicide. Many fishes and shellfishes that bred in restricted areas along the coasts followed them as onshore pollution escalated.

By 1977 the annual yield of fish from the sea was down to 30 million metric tons, less than one-half the per capita catch of a decade earlier. This helped malnutrition to escalate sharply in a world where an estimated 50 million people per year were already dying of starvation. The United Nations attempted to get all chlorinated hydrocarbon insecticides banned on a worldwide basis, but the move was defeated by the United States. This opposition was generated primarily by the American petrochemical industry, operating hand in glove with its subsidiary, the United States Department of Agriculture. Together they persuaded the government to oppose the U.N. move—which was not difficult since most Americans believed that Russia and China were more in need of fish products than was the United States. The United Nations also attempted to get fishing nations to adopt strict and enforced catch limits to preserve dwindling stocks. This move was blocked by Russia, who, with the most modern electronic equipment, was in the best position to glean what was left in the sea. It was, curiously, on the very day in 1977 when the Soviet Union announced its refusal that another ominous article appeared in *Science*. It announced that incident solar radiation had been so reduced by worldwide air pollution that serious effects on the world's vegetation could be expected.

II

Apparently it was a combination of ecosystem destabilization, sunlight reduction, and a rapid escalation in chlorinated hydrocarbon pollution from massive Thanodrin applications which triggered the ultimate catastrophe. Seventeen huge Soviet-financed Thanodrin plants were operating in underdeveloped countries by 1978. They had been part of a massive Russian "aid offensive" designed to fill the gap caused by the collapse of America's ballyhooed "Green Revolution."

It became apparent in the early '70s that the "Green Revolution" was more talk than substance. Distribution of high yield "miracle" grain seeds had caused temporary local spurts in agricultural production. Simultaneously, excellent weather had produced record harvests. The combination permitted bureaucrats, especially in the United States Department of Agriculture and the Agency for International Development (AID), to reverse their previous pessimism and indulge in an outburst of optimistic propaganda about staving off famine. They raved about the approaching transformation of agriculture in the underdeveloped countries (UDCs). The reason for the propaganda reversal was never made clear. Most historians agree that a combination of utter ignorance of ecology, a desire to justify past errors, and pressure from agro-industry (which was eager to sell pesticides, fertilizers, and farm machinery to the UDCs and agencies helping the UDCs) was behind the campaign. Whatever the motivation, the results were clear. Many concerned people, lacking the expertise to see through the Green Revolution drivel, relaxed. The population-food crisis was "solved."

But reality was not long in showing itself. Local famine persisted in northern India even after good weather brought an end to the ghastly Bihar famine of the mid-'60s. East Pakistan was next, followed by a resurgence of general famine in northern India. Other foci of famine rapidly developed in Indonesia, the Philippines, Malawi, the Congo, Egypt, Colombia, Ecuador, Honduras, the Dominican Republic, and Mexico.

Everywhere hard realities destroyed the illusion of the Green Revolution. Yields dropped as the progressive farmers who had first accepted the new seeds found that their higher yields brought lower prices—effective demand (hunger plus cash) was not sufficient in poor countries to keep prices up. Less progressive farmers, observing this, refused to make the extra effort required to cultivate the "miracle" grains. Transport systems proved inadequate to bring the necessary fertilizer to the fields where the new and extremely fertilizer-sensitive grains were being grown. The same systems were also inadequate to move produce to markets. Fertilizer plants were not built fast enough, and most of the underdeveloped countries could not scrape together funds to purchase supplies, even on concessional terms. Finally, the inevitable happened, and pests began to reduce yields in even the most carefully cultivated fields. Among the first were the famous "miracle rats" which invaded Philippine "miracle rice" fields early in 1969. They were quickly followed by many insects and viruses, thriving on the relatively pest-susceptible new grains, encouraged by the vast and dense plantings, and rapidly acquiring resistance to the chemicals used against them. As chaos spread until even the most obtuse agriculturists and economists realized that the Green Revolution had turned brown, the Russians stepped in.

In retrospect it seems incredible that the Russians, with the American mistakes known to them, could launch an even more incompetent program of aid to the underdeveloped world. Indeed, in the early 1970's there were cynics in the United States who claimed that outdoing the stupidity of American foreign aid would be physically impossible. Those critics were, however, obviously unaware that the Russians had been busily destroying their own environment for many years. The virtual disappearance of sturgeon from Russian rivers caused a great shortage of caviar by 1970. A standard joke among Russian scientists at that time was that they had created an artificial caviar which was indistinguishable from the real thing—except by taste. At any rate the Soviet Union, observing with interest the progressive deterioration of relations between the UDCs and the United States, came up with a solution. It had recently developed what it claimed was the ideal insecticide, a highly lethal chlorinated hydrocarbon complexed with a special agent for penetrating the external skeletal armor of insects. Announcing that the new pesticide, called Thanodrin, would truly produce a Green Revolution, the Soviets entered into negotiations with various UDCs for the construction of massive Thanodrin factories. The USSR would bear all the costs; all it wanted in return were certain trade and military concessions.

It is interesting now, with the perspective of years, to examine in some detail the reasons why the UDCs welcomed the Thanodrin plan with such open arms. Government officials in these countries ignored the protests of their own scientists that Thanodrin would not solve the problems which plagued them. The governments now knew that the basic cause of their problems was overpopulation, and that these problems had been exacerbated by the dullness, daydreaming, and cupidity endemic to all governments. They knew that only population control and limited development aimed primarily at agriculture could have spared them the horrors they now faced. They knew it, but they were not about to admit it. How much easier it was simply to accuse the Americans of failing to give them proper aid; how much simpler to accept the Russian panacea.

And then there was the general worsening of relations between the United States and the UDCs. Many things had contributed to this. The situation in America in the first half of the 1970's deserves our close scrutiny. Being more dependent on imports for raw materials than the Soviet Union, the United States had, in the early 1970's, adopted more and more heavy-handed policies in order to insure continuing supplies. Military adventures in Asia and Latin America had further lessened the international credibility of the United States as a great defender of freedom—an image which had begun to deteriorate rapidly during the pointless and fruitless Viet-Nam conflict. At home, acceptance of the carefully manufactured image lessened dramatically, as even the more romantic and chauvinistic citizens began to understand the role of the military and the industrial system in what John Kenneth Galbraith had aptly named "The New Industrial State."

At home in the USA the early '70s were traumatic times. Racial violence grew and the habitability of the cities diminished, as nothing substantial was done to ameliorate either racial inequities or urban blight. Welfare rolls grew as automation and general technological progress forced more and more people into the category of "unemployable." Simultaneously a taxpayers' revolt occurred. Although there was not enough money to build the schools, roads, water systems, sewage systems, jails, hospitals, urban transit lines, and all the other amenities needed to support a burgeoning population, Americans refused to tax themselves more heavily. Starting in Youngstown, Ohio in 1969 and followed closely by Richmond, California, community after community was forced to close its schools or curtail educational operations for lack of funds. Water supplies, already marginal in quality and quantity in many places by 1970, deteriorated quickly. Water rationing occurred in 1723 municipalities in the summer of 1974, and hepatitis and epidemic dysentery rates climbed about 500 per cent between 1970-1974.

III

Air pollution continued to be the most obvious manifestation of environmental deterioration. It was, by 1972, quite literally in the eyes of all Americans. The year 1973 saw not only the New York and Los Angeles smog disasters, but also the publication of the Surgeon General's massive report on air pollution and health. The public had been partially prepared for the worst by the publicity given to the U.N. pollution conference held in 1972. Deaths in the late '60s caused by smog were well known to scientists, but the public had ignored them because they mostly involved the early demise of the old and sick rather than people dropping dead on the freeways. But suddenly our citizens were faced with nearly 200,000 corpses and massive documentation that they could be the next to die from respiratory disease. They were not ready for that scale of disaster. After all, the U.N. conference had not predicted that accumulated air pollution would make the planet uninhabitable until amost 1990. The population was terrorized as TV screens became filled with scenes of horror from the disaster areas. Especially vivid was NBC's coverage of hundreds of unattended people choking out their lives outside of New York's hospitals. Terms like nitrogen oxide, acute bronchitis and cardiac arrest began to have real meaning for most Americans.

The ultimate horror was the announcement that chlorinated hydrocarbons were now a major constituent of air pollution in all American cities. Autopsies of smog disaster victims revealed an average chlorinated hydrocarbon load in fatty tissue equivalent to 26 parts per million of DDT. In October, 1973, the Department of Health, Education and Welfare announced studies which showed unequivocally that increasing death rates from hypertension, cirrhosis of the liver, liver cancer and a series of other diseases had resulted from the chlorinated hydrocarbon load. They estimated that Americans born since 1946 (when DDT usage began) now had a life expectancy of only 49 years, and predicted that if current patterns continued, this expectancy would reach 42 years by 1980, when it might level out. Plunging insurance stocks triggered a stock market panic. The president of Velsicol, Inc., a major pesticide producer, went on television to "publicly eat a teaspoonful of DDT" (it was really powdered milk) and announce that HEW had been infiltrated by Communists. Other giants of the petro-chemical industry, attempting to dispute the indisputable evidence, launched a massive pressure campaign on Congress to force HEW to "get out of agriculture's business." They were aided by the agro-chemical journals, which had decades of experience in misleading the public about the benefits and dangers of pesticides. But by now the public realized that it had been duped. The Nobel Prize for medicine and physiology was given to Drs. J. L. Radomski and W. B. Deichmann, who in the late 1960's had pioneered in the documentation of the long-term lethal effects of chlorinated hydrocarbons. A Presidential Commission with unimpeachable credentials directly accused the agro-chemical complex of "condemning many millions of Americans to an early death." The year 1973 was the year in which Americans finally came to understand the direct threat to their existence posed by environmental deterioration.

And 1973 was also the year in which most people finally comprehended the indirect threat. Even the president of Union Oil Company and several other industrialists publicly stated their concern over the reduction of bird population which had resulted from pollution by DDT and other chlorinated hydrocarbons. Insect populations boomed because they were resistant to most pesticides and had been freed, by the incompetent use of those pesticides, from most of their natural enemies. Rodents swarmed over crops, multiplying rapidly in the absence of predatory birds. The effect of pests on the wheat crop was especially disastrous in the summer of 1973, since that was also the year of the great drought. Most of us can remember the shock which greeted the announcement by atmospheric physicists that the shift of the jet stream which had caused the drought was probably permanent. It signalled the birth of the Midwestern desert. Man's air-polluting activities had by then caused gross changes in climatic patterns. The news, of course, played hell with commodity and stock markets. Food prices sky-rocketed, as savings were poured into hoarded canned goods. Official assurances that food supplies would remain ample fell on deaf ears, and even the government showed signs of nervousness when California migrant field workers went out on strike again in protest against the continued use of pesticides by growers. The strike burgeoned into farm burning and riots. The workers, calling themselves "The Walking Dead," demanded immediate compensation for their shortened lives, and crash research programs to attempt to lengthen them.

It was in the same speech in which President Edward Kennedy, after much delay, finally declared a national emergency and called out the National Guard to harvest California's crops, that the first mention of population control was made. Kennedy pointed out that the United States would no longer be able to offer any food aid to other nations and was likely to suffer food shortages herself. He suggested that, in view of the manifest failure of the Green Revolution, the only hope of the UDCs lay in population control. His statement, you will recall, created an uproar in the underdeveloped countries. Newspaper editorials accused the United States of wishing to prevent small countries from becoming large nations and thus threatening American hegemony. Politicians asserted that President Kennedy was a "creature of the giant drug combine" that wished to shove its pills down every woman's throat.

Among Americans, religious opposition to population control was very slight. Industry in general also backed the idea. Increasing poverty in the UDCs was both destroying markets and threatening supplies of raw materials. The seriousness of the raw material situation had been brought home during the Congressional Hard Resources hearings in 1971. The exposure of the ignorance of the cornucopian economists had been quite a spectacle—a spectacle brought into virtually every American's home in living color. Few would forget the distinguished geologist from the University of California who suggested that economists be legally required to learn at least the most elementary facts of geology. Fewer still would forget that an equally distinguished Harvard economist added that they might be required to learn some economics, too. The overall message was clear: America's resource situation was bad and bound to get worse. The hearings had led to a bill requiring the Departments of State, Interior, and Commerce to set up a joint resource procurement council with the express purpose of "insuring that proper consideration of American resource needs be an integral part of American foreign policy."

Suddenly the United States discovered that it had a national consensus: population control was the only possible salvation of the underdeveloped world. But that same consensus led to heated debate. How could the UDCs be persuaded to limit their populations, and should not the United States lead the way by limiting its own? Members of the intellectual community wanted America to set an example. They pointed out that the United States was in the midst of a new baby boom: her birth rate, well over 20 per thousand per year, and her growth rate of over one per cent per annum were among the very highest of the developed countries. They detailed the deterioration of the American physical and psychic environments, the growing health threats, the impending food shortages, and the insufficiency of funds for desperately needed public works. They contended that the nation was clearly unable or unwilling to properly care for the people it already had. What possible reason could there be, they queried, for adding any more? Besides, who would listen to requests by the United States for population control when that nation did not control her own profligate reproduction?

Those who opposed population controls for the U.S. were equally vociferous. The military-industrial complex, with its all-too-human mixture of ignorance and avarice, still saw strength and prosperity in numbers. Baby food magnates, already worried by the growing nitrate pollution of their products, saw their market disappearing. Steel manufacturers saw a decrease in aggregate demand and slippage for that holy of holies, the Gross National Product. And military men saw, in the growing population-food-environment crisis, a serious threat to their carefully nurtured Cold War. In the end, of course, economic arguments held sway, and the "inalienable right of every American couple to determine the size of its family," a freedom invented for the occasion in the early '70s, was not compromised.

The population control bill, which was passed by Congress early in 1974, was quite a document, nevertheless. On the domestic front, it authorized an increase from 100 to 150 million dollars in funds for "family planning" activities. This was made possible by a general feeling in the country that the growing army on welfare needed family planning. But the gist of the bill was a series of measures designed to impress the need for population control on the UDCs. All American aid to countries with overpopulation problems was required by law to consist in part of population control assistance. In order to receive any assistance each nation was required not only to accept the population control aid, but also to match it according to a complex formula. "Overpopulation" itself was defined by a formula based on U.N. statistics, and the UDCs were required not only to accept aid, but also to show progress in reducing birth rates. Every five years the status of the aid program for each nation was to be re-evaluated.

The reaction to the announcement of this program dwarfed the response to President Kennedy's speech. A coalition of UDCs attempted to get the U.N. General Assembly to condemn the United States as a "genetic aggressor." Most damaging of all to the American cause was the famous "25 Indians and a dog" speech by Mr. Shankarnarayan, Indian Ambassador to the U.N. Shankarnarayan pointed out that for several decades the United States, with less than six per cent of the people of the world had consumed roughly 50 per cent of the raw materials used every year. He described vividly America's contribution to worldwide environmental deterioration, and he scathingly denounced the miserly record of United States foreign aid as "unworthy of a fourth-rate power, let alone the most powerful nation on earth."

It was the climax of his speech, however, which most historians claim once and for all destroyed the image of the United States. Shankarnarayan informed the assembly that the average American family dog was fed more animal protein per week than the average Indian got in a month. "How do you justify taking fish from protein-starved Peruvians and feeding them to your animals?" he asked. "I contend," he concluded, "that the birth of an American baby is a greater disaster for the world than that of 25 Indian babies." When the applause had died away, Mr. Sorensen, the American representative, made a speech which said essentially that "other countries look after their own self-interest, too." When the vote came, the United States was condemned.

This condemnation set the tone of U.S.–UDC relations at the time the Russian Thanodrin proposal was made. The proposal seemed to offer the masses in the UDCs an opportunity to save themselves and humiliate the United States at the time; and in human affairs, as we all know, biological realities could never interfere with such an opportunity. The scientists were silenced, the politicians said yes, the Thanodrin plants were built, and the results were what any beginning ecology student could have predicted. At first Thanodrin seemed to offer excellent control of many pests. True, there was a rash of human fatalities from improper use of the lethal chemical, but, as Russian technical advisors were prone to note, these were more than compensated for by increased yields. Thanodrin use skyrocketed throughout the underdeveloped world. The Mikoyan design group developed a dependable, cheap agricultural aircraft which the Soviets donated to the effort in large numbers. MIG sprayers became even more common in UDCs than MIG interceptors.

Then the troubles began. Insect strains with cuticles resistant to Thanodrin penetration began to appear. And as streams, rivers, fish culture ponds and on-shore waters became rich in Thanodrin, more fisheries began to disappear. Bird populations were decimated. The sequence of events was standard for broadcast use of a synthetic pesticide: great success at first, followed by removal of natural enemies and development of resistance by the pest. Populations of crop-eating insects in areas treated with Thanodrin made steady comebacks and soon became more abundant than ever. Yields plunged, while farmers in their desperation increased the Thanodrin dose and shortened the time between treatments. Death from Thanodrin poisoning became common. The first violent incident occurred in the Canete Valley of Peru, where farmers had suffered a similar chlorinated hydrocarbon disaster in the mid-'50s. A Russian advisor serving as an agricultural pilot was assaulted and killed by a mob of enraged farmers in January, 1978. Trouble spread rapidly during 1978, especially after the word got out that two years earlier Russia herself had banned the use of Thanodrin at home because of its serious effects on ecological systems. Suddenly Russia, and not the United States, was the bête noir in the UDCs. "Thanodrin parties" became epidemic, with farmers, in their ignorance, dumping carloads of Thanodrin concentrate into the sea. Russian advisors fled, and four of the Thanodrin plants were leveled to the ground. Destruction of the plants in Rio and Calcutta led to hundreds of thousands of gallons of Thanodrin concentrate being dumped directly into the sea.

Mr. Shankarnarayan again rose to address the U.N., but this time it was Mr.

Potemkin, representative of the Soviet Union, who was on the hot seat. Mr. Potemkin heard his nation described as the greatest mass killer of all time as Shankarnarayan predicted at least 30 million deaths from crop failures due to overdependence on Thanodrin. Russia was accused of "chemical aggression," and the General Assembly, after a weak reply by Potemkin, passed a vote of censure.

It was in January, 1979, that huge blooms of a previously unknown variety of diatom were reported off the coast of Peru. The blooms were accompanied by a massive die-off of sea life and of the pathetic remainder of the birds which had once feasted on the anchovies of the area. Almost immediatey another huge bloom was reported in the Indian ocean, centering around the Seychelles, and then a third in the South Atlantic off the African coast. Both of these were accompanied by spectacular die-offs of marine animals. Even more ominous were growing reports of fish and bird kills at oceanic points where there were no spectacular blooms. Biologists were soon able to explain the phenomena: the diatom had evolved an enzyme which broke down Thanodrin; that enzyme also produced a breakdown product which interfered with the transmission of nerve impulses, and was therefore lethal to animals. Unfortunately, the biologists could suggest no way of repressing the poisonous diatom bloom in time. By September, 1979, all important animal life in the sea was extinct. Large areas of coastline had to be evacuated, as windrows of dead fish created a monumental stench.

But stench was the least of man's problems. Japan and China were faced with almost instant starvation from a total loss of the seafood on which they were so dependent. Both blamed Russia for their situation and demanded immediate mass shipments of food. Russia had none to send. On October 13, Chinese armies attacked Russia on a broad front....

V

A pretty grim scenario. Unfortunately, we're a long way into it already. Everything mentioned as happening before 1970 has occurred; much of the rest is based on projections of trends already appearing. Evidence that pesticides have long-term lethal effects on human beings has started to accumulate, and recently Robert Finch, Secretary of the Department of Health, Education and Welfare expressed his extreme apprehension about the pesticide situation. Simultaneously the petrochemical industry continues its unconscionable poison-peddling. For instance, Shell Chemical has been carrying on a high-pressure campaign to sell the insecticide Azodrin to farmers as a killer of cotton pests. They continue their program even though they know that Azodrin is not only ineffective, but often increases the pest density. They've covered themselves nicely in an advertisement which states, "Even if an overpowering migration [sic] develops, the flexibility of Azodrin lets you regain control fast. Just increase the dosage according to label recommendations." It's a great game—get people to apply the poison and kill the natural enemies of the pests. Then blame the increased pests on "migration" and sell even more pesticide!

Right now fisheries are being wiped out by over-exploitation, made easy by modern electronic equipment. The companies producing the equipment know this. They even boast in advertising that only their equipment will keep fishermen in business until the final kill. Profits must obviously be maximized in the short run. Indeed, Western society is in the process of completing the rape and murder of the planet for economic gain. And, sadly, most of the rest of the world is eager for the opportunity to emulate our behavior. But the underdeveloped peoples will be denied that opportunity—the days of plunder are drawing inexorably to a close.

Most of the people who are going to die in the greatest cataclysm in the history of man have already been born. More than three and a half billion people already populate our moribund globe, and half of them are hungry. Some 10 to 20 million will starve to death this year. In spite of this, the population of the earth will increase by 70 million souls in 1969. For mankind has artificially lowered the death rate of the human population, while in general birth rates have remained high. With the input side of the population system in high gear and the output side slowed down, our fragile planet has filled with people at an incredible rate. It took several million years for the population to reach a total of two billion people in 1930, while a second two billion will have been added by 1975! By that time some experts feel that food shortages will have escalated the present level of world hunger and starvation into famines of unbelievable proportions. Other experts, more optimistic, think the ultimate food-population collision will not occur until the decade of the 1980's. Of course more massive famine may be avoided if other events cause a prior rise in the human death rate.

Both worldwide plague and thermonuclear war are made more probable as population growth continues. These, along with famine, make up the trio of potential "death rate solutions" to the population problem—solutions in which the birth rate-death rate imbalance is redressed by a rise in the death rate rather than by a lowering of the birth rate. Make no mistake about it, the imbalance will be redressed. The shape of the population growth curve is one familiar to the biologist. It is the outbreak part of an outbreak-crash sequence. A population grows rapidly in the presence of abundant resources, finally runs out of food or some other necessity, and crashes to a low level or extinction. Man is not only running out of food, he is also destroying the life support systems of the Spaceship Earth. The situation was recently summarized very succinctly: "It is the top of the ninth inning. Man, always a threat at the plate, has been hitting Nature hard. It is important to remember, however, that NATURE BATS LAST."

C
The Way We Live

The definition of wealth is, in part, a social one. Since this is the case, the roles of rich man and poor man vary from generation to generation. What is regarded as affluence in one age is poverty in another. Given an American belief in the inevitability of rising standards of living, the riches of yesterday are inadequate for today. Even poor people now may have more absolutely than middle-class individuals of a century ago. Varying expectations make material standards an uncertain base for social analysis and complicate the eradication of the sense of being poor. The social-psychological elements in the role conception of the poor or the rich person may be as significant as his quality of life. In this section we wish to point out some of these changing elements.

The problem of the role of the poor person is that it has been defined as a necessary and desirable role from the larger viewpoint of society. In nineteenth century America, for example, poverty was assumed to have useful functions. The first function was a moral one. Poverty was often the result of immorality. Those who were slothful, intemperate, and otherwise worthless deserved to be poor. Their lack of ambition and self-control made them fine examples to hold up to children. Wealthy persons, on the other hand, were rewarded for their hard work and conserving habits. There were exceptions to these rules. Not all paupers were responsible for their misfortunes; widows and orphans were innocent victims of natural or social disasters. Some rich persons were fortunate and had quite undeservedly become affluent. Nonetheless, in general, wealth and poverty were the results of individual, not social, effort.

Poverty was a necessary element in prevailing economic theories, the fear of which acted as an engine to drive the system. The same fear that kept children working in mines made business success possible. Economist David Richardo's "iron law of wages" counted upon the lack of adequate sustenance to serve as balance on the supply-demand scale of worker's wages. In this sense, poverty had no necessary moral connotation, but it did have utilitarian value.

Finally, poverty in the nineteenth century was often regarded as a temporary condition through which almost all individuals passed. It was assumed by both the serious and popular writers of the day that this stage in life was occupied by the young, who could transcend it by hard work, individual effort, and luck. Such was the message of the Horatio Alger books, although, as Irvin G. Wyllie points out in his *The Self-Made Man in America,* the element of luck that was so significant in the Alger books tended to diminish in the rags-to-riches myth. The impermanence of poverty was a persistent theme; the poor farm boy who did his chores while dressed in ragged overalls would end his life of hard work dining on champagne and caviar while dressed in a frock coat. Neither was wealth secure; shirtsleeves to shirtsleeves in three generations was a widely used and believed precept. The almost universal consensus about the possibility of individual social mobility in nineteenth century society made poverty more acceptable.

Not all nineteenth-century thinkers hailed poverty as a blessing. The Irish playwright, George Bernard Shaw, argued that poverty was "a public nuisance as well as a private misfortune." Others, like Edward Bellamy, looked to a future where poverty would be eliminated by the continued material and social progress of the United States. By the beginning of the twentieth century, a general change in attitude toward poverty had occurred. Robert H. Bremner has outlined this change in his *From the Depths: The Discovery of Poverty in the United States.* Bremner contends that reformers of the period, men like Robert Hunter whose classic study, *Poverty,* was published in 1904, conceived of poverty for the first time as the result of a malfunctioning system and not as an individual's fault. The role of the poor person was not shed in later life; people who were imbued with a work ethic and who worked hard all of their lives remained poor. Pauperism was seen as the cause of individual demoralization instead of the product of it.

The concern about the poor person as locked in a fixed social role tended to be an urban one. It concentrated on the plight of the European immigrant in American city slums and overlooked the plight of the small-town or rural poor. The disparities in wealth that existed in these areas were either less sharp or less evident, so the roles of rich and poor tended to be found in the cities. The contrast here was between the native American and the recent immigrant and it went beyond class to cultural differences. The poor were regarded with a kind of paternalism that fitted their late arrival in this country and their lack of knowledge of American ways. Although the poor could be revolutionists, more commonly the role was defined and assumed in terms of social docility. Despite the definition and the lack of sustained urban violence, the fear of such violence remained to add urgency to reform efforts.

The poverty discovered in the Progressive Era has not disappeared, nor has the wealth of the "Guilded Age" vanished, but the issues brought up by these excesses have waxed and waned in the public forum. Gabriel Kolko, a New Left historian, maintains in *Wealth and Power in America* that the proportion of rich and poor in this country has remained about the same from the 1900s to the 1950s. Despite this lack of change, concern over the behavior of the rich or the problems of the poor emerges periodically. The 1920s were a time when the plight of the poor was not obvious. But the 1930s can be characterized as an era of intense interest in the deprived. The New Deal, with all its efforts at social security, make-work, and pump priming, did not share the wealth nor overthrow the capitalistic system, despite the claims of its severest critics. World War II ended the depression with its demands for labor to manufacture arms or to use them. The war also affected the more prosperous middle class as well, in that it provided the excuse to extend income-tax obligations to this group for the first time. The shifting of the tax burden downward had several consequences, among them the prevention of greater affluence among the middle class and, through loopholes politically derived, the creation of a newly rich class. The oil millionaire with his depletion allowance and the real-estate speculator with his lower capital-gains taxes remain familiar figures in our times.

The Truman and Eisenhower years were also ones in which affluence seemed to be most noteworthy. The scandals of the Truman administration reenforced the already common knowledge that political favors returned economic rewards. The Eisenhower years were ones of seeming tranquillity, of cold war anti-Communism, and of lack of concern for the very poor. The rich man became, as in the 1920s, a symbol of political as well as economic wisdom. President Eisenhower's first cabinet was described as being composed of seven millionaires and one plumber. The most outspoken of the millionaires, Charles E. Wilson, represented cabinet philosophy when he said that what was good for General Motors was good for the country.

Poverty was discovered again in the 1960s. Part of the credit for this must go to the invigorated civil-rights movement. In part, credit belongs to a President, John F. Kennedy, who, in order to get the country moving again, desired to know where it was. Finally, a book appeared that had considerable impact. This was Michael Harrington's *The Other America: Poverty in the United States.* It typified the mood of the early 1960s as John Kenneth Galbraith's *The Affluent Society* had in the late 1950s. Galbraith, mirroring the optimism of his time, had described American society as having achieved affluence and had pictured poverty as an aberration, the lot of those few out of the mainstream of economic life. Harrington, on the other hand, found much more poverty. He also offered an explanation of why others had not discovered it. Poverty was invisible; the poor lived in the slums of cities unseen by the commuters who passed through but did not stop, or in rural isolation that was regarded by passing motorists as picturesque and romantic. When the poor came to the major shopping or commercial areas of the cities, they successfully disguised their poverty through the abundance of cheap clothing. By 1963, the stage was set for a program to attack poverty.

John F. Kennedy's aims were unrealized at the time of his death in late 1963, although he had indicated that he was interested in "rehabilitation and not relief."

President Johnson began the War on Poverty when he signed the Economic Opportunity Act in 1964. The War on Poverty was not won by Johnson nor has it been vigorously fought by his successor, Richard Nixon. The issue of poverty remained a significant one. The role of the poor, however, had changed.

Selection 18 is from Jacob Riis' *A Ten Years' War*. Although not as well known as *How the Other Half Lives, A Ten Years' War* did awaken demands for slum clearance and housing reform. Riis began his life in Denmark; he grew up in a village there and mastered the craft of carpentry. He came to the United States in 1870, eventually finding work as a police reporter in New York City. For 13 years Riis roamed the city searching for newsworthy stories and, in the process, became an expert on the slums and their inhabitants. As a result of his experiences, Riis grew to sympathize with the poor and to write about their problems.

In the chapter entitled "The Tenant," Riis portrays the poor as consisting essentially of noble people who share a work ethic with their middle-class neighbors. The hard-working Irishman who supports the corrupt Tammany machine wishes to give his gold to the government, which he fears is in need. The starving daughter of a German peddler refuses an offer of money, while the family shares its meager fare with one whose plight is worse. The teacher whose sister is dying spends her time with her students instead of with her sister, to provide them with some semblance of Christmas. One expects sentimentality in the nineteenth century; indeed, it was the standard fare. But sentimentality is unexpected from a hard-bitten police reporter.

Riis also emphasizes the morality of the poor. Despite their squalid environment and their close contact with crime and lawlessness, the poor respect the law and maintain a standard of behavior that shames those who exploit them. They do this in spite of a society that has ignored them, failed to provide them with necessary services, and permitted them to exist almost as animals in slums. The poor, to Riis, are like their more fortunate fellow Americans; they believe in work, self-sufficiency, and charity to others. Above all, they are uncomplaining.

The contrasting life of the very rich appears next in Selection 19, taken from *The Good Years* by Walter Lord. Lord concentrates on the parties given by the wealthy to amuse themselves. He finds much excess. One host had an artificial waterfall built for a single party; another surprised guests with a flock of nightingales; a third gave a party in which all the participants were on horseback; and a fourth used a monkey—given the title of Prince del Drago of Corsica—as the guest of honor. The culmination is the fancy-dress ball given by the Frenchified James Hagen Hyde, the heir to the Equitable Life Assurance Society fortune. Hyde's party was ill-timed; his executive rivals seized on the resultant bad publicity to help them remove Hyde from the company. Yet Hyde was typical of the newly rich in that the only restriction on his extravagance seemed to be an internal one. The education that should have provided an internal guide, however, was lacking. Hyde was atypical in that his actions caused business difficulties; others gained social and economic advantage from theirs.

The rich provided material for the scandal sheets of the day with their active sex lives and their antics with their new toy, the automobile. The toys have changed, but little else has save attitude. Then, the very rich did not care about public opinion; they had no notion of being discreet. They wore their diamonds, they drove their automobiles, they displayed their wives and mistresses. Today, the rich seem more self-conscious.

The role of the rich in setting styles for others to follow has also changed. Lord shows two of the avocations of the rich at the beginning of the century, football and automobile racing. These sports, which were then exclusive ones, have been taken over by middle- and lower-class persons. Football is no longer the game played for recreation by the sons of the rich; it is the path of social mobility for the sons of the Polish coal miner and the black tenant farmer. While it is true that automobile racing of the Indianapolis 500 variety requires substantial financial backing, stock-car racing reputedly originated in the South from lower-class white moonshiners testing their cars against each other in a dirt field outside a hamlet. What were rich men's games and toys have become common property. The rich, then, led the way.

Selection 20 details life in the Midwest in a country town and comes from Louis Atherton's *Main Street on the Middle Border.* This way of life was not conceived primarily in terms of richness or poorness. While the country town was not classless, it often seemed that way because of community closeness and the lack of visible standards of wealth or poverty. The contrast seemed instead to be between a rural, older way of life and a newer, urban style. The selection, "The City Comes to Main Street," shows how the urban style won.

There is a quality of nostalgia in Atherton's work, combined with a sense of unreality. The past may be covered with an aura of romance so that the democratic qualities of small-town life may be as much imagined as experienced: Despite this sense of unreality, there is a sense of rightness in the permanence of role. There is the example of the retired farm couple who have declined in status because of their age and reduced income, who live out their lives in memory, unconsciously lamenting the loss of meaningful work. But they, like their neighbors, live as convention dictates, as their parents had lived before. Roles are connected with age and work and are slow to change. The small town had well-defined roles that were the obverse side of the neighborliness of the community.

The advent of technology, which made possible intimate contact with urban ways—either directly through better transportation facilities or indirectly through improved communication networks—helped bring about the end to an older way of life. The movies replaced the Chautauqua and television diminished the appeal of church and lodge. While the older institutions sometimes coexisted along with the new ones, the older roles died out. As the generations passed, roles that had remained relatively unchanged since the nineteenth century disappeared. The role of farmer or small-town person, differentiated from a city dweller by lack of sophistication and ignorance, has become a relic of the past. In ways of behavior, we are all urbanites.

Selection 21 returns us to contemporary times. It is taken from a Congressional committee hearing on nutrition and shows a different conception of the role that the poor should take. This role has changed considerably from the one described by Riis. For Riis the poor were self-denying, stoical in the face of adversity, and undemanding, and they shared a value system based on individual responsibility.

The new role is exemplified best by Mrs. Jeanette Washington of the National Welfare Rights Organization who testified before this committee. (The name of the organization is as good a clue to the changed role of the poor as any.) Mrs. Washington represents the poor who share an identity with other poor; they are no longer too proud to admit their poverty. They no longer accept welfare as a privilege but instead regard it as an inherent right of citizens of the United States. They are no longer self-punitive about their circumstances, blaming instead the social system for having failed them. They are no longer patient, no longer content to wait for a better tomorrow. They are, in short, active, aggressive, and vocal.

Not all poor people identify with the National Welfare Rights Organization. Many still conceive of the role of the poor as it was in nineteenth-century urban America. The mere fact of the existence of this organization, however, must give pause to the majority of Americans who hold the older view. The new militance of some of the poor and their unwillingness to accept the blame for their poverty threatens middle-class Americans who use the specter of poverty and the shame attached to it to motivate themselves and their children. If being poor no longer accurately mirrors character, how will society operate? If being poor is not bad, how will the next generation gain an enthusiasm for work? These questions account for much uneasiness on the part of the more affluent majority.

The very rich are not as troublesome to the rest of America as are the very poor. In part, this is because they have become less visible than in the past. Selection 22 documents the changes in role through a discussion of five places in New York City that are frequented by the new aristocracy. Peter Benchley points out in this article that this new aristocracy is not the same as the old aristocracy. Nor are the rules the same. The clothes worn and the manners used have become so varied that judgment of them is difficult. There are those who cling to older rules. The admission committee at Raffles is composed in part, of names long in the social register—Drexel, Vanderbilt, and Whitney—and the curtained rooms for members to entertain women other than their wives speaks for some discretion. The snobbishness remains and is, perhaps, intensified; would the proper clubs in Newport in 1905 have turned away the Prince of Wales or President Theodore Roosevelt and his daughter Alice?

The new elite, for the most part, is more ephemeral than the old. This is reflected in the success of Raffles and Le Club. To become a celebrity, one must associate with other celebrities. Raffles and Le Club are where the celebrities are—despite the darkness of Le Club, where the celebrities, or anyone else, cannot be distinguished. The attraction of the Hippopotamus is different. Obviously catering to a younger generation more involved in sex and less in alcohol, the Hippopotamus is the place for the would-be notorious. The genuine celebrities on owner Olivier Coquelin's list are for publicity purposes at the opening but are not counted on for continued business. While the Hippopotamus relies upon people with money, it disdains middle-class bachelors and single girls, aiming at a clientele a cut under Le Club and Raffles.

Not so Maxwell's Plum, which encourages middle-class swingers. The attraction here is the mix of celebrities with noncelebrities, and this attraction is testimony to the changed attitudes of the 1970s. It is now fashionable to associate with the young, the black, and the artsy-craftsy crowd. Another club, Elaine's, caters to the intellectuals and writers. Unlike Maxwell's Plum, Elaine's has a more homogeneous clientele; celebrities are welcome, but they are celebrities of another kind. There is a mix, but it is a mix of the talented and the rich.

In 1900, there was an identifiable society that had recognizable standards to which individuals had to conform. It was dominated by the rich, who were not synonymous with the famous. Society was made up of persons who originated fads and who were indifferent to public opinion. By 1970, this society, as Cleveland Amory has shown, was dead. The rich survived but their behavior changed. No longer did they set the fashion in clothes, sports, or parties. In many instances, they followed fads. Behavior appropriate to certain classes has blended, so the casual observer may have trouble distinguishing between the duke and the commoner. They wear the same clothes and can be found at the same places. Not all the rich have changed; like the old poor, the old rich may cling to an older role. They still collect art, urge their daughters to go to debutante balls and join the Junior League, and live in Palm Springs in the winter. Despite these conservative examples, the rich have more alternatives to behavior and can take on a new life-style.

In this section we have suggested that there has been considerable change in attitudes of rich and poor toward themselves and their role in society in the twentieth century. The rich have assumed less exclusive and less arrogant roles; the poor have become less humble. While the poor may still look with envy on the rich and imitate their ways, the rich may take from the poor such things as clothes, dances, and slang. The rich may wear the red shirts of the ghetto with their tuxedos, and may reject a high culture orientation for a camp-art one. All of this occurs while the poor are becoming an interest group and are taking on the moral assurance of the middle-class American. Although the roles of rich and poor are still aeons apart, they are now borrowing more from each other.

18 THE TENANT

Jacob Riis

When the country was in the throes of the silver campaign, the newspapers told the story of an old laborer who went to the subtreasury and demanded to see the "boss." He undid the strings of an old leathern purse with fumbling fingers, and counted out more than two hundred dollars in gold eagles, the hoard of a lifetime of toil and self-denial. They were for the government, he said. He had not the head to understand all the talk that was going, but he gathered from what he heard that the government was in trouble, and that somehow it was about not having gold enough. So he had brought what he had. He owed it all to the country, and now that she needed it he had come to give it back. The man was an Irishman. Very likely he was enrolled in Tammany and voted her ticket. I remember a tenement at the bottom of a back alley over on the East Side, where I once went visiting with the pastor of a mission chapel. Up in the attic there was a family of father and daughter in two rooms that had been made out of one by dividing off the deep dormer window. It was midwinter, and they had no fire. He was a peddler, but the snow had stalled his pushcart and robbed them of their only other source of income, a lodger who hired cot room in the attic for a few cents a night. The daughter was not able to work. But she said, cheerfully, that they were "getting along." When it came out that she had not tasted solid food for many days, was starving, in fact—indeed, she died within a year, of the slow starvation of the tenements that parades in the mortality returns under a variety of scientific names which all mean the same thing—she met her pastor's gentle chiding with the excuse, "Oh, your church has many poorer than I. I don't want to take your money."

These were Germans, ordinarily held to be close-fisted; but I found that in their dire distress they had taken in a poor old man who was past working, and had kept him all winter, sharing with him what they had. He was none of theirs; they hardly even knew him, as it appeared. It was enough that he was "poorer than they," and lonely and hungry and cold.

It was over here that the children of Dr. Elsing's Sunday school gave out of the depth of their poverty fifty-four dollars in pennies to be hung on the Christmas tree as their offering to the persecuted Armenians. One of their teachers told me of a Bohemian family that let the holiday dinner she brought them stand and wait, while they sent out to bid to the feast four little ragamuffins of the neighborhood who else would have gone hungry. I remember well a teacher in one of the Children's Aid Society's schools, herself a tenement child, who, with breaking heart, but brave face, played and sang the children's Christmas carols with them rather than spoil their pleasure, while her only sister lay dying at home.

SOURCE: From Jacob Riis, *A Ten Years' War, an Account of the Battle with a Slum in New York* (Boston: Houghton, Mifflin, 1900).

I might keep on and fill many pages with instances of that kind, which simply go to prove that our poor human nature is at least as robust on Avenue A as up on Fifth Avenue, if it has half a chance, and often enough to restore one's faith in it, with no chance at all; and I might set over against it the product of sordid and mean environment which one has never far to seek. Good and evil go together in the tenements as in the fine houses, and the evil sticks out sometimes merely because it lies nearer the surface. The point is that the good does outweigh the bad, and that the virtues that turn the balance are after all those that make for good citizenship anywhere, while the faults are oftenest the accidents of ignorance and lack of training, which it is the business of society to correct. I recall my discouragement when I looked over the examination papers of a batch of candidates for police appointment—young men largely the product of our public schools in this city and elsewhere—and read in them that five of the original New England States were "England, Ireland, Scotland, Belfast, and Cork;" that the Fire Department ruled New York in the absence of the Mayor—I have sometimes wished it did, and that he would stay away awhile; and that Lincoln was murdered by Ballington Booth. But we shall agree, no doubt, that the indictment of these papers was not of the men who wrote them, but of the school that stuffed its pupils with useless trash, and did not teach them to think. Neither have I forgotten that it was one of these very men who, having failed, and afterward got a job as a bridge policeman, on his first pay day went straight from his post, half frozen as he was, to the settlement worker who had befriended him and his sick father, and gave him five dollars for "some one who was poorer than they." Poorer than they! What worker among the poor has not heard it? It is the charity of the tenement that covers a multitude of sins. There were thirteen in this policeman's family, and his wages were the biggest item of income in the house.

Jealousy, envy, and meanness wear no fine clothes and masquerade under no smooth speeches in the slums. Often enough it is the very nakedness of the virtues that makes us stumble in our judgment. I have in mind the "difficult case" that confronted some philanthropic friends of mine in a rear tenement on Twelfth Street, in the person of an aged widow, quite seventy I should think, who worked uncomplainingly for a sweater all day and far into the night, pinching and saving and stinting herself, with black bread and chicory coffee as her only fare, in order that she might carry her pitiful earnings to her big, lazy lout of a son in Brooklyn. He never worked. My friends' difficulty was a very real one, for absolutely every attempt to relieve the widow was wrecked upon her mother heart. It all went over the river. Yet one would not have had her different.

Sometimes it is only the unfamiliar setting that shocks. When an East Side midnight burglar, discovered and pursued, killed a tenant who blocked his way of escape, a few weeks ago, his "girl" gave him up to the police. But it was not because he had taken human life. "He was good to me," she explained to the captain whom she told where to find him, "but since he robbed the church I had no use for him." He had stolen, it seems, the communion service in a Staten Island church. The thoughtless laughed. But in her ignorant way she was only trying to apply the standards of morality as they had been taught her. Stunted, bemuddled, as they were, I think I should prefer to take my chances with her rather than with the woman of wealth and luxury who, some years ago, gave a Christmas party to her lap-dog, as on the whole the sounder of the two, and by far the more hopeful.

All of which is merely saying that the country is all right, and the people are to be trusted with the old faith in spite of the slum. And it is true, if we remember to put it that way—in spite of the slum. There is nothing in the slum to warrant that faith save human nature as yet uncorrupted. How long it is to remain so is altogether a question of the sacrifices we are willing to make in our fight with the slum. As yet, we are told by the officials having to do with the enforcement of the health ordinances, which come closer to the life of the individual than any other kind, that the poor in the tenements are "more amenable to the law than the better class." It is of the first importance, then, that we should have laws deserving of their respect, and that these laws should be enforced, lest they conclude that the whole thing is a sham. Respect for law is a very powerful bar against the slum. But what, for instance, must the poor Jew understand, who is permitted to buy a live hen at the market, yet neither to kill nor keep it in his tenement, and who on his feast day finds a whole squad of policemen detailed to follow him around and see that he does not do any of the things with his fowl for which he must have bought it? Or the day laborer, who drinks his beer in a "Raines law hotel," where brick sandwiches, consisting of two pieces of bread with a brick between, are set out on the counter, in derision of the state law which forbids the serving of drinks without "meals"? (The Stanton Street saloon keeper who did that was solemnly acquitted by a jury.) Or the boy, who may buy fireworks on the Fourth of July, but not set them off? These are only ridiculous instances of an abuse that pervades our community life to an extent that constitutes one of the gravest perils. Insincerity of that kind is not lost on our fellow citizen by adoption, who is only anxious to fall in with the ways of the country; and especially is it not lost on his boy.

We shall see how it affects him. He is the one for whom we are waging the battle with the slum. He is the to-morrow that sits to-day drinking in the lesson of the prosperity of the big boss who declared with pride upon the witness stand that he rules New York, that judges pay him tribute, and that only when *he* says so a thing "goes;" and that it is all for what he can get out of it, "just the same as everybody else." He sees corporations to-day pay blackmail and rob the people in return, quite according to the schedule of Hester Street. Only there it is the police who charge the peddler twenty cents, while here it is the politicians taking toll of the franchises, twenty per cent. Wall Street is not ordinarily reckoned in the slum, because of certain physical advantages; but, upon the evidence of the day, I think we shall have to conclude that the advantage ends there. The boy who is learning such lessons—how is it with him?

The president of the Society for the Prevention of Cruelty to Children says that children's crime is increasing, and he ought to know. The managers of the Children's Aid Society, after forty-six years of wrestling with the slum for the boy, in which they have lately seemed to get the upper hand, say in this year's report that on the East Side children are growing up in certain districts "entirely neglected," and that the number of such children "increases beyond the power of of philanthropic and religious bodies to cope properly with their needs." In the Tompkins Square Lodging House the evening classes are thinning out, and the keeper wails: "Those with whom we have dealt of late have not been inclined to accept this privilege; how to make night school attractive to shiftless, indifferent street boys is a difficult problem to solve."

Perhaps it is only that he has lost the key. Across the square, the Boys' Club of St. Mark's Place, that began with a handful, counts five thousand members today, and is seeking a place to build a house of its own. The school census man announces that no boy in that old stronghold of the "bread or blood" brigade need henceforth loiter in the street because there is not room in the public school, and the brigade has disbanded for want of recruits. The shop is being shut against the boy, and the bars let down at the playground.

19 THE GOLDEN CIRCUS

Walter Lord

A man who has a million dollars is as well off as if he were rich.
John Jacob Astor

New inventions, glittering fairs, the excitement of a country bursting at the seams held little appeal for a courteous, reserved New Englander whom everyone assumed to be French—Louis Sherry of St. Albans, Vermont. As New York's favorite caterer and restaurateur, Sherry naturally leaned toward preserving the Established Order. And Society responded—they all came to his handsome restaurant on Fifth Avenue or engaged him to handle the sparkling parties that filled their leisure.

Sherry's big leather-bound order book suggested that the 1905 season would be one of his busiest. It began auspiciously with Mrs. Astor's ball, to which some 450 guests (not Ward McAllister's Four Hundred) dutifully reported on the evening of January 9. They came at 11:00, arriving from heavy, richly served dinners all over town—a centerpiece of 3,000 roses graced the Harry Lehrs' table at the St. Regis. Already buried under ten courses, the Lehrs' 100 guests now embarked on a nine-course midnight supper at Mrs. Astor's—terrapin, fish, canvasback duck, *pâté de foie gras* and so on.

SOURCE: "1905: The Golden Circus" from *The Good Years* by Walter Lord. Copyright © 1960 by Walter Lord. Reprinted by permission of Harper & Row, Publishers, Inc.

With this foundation, they had to dance a cotillion. But perhaps Mrs. Astor's favors made it all worth while—everyone got Directoire canes, paper weights, leather pen wipers, rubber-bulb automobile horns, gold pencil cases, china figurines, whips, jardinieres, and leather letter cases.

When it was over, the guests sat down for another supper—more terrapin and four other courses. By now there were only fifty survivors. Possibly Ward McAllister was right after all—there were only "the Four Hundred" and they had gone home, leaving only the social climbers to battle on to the end. More likely, most of the guests were just worn out.

For this was the era of massive entertainment. Night after night the rich and fashionable vied with one another in achieving the spectacular. Two weeks after Mrs. Astor's ball, James Stillman installed an artificial waterfall in his dining room for a dinner dance. On another occasion Rudolf Guggenheimer stocked the Waldorf's Myrtle Room with nightingales borrowed from the zoo. The Cornelius Vanderbilts imported the first act from the Broadway musical *The Wild Rose,* complete with cast and scenery, for an "at-home" during one of Newport's famous tennis weeks.

In the competitive whirl, some hosts simply turned to the bizarre. Cornelius K. G. Billings marked the completion of his $200,000 stable by giving a Horseback Dinner at Sherry's. Livery stable nags were brought by freight elevator to the grand ballroom. The honored guests mounted them and dined in the saddle from precariously balanced trays. The dinner was served by waiters disguised as grooms, while grooms (perhaps disguised as waiters) hovered in the rear to clean up any mess.

At Newport, society was invited to a formal dinner to meet a new arrival, Prince Del Drago of Corsica. The "prince" turned out to be a monkey in full evening dress—the joint inspiration of Mrs. Stuyvesant Fish and her personal jester, Harry Lehr. The dinner went on, and as the monkey sipped his champagne, all agreed it was one of Mrs. Fish's cleverest ideas yet.

In the search for something new, the fashionable naturally turned to fancy-dress balls. While Newport amused itself with the exotic ("come-as-one-of-your-servants"), New York went for the lavish, and even the outlandish. In 1904, Mr. Lloyd Warren gave a Far Eastern masquerade that almost touched the high-water mark set by the Bradley Martin ball of the '90s. At Mr. Warren's dance the guests were told to come in Oriental costume. Some were a little vague on their geography—a good many Turks, Egyptians and Greeks showed up—but it was still a brilliant spectacle.

As the gay 1905 season got under way, invitations went out for another fancy-dress ball. The host was a dark, sensitive, twenty-eight-year-old New Yorker named James Hazen Hyde. Like Louis Sherry, he had little interest in mechanical contraptions like flying machines. His tastes ran to eighteenth-century coaching, *faisan piqué Louis XV,* 1830 beaver hats, royal purple ascots, embroidered French dressing gowns. And in the winter of 1905, he could afford them all.

His father, Henry B. Hyde, had made a vast fortune in the insurance business. Feeling that most of the companies lacked imagination, the elder Hyde formed the Equitable Life Assurance Society in 1859. He began with little more than a large sign and a box of cigars for the customers he hoped would come, but the very first day he wrote $100,500 in policies. From this promising start he built the Equitable into a mammoth organization of 600,000 policyholders and $400 million in assets. The company became an obsession—it was more than a business, it was a hobby, a monument, a cherished possession.

Originally he hoped to leave this prize to his first son, Henry B., Jr., but the lad died at the age of ten. So he transferred his attention to the younger James Hazen. With loving care he trained the boy, taught him to be proud of the Equitable ... to think of it as his own.

There was only one trouble. Young James Hazen Hyde was not what is normally called the business type. His tastes ran more to literature, music, good food, fine living. Early in his teens he visited France and fell in love with the country. Not with the gaiety of Paris—or the attractions other boys smirked about—but with the exquisite culture of French civilization. He loved the salons, the poets, the theatre and ballet. In his enthusiasm he soon adopted French clothes, mannerisms, even what he considered to be a French appearance.

He grew a sharp-pointed little Henry IV beard, combed his thick black hair in a wavy pompadour, affected tight-fitting black frock suits. His spats, gloves and waistcoats lent generous splashes of color to the ensemble. Usually he capped it off with an immaculately ironed silk hat—not in the jaunty Edwardian style, but with the brim flat and turned down. It reminded unsophisticated people of the hats traditionally worn by French villains on the stage.

This was the young man who suddenly inherited controlling interest in the Equitable, when his father died of overwork in 1899. At the time James Hazen Hyde was only twenty-three—just one year out of Harvard. Realizing this, the old man had arranged for James Alexander—a loyal long-time official of Equitable—to serve as president and trustee for the boy until he reached thirty. Still, it was a pretty sharp transition. As first vice president, Hyde found himself with an annual salary of $100,000 and the prospect of limitless power.

It was enough to turn the head of anybody his age, and Hyde was perhaps more vulnerable than others. He already had extravagant tastes, and he was quite impressionable. Seeing this innocent young sentry guarding the Equitable's $400 million, the sharper denizens of Wall Street swooped in with all kinds of flattering proposals.

They made him director of forty-six companies, including nineteen banks and fourteen railroads. They let him in on all sorts of promotions and schemes. They persuaded him, in return, to deposit the Equitable's money in their banks, to invest the Equitable's funds in their ventures. And they showed him how that could earn him a little extra. For instance, the Oregon Short line, on which Hyde served as director, sold $1,250,000 in bonds to "James H. Hyde and Associates" at 96, which in turn sold the bonds to Equitable at 97—clearing a $25,044 profit in five days.

Hyde's problem was not getting but spending his money. And it was that way with most of the rich. These were the days before taxes and high living costs. Nor were there any brakes on the desire to spend. No recent depression left a lingering fear that conspicuous wealth might be in poor taste. No carefully trained sense of propriety curbed the natural inclination of rich people to act that way. There were exceptions of course—take those quiet Rockefellers—but they were few. For the most part, the privileged poured their money into projects that amused or interested them, while the not-so-privileged watched the splash.

And it was quite a splash. William K. Vanderbilt's palace on Long Island boasted a garage for one hundred motorcars. His brother George used more men on his North Carolina estate than the Department of Agriculture had for the entire country. Pierpont Morgan spent over a million dollars in one year for old scrolls and tapestries. William Fahnestock decorated the trees around his Newport "cottage" with artificial fruit made of fourteen-carat gold. Mrs. John Jacob Astor enjoyed a two-ton bathtub cut from a solid block of marble. The O. H. P. Belmonts treated their horses at Newport to pure linen sheets embroidered with the family crest. Running out of ideas, financier Thomas Lawson paid $30,000 to have a carnation named after his wife.

James Hazen Hyde's tastes weren't as sumptuous, but in his way he was more eye-catching. He loved, for instance, coaching and was perhaps the country's best four-in-hand whip. Clattering along New York's avenues, he cut quite a sight, sporting a fawn-colored driving coat with large pearl buttons. On these occasions he discarded his shiny topper for a tall fuzzy beaver, but this made him no less conspicuous.

At one point Hyde established a regular stage run from Holland House to the front of George Gould's estate at Lakewood, New Jersey, seventy-eight miles away. To make the trip more attractive, he had a little inn at New Brunswick done over in the style of Olde Englande. Here the paying passengers could descend for an appropriate luncheon. Not exactly profitable but certainly spectacular.

His taste in entertaining ran along similar lines. He loved the cosmopolitan, the flashy, any occasion that could be considered part of the good life. He undoubtedly enjoyed taking Alice Roosevelt to the Horse Show in 1904—she was as worldly as they came. And it must have been pleasant to be seen with the President's daughter.

Not that there weren't less public occasions. For instance, the sophisticated little suppers he sometimes gave in his stables at Bay Shore. The French writer Jules Hurst vividly recalled one "where ladies donned old postillion hats or bull fighters' bonnets and blew hunting horns while everybody danced the cake walk."

Best of all, however, were the big parties. Who could forget his 1902 dinner for Ambassador Cambon of France? It cost the Equitable $12,600, but it was a brilliant affair—everybody came—and any young man couldn't help but enjoy being the center of so much attention.

Perhaps that triumph was in the back of his mind as he labored over plans for his 1905 masquerade. Ostensibly it would honor his niece, Annah Ripley, but she was rarely mentioned in the notices that appeared in the Society columns. It seems more likely that he just wanted to make a magnificent gesture.

The ball's motif was almost inevitable: the Court of Louis XV. As a special attraction—these days you had to give your guests more than just a party—he would import Madame Gabrielle Réjane, the current toast of Paris. She agreed to appear in a *commedietta* written especially for the occasion. He then recruited his friend Whitney Warren, an architect trained at the Beaux Arts, to convert Sherry's into a reasonable replica of Versailles.

New York Society began preparing for the great day—"le Mardi 31 Janvière 1905," according to the programme—with the varied emotions people have always approached costume parties. Mrs. George Gould went all-out, happily choosing the role of Marie Leczinska, the wife of Louis XV. She ordered a glittering ensemble of satin and pearls, trailing a long train of green velvet lined with ermine and embroidered with gold and emeralds. On the other hand, Mrs. F. Egerton Webb couldn't be bothered and felt she could get by with a powdered wig.

A few of the men self-consciously ordered court costumes; a good many more rummaged through trunks in the attic. Major Creighton Webb found an old toreador suit—not exactly right, but it would do. Georges A. Glaenzer salvaged the sheets of a Bedouin; it looked suspiciously like one of the costumes at Lloyd Warren's party last year. Most took the easy way out, settled for hunting pinks of the evening dress of their coaching club. History does not record how one of the young extra men, Franklin D. Roosevelt, solved the problem.

Starting at 10:30 that Tuesday evening, a steady stream of carriages and electrics rolled up to Sherry's. The young host had ordered all to be there by eleven o'clock, and even Mrs. Stuyvesant Fish managed to shepherd her small dinner party of sixty to the restaurant on time.

Straight to the third-floor ballroom they trooped. Before entering, a moment's pause to pay their *devoirs* to the splendid young man who made it all possible. Looking at him in his uniform of the New York Coaching Club—coat of myrtle green, black satin knee breeches, black silk stockings, and assorted medals—the insurance business seemed very, very far away.

Now to the ballroom and a breathtaking sight: Whitney Warren had gone wild with roses. Bushes, arbors, trellises, vines—every way a rose could grow. A latticework of roses crossed the south side of the room, screening both wings of the stage that had been built for the evening's performance. Rosebushes banked the ballroom floor itself. Rose trellises covered the galleries overlooking the room. Just like a real *loge grillée*, the savants said. From here reporters could watch the party without the guests having to look at them.

Promptly at eleven, conductor Nahan Franko tapped his baton, and the room swelled with the beautiful music of the Metropolitan Opera House's forty-piece orchestra. Eight of the season's debutantes advanced uncertainly to the center of the floor. There they were joined by eight equally uncertain young swains. The girls were dressed *à la Carmargo* (with baskets of roses, garlands or roses, wreaths of rosebuds) and the young men were predictably clad as Pierrots. Together they struggled through a gavotte. "Hearty applause was their reward."

Next, with unintentional cruelty, the ballet corps of the Metropolitan Opera showed how it should be done. Mlle. Enrichetta Varasi whirled gracefully through an intricate eighteenth-century figure, assisted by Herr Conreid's finest dancers.

Now it was almost midnight. A hum of excitement filled the room. Then, through the west portal, came four court lackeys carrying a *vernis Martin* sedan chair. Midway across the room they gently lowered it and out stepped Madame Réjane herself to the shrill delight of the 350 guests. She was, of course, dressed in the eighteenth-century fashion, but she was wise enough not to outdo any of the Society matrons.

A gracious greeting from the host ... a few final adjustments ... and the rose-tinted curtain went up. The *commedietta* turned out to be a little French bedroom farce called *Entre deux Portes*, written by Dario Nicodemi especially for the occasion. The plot involved a couple who tried to make each other jealous by staging separate flirtations in their neighboring bedrooms. The final curtain found all misunderstandings forgotten and the lovers locked in each other's arms.

This rickety vehicle was handled with tolerant skill by Madame Réjane and her company. A generous critic called the plot "ingenious" and all agreed that at least the scenery was wonderful. It had been imported from Paris by Mr. Hyde especially for the evening. The *Metropolitan Magazine* later called this "a very wise precaution when one remembers the rattle-trap settings to which Réjane treated her American audiences this season."

A blast of bugles followed the show and Hyde led his guests down to the supper room on the second floor. Here they found that Whitney Warren had again outdone himself. The room had been turned into a Versailles garden. Overhead was a rich canopy, under foot a rolling lawn. Along the sides were trellises, marble statues, even running fountains.

And, of course, there were more roses than ever. They lined the walls. They rambled over the gilt latticework. They bloomed on the trees that sheltered the sixty tables. And through them all peeped thousands of colored light bulbs, making the rosy vista even rosier.

A bell tinkled. The diners fell silent, and Madame Réjane arose from her gilded chair at the host's right. Charmingly she recited a little poem called "Apropos." It turned out to be another creative effort written just for the evening and dwelt, fittingly enough, on Franco-American friendship. After this salute to the *entente cordiale,* the guests plunged into *consommé Voltaire.*

The dawdlers were still sipping their Pol Roger '89 when the music began again upstairs. Now it was dancing for everyone. As the glittering couples swirled about, the twinkling lights were easily eclipsed by Mrs. Fish's turquoises, Mrs. Belmont's *parure* of emeralds, and especially by Mrs. Potter Palmer's diamond tiara, diamond dog collar, and diamond breastplates.

At three o'clock everybody came downstairs again for another supper. After the guests had their fill of bouillon, sausages, ham, and chicken, the survivors mounted to the ballroom for more dancing.

Wistfully looking on from the sidelines was Mrs. Clarence Mackay. She had so burdened herself with props and equipment that she was completely immobilized. In a moment of excess ambition, she had decided to come as the eighteenth-century actress Adrienne Lecouvreur playing her great role of Phèdre. Now she found herself equipped with a scepter, tangled in folds of silver cloth and turquoise, and trailing a train so long that it had to be carried by two little Negro boys in pink brocade. When she managed to move at all, they trudged wearily after her most of the night.

Dawn found Mrs. Mackay still holding out, but with train unhooked and pages gone. In the debris of torn vines and withered rose petals, she joined Mrs. Joseph Widener in thanking an ever-radiant James Hazen Hyde.

"You have given us a most delightful eighteenth-century dinner, but I think the time is ripe for a little twentieth-century breakfast," hinted Mrs. Widener.

It seemed a fine idea, and Hyde gallantly asked what she would like.

"Fishballs!" said Mrs. Widener, and for those who heard it, her earthy response broke the spell of Versailles for good.

The ball was over. Madame Réjane lay exhausted, unable to appear at the benefit for St. Mary's Hospital Wednesday afternoon. Society showed greater recuperative powers. The diamond-studded Mrs. Potter Palmer got to the same benefit, wearing a toque of golden grapes. Thursday she was still going strong at a charity ball at the Waldorf—this time clad in white gauze with straps of bronze spangles.

The press dutifully reported every detail. Its attitude toward the ball was favorable, even envious. The New York *World* especially approved the invitation list. The paper pointed out that this was more than just another gathering of the Four Hundred: the guests included names from the opera and stage. On February 5, the *World's* Society editor paid Hyde another compliment: "Unlike many of those who do Society, he is serious and an excellent man of business."

At the Equitable there was some difference of opinion. Old James Alexander had long been upset by Hyde's deals and associates; he considered them reckless and irresponsible. The young man's social life somehow confirmed his worst suspicions. And now this ball: it was the last straw. Bitter dissension racked the firm: Hyde and his imaginative friends like E. H. Harriman on one side; Alexander and old-line management on the other.

On February 9 one of the Alexander faction demanded that Hyde resign, arguing among other points that he had put on a cancan at the ball. (Ironically, no one would have shuddered more than Hyde if such a breach of decorum had occurred.)

At another meeting the Hyde clique grew so excited that at one point Harriman was literally speechless. For a few seconds all he could do was yelp, "Wow! Wow! Wow!" This caused Judge William Cohen, one of the opposition, to remark coldly: "Mr. Harriman, that is one aspect of the situation which had quite escaped my attention."

Such blazing dissension soon reached the *World*. Publisher Joseph Pulitzer quickly forgot his Society editor's little paeans to the imaginative host who was also "serious and an excellent man of business." He smelt a far hotter story.

By mid-February all New York was lapping up the *World's* exposé of "High Life Insurance" at the Equitable. On February 19 the paper's Sunday supplement printed stolen pictures of guests at the ball. And in the merciless lens of photographer Byron's camera, the impression was devastating. There was no suggestion of an evening of old-world culture; only shot after shot of bewigged lackeys, foppish young men, and spoiled-looking girls, their powdered hair lumped clumsily above their bland, patched faces.

Looking at them, it was easy to believe the rumors of scandalous goings-on. And the denials only focused greater attention on the stories. When one flustered Hyde spokesman announced that the ladies' costumes were not "diaphanous," eager readers raced for their dictionaries. Estimates on the cost of the ball soared from $75,000 ... to $100,000 ... to $200,000. Whatever it was, the *World* darkly (though mistakenly) hinted that the Equitable policyholders were the real hosts.

Matters came to a head March 31. The Equitable's contending factions met face to face at the offices of the Superintendent of Insurance. Alexander "trembled with rage and indignation." He demanded that Hyde agree at once to a mutualization plan that in effect would end his control of the company. The alternative: Alexander would go to the Attorney General and demand a public investigation. Hyde, described as "almost wild with anger," had overnight to think it over.

The following morning at ten o'clock, a brightly polished hansom set out from the Hyde residence on East Fortieth Street. On either side of the horse's bridle, a rosette of artificial violets nestled in a frame of green leaves. The coachman, splendid in tan livery, wore a bouquet of violets in his buttonhole. The young gentleman inside sported no violets but did wear a royal purple cravat. In this way James Hazen Hyde drove downtown for what amounted to an abdication ceremony —he agreed to the mutualization plan.

Now to get him out completely, the *World* stepped up its din. It found elevator men who recalled that Hyde wouldn't say good morning to them. It interviewed Bay Shore merchants who said, or were persuaded to say, "He's a little too Frenchified for us plain people." It printed a dandified picture of H. Rogers Winthrop, the inexperienced thirty-year-old whom Hyde appointed financial manager of the Equitable. It joyfully reported the appalling analogy offered by a loyal adherent: this inept soul explained that Hyde's activities were really no different from those pursued by a successful champagne salesman.

No one could stand this sort of drumfire. Hyde soon resigned. By then there had been so many charges and countercharges that the state investigated the whole insurance business. From September 6 to December 30, 1905, the Armstrong Committee's bright young counsel Charles Evans Hughes patiently chipped at the facts. He discovered how interlocking directorates worked—George W. Perkins of Morgan & Company sold George W. Perkins of New York Life $8 million worth of shaky International Mercantile Marine bonds floated by Morgan & Company. He discovered what politics could do—Mutual spent thousands on a mysterious "House of Mirth" located conveniently near the Albany legislature. He discovered that the very symbols of virtue can be tainted—old James Alexander, Equitable's shining knight, had played around with a few syndicates himself. (He also had six relatives on the payroll.) The following year, new regulations reformed the whole business.

To many, the most interesting result came sooner. On December 28—two days before the investigation closed—James Hazen Hyde boarded the French liner *La Lorraine*. "I wish to deny emphatically that I am going to live abroad," he told the reporters who saw him off. But thirty-five years passed before the period's most gilded youth—finally driven by the Nazis from his beloved France—quietly returned to his native land.

The pratfalls of the privileged gave ordinary people a steady diet of excitement. They loved watching Charlie Schwab squirm, when the president of U.S. Steel was discovered gambling at Monte Carlo. They lapped up stories of fantastic poker games on the Atlantic—it was said one millionaire lost $90,000 in a friendly session on the *Kaiser Wilhelm II*. They savored the antics of Harry Thaw, who wrecked cafés and rode a horse up the steps of the Union League Club.

The very week of the Equitable crisis, young Thaw married the lovely show girl Evelyn Nesbit. Everyone wondered whether this new responsibility would quiet him down. The question was answered a year later on the roof of Madison Square Garden. It was the opening night of the musical *Mamzelle Champagne*. Thaw was there with his wife, as was the country's leading architect, Stanford White. While a sextet called the "Big Six" sang "I Could Love a Million Girls," Thaw slipped away from his table, walked over to White, and shot him dead.

"You deserve this. You have ruined my wife!" he cried, and at the trial that followed, the public hung on the lurid details. There was little sympathy for Thaw, who eventually got off by pleading insanity, but enormous interest in the stories of high jinks in high places. The murdered White seemed almost a stage roué—a wicked hide-out, a velvet swing to allure innocent girls, the inevitable glass of drugged champagne.

Nor were the vagaries of the rich just something to watch. Sometimes they affected people directly. Especially the growing number of cases where automobiles were concerned. The "bubble"—as everybody called it—was still considered a rich man's toy, and he certainly treated it that way.

Alfred G. Vanderbilt made a sport of eluding New York policemen in his big red touring car. One day in 1905 he dashed past patrolman Hanlon going eighteen miles an hour. This, of course, was well above the ten-miles-an-hour speed limit. Hanlon gave pursuit on a bicycle. He scored a rare triumph by nabbing Vanderbilt when the millionaire bogged down in a Harlem mudhole.

About the same time Pierpont Morgan's coupé struck a Mrs. Mary Socco on Park Row ... and drove on downtown without bothering to stop. Police eventually caught up with the driver but Mrs. Socco withdrew her complaint, according to the *World*, "when she learned of the wealth of the occupant in the coupé." On another occasion Mrs. Stuyvesant Fish managed to run down the same Negro three times with her electric. Incredibly the man emerged unhurt and ran off. There was no question of legal redress. He was only too happy to escape.

When local authorities tried to establish some sort of order, the automobilists quickly bristled. The Duke of Manchester, visiting New York with his bride, was politely indignant to find he couldn't have a driver's license for the asking. "A duke who is fit to be trusted with an American wife," he complained, "is certainly fit to be trusted with a 'bubble' in New York, provided he knows how to run it."

He missed the point. It was not a question of ability, but behavior. And the only thing more lethal than one automobilist was a collection of them. This was immediately apparent when the first Vanderbilt Cup Race was staged in 1904. The world's best cars and drivers competed over a course that ran through the quiet lanes and hamlets of Long Island. There were thrills galore, and word quickly spread that this was something to see.

When the second race was staged in 1905, Society went en masse to the scene. Starting time was set at 6:00 A.M., and the morning star still shone as the long line of autos and carriages crept toward the shaky grandstand on Jericho Turnpike. In the first gray light of dawn, the elite stood nervously around, listening to the motors warm up, watching blue fire spout from the exhausts.

The scene reminded some of early-morning hunt meets, others of a Roman chariot race. In any case, they had never known anything quite like it—which was obvious from their dress. Mrs. Tiffany Belmont chose tweed; Mrs. Oliver Harriman dripped pearls. Miss Catherine Cameron's Gainsborough hat seemed better suited to a Buckingham Palace lawn party. Perhaps the most remarkable sight was Mrs. Reginald Brooks, who blended together a Persian veil, Panama hat, and Scotch knockabout suit.

The gentlemen too were uncertain. Most wore riding clothes, as though going to a hunt, but Herman B. Duryea wore a splendid gray cutaway, gloves and mauve tie. Only W. K. Vanderbilt, Jr., seemed sure what to do—he wore a black satin Norfolk jacket, black leather trousers, and thoroughly professional-looking automobile goggles.

As the twenty cars roared off on the twenty-eight-mile course, the fashionable cheered and waved. Pietro Lancia, the daredevil Italian driver, stood up in his big Fiat and saluted them back. The race was ten laps—with not much to look at in between—so most of the time the spectators gossiped, or gaped at the Duchess of Marlborough's box, or nibbled at sandwiches supplied by enterprising farmers at Delmonico prices. All agreed that the local people were outrageous—charging as much as $50 for a parking space near the course.

And yet there was something to be said on their side. The racers roared through Jericho, Brookville, Greenvale, Lakeville, other towns at over sixty-five miles an hour. The dashing American Foxhall Keene clipped off a telegraph pole. Louis Chevrolet broke an axle and veered into a ploughed field, scattering fans and farmers alike. Joe Tracy, the plucky American who finished third, conceded that he saw "some dogs lying on the track near Mineola." Auguste Hemery, the Frenchman who ultimately won, coolly calculated, "Someday a dozen people will be killed if means are not found for keeping American courses free." The emotional Lancia was more complaining: "Thousands ... all in the way."

It spelled a grave problem to Woodrow Wilson, the president of Princeton. Several months later he declared, "Nothing has spread socialistic feeling in this country more than the use of the automobile. ... To the countryman they are a picture of arrogance of wealth, with all its independence and carelessness."

Wilson was right about autos but wrong about people. Except for a small, smoldering minority, Americans felt no resentment toward the little world of Privilege that lived this special life. Far from turning "socialistic," some were frankly envious. Four days after the Hyde Ball, Katy Cogan and Sophia Peterson—a pair of impressionable Harlem teenagers—were so overwhelmed by the press accounts that they ran away from home. Their avowed purpose: "not to return until they had gained a place in Society." A generation later, girls might run off to Hollywood, or to become "models," but at this time the epitome of glamour was the Social Register.

On a slightly more dignified scale, the same sort of thing was going on all over the country. Everywhere the newly-rich were battering at the gates of local Society—the best fruit of success they could imagine. Charles Dana Gibson depicted these climbers in searing cartoons. Frederick Townsend Martin was more philosophical: "I remember very well the first great march of the suddenly rich upon the social capitals of the nation. Very distinctly it comes back to me with what a shock the fact came home to the sons and daughters of what was pleased to call itself the aristocracy of America that here marched an army better provisioned, better armed with wealth, than any other army that had ever assaulted the citadels of Society."

Most people were less ambitious. They didn't expect to make Society, but they didn't feel downtrodden either. On the contrary, they were content to sit back and enjoy the show. The average American has always enjoyed watching conspicuous spenders in action, and until the discovery of TV, screen and sports stars, Society filled the role. The press realized this and served what amounted to a minute-by-minute account of fashionable doings.

So in 1905 it was front-page news when, during Robert Goelet's dinner at Sherry's, Miss Laura Swann's hat caught on fire ... or when a group of stately Boston ladies abandoned side saddle ... or when Yale and Princeton played football that November in New Haven.

For football was another Society monopoly. True, all sorts of schools played it, but the only ones that counted were Yale, Harvard, and Princeton. They won the headlines, dominated the All-American teams, and provided a steady flow of heroes—usually bandaged and limping—who had an enthusiastic national following. The Saturday of the 1905 Yale-Princeton game, the New York *Tribune* bothered to mention only one game west of the Hudson—those interesting Carlisle Indians were playing the University of Cincinnati.

But all eyes watched the fashionable converge on New Haven. They rolled north in fifty special parlor cars, their needs recorded in page after page of Louis Sherry's order book. *Gumbo passé* led off the seven courses served in Captain R. B. McAlpin's car ... *huîtres à la Camile* for Mr. McCall ... *croquettes exquise* for E. S. Auchincloss. The best Sherry waiters went along to serve the Krug '98 and Apollinaris water for the ladies.

That afternoon Yale routed Princeton 23 to 4, and as the private cars lumbered back to New York, the Sherry waiters were again on the job. In Car No. 2126 the Auchincloss party enjoyed post-game refreshments that might seem strange to a later generation—they had sandwiches, tea, and lady fingers.

Crowds jammed Grand Central as the specials pulled in, apparently content just to gape at the people who had been on the scene. Accounts of the game filled the front page Sunday, and everyone suffered with Captain Cooney of Princeton, who was so shattered by the disaster that he couldn't face the press.

No doubt about it, Society put on a wonderful show—whether football, parties, regattas, or automobiling. Everyone was entertained, and no one seemed bitter. Let Professor Wilson shake his head, most people went along with the New York *Tribune's* salute to the end of 1905: "Never did a year close with a better record —never did a new year dawn with prospect brighter—Good times go marching on!"

20 THE CITY COMES TO MAIN STREET

Louis Atherton

In material ways, midwestern country towns have become more and more like cities, and have departed radically from former patterns of living. Rockville, Indiana, advertised a surprisingly large number of modern services in 1948, including a "mortuary" prepared to handle every detail of funerals, and appliance stores selling various national brands of electric refrigerators and home freezers. Hatcheries, garages, filling stations, home-and-auto radio repair shops, dry cleaners and pressers, a battery shop, a "Beauty Shoppe," and moving-picture houses contrasted sharply with nineteenth-century services. Advertisements mentioned electric sweepers, floor polishing machines, electric wiring and maintenance, ambulance service, and nationally publicized brands of insulating materials. For the term "country town" to continue to have real meaning under such circumstances, Rockville and other claimants to that title need more than a small population in a rural setting, and that need has been expressed in the word "togetherness."

A real country town continues to be a community in which people speak to one another as they pass along the street and a stranger is recognized as such the minute he arrives. In such places people feel that all "belong" and all should be acquainted. When Mrs. Maggie Fugate asked the Gallatin, Missouri, editor to continue to send the paper to Viola, Illinois, where she then lived, she explained that her husband had recently died from a stroke and that she needed something to remind her of other days, and, as Mrs. Fugate said, there were people around Gallatin whom she once knew. Mrs. Fred Snyder of Altamont felt much the same way. On a Tuesday shopping trip to Gallatin she took time out to renew her subscription because her husband, "the late Fred Snyder," had been a lifelong reader of that paper, and she expected to continue the custom as long as she lived.

In real country towns people know one another well enough to recognize the unique in every personality, town "characters" being common for that reason. "Uncle Pat" Snider of Altamont, Missouri, had all kinds of trouble in 1909. Boys first stole his knife and tobacco while he was "taking in the sights" at the local depot; then, while "up town" one evening, he received a handful of "cow itch" down his neck. Although Uncle Pat could not identify the culprit, he swore vengeance on his tormentor. For the moment, however, he could only itch. August Derleth speaks of the "Town Characters Club" which he and another citizen of Sauk City, Wisconsin, have mentally called into being. It includes such likable characters as Mr. Elby, the bibulous pants-presser, Mr. Syllaber, the salesman, Mr. Elgy, the incomparable justice of the peace, Mr. Elky, the kindly religious fanatic, and even Derleth himself. Out of such familiarity with one's neighbors comes the small-town urge to employ nicknames. In Sauk City they generally emphasize physical traits or personal mannerisms. "Butch" is a tough guy, ready to fight; "Dutchy" has a German accent; "Stub" and "Shorty" are simply short; "Pipe" once became ill from smoking; and "Duke" puts on airs.

In a real country town citizens identify themselves with the place through participation in informal social activities which are open to all. When the Clinton, Wisconsin, editor wanted to recall his own days of fun in the local community he remembered the strawberry patch on "Quality Hill," the melon patch near the Northwestern railroad tracks which the boys raided until Old Doc Calvert "doctored" the watermelons, and the swimming hole at the Wyman farm. He recalled the local fires which he had attended as a breathless youngster, the local home-run hitter in baseball, Ed Klenigbeil, the raft on Case's pond, hunting, annual school picnics in Wyman's Woods, and the place in town where one could put on skates and slide all the way to the marsh.

In spite of the tremendous upsurge of organized life and the organizational spirit, informal life still remains important in country towns. Residents have their memories made warm and vibrant by what they see. In Derleth's words,

> *Coming home this evening, I heard and saw children playing hide and seek in the park, and others playing about a bonfire in the street not far away; and at once I was struck with a pleasant nostalgic memory of how at one time I too played blindman's buff, statue, run-sheep-run, and hide-and-go-seek, always waiting apprehensively for the streetlights to come on, knowing soon we would be called to bed.*

Though one cannot determine the relative amounts of formal and informal social life in cities as contrasted with country towns, available figures and estimates indicate that informality exists most of all in small communities. Grownups belong to casual congeniality groups and youngsters make eating a hot dog or a noonday lunch at a local restaurant or having a coke at the local drug store a major part of their commercial recreation.

Several factors help explain why smaller places emphasize informal social life. For one thing, community-wide participation without extensive planning is much easier to achieve in villages. Moreover, rural towns have been slow to extend organizational activities to children. In the 1920's, 19 per cent of the population in a considerable number of midwestern towns, selected as average for their section, consisted of boys and girls aged ten to twenty, but only 2 per cent of all people enrolled in organizations in these same villages were members of girls' and boys' groups. Lastly, as the home of old people, country towns have been slow to abandon the more informal life of earlier days.

No historian can surpass Ruth Suckow's book, *Iowa Interiors*, in portraying the social life of elderly village people. In spite of airing and cleanliness, their homes are likely to retain an air of mouldiness, of autumn shade, emphasized

still more by the old-fashioned look of brown-painted woodwork. Suckow's
photographic mind evokes pictures of ancient organs, ingrain carpets, geraniums
in tin cans and jars, faded religious mottoes on the walls; of blue, plush-covered
albums with steel clasps on center tables, pink shells near the door, and black
walnut bedroom furniture; of "shut-off" chilly rooms and front-door screens
covered with black oilcloth in the winter season to reduce heating costs.

Suckow sees the tragedy in the lives of these elderly people. Instead of stress-
ing the usual theme of peace, security, and contentment in the little town, she
points out that many homes are haunted with fear of poverty and that all face
the grim reality of declining independence in old age. Since even the "well-fixed"
have worked hard in early life in order to be able to "sit" in later years, they
lack the necessary interests to enjoy their new-found leisure. Women fare better
with their sewing, cooking, canning, and housecleaning. But husband and wife
rise early as they did on the farm, and "she" waits on him at the table as she
did in more hurried days until "he" has finished his meal. Beyond attending
church functions he and she depend on informal activities for their social life.
She may attend a birthday club of elderly women even before she becomes a
widow, but does not turn to clubs otherwise. He goes to town for the mail and
a package of yeast. Going and coming he stops at the poultry house to chat
with his cronies. In a big dingy room littered with slatted poultry crates, a
wooden settee and some battered chairs around a pot-bellied stove compete with
similar accommodations for retired farmers in stores all over town. Most of the
loafers wear woolen caps, old coats, and sweaters which seem to go with their
white hair and rough, weather-stained complexions. These people live in the
past, and thereby help dilute the heavy emphasis on organizational life.

A real country town also continues to demand obedience to local customs
and beliefs from those who expect to share in its spirit of "togetherness." In
1905 a Rockville, Indiana, couple became incensed when their wedding plans
were marred by local "hoodlumism." In an effort to stage a fashionably correct
ceremony, male members of the wedding party had worn dress suits and a satisfactory number of out-of-town guests had been present. Unfortunately for the
peace of mind of those participating, a crowd gathered outside the gates of the
home, and, worse still, some of the bolder spirits insisted on using that "relic of
barbarism," the charivari, to serenade the bride and groom with raucous noise
and village joviality.

Even nostalgic articles recognize that knowing and being known exact the
penalty of conformity to local custom. A Mount Pleasant, Iowa, family received
gifts of chocolate cake, apple pie, a jar of home-made strawberry preserves, and
half of a fried chicken from immediate neighbors their first day in town, an introduction to many happy, satisfying years which lay ahead. Nonetheless, they
knew that friendship extended to them on arrival in a new community could
rapidly vanish unless they kept "clean," went to church most of the time, and
spoke to everybody. Another defender of the small town has recorded examples

of disciplinary force in action. When "Judith" in a moment of sentimental for-
getfulness said to her friends "Tom and I have such a wonderful love," she was
not allowed to forget the comment for a whole year. As the writer remarked,
Judith would be an old lady with snow-white hair before she allowed herself to
become audibly sentimental again:

> *After a few years of this, one is trained for the diplomatic service, for court
> intrigue, for a master's degree in tact, self-control, and valiance. For you have
> to take it. You have to profit by it. And, at times, you must hand it out.
> So, only, can the local social group survive without being bored, and so is the
> whole state enriched by discipline.*

Many factors have combined to weaken small-town "togetherness." Rural and
village youngsters know and participate in a larger world which no longer thinks
of them in unkind moments as rubes, hicks, or hayseeds. In describing the Iowa
State Fair of recent years, Phil Stong has stressed the poise and polish of 4-H
club boys and girls. Though busy showing livestock and household products during the day, these farm youngsters leave their dormitories on the fair grounds
each evening on pleasure bent, the girls garbed in stylish pink and yellow dresses
and the boys in clean white flannels—marked contrasts to the daytime blue jeans
of both sexes. As Stong says, they look like city folks, and an English photographer, covering the fair for a New York magazine, keeps asking why only city
people are present and no farmers in sight.

An expanded curriculum in consolidated rural and village high schools and
easy access to cities by automobile put youngsters in immediate contact with
urban life as early as the 1920's. Within another decade visits to cities even in
the dead of winter became routine. One Monday night in January, 1935, Ber-
nays Seymour and James Cooper of Hillsboro, Illinois, drove to St. Louis, fifty
miles away, to attend a performance of "Roberta," and Mrs. H. H. McHugh
took her daughters and their chums to the city to spend the night and see the
Russian ballet. Unfortunately, the true cosmopolitan has difficulty in developing
any feeling for small-town "togetherness." As small towns have become more
cosmopolitan, they have lessened their bonds of local unity.

From Peep Show to Movie

In 1887 Edison began work on the kinetograph, the first motion-picture
camera capable of photographing a few seconds of continuous action, and the
kinetoscope, the popular peep-show device which brought magic-shadow art to
the public. Edison concentrated on the kinetoscope, which retailed to showmen
at three hundred to three hundred and fifty dollars each, because he feared that
screen projections, enabling many people to see pictures from one machine,
would quickly destroy the novelty of his inventions. Nevertheless, the motion
picture soon invaded vaudeville programs, where it replaced one of the ordinary
acts because of its lower price or served as a "chaser" to clear the house when

the show ended. In the absence of titles or explanatory phrases, an announcer, garbed in a frock coat, stood at the side of the screen to make appropriate remarks and to identify objects as they flickered into view. As films lengthened, this functionary evolved into a "lecturer," whose services were necessary until producers began to substitute titles to explain the film.

Western audiences, including church societies and Chautauquas, showed an avid curiosity in moving pictures; an interest which travelling showmen from the older carnival, patent medicine, and phonograph fields began to meet with machines, lectures, and films purchased from the Michigan Electric Company of Detroit or Montgomery Ward. They were tall, gaunt personages, addicted to Prince Alberts—often turned slightly green at the back and shoulders by age. Although dependent on novelty and change for audience appeal, such exhibitors must have been astounded at the rapid growth of movies. By 1915 Louella O. Parsons and others were established film critics, stars were becoming nationally known, and movies were rapidly destroying the old opera-house regime.

Old country newspapers—yellow and fragile with age—reveal the ease with which moving pictures invaded older or better established mediums of entertainment. In 1905 the Terre Haute, Indiana, Chautauqua featured a vitascope production of the Russo-Japanese war in appealing to small neighboring towns for patronage. The following year, during a week's stay at Monroe, Wisconsin, the Mardi Gras Carnival Company introduced an "electric theatre" as one of its midway attractions. This showed pictures of the San Francisco fire, of Buster Brown and his dog "Tige" in comical feats, of the Old Maid's mad chase for a husband, of a bank robbery, a train robbery, a holdup of the Denver stage, and the capture of the fugitives who committed the crimes. A company of professional actors who presented a week of old-style plays to a Gallatin, Missouri, audience in January, 1909, gave a Saturday afternoon ten-cent matinee for children which featured moving pictures and illustrated songs.

The mixture of the old and the new was much in evidence at Algona, Iowa, in 1908. Jubilee singers performed at the Algona Chautauqua; Ringling Brothers circus came to town; and the local opera house featured old favorites like "Uncle Tom's Cabin" and "The Count of Monte Cristo." A brash, new "Broadway Electric Theatre" offered a program opening with a city "fire run" by a dozen or more fire engines, and involving scenes of daring rescues and hazardous positions taken by firemen. This was labelled "pathetic and sensational." In addition, patrons could see "The Talisman," called "mystic," "The Orphan," described as "pathetic," and a "Quiet Hotel," said to be "very comic." The program closed with an illustrated song, "Just Because I Loved You So," by Mr. Arthur Smith. Admission was ten cents—half-price for children under twelve—with shows starting at 7:30, 8:30, and 9:30. Shortly afterwards, the Broadway Electric Theatre responded to complaints against noisy children in the audience by charging them adult prices, except on Saturday nights, unless they were accompanied by their parents. All were urged not to miss the pictures "Are you an Elk?" and "The

Masher." Algonans were debating whether movies were just a fad of which the public would rapidly tire, but the local editor insisted that people would always be interested in unusual sights and would look at copies when originals were unavailable.

Even by 1916 touring play-companies and Chautauqua programs were beginning to seem dated in comparison with movie offerings. The Chatfield, Minnesota, Chautauqua in 1916 featured a lecture on "Unseen Forces" by Judge Manford Schoonover, "a rugged, manly man with a virile message." By then, the local Gem Theatre was advertising Vitagraph's "great five reel masterpiece, the Colossus of Modern Railway Drama—The Juggernaut," containing a train wreck, actually staged at a cost of $25,000. Though Chautauquas seemed solidly entrenched in public favor, within another ten years they were virtually gone because audiences preferred colossal train wrecks to virile messages.

Those were the days when serials were popular. Pearl White appeared in "The Perils of Pauline" in 1914, and the rage was on. In 1915 youngsters at Gallatin, Missouri, could see the first two reels of "The Master Key" simply by presenting a picture of a key, cut from the local advertisement, at the ticket window of the "Duchess Photoplay House." The remaining twenty-eight reels were strung out over the course of the next fourteen weeks. On Saturday nights Gallatin youngsters gathered on the front rows to chew popcorn, scream at chilling dramatic moments, and cheer when the hero overcame seemingly insuperable difficulties with nothing more than the pulsating music of the piano player at the front of the show house as an aid. In the end, movies completely eliminated some of the old rivals and surpassed all others in popularity. When Walworth County, Wisconsin, high school students were asked in 1950 to list their favorite pastimes, movies were an easy first choice, with 93 per cent naming picture shows as their favorite form of recreation.

Church and Lodge

Automobiles, movies, radio, television, and other mechanically reproduced mediums of entertainment now operate throughout the calendar year with no interruption from the marked midwestern variation in seasons. In doing so, they compete with churches and lodges which almost alone among nineteenth-century, small-town organizations maintained their major activities every month in the year. Basic church activities of a continuous nature have expanded very little over the years. The calendar for the Gallatin, Missouri, Christian Church in March, 1915, announced Bible School at 9:45, morning worship at 11:00, Junior Christian Endeavor at 3:00, Senior Christian Endeavor at 6:30, and an evening sermon at 7:30 on Sundays, with Ladies' Aid on Tuesday afternoons and prayer meetings on Wednesday evenings at 7:30. The United Brethren, the most active church in Ashville, Ohio, in July, 1926, had Bible School, morning preaching and afternoon Christian Endeavor on Sundays, orchestra and choir practice on Tuesday evenings, prayer meeting on Wednesday evenings, and meetings of the "Sisterhood" each Friday evening. Even in the smallest places, Sunday school, a Sunday morning preaching service, and midweek prayer meetings are maintained around the calendar, if at all possible.

Although lodges have suffered from new and competing forms of recreation, they have held on exceedingly well in the Middle West. In 1925, midwestern towns averaged over eight lodges each, considerably higher than the rate in comparable communities elsewhere. At the time, Masons, Eastern Stars, Odd Fellows, and Rebeccas were the most numerous. Lodges continue to appeal to middle-class groups and have emphasized social activities more with the passing of the years. Eastern Star receptions, installations, initiations, and entertainments are leading social events of the season, at which women often appear in evening clothes and the men in business suits.

21 NUTRITION AND HUMAN NEEDS–1970

MR. WILEY.[1] I would like to introduce Mrs. Jeanette Washington who is one of the members of the executive committee of the National Welfare Rights Organization and vice chairman of the citywide organization in New York City, and a recipient, herself, and one of the leaders from the beginning in the National Welfare Rights Organization.

I want to say at the outset, No. 1, that I had asked Senator Harris if he could possibly stay and hear this testimony because in many senses we have what we regard a very cogent message for the liberals in the House and in the Senate and we regard Senator Harris as a friend who has fought against repressive welfare legislation in and along with the late Senator Kennedy and yourself, Senator McGovern, who have brought out the serious problem of hunger and malnutrition in this country.

We have appreciated and admired the work you have done.

We feel especially concerned that we get the support of the liberal Senators and Congressmen around the issues that poor people have identified as their No. 1 issue in dealing with the problem of hunger and that is an adequate income and getting a drive for an adequate income for every citizen in this country.

We do not stress a guaranteed income. We stress adequate income. When we say adequate income, we are talking about an income to meet the real necessities of life in this country.

SOURCE: *Hearings Before the Select Committe on Nutrition and Human Needs of the United States Senate, Ninety-First Congress, Second Session* (Washington, D. C.: U. S. Government Printing Office, 1970).

[1]Dr. George A. Wiley, Executive Director, National Welfare Rights Organization.

We want to talk a little more about that but I would like to introduce Mrs. Washington to say something about the problem as we see it.

SENATOR McGOVERN. We are happy to welcome you to the committee, Mrs. Washington.

MRS. WASHINGTON.[2] Thank you very much.

I am a welfare recipient. I was raised on welfare and I am raising children on welfare. I have eight children. It is not an easy job. And I live in the State of New York which is supposed to be the Empire State of the world.

Poverty Amid Plenty

The cutback in the budget in New York State has affected my family and all families not only in New York City but all across the country.

My involvement in the National Welfare Rights Organization took my concern of myself primarily and put it on people, black people, white people, Mexican-Americans, Indians, people in general who are poor, who are hungry, who were in need and asking for redress from this American Government that has said we have a right.

Yet, when we went to the door, they said, "Don't knock; just walk in." When we get to the door, it is locked. We have seemed to find that during the course of the whole 30 years of this whole welfare program it is not doing the job it is supposed to do. It is supposed to get people on their feet and back into the American mainstream.

I am an example of that. I went to school in New York. I did not get educational opportunities; job opportunities were not there. As far as my children right now, there are not educational opportunities.

Since I have been involved in this movement, I have had problems with my children but I have let that not be a big thing in my life. But I have one that has been kicked out of school and become what you call another "problem" to society as far as drugs are concerned.

So, therefore, you see the cycle of poverty is not just money and giving us some food and a place to live, but it is many more things, the whole environment in which our children are to be raised, also.

I would just like to make a little statement from this printed statement here concerning how we feel because, as a mother, I have been out here struggling many days and I have said, "What is the use? Why should I go out again tomorrow because every day we go out we knock on doors and people say 'OK'"; always the promise of a package.

I have gotten to the point where I am a little tired of hearing about the promises and I have asked the Governor of New York State and the mayor of New York City and the commissioner of welfare, "What do you expect us to do?

[2] Mrs. Jeanette Washington, member of the Executive Committee, National Welfare Rights Organization.

Continue to be nice and passive and law-abiding citizens and orderly people when we are seeing hunger, we are seeing children without proper clothing, we are seeing elderly people who cannot go to a clinic, we are seeing blind people who cannot come out of homes, we are seeing pregnant mothers that do not have adequate clothing or diets to have a child in a good healthy condition.

"We are getting maltreatment from the doctors who are getting a lot of money from medicaid.

"Do they expect us to continue to be passive?"

I ask myself that many days why have I not wrecked a place where I can get my anger off. Again I think like so many poor people that may not be the same feeling, you know, the same level of feeling that I am at. Breaking up a place certainly is not going to feed the people, certainly is not going to make the Government give it to us tomorrow. So, I think twice.

But many days the emotions of the moment make you not think.

I would just like to make this statement here.

I am just wondering, how long can poor people stand on the outside of affluent America and be told to quietly watch and wait, to be still while their children starve? Poor people see the affluence around them. Poor people see the millions and billions being spent on everything from moon rockets to Merry Widow uniforms for the White House guards. How can the poor relate to a country where newspapers spend pages describing Mrs. Pompidou's hemlines while children in Wisconsin are without winter coats?

Government officials and average citizens alike are allegedly concerned about the fragmentation and polarization of our country. The biggest gap, gentlemen, is not generational, political, or even racial. The biggest gap is between the poor and the nonpoor.

We have a big struggle going on at this moment, not just organizing poor people to learn their rights, their constitutional rights and their rights as human beings. We are also involved in a struggle to educate the middle class. They have also been told the lie that poor people live at their expense.

Because I happened to live in a community which pays high taxes for the food that we buy, the prices go up when the checks come, we pay taxes in our rents, we pay water taxes; we purchase cigarettes, taxes are involved in that, also. But these taxes do very little for poor people.

As far as even education, our pennies go to education and yet our children never are allowed to get a student loan to further their education.

So, we question many times the fact that middle class is always told that poor people live at their expense and we are not tax-paying citizens so we don't have any rights to say what we need and what we want.

I look around and see middle-income co-ops going up at Federal Government expense. I see children getting educational opportunities in college in New York City at the expense of poor people's children who never get a chance to finish high school.

I just question who is living on welfare and are we really living at the expense of middle-class folks. I question Governor Rockefeller being so rich and involved in so many corporations and they have not been taxed for years but yet our taxes are continuing to go up. When they give us our welfare checks, we still have to pay those taxes and they increase.

Carfare is being eliminated. Transportation prices are going up. We are being concentrated in our area because people cannot travel in those areas. They are confined to the communities.

I thank you very much for speaking to you, sir, and to this body. I hope in summary you will be able to make good your promises and do some effective work, because I tell you a lot of us are tired of being studied and talked to, committee meetings are called, conferences are called, and nothing ever ends up.

Now the President is talking about air pollution and environment, the conditions of the slums, lead poisoning the children in our community. If we are given enough money to provide decent places for our children, many of those problems will be erased because lead poisoning does not vanish; it is still there even though you cover it up with another coat of paint in those old buildings, because that is the only place that people have to live.

Thank you, sir.

SENATOR McGOVERN. Thank you, Mrs. Washington.

Did I understand you to say that, in your judgment, the most important gap that we need to concentrate on is the gap between the rich and the poor?

Recognizing that there is a continuing civil rights inequality, that there is a gap between blacks and whites, what you are suggesting is that the most important problem to focus on is to close that gap between the poor and the rich. Is that a correct statement?

MRS. WASHINGTON. Yes. It takes a lot of education on that from our point. First of all, people are quite hostile to poor people coming in and telling them they have been wrong. They have always told us about the financial cushion. We don't know anything about financial cushion. That is for rich folks, you know. We have said that we feel that education must go on but people need something in the meantime: we need to be given things that are already here on the statute books, such as given basic things to survive until the country decides to getting down to really take care of business, you know.

Poor people are saying the middle-class people are a bigger problem than rich folks because they think we are enemies.

SENATOR McGOVERN. Beyond that, you are also suggesting, as I understand the import of your point, that many times poor blacks and poor whites are in combat with each other.

MRS. WASHINGTON. That has been the history of black people and white people fighting each other.

Since I have been involved in the National Welfare Rights Organization and I have been speaking to a lot of people, especially poor people, I have tried to make them understand that it is not a black and white situation. It is a poor people situation and we must rally our support and our strength together to confront this country with the problems of the poor people, be they black, white, Puerto Rican, Mexican-Americans, or Indians, because we have the problems even as far as the Indians are concerned.

SENATOR McGOVERN. Don't you think one of the reasons for the continuing tensions and combat that exists in some areas between poor white and poor blacks stems from that very point, that they are competing with each other for jobs that are too few, for decent houses that are too few? They are in a poverty grip in which, without regard to color, people are thrown into combat with each other.

MRS. WASHINGTON. It is the same thing as far as black and white competing for jobs, competing for housing. Yet, they are both in the same situation. I think the misinformation that has been going around has caused that to happen. We have a big job to do. The middle class have a job to educate their people to really know what is going on in the society.

We have to eventually hurry up, otherwise, many problems will arise that we will not even begin to find a solution to.

MR. WILEY. Senator, could we finish the statement and then answer the questions?

One of the things that is very basic to what Mrs. Washington said is that poor people are organizing and trying to press to change this terrible welfare system and the rotten way in which poor people are treated. There has been little but promises, studies, and phony programs that have not dealt with the basic problems of poverty in this country and that people in the poor communities, black and white, Chicano, Indian, Puerto Rican, poor people are tired of waiting for programs that are supposed to help them, that don't really help them.

We are concerned that the Nixon welfare program nor any of the other programs that we have seen deal with the fundamental problems that organized poor people have raised and that is inadequate income for all poor people. The Government's own figures, the Bureau of Labor Statistics figures, can clearly be demonstrated to show that it takes at least $5,500 a year for a family of four to meet the basic necessities of life.

Where are the programs that have been advanced and where are the Congressmen and Senators who are out fighting for a $5,500 income for every citizen?

The Nixon "illfare," workfare program is a totally inadequate program. A $1,600 program is inadequate. But any program that talks about levels of $2,400, $3,200, $3,600, are thousands of dollars away from what is necessary to meet the basic necessities of life, do not come anywhere near the basic proposals that organized poor people across the country have been making as what they see is necessary to meet their minimum needs.

Now the proposals for an adequate income have risen in all of the 300 welfare rights organizations across the country. The questions of adequate money to meet the needs of families, for food, for clothing, for shelter, are regarded as basic for all poor people for meeting the problems that they face.

This is something that the welfare rights organizations all across the country have come up time and time again is how can we get more money to meet the basic needs of our families? Look at the history. The Government fought a war on poverty and the poor people lost. Both modern and liberal candidates for public office continuously promised to help poor people but no matter what candidate wins, poor people lose.

The only programs that poor people believe in, the only programs that poor people want, are action programs now to produce adequate income to meet the necessities. Hunger is not an academic problem. There has been sufficient time studying the problem, preparing reports, gathering statistics, making statements, holding hearings.

What we are saying is that we are tired of this and that we need a solution and a solution means action now and motion now toward an adequate income.

I think that it is important that poor people begin to speak out and expose the inadequacy of President Nixon's proposals. The fact is that a $1,600 proposal comes nowhere near meeting basic needs but the fact is also that none of the other proposals that are advanced that I have heard come anywhere near meeting basic needs.

It is remarkable to me that we have had a White House conference on food, nutrition, and health, a White House conference where poor people came to that conference and appealed to citizens from all walks of life around what poor people felt were the basic problems and the basic solution to hunger and that conference came out with a recommendation for immediate emergency action to distribute free food stamps now and free food now to all the hungry people. It came out as a more basic solution the guaranteeing of a $5,500 adequate income for all citizens.

Yet, there has been no action around those proposals. The President has ignored those proposals. The people on Capitol Hill have appeared to prefer to ignore those proposals. We in the welfare rights organizations are deeply concerned about the fact that the voices of poor people are not being heard, that we do not have a coalition of liberal and moderate Senators and Representatives in the House rallying around the issues as identified by the people.

I think that what you are going to have is as poor people are organizing, we have now more than 75,000 members across this country, people in the ghettos, and barrios, people who are black and white and Chicano and Mexican-American, who are organizing and prepared to wage a political struggle around the issues that we see as important to our survival.

Let no one mistake and let no candidate for political office, be they local or State or congressional or senatorial or the President of the United States, let no candidate for political office fail to recognize that we are organized and building and intend to have a base of power that can deal with these people who don't respond to our issues.

In New York State right now, there is a race going on for Governor. I want you to know that people, that candidates and their representatives have been sitting on door steps of the welfare rights organization asking how they can get our support. What is going to happen today in the political arena is that liberal candidates and people who say that they have been with us and they are for us, they are going to come to our door, and we are going to be somewhere else.

We are going to be putting our support, we are going to be withholding our support from those people who do not take a stand around the basic issues that we believe are vital to the survival of poor people and that is for an adequate minimum income of at least $5,500 for a family of four.

We think this is the only true commitment to end hunger in this country. We think that the country has to make this commitment. We think that the commitment has to be through an adequate income guarantee system for every person in the United States.

I think that many people are going to be fooled by the Nixon proposals. I think that many people are going to think that a proposal that offers $1,600 income is a proposal that deals with the welfare problem. I want to say that this proposal we regard as a proposal simply to help people live like a dog.

The Nixon welfare proposals provide something like 19 cents per meal per person as an average money payment for people in the United States. You can extrapolate that and see what that would mean with other proposals that would suggest that the benefits be higher by $1,000 or $1,500 beyond the Nixon proposal.

These are totally inadequate proposals because they do not meet basic human needs. Poor people live in a society of continuing injustice. We have a situation where case workers harass recipients, where there is the frustration of people having to beg for emergency food orders to meet their basic needs at the end of the month.

We have a situation where working people, thousands and thousands of working people, do not have adequate income from wages to meet their basic needs, and we feel that for those as well as for the people on welfare, as well as the millions of people who have no jobs and are denied welfare because of illegal application, of requirements, because of the categorical and arbitrary nature of welfare requirements at the time, requirements that in many senses would be continued under the Nixon proposals, we feel that the continuation of such practices are something that are going to continue to a deep division in America.

We think that as long as there is this terrible income gap between the people who have and the people who have not, that our Nation is always going to be divided and that we think until this Nation can bring itself and can speedily bring itself to the point of recognizing the need for a guaranteed adequate income for every citizen that we are going to have tension, that we are going to have conflict, that we are going to have disorders.

We think that the time is now for action. The time is now for people to rally while the debate is fresh around welfare reform proposals. The time is now to act and to speak out and to move in behalf of an adequate income proposal lest we get an inadequate Nixon "illfare" proposal and the country return for many years to sleep on the feeling that the problems of poor people are solved.

Thank you.

(The prepared statement of Dr. Wiley follows:)

PREPARED STATEMENT OF GEORGE A. WILEY, EXECUTIVE DIRECTOR, NATIONAL WELFARE RIGHTS ORGANIZATION, ACCOMPANIED BY MRS. JEANETTE WASHINGTON, MEMBER OF THE EXECUTIVE COMMITTEE

Today, once again, as we have in past years, representatives of the National Welfare Rights Organization[3] come before a congressional committee to make the case for the poor.

I understand that you are interested and anxious to end hunger in this country. Let me then begin by saying that action towards ending hunger had better come soon.

Just how long can poor people stand on the outside of affluent America and be told to quietly watch and wait, to be still while their children starve?

Poor people see the affluence around them. Poor people see the millions and billions being spent on everything from moon rockets to Merry Widow uniforms for the White House guards. How can the poor relate to a country where newspapers spend pages describing Mrs. Pompidou's hemlines while children in Wisconsin are without winter coats?

Government officials and average citizens alike are allegedly concerned about the fragmentation and polarization of our country. The biggest gap, gentlemen, is not generational, political or even racial. The biggest gap is between the poor and the non-poor.

Last month, in Jackson, Mississippi, 15 welfare recipients were arrested. They had participated in a sit-in at the local welfare office, part of a group of some 200 recipients protesting a week-long delay in welfare checks. The delay caused recipients to miss their rent and utility payments. Hundreds were evicted. Thousands more had their gas and electric shut off.

The meager welfare payments to Mississippi recipients left them with no surplus to tide them through the week when the checks did come. And the state welfare department refused to inform landlords and utility companies that bills could not be paid because the checks had not been sent out. The reason for the delay was minor—the department was switching to computerized payments.

How can those recipients in Mississippi relate to a country whose technology can put a man on the moon—but which refuses to use that technology to get those drastically needed checks out on time.

It is quickly apparent why poor people find it hard to believe that this government wants to help them—hard to believe that the United States wants to end hunger. And it gets harder every day.

[3] The National Welfare Rights Organization is a grassroots, poor people's organization with 75,000 members in 300 local groups throughout the United States.

If we do not want American society to permanently fragment into two distinct societies, then the promises made to the poor must soon be kept.

Look at the history. The United States government fought a War on Poverty. The poor lost. Both moderate and liberal candidates for public office continually promise to help the poor. No matter which candidate wins, the poor person always loses. The only program that poor people will believe in, that poor people want, is a program of action and adequacy.

Hunger is not an academic problem. Sufficient time has been spent preparing endless studies, reports, conferences, statements, promises, plans and programs.

An adequate income is the only answer—not the half-solutions of pushing mothers out of their homes for jobs that are demeaning and ill-paid—not the half-solutions of inadequate funds for insufficient food and a way of life that is in its horror un-American.

Figures taken from reports from the Bureau of Labor Statistics show that a family of four needs $5,500 annually to live adequately—not well, merely adequately. And until that family receives that $5,500, the basic problems remain.

Free food stamps, a national hunger emergency as recommended by the recent White House Conference—these will certainly help to end hunger on a stop-gap basis.

But the second conference recommendation shows the only way to a permanent end to hunger, the only way to integrate the poor into our society and the only way to stop the class polarization that is occurring in our country. That solution is $5,500 a year.

There will be a permanent end to hunger in this country when, and only when all people are given the same chance. That means a proper education, a decent home, clothes for school—and enough food so that worrying about being hungry doesn't keep a child preoccupied through the day and awake at night.

This country must make a true commitment to ending hunger. The only realistic approach is making a guaranteed adequate income a national goal—and then making that adequate income a national reality.

There are working people in this country who are entitled, even under the present inadequate system, to welfare benefits. We are helping them get those benefits. There are millions more who should receive wage supplements. We plan to see a program enacted that makes those supplements possible.

We see an adequate welfare plan as the only means of integrating the disinherited into the American way of life—as a means of allowing all citizens their very right to live.

Who can participate in government when he is facing a day-to-day fight for survival?

That is no exaggeration. Let me remind you that the inadequate Nixon plan allows only 19 cents a meal in many states. A recipient is still forced to feed her family mainly rice, beans, peanut butter and greens while trying to scrounge together the money for toothpaste so her children's teeth don't rot as early as her's did.

I do not believe that the American people, once presented with the true facts of how little the present proposed legislation really does to help people can see it as a landmark in aiding the poor. An inadequate plan just doesn't solve any problems.

Either the government is concerned with really helping people to live a decent life—or it is content to allow millions of people to go through years of suffering and want. That is the simple correct set of alternatives. Passing programs that are inadequate just to give a family a few more cents a day is cruel; telling the middle class that these proposals will really help people is more than dishonest.

Poor people live in a society of continuing injustice. The case workers whose case loads are so heavy mothers are forced to wait six and eight hours to get a simple form. The continuing frustration of begging for emergency food orders, in states where recipients consider themselves lucky to be allowed emergency food orders. The bureaucracy that frequently loses a letter requesting a special diet allowance for a child, thus sending the mother back on the rounds of doctor's visits and trips to the welfare office.

To be poor in this country is not to live in "another America"—how could any America treat people with the injustice and disdain that poor people suffer every day.

So I come here to tell you that poor people are waiting, waiting for you to fulfill your promises. None of the present plans proposed in Congress end that wait. All are inadequate. All are efforts which do not confront the problem realistically or with justice.

Poor people have been lied to so many times, though, that no longer do we merely wait. We are organized. And we intend to keep on organizing and protesting inadequate solutions until our plan—a guaranteed adequate income for all Americans—becomes a reality.

SENATOR McGOVERN. Thank you very much, Dr. Wiley.

Senator Harris, we appreciate your staying on to hear Dr. Wiley and Mrs. Washington.

Dr. Wiley, it seems to me that there is really a question that you and I and other people who are concerned about this problem must answer and that is this:

Let us grant, to begin with, that the figure that you suggest as an adequate income, somewhere around $5,500 a year, and I think there is support for that estimate in the Bureau of Labor Statistics concerning what it costs to support a family of four in this inflated economy of ours, let us suppose that that is an agreed-upon objective and that people in the Congress across the country who are concerned about this problem would like to move toward that goal.

MR. WILEY. I can't allow that supposition because that supposition does not exist.

I think one of the basic problems we have to do immediately is that we have to rally support for that supposition. Is it a supposition or is it a fact that peoplc need some kind of adequate income around $5,500. I think that there are very few people who have been speaking out and who have been saying that that is what is necessary.

SENATOR McGOVERN. That brings me to my question.

What do you think is the program that is best designed to get the political support that is needed? In other words, as you yourself have said, it is all well and good to have a national conference and have the delegates agree on a figure, $5,500. That is the rhetoric. Now, the question is, how do you put together the political strategy or the public understanding, the congressional understanding, that will make that more than rhetoric?

MR. WILEY. To me, the first thing you have to do is that you have to recognize that as the need, you have to recognize that as the goal. You have to initiate a fight to reach that goal. It seems to me until the leadership of the country recognizes the need for a struggle toward that goal, that we are not going to have any motion toward that. To me, and I think to all of us in the welfare rights organization, we have felt that the question of whose plan is the least important question to the question of getting an adequate income.

We have said that adequate income, some way of getting adequate income to people, is the basic necessity. We feel that the decision about what plan and what strategy are in a sense political decisions that have to be assessed and have to be made.

I could make it seem that most every plan could be fitted to make an adequate proposal out of it. The basic thing you have to do with President Nixon's proposal is to raise the benefit level for family assistance to $5,500 and broaden the coverage to every citizen and not simply families with children, and then you would have the framework for a plan that deals with the basic problem of poverty, hunger, and malnutrition.

You could take Senator Harris's proposal and instead of talking about a proposal that goes in 3 years to the poverty, talk about a proposal that goes to an adequate income level in the earliest possible time. I don't think we need 3 years. I don't think we need 3 years to reach that point.

The amount of money necessary is less than the amount of money we spend on defense, is about equivalent to the amount of money we are spending on the war in Vietnam, is far less than the aggregate of tax exemption and tax loopholes through which we subsidize businesses and middle- and upper-class people in this country.

There is plenty of money, in short, to deal with the basic problem of poverty. What there is not is the political commitment and the drive on the part of people and political leadership to reach that goal and that seems to me to be the basic thing we need.

SENATOR McGOVERN. So the thrust of your testimony is that you are not particularly wedded to any one formula. The key fact is to center on adequate income and you believe that to be $5,500 or somewhere in that area. This is your goal and what you are calling on this committee to do is to accept that adequate income level, defined as $5,500 a year, and then find some kind of legislative formula that will achieve that with a measure of dignity to the recipient.

Is that a fair statement of your position?

MR. WILEY. Yes; it is.

SENATOR McGOVERN. Your chief critique, then, of the administration's proposal and of others is that they simply do not measure up to the adequate income criteria?

MR. WILEY. That is right. They do not provide adequate income and they do not provide, in my opinion, any of the proposals I have seen, they don't provide a mechanism for achieving adequate income. They do not provide the possibility or the likelihood that we are going to reach an adequate income level.

SENATOR McGOVERN. Let me ask you this, Dr. Wiley.

While I have not introduced a legislative proposal, I think you are generally familiar with the rough outline of the proposal we have been thinking about, the children's allowance, guaranteed public service job to those unable to find employment in the private sector, lifting the social security guarantees for the elderly and disabled to an adequate level and then covering in people who are not covered by those three provisions with direct assistance.

Do you believe that that formula, once it were targeted at an adequate income level that you referred to, would be one possible alternative that would be generally acceptable?

MR. WILEY. No.

SENATOR McGOVERN. Why is that?

MR. WILEY. The reason is that at the heart of our proposal is getting an adequate income for every citizen. I do not see a mechanism in those sets of proposals for achieving that end.

I think that the proposals are fine proposals and are perhaps supplementary to achieving adequate income. That is to say, they would help some people who are working or some people who are old, whose benefits were inadequate, or they would help some—for example, the children's allowance tends to help families of working poor people who are working but whose income does not measure up for one reason or another and the children's allowance tends to supplement those people and therefore get them to a more adequate income.

An example. A family of four with two children. If they got a $50 a month children's allowance, that would be $1,200 a year. Our sense of that is that if they had a net income, earned income, of say, $4,300 a year, then the $1,200 would bring them to $5,500 and they would be in good shape.

If, however, they had no income, the $1,200 would bring them to $1,200 and they would have to turn to welfare or some form of public assistance, some other form of public assistance, for help.

What we say is that the children's allowance is a strategy, much like social security, talking about full employment and wages our strategies in themselves are valid and valuable but the basic thing at the heart of the matter is seeing to it that there are no cracks and that there is a floor that insures that every family will get a basic minimum income and the plan that does that, and I think your proposal if it incorporated a $5,500 guaranteed income for everybody who was left out and did not have an adequate income from children's allowance, social security of whatever else, then there would be a first-rate set of proposals.

SENATOR McGOVERN. If the fourth section of our bill were adequately stretched, it would then become more compatible with what you are saying.

MR. WILEY. If the fourth section were an adequate income proposal rather than would hint to that—I hope the debate is still open—

SENATOR McGOVERN. The debate is wide open.

MR. WILEY. Rather than what is hinted at as a categorical welfare program, which to me would insure the isolation, would insure the inadequacy for the people in situations such as Mrs. Washington and many others, particularly the women and children on welfare, that I think it would insure an adequate program. I think that there is no reason to think that a welfare program just because it is small, just because it applies to a small number of people, is likely to be an adequate program.

So we say this has to be a guaranteed floor that includes everybody in it and assures everybody of an adequate income level. Then I think family assistance, full employment, higher wages, better social security, all of those things are important antipoverty measures, but the basic thing of adequate income is the thing on which we must maintain our central focus.

SENATOR McGOVERN. Let me just put it to you this way, Dr. Wiley.

One of the reasons why I thought that the first three sections of my proposal were important is that they would reduce the very problem that you have referred to here, which is the isolation of the poor. Those first three provisions of the bill apply to everyone, rich and poor alike. Everybody would qualify for a children's allowance. Everyone who wants to work in public service employment, who doesn't have a job in private employment, would be given a useful job, something the country needs. Everyone would automatically qualify for the improved social security protection.

It was precisely to reduce the image of a welfare poor people's program that led me to structure this proposal as I did.

I just wanted to make that observation.

MR. WILEY. I think we understand that strategy. I think we disagree. If that turns out to be your strategy, which I hope it is not, I think it would be a basic mistake to pursue that strategy as the main-line attack on the problem because I think without a guaranteed adequate income floor so that nobody could slip through the crack, of what you have to admit is a categorical program, you have four major categories of programs that would deal with these problems and there could be cracks in those programs.

If you say full employment, you may be disabled, you may be unable to work.

You may not qualify for social security for whatever reason. You may not qualify for a children's allowance. Maybe you don't have any children. So there is a crack for you to slip through.

Then your reliance must be on some kind of fourth alternative. We say the fourth alternative must be something that guarantees for everybody that they are going to have the right to live, they are going to have food and clothing and shelter at an adequate level and that means an adequate income.

SENATOR McGOVERN. Well, Dr. Wiley, I want you to know that you are giving me pause, as you have for a long time, for some serious thought on this matter.

What you say here is presented persuasively and convincingly as it always is. I want you to know that your proposal is going to be very, very seriously evaluated by me and I am sure will be by other members of this committee.

We hope that we can get together on a formula where people concerned about this problem can stand together. If that happens, you are going to deserve a great deal of credit.

We do want to thank you and Mrs. Washington for appearing here today.

MR. WILEY. Let me say as a final thing that I think all of us in the Welfare Rights Organization have looked to you, Senator McGovern, for leadership in this area. We have admired the things you have done on hunger, malnutrition, your crusading efforts in these areas.

We hope that you will be a leader in this program of directly helping poor people on issues as poor people see it.

We think that an adequate income is really the basic thrust of something that must be done.

We are looking forward to having our executive committee meet with you in the near future.

SENATOR McGOVERN. I would like very much to do that.

MR. WILEY. If such a meeting can be arranged, it can lead to a profitable program.

22 FIVE IN SPOTS FOR THE MIDNIGHT CHIC

Peter Benchley

Once upon a time, before technology gave us the Jet Set and before Diana Vreeland ordained a generation of Beautiful People, when Cafe Society was still a viable phrase, New York's night life was orderly. There were, it was said (and said and said) only 400 people worth writing about, and columnists knew where to find their prey at play: El Morocco or, upon an even farther distant time, the Stork Club.

But then, along about 1960, the order began to decay. It became as fashionable to *do* things as to *have* things, and meritocrats replaced aristocrats in the social hierarchy. As admirable as this democratizing of New York was, it played hob with accepted standards, for at the same time the social base broadened, so did tastes.

People were no longer predictable. They did freaky things that gave the chroniclers of the night scene the yips from trying to keep up with frantic changes. When a fat little man called Chubby Checker started doing a weird routine called The Twist in a dreary midtown *boîte* called the Peppermint Lounge, who should show up but the Bedfords (Duke and Duchess), the Pagliais (Merle Oberon and Bruno) and scribes like Tennessee Williams and Norman Mailer.

When the ex-wife of an actor named Richard Burton opened a joint named Arthur after a hairdo coined by some cats named the Beatles, the town went nuts.

And so through the decade of the sixties the vortex kept spinning, with entrepreneurs stumbling over each other in their greedy rush to capitalize on the whims of the people who follow each other—and who, in turn, are tailed by legions of well-heeled gawkers. A few succeeded. Arthur is said to have made some money for its backers, who were once described as 70 celebrities in search of a tax loss.

Most did not, of which there is ample archeological proof. Because, regardless of their interior décor, most night spots require generally identical facilities, new ones are usually built—like ancient cities—atop the ruins of their predecessors. Hippopotamus stands on the site of Arthur, which once housed the old El Morocco. Thursday's 24 just opened in the same place Escadrille enjoyed its short, splashy stand.

Now, in the dawn of the seventies, the cry is abroad that New York night life is finished, that the recession has forced people to stay at home, that it isn't fashionable to be seen any more, that no one cares, that dancing is a dead art, that, in the words of one dapper young bachelor, "it's much more fun to stay indoors and get stoned."

To some extent, the cry is a hoary truism, for New York's swinging night life has always been something of a myth. Never, not in the flushest of times, has this city of almost 8 million souls supported more than a handful of night clubs elegant enough or crazy enough or "fun" enough to lure—and, more important, keep—the chic trade.

But the cry is mostly pure cant. Accepting the fact that the vast majority of New Yorkers don't give two hoots where Jacqueline Onassis (to cite only the most obvious name) goes for her postprandial jollies, a few thousand do, and at least a few hundred want to be there too. Of the 8,442 establishments reckoned by the city as legal hard-liquor licensees, at least five have whatever magic it takes to command the profitable patronage of that motley band of special names and faces.

Two are private clubs. One is a public discothèque that has engineered the clever trick of making itself seem private. Two are restaurants—one slightly seedy and one sublimely gaudy.

Now that all traditional mores have vanished, social climbing is a very nerve-racking avocation. In the days when the only individual stamp a man could put to his evening clothes was the monogram on his cufflinks, there was no taste factor in attire. You either dressed properly or you didn't. But here in the age of the peacock, an aspiring member of one in-group or another is unpleasantly vulnerable to the judgment of every maître d' and doorkeeper as to whether his plumage is acceptable.

If you happen to be George Plimpton, you could probably gain admittance to any saloon in town wearing a posing strap and a *babushka*. But if, as is more likely, you happen to be just a normal good-time charlie, you may be thrown out of a place for not wearing a tie, for wearing a tie that is deemed too loud or too thin, for having scuffed shoes, baggy pants or a *déclassé* cast to your beady eye.

One of the strictest arbiters of fashion is an Englishman named Derek Hall-Caine, who runs Raffles, the club in the basement of the Sherry-Netherland that is by all odds the most exclusive restaurant-*cum*-discothèque in New York. (That is, "exclusive" in the time-honored, socioreligious sense of the word, not the sense used by the furniture companies in blatting about their "exclusive ottomans.") At the moment, there are—worldwide—about 1,900 members of Raffles, and about 1,000 more are waiting eagerly to be afforded the privilege of paying a $600 initiation fee and $350 in annual dues. (There are cheaper memberships: for a $300 initiation fee and $250 a year, for instance, one may be permitted to use the club just for lunch.)

An applicant must be recommended, in writing, by three club members, but even the most effusive recommendations are no guarantee of entry. "We never actually say no," says Hall-Caine. "But by the same token, someone can stay on the waiting list forever."

The "we" refers to a select admissions committee, whose members include

Plimpton, John R. Drexel 3d, Charles Addams, Cornelius Vanderbilt Whitney and Douglas Fairbanks Jr., and which meets once a month in a small room adorned with baby pictures of the committee members. Perhaps because it takes a certain degree of *hubris* to rule on the social graces of Truman Capote, the Maharaja of Jaipur and the Richard Burtons, such rulings are conducted in discreet secrecy.

The rest of the club is bedecked with photographs of other famous members, obtained by Cecil Beaton, who decorated Raffles at a cost rumored to be around $750,000. Beaton once said he wanted Raffles to be a "tongue-in-cheek version of the traditional 18th-century club," and as he dispensed owner Jerry Brody's (of the Brody Corp.) cash, his tongue must have been welded to his cheek. He first, in fact, thought of calling the place The Dogs, because it might have been amusing to say, "I'm going to the dogs tonight," and there was also a suggestion that the club be named The Pugs, in tribute to ugly people.

The décor is, to say the least, close and clubby—hunting prints on flocked wallpaper, plush carpeting, velvet banquettes, polished brass fixtures and a magnificently polished bar, sedate red curtains separating tables, and a row of small private dining rooms that can be curtained off—"in case a man is married but is taking someone else out—sort of *demi-mondiale*," says Hall-Caine. "He can pull the curtains so no one can see who he's with."

The ceiling over the dance floor, which has aroused both ire and admiration in members, is an assemblage of shards of colored glass.

From the moment it opened two years ago, Raffles has been jammed, a happy circumstance that Hall-Caine attributes, at least in part, to the fact that he has been "awfully strict about letting only members in, running it like a private club," which it most emphatically is. Writing not long ago about Annabel's, London's counterpart to Raffles, Auberon Waugh observed, ". . . it is extraordinary what a close resemblance bank notes have to membership cards when the light is dim." But Hall-Caine swears the resemblance is not recognized at Raffles. He likes to tell a tale of informing a clutch of Secret Service men that President Johnson and one of his daughters would not be admitted unless they could latch onto a member.

"I told them that, after all, I had had to turn away Lord Snowdon, the brother-in-law of my Queen. Nobody impresses me. I'm too old. I've had too much money. I can't be bribed. I've been offered $500 in cash to use my influence to get a man a membership. And I don't take tips. My maître d' makes far more money than I do."

Tips to the maître d' are the only cash transactions condoned at Raffles, which is probably just as well, for a cozy evening for two can set a man back much more than the American Express Company says is safe to tote on one's person.

One might start with a late dinner (edible food at *prix fixe* $15.50; a modest wine $14 or so, an immodest one $65 or so), then sit around over coffee waiting for the action to start. At about 10:30, Slim Hyatt, the disc jockey who, legend has it, was once Peter Duchin's butler, peeks out from his control room, gauges his crowd, and starts the music—usually slowly. The dinner crowd is relatively elderly, and an occasional waltz is appreciated.

By 12 or 1 o'clock, the joint is as jumping as it's going to get. The lights are low and the music loud—raucous rock, throaty ballads. Stockbrokers thrash around with mididressed young sylphs, performing Terpsichorean rituals that no longer have any names.

"Most of these dances are adlibbed," one thoughtful roué told me. "I guess if they're descended from any one thing, it's The Chicken." (O noble forebear!)[1]

Between dances, there is always the relaxing pastime of stargazing, for, as Hall-Caine is the first to insist, "We do have the people. You name 'em, we've got 'em. And no matter who they are, they come here to see and be seen. Frank Sinatra likes to look at Henry Ford as much as Henry Ford likes to look at Sophia Loren. Mrs. Onassis likes to be told that over there, Bob Hope and Bing Crosby are sitting together."

The real thrill of celebrity-watching, of course, is reserved for those who believe that luster can be rubbed off and assimililated by proximity. And who is to say that by 3 in the morning, when the lawyer and his young lovely lurch homeward, they have not gotten full emotional value for their $75 or $100?

"They want to be told they're the Beautiful People," says Hall-Caine, who spent 20 years in the Gordon Highlanders before embarking on his restaurant career three years ago.

"They want to see it in print. They feel they're important and sitting next to a big name makes them believe it. When they see in the paper that so-and-so was at Raffles last night, they can say, 'I was there, too,' and they feel good. Obviously, there's a great deal of insecurity in all this."

There sure is. Raffles could collapse almost overnight if suddenly some other place opened that touched and held the fancy of the right people. But so far, Raffles has demonstrated a staying power that may let it live as long as the only other club with which it shares (however reluctantly) its cachet: Le Club, the dowager queen of discothèques that has been open to members for a dozen years.

A few of Le Club's regulars dropped their memberships when Raffles opened, but many more simply joined Raffles, too. It is a safe guess that 25 per cent of the members of each place are also on the other's rolls. Martin Revson, the cosmetics millionaire, belongs to both, as do the ubiquitous Mr. Plimpton and Col. Serge Obolensky, the world's most elegant public-relations man.

Le Club, which the cognoscenti are careful to pronounce "club," not "cloob," has about 1,100 members—including, as a sort of *primus inter pares,* Oleg Cassini, the leonine promoter of things social who has been president of the club for the past nine years. Six hundred owner-members have a piece of the action. The other 500 pay dues (about half what it costs to belong to Raffles) and are listed

---

[1] The Chicken is a non-contact dance in which the performer extends his elbows horizontally, winglike, and shakes his glutei.

as senior members, international members or junior members.

If one chose to spend an evening at Le Club with his eyes closed, he might well imagine he was at Raffles. The music in one place is indistinguishable from that in the other. So is the quality of the food. The muted voices of patrons of Le Club might sound a touch younger, but basically the clientele is from the same monied mold.

There, however, the similarity stops. Le Club is decorated to look like the living room of a tiny castle. The ceiling is high, the walls apparently of rough stone. An ancient-looking tapestry hangs on the wall behind the dance floor. Altogether, the club is about a third the size of Raffles—"definitely a sexier place," says one member of both.

Well, perhaps—if sexiness can be generated by a bunch of people writhing around to deafening sounds in near-pitch blackness. It is said that at Raffles, Truman Capote's special booth has a peephole cut into the wall so he can peek at the dancers in the dark corners. If there were private booths at Le Club, which there aren't, Capote would have to use a flashlight to find his peephole.

The place is so dark that one has to take the word of someone who stepped on a celebrity that the famous presence was, indeed, there. Anyone who went to Le Club to marvel at movie stars would have to employ an infrared sniper-scope.

"I was sitting in here one night," the dark shadow of a friend murmured at me across a table at Le Club, "and a guy at my table pointed to a woman two tables away and asked if I knew who she was. I must have looked at her for 30 seconds before I realized it was my sister."

Le Club's newest attraction isn't even in the same building. It is a brown-stone annex on East 48th Street, seven blocks downtown from the main club, which features gaming rooms for backgammon and bridge, sauna and steam rooms, and a discothèque that may be rented for private parties. (When it gets a liquor license, it may be open to members on Sundays, the night the uptown club is closed, though the annex is primarily a daytime operation.) Supposedly, when Le Club's uptown lease expires in a few years, the whole establishment will move into the annex.

One of the motive forces behind Le Club was Olivier Coquelin, a charming Gaul who must rank by now as the Sol Hurok of the discothèque set. Over the years, he and a group of friendly backers (including, at various times, Stavros Niarchos and Michael Butler, producer of "Hair") have launched Le Club, On-dine, Cheetah, Sugarbush (the ski resort) and their current pet, Hippopotamus.

Whether Coquelin follows or creates fashion is a matter of some dispute, but he is ever in its vanguard. When he started Cheetah a few years ago (with $150,000 of Borden Stevenson's money), a photograph showed him with short hair, horn-rimmed glasses and a dark necktie. Today his hair is down to his shoulders, his glasses are huge, slim-rimmed and tinted, and his bellbottom suits come from Saint-Germain.

Not surprisingly, Coquelin thinks Raffles is a drag—that the music is too slow and too dated, that the atmosphere is too formal. (It is axiomatic that every night club owner or manager avers that there is no night life in town except that served up by himself.) Derek Hall-Caine, for his part, does not even consider Hippopotamus competition, suggesting that the clientele is bourgeois and tainted with Brooklyn secretaries—the villains of every piece and surely the most maligned group of people in New York.

Technically, Hippopotamus is a public place, but the general public is hardly encouraged. Coquelin has been accused of refusing admission to people he doesn't like and of refusing to make reservations for people he doesn't know. True or not, there is no welcome mat outside Hippopotamus's door. There isn't a sign of any kind, in fact, and the door is often locked.

The result is that Coquelin has cultivated the clientele he wants—a few sprinklings of the Raffles-type celebrities, but mostly a much younger crowd who, to Coquelin's chagrin, don't drink much. "It's tragic, but it's a fact," he says. "They all turn on with something—mostly pot, though not in here—but they don't drink." To cope with teetotaling youth, he charges a $5 minimum ($7 on weekends) which buys two drinks and entitles a reveler to dance away the night. (The price structure guarantees that the only drunks ever seen in Hippopotamus are very rich indeed.)

If Raffles can be said to treasure its aura of celebrity-chic, Hippopotamus thrives on being sort of freak-chic. The sartorial whims of Coquelin's clients make the elegant folk at Raffles seem to be dressed in Dr. Denton's. One night an epicene young man strolled in wrapped in a white fur cape and shod with high furry boots. Another sported a velvet jerkin, thigh-high boots and random patches of facial hair—scraggly and black—that might have been pasted on by some sadistic cosmetician.

Hippopotamus also features a social curiosity that would no more occur to the directors of Raffles than would the idea of adding frozen pizza to the menu— something that for lack of a better phrase must be catalogued as porno-chic. Copies of Screw and other dubious journals hang from a hallway newspaper rack. An exhibition of full-front nudes ripped from magazines is mounted in a glass cage. And in the ladies' room, above a mirror before which hair is combed, there is a huge stained-glass painting, reminiscent of Hieronymus Bosch, filled with countless figures, most of them human, performing acts on and with each other that would have given pause to Bosch, Henry Miller and the authors of the Kama Sutra, let alone your garden-variety consenting adult.

To complement the freaks, however, it must be said that Coquelin manages to attract the most dazzling array of lovely women—attired in everything from plastic to stainless steel—to grace any joint in the city. Furthermore, he maintains an atmosphere of easy camaraderie that makes repeaters of his patrons; they know they will always see a friendly face.

A man as savvy as Coquelin is to the vagaries of the night club business leaves little to chance when he opens a new place. There are definite economic formulas that must be followed. "In a restaurant, if you have good food, a nice atmosphere and good service, you have no reason to fail," he told me one afternoon. "But a night club audience is so fickle. You have to get your money back within six months or you're taking a terrible risk. So to spend more than $200,000 on a night club is pure madness."

By no coincidence at all, Hippopotamus was capitalized at precisely that figure: $150,000 for the décor and sound system, $100,000 to Sybil Burton Christopher—of which only half had to be paid on the spot—for the skeleton and some of the innards of Arthur.

"Once you are open," he said, "if it's well-run, you should double your money every year—as long, that is, as it's run by the proprietor at least 14 to 16 hours every day. Basically, there are two things that are critical—the charisma of the host and the quality of the sound system. We spent $27,000 on ours."

Running it well also means knowing what percentage of the sale prices of a drink (75 per cent) and of food (65 per cent) should be profit, and how much staff salaries should total ($3,000 to $5,000 a week, presuming there is no band).

Finally, it means picking and choosing clientele as best as one can. Coquelin has a standing mailing list of 14,000 people with whom he has dealt and who receive announcements of every new venture he launches, and he can usually drum up enough early celebrity trade to give a place an initial impetus.

There are, to be sure, just as many people to be avoided as courted. The poor Brooklyn secretary heads the list, but right behind her comes the mass of middle-class young people known derisively as "singles." They are the bankers and businessmen who spend their days dressed in conservative suits, pursuing all the honorable goals of commerce, and their evenings in splendid mod clothes and store-bought mustaches, pursuing single girls. The pursued are secretaries, stenographers, TV production assistants, junior ad-agency executives. They congregate at bars named after every day of the week, several fruits and an animal or two. Pressed together in enforced, sweaty familiarity they engage in randy dialogues that one Manhattan psychologist has called "nothing but a bad ego trip. The men are desperate to assert their masculinity by latching onto the best-looking girl in the place and hustling her to bed. The women are desperate to convince themselves and their peers of their seductive powers."

From a look at the crowd of young people jamming the sidewalk on the north side of 64th Street and First Avenue, one would be forced to conclude that Maxwell's Plum is but another marcher in the endless parade of singles bars. It is, instead, one of the true paradoxes of the city's night life. By being consciously—almost self-consciously—democratic, by avoiding all pretense to exclusivity, it has become one of the most smashingly successful places in the city, attracting everyone from movie stars to restaurateurs to—yes, even the fabled Brooklyn secretary. And contrary to the social imperative, they all seem to coexist in relative bliss.

Maxwell's Plum was started five years ago by Warner LeRoy, son of Mervyn and himself a producer-writer of some modest renown. He was trying, he says, to "create an American cafe," and for almost four years it was just that—a small, cozy, profitable cafe.

Then, a little over a year ago, LeRoy decided to expand, and he took on a partner, Hardwicke Companies Inc., to help him with the financing. Today, Le-Roy's plum is a massive, sprawling money machine that generates between $2.5- and $3-million worth of business a year (with a nice profit of about 10 per cent) and is suddenly, in dollar volume, one of the four biggest restaurants in New York.

LeRoy serves meals from noon until 3 A.M., and on a slow day he will dish up 1,000 lunches and dinners. A fast day means turning over each of the 250 seats six times, for a total of 1,500 meals, which taxes the staff of 160 just about to its limit. At any given mealtime, there are 24 waiters (earning between $300 and $400 a week) on the floor, and 10 bus boys. LeRoy has 22 cooks (a sauce cook, a roast cook, a fish cook, and so forth). 20 assistant cooks and a private bakery. To keep an eye on his legions, he has arrangements with three detective agencies, which staff the Plum with anonymous diners and drinkers to make sure the help isn't cheating the customers or the house. In the past year, LeRoy has had to fire about 30 waiters for various chicaneries.

The reasons for Maxwell's Plum's enormous success are partly demonstrable, but partly not. The food is good. ("Much of it is amusing," Craig Claiborne wrote, "and much of it is more than merely palatable.") The drinks are better than in many saloons. LeRoy serves an ounce-and-a-quarter shot—which, incidentally, means that he serves 24 to 26 drinks a bottle and, at $1.35 a drink (for the bar Scotch), clears something like $30 per quart.

The décor has much to do with the Plum's allure. LeRoy says it cost over $1-million, which I suppose is as good a figure as any. The huge room is an explosion of brass, polished wood, flowers (all fresh), honest-to-God gas lamps and Tiffany glass (real and copies)—10,000 sheets of it in all, many of which are in the ceiling. The overall effect is something like the Edwardian park in "Yellow Submarine"—funny, slightly kicky, friendly and comfortable.

Despite a slight chill emanating from the rotating crew of six myrmidons who guard the door, the atmosphere is relatively congenial, which LeRoy insists is the secret of his cafe ambiance. "An attractive girl can come in here alone and not feel conspicuous," he says. "In most places, you sort of assume that if someone is in the bar alone he's lonely, and I guess that's true. But we've tried here to make the atmosphere genial enough so loneliness isn't conspicuous. You may be lonely, sure, but you can feel sort of at home here."

Evidently. Not long ago, a party of four suddenly took off all its clothes. One of the girls jumped up on the table and gyrated a bit, then everybody got dressed again. The four were sitting in the front of the Plum, in the cafe area, but their performance was visible to the diners in the rear of the room, which suggests another important reason for LeRoy's success. He has carefully separated the place into three distinct areas, which interact synergistically.

The main dining room, where one may pick from an extensive menu and pay $7.85 for a steak, is raised, affording a clear view of the rest of the room, including the bar, which attracts the singles trade. You may eat in peace and luxury, therefore, while enjoying the sight of the youngsters doing their predatory thing, jammed four-deep in an area tightly enclosed by a brass railing. The bar ("very sex-oriented," says LeRoy) is elevated above the cafe area, which has its own, much less expensive menu.

"The three feed off each other," says LeRoy, who looks as if he feeds off quite a bit himself, "and it's really quite a show. It's what keeps people here until 3 A.M. We couldn't do this if we tried to be an 'in' place. We have to keep it open to keep its mix, which is its fun and excitement."

A mile to the north of Maxwell's Plum, in an out-of-the-way neighborhood known for absolutely nothing, sits an establishment that in its own quiet way is at least as phenomenal as LeRoy's miracle. It has a staff of 12, a legal capacity of 98, and a practical serving capacity of about 200 dinners a night. The décor is a nondescript hodgepodge of posters and pictures. The food is all right—easily worth the reasonable prices charged. This unpretentious carapace shelters the only place in the city that even faintly resembles a *salon littéraire*.

It is called Elaine's, and if its locale (88th and Second) is unlikely, its proprietress is even more so. Her name is Elaine Kaufman, and Madame Récamier she isn't. She is tough, salty, wry, shrewd, earthy, unimpressible and immense—the latter quality having been exploited in a curious fashion by Braniff International airlines, which employed her in its "If you've got it, flaunt it" campaign.

I presume the reference was supposed to be to her clientele, and though the thought of her flaunting it is unimaginable, she's got it, all right. Perhaps the most telling testimony to Elaine's cachet was delivered by a fictional character, the insufferable Jonathan Balser in Frank Perry's "Diary of a Mad Housewife." Elaine's was the place he insisted on going when he wanted to see and be seen by the artsy-craftsy crowd.

Rolls-Royces are common incongruities in the dingy street outside Elaine's. Mrs. Onassis has made the scene. ("Fun slumming," was one acid comment; "masochism-chic," another.) So have Sinatra, Leonard Bernstein, Joe Namath and John Kenneth Galbraith. Suzy, the columnist for The Daily News, reported with glee that Henry Ford and his wife had to stand around the packed bar at Elaine's and wait for half an hour for a table, just like ordinary mortals.

Indeed he did. He got his table but no faster than anyone else would have, for Elaine does not court any man's patronage. "Henry Ford doesn't make a place," she says. "He's a one-shot. He and his wife came in here that one night. She's just a middle-class Italian. She loves to crane her neck and look around, just like everybody else. I built this place around regulars, not around tourists— you know, the guy who says to me, 'I really wanted to go to so-and-so but my wife says let's go to Elaine's.'"

A customer is a customer. If he comes once or twice, he is treated with what could generously be called civility. If he becomes a regular, he is treated well—

seated at a front table and mothered by Elaine, who has a genius for remembering not only names but preferences in drink, food and company.

The regulars are from no particular field, but the most conspicuous ones are journalists (David Halberstam), writer-editors (Willie Morris), playwrights (Arthur Kopit) and musicians (Bobby Short, who is probably New York's most adored pianist). Those of lesser luminescence communicate their talent on the walls of the men's room, scribbling messages like "Chekhov loves Genoa" and "Norman Norell is a *yenta*."

Elaine presides over her territory like a drill sergeant, which she admits has contributed to her reputation for brusqueness. "People keep hassling me for this," she says, "but I just want to make sure everybody gets seated. So if you've finished dinner and have ordered everything you want, I'll give you the check. I want to keep the room moving."

It is not difficult to get thrown out of Elaine's. A few weeks ago, a man came in, plopped himself down at a table to which he hadn't been assigned, and demanded that a passing waiter clean it off.

"That's not your table," said the waiter.

"Clean it off," said the man.

"Out," said the waiter, and in a few brief moments the man was out on the street.

On another occasion, a writer (and something of a regular) came in with a date. When Elaine heard it was his birthday, she asked him up to the bar for a glass of champagne. "I was sipping my champagne," he remembers, "when I happened to look through the smoke and the crowd and what should I see but my date being thrown out. I don't know whether they thought she was being too noisy or was just taking up too much space. Anyway, I paid my check and left."

Elaine's does have its knockers among writers, particularly those who do not cherish the rather restricted fraternity of their fellows. "The place is just a one-up put-down," says one such (who was almost willing to be quoted, until he decided, "What the hell, why tee off Elaine?"). "It's a bunch of insecure writers fighting to be the center of attention."

The criticism may be unfair, for attributions of failure imply lofty ambitions, and Elaine has few. She runs a successful restaurant. If people like it, they can come in. If they don't, the hell with them. And again, anyone who is willing to put up with the crowds and the wain can come in.

Well, almost anyone. Not the singles crowd, who make occasional forays into Elaine's. "You can have 'em," she says. "I tell 'em to go someplace else, like where they give you a ticket worth two drinks for $3. We get a lot of the little girls who come in here to use the bathroom just so they can cruise the place. No, thanks." (This is not to say that unattached males are denied entry. Elaine's is a haven for the single—or, as common, divorced—intellectual [whatever that may mean] who wants to come in and have a drink with his chums and, perhaps, play backgammon into the morning hours.)

Occupied though she is with her own establishment six nights a week, Elaine is a student of the whole New York night scene—both vicariously, through her clients, and firsthand. (Indeed, Suzy took pleasure in reporting that even Elaine was turned down at one of Bobby Short's performances at the Carlyle. No room.) And since no one really knows better than anyone else what will be the next cynosure to strike the landscape, her thoughts are as valid as anyone's.

Greenwich Village, she thinks, will create no interesting new places until it regains some of the identity it lost during the building boom and social sprawl of the sixties. The current, amorphous dance styles are on the way out, the strong bloodline of The Chicken notwithstanding. "It's no good," she says. "You can't feel anybody. You're no better off than you were before. It's like looking in a mirror." She is convinced that the Latin *boîtes*, like the Corso on East 86th Street, are the comers of the seventies—with their comprehensible and danceable beat.

Maybe she's right. Maybel El Morocco will reopen (again) as a private club. Maybe Olivier Coquelin will come up with some outrageous new spot when the bloom is off the Hippopotamus.

The only certainty, of course, is change. And every man or woman who aspires to run a night spot in Fun City should hang above his cash register a copy of something Sybil Burton Christopher said on the occasion of Arthur's first birthday in 1966. Flushed with success, contemplating lucrative franchise agreements, the savvy lady muttered quietly: "The trouble with being listed as in is that if you're in, sooner or later you must be out."